THE COMPLETE GUIDE TO THE

NATIONAL
PARK LODGES

Fifth Edition

\|/

DAVID L. SCOTT

KAY W. SCOTT

INSIDERS' GUIDE®

GUILFORD, CONNECTICUT
AN IMPRINT OF THE GLOBE PEQUOT PRESS

The dollar cost of rooms and meals is for summer 2005. Taxes are not included. The prices and rates listed in this guidebook were confirmed at press time. We recommend, however, that you call establishments before traveling to obtain current information.

Maps provided are for reference only and should be used in conjunction with a road map. Distances suggested are approximate.

Other Globe Pequot Press books by
David L. Scott and Kay Woelfel Scott
Guide to the National Park Areas, Eastern States
Guide to the National Park Areas, Western States

To buy books in quantity for corporate use
or incentives, call **(800) 962–0973, ext. 4551,**
or e-mail **premiums@GlobePequot.com.**

INSIDERS' GUIDE®

Text design: Sheryl Kober
Text illustrations: Carole Drong

ISSN: 1537-3312
ISBN-13: 978-0-7627-3891-5
ISBN-10: 0-7627-3891-X

Manufactured in the United States of America
Fifth Edition/First Printing

CONTENTS

CONTENTS

CONTENTS

CONTENTS

CONTENTS

CONTENTS

Overview of National Parks

HELP US KEEP THIS GUIDE UP TO DATE

Every effort has been made by the authors and editors to make this guide as accurate and useful as possible. However, many things can change after a guide is published—establishments close, phone numbers change, facilities come under new management, and so on.

We would love to hear from you concerning your experiences with this guide and how you feel it could be improved and be kept up to date. While we may not be able to respond to all comments and suggestions, we'll take them to heart, and we'll also make certain to share them with the authors. Please send your comments and suggestions to the following address:

The Globe Pequot Press
Reader Response/Editorial Department
P.O. Box 480
Guilford, CT 06437

Or you may e-mail us at:
editorial@GlobePequot.com

Thanks for your input, and happy travels!

INTRODUCTION

Have you ever thought about waking up, looking out your window, and viewing the morning sun shining on the north face of the Grand Canyon? How about a walk down a dirt road from the historic hotel where you just had a dinner of walleye pike, and standing where French fur trappers portaged their canoes around a waterfall? Maybe you would enjoy sitting on a wooden deck outside your room, listening to the roar of a mountain stream. Perhaps you are a closet cowboy who has always wanted to spend a week riding horses at a dude ranch. Maybe you would like to walk outside your lodge and view a dormant volcano. These are just a few of the dreams that can be brought to life by staying at a national park lodging facility.

The two of us have devoted more than two dozen summers and numerous Christmas vacations to exploring America's national parks. Most of the trips took place in a series of four Volkswagen campers that accumulated nearly a quarter of a million miles. Trust us, twenty summers living in VW campers is marital devotion with a capital D. We dedicated four summers to experiencing the national park lodges. Our latest lodge trip during the summer of 2005 consumed ninety-two days during which we drove 11,000 miles through thirty states. We visited sixty-six national park lodges and stayed fifty-six nights in forty-six different lodges, many of which for the third or fourth time. At each lodge we walk the property, view as many rooms as possible, talk with the employees, and sample the food. We gather information that we believe will be of value to you in planning a trip.

Most national park lodges are in the well-known and heavily visited parks, such as Grand Canyon, Death Valley, Everglades, Yosemite, Yellowstone, Olympic, and Glacier. However, some lesser-known park areas, including Oregon Caves National Monument, Isle Royale National Park, Big Bend National Park, and Lassen Volcanic National Park, each offer comfortable and interesting lodge facilities. Some of the biggest and busiest parks do not have lodges. For example, Great Smoky Mountains National Park, Rocky Mountain National Park, and Acadia National Park do not offer conventional lodging inside the park boundaries, although accommodations are available directly outside each of these parks.

Not all areas managed by the National Park Service are classified as national parks. In fact, only about 15 percent of the areas officially carry the title "national park." The National Park Service also manages many national monuments, national lakeshores, national historic sites, national recreation areas, national memorials, and several other types of facilities. Each of these areas has something unique to offer or it wouldn't be included in the system. Some of them even have lodging. We mentioned Oregon Caves National Monument, in which a classic old lodge awaits you. Lodging is also available at Canyon de Chelly National Monument, Blue Ridge Parkway, Cumberland Island National Seashore, Ozark National Scenic Riverways, Glacier Bay National Monument, and Buffalo National River.

Staying in a park lodge during your trip to a national park area will almost surely enhance your park experience. It certainly did ours. Spend some time talking to the employees and learning about the history of the building where you are staying. Most of all, travel and enjoy.

CONSIDERATIONS IN PLANNING A STAY AT A NATIONAL PARK LODGE

National park lodges provide a different kind of vacation experience. Most of the lodges are in close proximity to the things you want to see, the places you want to visit, and the facilities you will want to use when you visit a park. At Crater Lake Lodge, you can sleep in a room with windows that overlook the crater rim. In Yellowstone's Old Faithful Inn, you can walk out the entrance and view an eruption of Old Faithful. At the Grand Canyon's El Tovar, you can walk a few steps outside the hotel and look down into the canyon. Many park lodges have large rustic lobby areas where you can relax with other guests in front of a blazing fireplace. The lodges are often near National Park Service visitor centers or campgrounds where guided walks originate and natural history programs are presented. Evening programs or other entertainment can be enjoyed in many of the lodges.

Most lodge facilities in national park areas are owned by the government but managed by private concerns subject to oversight by the park in which they are located. Managements of these lodges operate as concessionaires and are required to obtain the approval of the National Park Service for room rates, improvements, and the prices charged for everything from food to gasoline. Some lodges remain under private ownership on private property within a park. In general, lodges under private ownership were in operation prior to the establishment of a park or prior to an expansion of the park boundaries. Lodges on private property are subject to fewer restrictions regarding what they can offer and the prices they can charge.

Some basic information regarding reservations, facilities, and policies can be helpful if you have never stayed in a national park facility or have stayed in only one or two lodges. Most national park lodges experience large public demand for a limited number of rooms, especially during peak season, when you are most likely to want a room. Thus, you should make a reservation as early as possible, especially if your planned vacation coincides with the park's busiest period. Try to book rooms at a popular lodge at least six months before your expected arrival. Several lodges in very busy locations such as Yosemite Valley should, if possible, be booked nearly a year in advance. Choosing to vacation in off-peak periods, normally spring and fall, will make it much more likely that you are able to obtain a reservation on the dates you desire. Other important factors regarding national park lodges are discussed below.

Facilities. National park lodges range from luxurious and expensive facilities, such as Yosemite National Park's Ahwahnee and Death Valley National Park's Furnace Creek Inn, to very rustic cabins without bathrooms, such as those at Grant Grove in Kings Canyon National Park. Some facilities call themselves lodges but are not what most of us picture when we think of a lodge. For example, Old Faithful Lodge Cabins (not the more famous Old Faithful Inn, which sits nearby) offers only cabins as overnight accommodations. Likewise, Signal Mountain Lodge in Grand Teton National Park does not have a main lodge building with overnight accommodations; rather, it has several types of cabins that rent at a fairly wide range of prices. The variation in facilities between and within parks makes it important that you understand exactly what types of accommodations are being discussed when you are making a reservation.

Most national park lodging facilities don't have amenities such as spas, swimming pools, game rooms, and some of the other niceties you may expect to find at commercial facilities outside the parks. In fact, most park lodges don't have telephones or televisions in the rooms, although public telephones are nearly always available somewhere in the facility. Several older lodges, including Old Faithful Inn and Lake Crescent

Lodge, offer some rooms without a private bathroom. Community bathrooms and shower rooms are available for occupants of these rooms. Some cabins do not have private bathrooms.

Rooms. Rooms in a lodge often vary considerably with regard to size, bedding, view, and rate. Likewise, a single lodging facility may offer rooms in the main lodge building, rooms in motel-type buildings, and a variety of cabin rooms. This is the case with Lake Crescent Lodge in Olympic National Park and with Big Meadows in Shenandoah National Park, for example. Potential differences in rooms mean that it is worthwhile to learn what options are available at a particular location where you plan to stay. If you wait to make a reservation near your planned arrival date, you are likely to find a limited variety of accommodations. For example, you may find that all the rooms with private bathrooms are already taken. On the other hand, call early and you are likely to have a wide choice of rooms that are offered at a wide range of rates. Ask about a view room, for example. Sometimes rooms with an excellent view are more expensive, and sometimes they are not. Some buildings do not have elevators, so the floor you are assigned may be important. Higher floors tend to offer better views but require more climbing. Rooms near the lobby may be noisy. Some lodges allow you to reserve a particular room, but most lodges guarantee only a particular type of room. Even when a particular room won't be guaranteed, a lodge will often make note of your preferences and attempt to satisfy the request when room assignments are made.

Wheelchair Accessibility. Most national park lodging facilities offer some type of wheelchair accessibility, but the degree of accessibility varies considerably among the lodges and among different types of accommodations at the same lodge. For example, Zion Lodge has two newer motel-type rooms that are fully wheelchair accessible with ramps, wide doorways, and roll-in showers. On the other hand, Western Cabins at the same lodge are only marginally wheelchair accessible. It isn't that the lodge managers don't care, but rather that many national park lodging facilities are historic and restrictions exist with regard to modifications that can be made. Keep in mind that lodging facilities are sometimes a distance from parking, and many facilities with two or more stories do not have elevators. In addition, some national park accommodations do not have telephones in the rooms. Be certain to have a clear understanding about the extent of wheelchair accessibility when booking a room.

Reservations. Reservations can generally be made by either telephone or mail, and sometimes by fax or the Internet. The disadvantage of using the mail is the uncertainty that a room will be available on the dates you request. If rooms are unavailable on the specified dates, you must wait for a reply and then start over again, but at a much later date, when even fewer rooms are available. This can sometimes be avoided by listing alternative dates that you find acceptable.

Choosing to make a reservation by telephone allows you to immediately determine room availability and, if necessary, choose alternative dates. Using the telephone will also allow you to discuss with the reservation agent the types of facilities that are available. The best bet is to write early for literature or study the lodge Web site so that you have a basic understanding of the facilities and rates prior to calling. This will allow you to know which type of room and building to ask for and what to expect regarding rates. Be aware that it is often difficult to get through to a reservation agent via telephone, especially if you call late in the spring, when everyone else in the country seems to be trying the same number. Try calling at odd hours, such as weekend mornings.

Most lodges require a deposit of at least one night's lodging when making a reservation. A few lodges permit you to guarantee the reservation with a credit card and to pay for the entire stay when you check out. When sending a deposit check or giving a credit card number, always ask for an e-mail or written confirmation to take on your vacation. In a couple of cases, our reservations have gotten lost. In the event your plans change, refund of a deposit requires advance notice, usually forty-eight hours, but this varies by lodge.

Rates. In general, accommodations in the national parks aren't cheap. You can expect to pay $100 and up for most double rooms, although some rustic cabins are much cheaper, while a room at one of the nicer facilities can run $150 and up. In addition, discounts for seniors, AAA members, and so on, that you expect at most commercial facilities are generally unavailable at national park lodges. Most lodges quote rates for two adults, which means that you must pay a double rate even if you travel alone. Additional adults pay extra, although young children are generally free when staying with adults. Some lodges allow children twelve years and under to stay free, while other facilities limit free stays to children three and under. Lodges sometimes offer reduced rates during their off-seasons or have special packages that include meals or a lower rate for multiday stays. Ask about specials when you book a reservation, but don't get your hopes too high. The dollar cost of rooms and meals for summer 2005 is used in this book. Expect somewhat higher prices in subsequent years.

Payment, Check-in, and Checkout. Most lodges accept major credit cards, but you should determine acceptable methods of payment when a reservation is made. For example, you may end up at a lodge that will accept only a few major cards, or will not accept a personal check.

Most lodges specify an 11:00 A.M. checkout and a 4:00 P.M. check-in, but the times can be different depending on which lodge you will be using. For example, some lodges specify a 2:00 or 3:00 P.M. check-in,

while some don't require a checkout until noon. The checkout time can generally be postponed by at least an hour with a request to the front desk the prior night or the morning of your planned departure. You may be able to check in prior to the specified time, but don't count on it. If you arrive early in the morning, you are likely to roam around without a room until late afternoon. Lodges that assign a particular room to each guest are less flexible in getting guests into rooms before the scheduled check-in time.

Obtaining a Room without a Reservation. Some national park lodges have space available, especially during off-peak periods. Even busy lodges experience cancellations or early departures that free up rooms. Thus, you may be able to obtain a room without an advance reservation. For example, you may locate a room in a busy park like Yellowstone during peak summer months just by dropping in at one of the nine lodges and asking about a vacancy. If rooms are available, they are unlikely to be the exact configuration, location, or price category you would choose. For example, you may have to accept a room without a private bathroom or a room that is more expensive than you would ordinarily reserve. In a large park like Yellowstone or Glacier, the only available rooms may be in a different facility that is many miles from the lodge where you are making the request. Taking a chance on a vacancy is a risky strategy. Being unsuccessful may result in a long drive to a distant location where you are likely to overpay for an inferior room. Hedge your bets by calling ahead.

Pets. National park lodges generally prohibit pets of all kinds except for seeing-eye dogs. There are exceptions, but not many. Some of the larger lodges such as those at Mammoth Cave National Park, the South Rim of Grand Canyon National Park, and Yosemite National Park have kennels available, but don't count on this convenience at the park you plan to visit. Ask about the policy regarding pets at the time you make a reservation. Each of the national parks requires that pets be kept on a leash at all times. In addition, pets are normally prohibited from park trails. The bottom line is that pets should be left at home if you are making a trip to a national park, especially if you plan to visit several parks during the same trip.

Reducing Expenses. Most national park lodges are pricey. If you are on a limited budget but want to experience a stay at one or more of the lodges, it is possible to take steps to reduce your expenditures. Accepting a room without a private bathroom (if available) can often save $40 to $50 per night compared to rooms with a private bath. These rooms also tend to be easier to reserve, because many individuals demand a private bath.

Another money-saving strategy is to spend every second or third night camping. Most parks with lodges also have campgrounds that charge $12 to $20 per night. Arrange the campground stays into your schedule when reservations are being made. For example, spend two nights in a lodge, then move to a campground for the third night. Keep in mind that some national park campgrounds operate under a reservation system.

Another strategy is to spend the night prior to arrival at an inexpensive commercial facility that is within an hour or two of the park. Staying in close proximity permits you to enjoy most of a full day in the park before checking in at the lodge. Likewise, obtain a reservation at a motel a couple of hours outside the park on your departure date so that you can spend most of an extra day finishing your park sightseeing.

Take along a cooler with some food and drink, including snacks such as pretzels, candy, soft drinks, and fruit. Most lodges have ice machines that can be used to resupply a cooler. Buy groceries outside the park, where they are likely to be cheaper. Eat a breakfast of fruit and cereal in your room, and have a picnic lunch or supper. If you take the trouble to visit a national park, you may as well enjoy nature. If you choose to eat in a lodge restaurant, keep in mind that lunch can be quite a bit less expensive than dinner. In parks that offer several restaurant facilities, examine the menus before choosing a place to eat because prices can vary a great deal from one restaurant to another. In general, cafeterias are considerably less expensive places to eat than dining rooms.

Play it safe by establishing a budget for your trip before you leave. Estimate how much you are going to spend for lodging, food, transportation, and incidentals, then make a real effort to stay within your budget. You might find that some things are more expensive than planned. You may be able to substitute a couple of picnic lunches for restaurant meals and save enough for a guided park tour. Using a budget may keep you from buying all the T-shirts during the first visit to a gift shop.

Take advantage of the many free things that are offered at virtually all the park areas. National Park Service personnel offer guided walks and programs, generally at no charge. These are fun and informative. Parks with campgrounds typically have evening history and nature programs that are offered without charge. Park visitor centers have exhibits and audiovisual programs to help you understand the park. Some of the lodges even offer free lodge tours. Many parks offer Junior Ranger programs for children. It is best to stop at the park visitor center and obtain a list of daily activities.

Park Fees. Many areas operated by the National Park Service charge an entrance fee. Visitors, including those staying in a lodge within a park, are required to pay the park entrance fee. Most parks charge a vehicle entry fee that covers everyone inside the vehicle. Hikers, motorcyclists, bicyclists, and visitors entering in commercial vehicles pay a separate fee applicable to individual entry. Entrance fees range from $10 to $20 per private vehicle, with the higher price charged at large national parks, including Yellowstone, Yosemite, and Grand Canyon. The park fee generally provides exit and entrance for three to seven days, depending on the park. Inquire about this at the entrance station if you may need to go outside the park during a stay of several days. The National Park Service sells four types of passes that provide free entrance at all national parks. The National Parks Pass ($50) allows unlimited entry to any and all areas operated by the National Park Service for one year from the month of purchase. For an extra $15 a hologram is attached and converts this pass to a Golden Eagle Passport that provides entrance to additional areas operated by the Bureau of Land Management, the National Forest Service, and the Corps of Engineers. For seniors (age sixty-two and over), the Golden Age Passport provides lifetime free entrance for a one-time fee of $10. The Golden Access Passport (no charge) is available to individuals who are disabled. Both the Golden Age and Golden Access passports, which must be purchased in person, also allow a 50 percent reduction in fees for parking, boat launching, and most tours. All four passes may be purchased at most National Park Service entrance stations and visitor centers. The National Park Pass is available by phone (1–888–GOPARKS), on the Internet (www .nationalparks.org), or via mail by sending a check or money order to National Parks Pass, 27540 Avenue Mentry, Valencia, CA 91355. A shipping charge of $3.95 applies to passes purchased by mail, phone, or via the Internet.

Getting the Most from a National Park Visit.
Staying in a national park lodge should enhance your visit to a park, but don't let it be your main activity.

National park areas offer numerous activities in which you can participate. Your first order of business should be to request information from the park areas you will be visiting. We have included addresses, phone numbers, and Web sites for each park that has lodging facilities. Parks are generally prompt in answering requests for information. Read about the parks so you will have a basic understanding of the history, geology, and activities prior to your arrival. At parks with an entry station you will be given a park newspaper and a mini-folder with a map of the park. These can be obtained at the visitor centers of parks without an entry station. Stop at a visitor center to determine what activities are scheduled during your stay. A visitor center may be near the lodge where you will be staying or it may be on the way to your lodge. Visitor centers generally have excellent video presentations that provide either an overview of the park or a story about some particular facet of history or geology. Visitor centers also generally post a list of daily activities including talks, demonstrations, guided hikes, and campfire programs. Take advantage of as many of these activities as time permits, for they are nearly always enjoyable and educational. You will have an opportunity to ask questions of an expert at the same time that you share information with other visitors who have interests similar to yours. Many parks offer junior ranger programs for children. These programs allow kids to earn a junior ranger patch while they learn about the park and its environment. Information on these programs is available at the visitor center.

ALASKA

Glacier Bay National Park and Preserve

P.O. Box 140 • Gustavus, AK 99826 • (907) 697-2230 • www.nps.gov/glba

Glacier Bay National Park and Preserve comprises approximately 3.3 million acres that include some of the world's most impressive examples of tidewater glaciers, rivers of ice that flow to the sea. The park is rich in plant and animal life and is the home to moose, black bears, mountain goats, seals, humpback whales, and porpoises. A short road links the small town of Gustavus and its airport with the lodge, but most of the natural features of the park can be seen only by boat or airplane. The park visitor center is located inside Glacier Bay Lodge. The park is in southeastern Alaska, approximately 65 miles northwest of Juneau. No roads lead to the park, and access is via plane or boat. **Park Entrance Fee:** No charge.

Lodging in Glacier Bay National Park: Glacier Bay Lodge offers the only overnight accommodations in Glacier Bay National Park. The rustic fifty-six-room lodge is located in the southeastern section of the park near the mouth of Glacier Bay, about 9 miles from the small town of Gustavus. There are several bed-and-breakfasts in Gustavus.

GLACIER BAY LODGE

P.O. Box 179 • Gustavus, AK 99826 • (907) 697–4000 • www.visitglacierbay.com

Glacier Bay National Park and Preserve

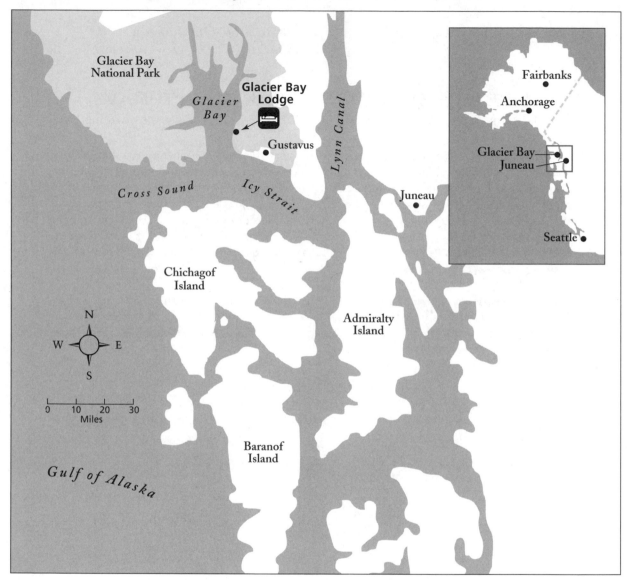

GLACIER BAY LODGE IS A WILDERNESS RESORT situated among Sitka spruce in a rainforest. The complex includes a two-story wooden chalet-type lodge building that houses a lobby that has a cathedral ceiling with wood beams, a large fireplace, registration desk, dining room with great views of the bay, theater, gift shop, and mezzanine with interpretive displays. This lodge building is connected by boardwalk to sixteen nearby one-story wooden buildings that provide guest accommodations. The lodge is located on Bartlett Cove, 9 miles from the town of Gustavus in the southeastern corner of the park. A road connects

The glaciers here remain from the Little Ice Age that began about 4,000 years ago. Glaciers form when mountain snowfall exceeds snow melt. Accumulating weight of the snow presses lower layers into solid ice that eventually flows slowly downslope. Glacier Bay National Park includes sixteen glaciers that terminate at the sea's edge. The most spectacular are the twelve glaciers that actively calve icebergs into the bay.

\\|/

the lodge with the town of Gustavus and its small airport, but no roads lead from the mainland into the park. Access is via boat or airplane.

The lodge offers fifty-six rooms in sixteen one-story wooden buildings that are close to but separate from the main lodge building. These buildings each have from two to six rooms. The rooms have radiant heat, telephone, and a private bathroom with either a shower or a combination shower-tub. All the rooms are the same size, and most have two double beds or two twin beds, although two rooms have a queen-size bed. The rooms have wood paneling and a vaulted ceiling.

Glacier Bay Lodge is certainly a place to get away from it all. It is in a very remote location that offers spectacular scenery, abundant wildlife, and a wild and unique environment. A deck attached to the main lodge allows guests to sit and watch the sun set over Bartlett Cove. A variety of activities are available, including guided nature walks, kayaking, hiking, and whale watching. Whale-watching excursions, overnight wilderness cruises, and sportfishing charters depart from a nearby dock. Films and slide programs about Glacier Bay are presented by National Park Service rangers each evening in the lodge auditorium.

Rooms: Singles, doubles, triples, and quads. All rooms in the lodge have private baths.

Wheelchair Accessibility: Two lodge rooms are ADA compliant, with wide bathroom doors, adjustable showerhead, and grab bars in the shower and near the toilet.

Reservations: Glacier Bay Lodge & Tours, 241 West Ship Creek Avenue, Anchorage, AK 99501. Phone (800) 229–8687. Cancellation is required at least seven days prior to arrival.

Rates: All rooms ($190). Rates quoted are for two adults. Each additional person is $10 per night. Children under twelve years of age stay free with adults.

Location: Approximately 9 miles northwest of Gustavus, on the shore of Bartlett Cove.

Season: Mid-May through mid-September.

Food: A dining room specializing in fresh Alaskan seafood, such as Dungeness crab, halibut, and salmon, serves three meals daily (dinner $17–$30). Lighter meals, including sandwiches, nachos, and halibut tacos, are served on the deck. A small grocery is in the town of Gustavus.

Transportation: Allen Marine Tours (888–229–8687; www.allenmarinetours.com) provides passenger ferry service from late May to early September between Glacier Bay and Auke Bay Public Boat Harbor in Juneau. The firm's 150-passenger catamaran departs from Juneau at 11:00 A.M. daily, except Wednesday, for the four-hour trip to Glacier Bay. The three-hour return trip to Juneau departs from Glacier Bay at 5:00 P.M. The trip to Glacier Bay includes extra time for whale and wildlife watching and costs $99 for adults and $69 for children ages three to twelve. The return from Glacier Bay to Juneau is $69 and $49, respectively. Round-trip cost is $149 and $99. Light food service is available on board. Two pieces of luggage are permitted without an extra charge. Alaska Airlines operates scheduled jet service to Gustavus during summer months. Charter airlines provide service between Glacier Bay and several Alaska towns. Charter air service between Juneau and Gustavus costs approximately $70 per person. A lodge shuttle (fee charged) operates between the lodge and the town of Gustavus. Gustavus transportation information is available at www.gustavus.com/gethere.html.

Facilities: Restaurant, cocktail service, auditorium, gift shop. A ranger station and boat dock are nearby.

Activities: Hiking, fishing, guided walks, fishing charters, wildlife and whale-watching cruises, and day cruises to the glaciers.

ARIZONA

Canyon de Chelly National Monument

P.O. Box 588 • Chinle, AZ 86503 • (928) 674–5500 • www.nps.gov/cach/

Canyon de Chelly (pronounced "d' SHAY") National Monument comprises nearly 84,000 acres of Navajo land that include ruins of Indian villages built between A.D. 350 and 1300 in steep-walled canyons. The visitor center is located near the park entrance. The canyon can be seen from scenic overlooks along North Rim Drive (36 miles round-trip) and South Rim Drive (34 miles round-trip). White House Ruin is accessible via a 2.5-mile (round-trip) trail that begins at a trailhead on South Rim Drive. All other trails and all four-wheel-drive travel within the park require a park ranger or authorized guide. Information is available at the visitor center. Canyon de Chelly is in northeastern Arizona, approximately 85 miles northwest of Gallup, New Mexico, near the town of Chinle, Arizona. **Monument Entrance Fee:** No charge.

Lodging in Canyon de Chelly National Monument: Thunderbird Lodge, near the monument entrance, is the only lodging facility in Canyon de Chelly National Monument. The lodge includes a cafeteria and gift shop. Guided tours of the canyons leave from the lodge. A Best Western and a Holiday Inn are in the town of Chinle and a short distance outside the monument entrance.

THUNDERBIRD LODGE

P.O. Box 548 • Chinle, AZ 86503 • (928) 674–5841
www.tbirdlodge.com

Canyon de Chelly
Units at Thunderbird Lodge

Canyon de Chelly National Monument

THUNDERBIRD LODGE IS AN ATTRACTIVE, WELL-maintained motor lodge, offering seventy-four rooms just inside the entrance to Canyon de Chelly National Monument. The lodge, situated in a grove of cottonwood trees, comprises a complex of several adobe and stone buildings, including four adobe units that contain most of the lodging rooms. The adobe registration building is separate but adjacent to the buildings containing the rooms. Separate stone buildings house a small number of rooms, a gift shop, and a cafeteria. Thunderbird Lodge is on Navajo Route 7, 3 miles east of the intersection with Highway 191 in the town of Chinle.

Thunderbird Lodge offers several types of rooms, although most are very similar. All rooms are decorated in an attractive Southwest style and have air-conditioning, heat, ceiling fans, television, and a telephone.

Thunderbird Lodge was originally constructed in 1902 as a trading post on the Navajo Reservation. The post served as a store, bank, post office, community meeting place, and courtroom. The owner began offering rooms and food service to accommodate an increasing number of tourists, who came to view the cliff dwellings and spectacular scenery. The present-day cafeteria is in the original trading post, while the building housing the gift shop originally served as home for the trading post's owner.

\\/

Most of the forty-one Adobe motel-type rooms have two queen beds and a full bath. The Adobe Rooms have beamed ceilings and are housed in two long buildings built into the back of a hill. Adequate parking is directly in front of a covered walkway that runs across the front of the buildings. Most of the twenty-eight De Chelly Rooms each contain two double beds and a full bath, although one has three full beds, and a few are available with a king bed. All but four of the De Chelly Rooms are in two buildings constructed around a grassy courtyard filled with trees. Rooms in these buildings back up to one another, with half facing the courtyard and half facing the parking lot. Four De Chelly Rooms are in two buildings, one stone and one adobe, that sit in the center of the complex. One suite in a stone building has a separate bedroom with one king bed, a living room area with a queen sofa bed and a refrigerator, and a full bathroom. Four smaller rooms in one stone building each have one double bed and are rented only on-site. We recommend you choose from De Chelly Rooms 14 through 18 or 25 through 29, all of which face the courtyard. These are quiet and front on a nice grassy area.

Thunderbird Lodge is an exceptionally well-maintained facility offering a relaxing atmosphere where guests visit from porch chairs directly outside their rooms. The green lawns are immaculate and the building exteriors always appear as if they were recently redone. Guests from a neighboring room told us during our 2005 visit that Thunderbird Lodge was their favorite stay during a two-week trip to the Southwest. The lodge cafeteria has an attractive interior with decorative Navajo rugs and offers inexpensive food, including the house specialty Navajo taco, from early morning to evening. The lodge gift shop features a large selection of handwoven Navajo rugs. The National Park Service visitor center with a variety of exhibits, including a Navajo home called a *hogan*, is an easy half-mile walk from the lodge. Interpretive programs at the visitor center include ranger presentations and guided walks. The lodge is also near the monument's campground where evening campfire programs are offered.

Half-day ($40 adults/$30 children) or full-day ($65) guided canyon tours are offered by the lodge. The half-day tours take approximately three and a half hours and cover the lower half of Canyon del Muerto and Canyon de Chelly. They depart at 9:00 A.M. and 2:00 P.M. April through October, and 1:00 P.M. the rest of the year. Full-day tours last approximately eight hours, departing at 9:00 A.M. The longer tour includes lunch and traverses Canyon del Muerto to Mummy Cave and Canyon de Chelly to Spider Rock. For reservations call (800) 679–2473. The Tseqi Guide Association offers guides to lead tours in your four-wheel-drive vehicle. Call (520) 674–5500 for information.

Rooms: Doubles, triples, and quads. All rooms offer a full private bath.

Wheelchair Accessibility: Seven De Chelly Rooms offer ramp access, one king bed, and a bathroom with a wide doorway, grab bars, and a combination shower-tub. These rooms are on the parking lot side of the building. The registration building and cafeteria also offer ramp access.

Reservations: Thunderbird Lodge, P.O. Box 548, Chinle, AZ 86503. Phone (800) 679–2473; fax (928) 674–5844. Reservations may be made up to a year in advance. Cancellation must be made twenty-four hours in advance for a full refund.

Rates: Summer rates (April 1 to October 31) for two people: Adobe units ($106); De Chelly units ($101); Suite ($145). Each additional person is $4.00 in rooms and $5.00 in suite. Winter rate for two persons: Adobe or De Chelly ($65). Rollaway, crib, and each additional person is $6.50. Special packages are available during winter months. Senior discounts and government rates are offered.

Location: The lodge is a short distance inside the park entrance.

Season: The lodge is open year-round. Heaviest season is from April through October, when reservations are advised.

Food: A lodge cafeteria offers basic food at reasonable prices from 6:30 A.M. to 8:30 P.M. during the summer months, with shorter hours the remainder of the year. Most meals range from $6.00 to $15.00, with steak dinners from $10.00 to $18.00. Alternative eating facilities are in the town of Chinle.

Transportation: No public transportation serves Canyon de Chelly National Monument or the town of Chinle.

Facilities: Cafeteria, gift shop, stable, National Park Service visitor center. Three miles west the town of Chinle has fast-food outlets, service stations, grocery stores, laundries, and a bank.

Activities: Hiking, canyon tours, National Park Service interpretive programs, horseback riding.

Glen Canyon National Recreation Area
P.O. Box 1507 • Page, AZ 86040 • (928) 608–6200 • www.nps.gov/glca/

Glen Canyon National Recreation Area comprises 1.25 million acres of high desert surrounding and including Lake Powell and its nearly 2,000 miles of shoreline. Lake Powell is formed by the Glen Canyon Dam near Page, Arizona, which backs up the Colorado River for nearly 200 miles. Most of the activities here, including boating, fishing, and waterskiing, are water-related. Houseboat rental is available at several locations on Lake Powell. Although nearly all of the recreation area is in southern Utah, the most accessible part is along U.S. Highway 89 near Page, Arizona, where the Glen Canyon Dam is located. **Recreation Area Entrance Fee:** $10.00 per vehicle or $3.00 per person, good for seven days.

Lodging in Glen Canyon National Recreation Area: Four locations in Glen Canyon National Recreation Area offer overnight lodging facilities. The largest and nicest facility by far is at Lake Powell Resort, 6 miles north of Page, Arizona, on US 89. The resort also has the largest marina on the lake. Overnight accommodations are offered by the same concessionaire at three other locations. The three facilities are on a much smaller scale than Lake Powell Resort and at relatively remote locations in southern Utah. Bullfrog Resort and Halls Crossing are located in the central section of Lake Powell, and Hite, in the northern section. Reservations are made using the same address and phone number listed for Lake Powell Resort. All of the locations permit pets. Houseboat rentals are available at all four locations.

LAKE POWELL RESORT

Box 1597 • Page, AZ 86040 • (928) 645–2433 • lakepowell@aramark.com
www.lakepowell.com

LAKE POWELL RESORT (FORMERLY WAHWEAP Lodge) offers 344 rooms as part of a marina resort complex on Lake Powell, just north of Page, Arizona. The resort comprises a separate registration building and eight identical two-story lodging buildings on a peninsula on Lake Powell. The landscaped stucco buildings are finished and decorated in a Southwest design. The complex also has two swimming pools, a well-equipped fitness room with sauna, a gas station, a restaurant, a coffee bar, a lounge, and a grocery/gift shop. An RV park and campground are a short distance away. A very large marina complex is beside the lodge, which is situated directly on Lake Powell.

All 344 spacious rooms (other than the four suites) in Lake Powell Resort are of identical size. The majority have two queen-size beds, while others have a king bed. All of the rooms have heat, air-conditioning, a television, a telephone, a refrigerator, a coffeemaker, a hair dryer, and a full bath. Each room has a private balcony or patio with chairs. The two-story buildings are constructed with rooms on both sides and access through an interior corridor that runs the length of the building.

The rooms on the second floor require climbing a flight of stairs, as none of the buildings has an elevator.

The lodge offers four categories of rooms. The least expensive Traditional Rooms face the parking area on

The stunning landscape surrounding Lake Powell Resort has served as a location for more than forty movies, including 1962's The Greatest Story Ever Told, *starring Charlton Heston, Carroll Baker, Pat Boone, and Jose Ferrer.* Maverick, *with Mel Gibson, Jodie Foster, and James Garner, was filmed here in 1993. Other movies filmed in the Lake Powell area include* Planet of the Apes, Sergeants Three, The Outlaw Josey Wales, Superman III, *and* Anasazi Moon. *John Travolta stayed in Lake Powell Resort suite 274 for a month in 1995 during the filming of* Broken Arrow.

Glen Canyon National Recreation Area

both first and second floors. Lakeview Rooms were renovated in 2004 and 2005 with substantially nicer furnishings, tiled bathrooms, and upgraded porch furniture. These rooms also have an iron and ironing board and enjoy a view of Lake Powell. Deluxe Lakeview Rooms in the two newest buildings have been completely refurbished with upmarket Southwestern-themed furnishings. These rooms are quite nice and rent for about $20 more than Lakeview Rooms. The lodge offers four second-floor Lakeview Suites, each twice the size of a regular room. The suites have a wet bar, a 32-inch LCD television, and a king bed plus a sofa bed in the sitting room. Two suites each have a wraparound balcony while the remaining two have whirlpool tubs.

Lake Powell Resort offers an upscale place to spend the night in a lakeside setting. It has two swimming pools, a pool bar, and an outdoor spa. The registration building has a large gift shop, a tour desk, a lounge with great lake views, a coffee bar, and a full-service restaurant. The attractive restaurant has a tiered circular dining area with a wall of windows that present a panoramic view of the lake. A gas station and general store are nearby.

The Adventure Cove beach area has cabanas, food

and beverage service, and water-related offerings including kayak rentals and water ski lessons. Various types of boats, from canoes to 59-foot houseboats, can be rented at the marina. A variety of half- and full-day boat tours can be arranged in the lobby of the registration building. Air tours are available at the Page Airport. Special packages that include a boat tour and room at the lodge are available.

Rooms: Doubles, triples, and quads. All rooms have private baths with a combination shower-tub.

Wheelchair Accessibility: Twelve wheelchair-accessible rooms (no suites), some Lakeview and some Traditional, have a wide bathroom door, a combination shower-tub with grab bars, and a regular door, rather than a sliding door, connecting with the patio.

Reservations: Lake Powell Resorts & Marinas, P.O. Box 56909, Phoenix, AZ 85079. Phone (800) 528–6154 or, from the greater Phoenix area, (602) 278–8888; fax (602) 331–5258; www.lakepowell.com. A deposit of one night's lodging is required. A cancellation notice of twenty-four hours is required for a refund.

Rates: Peak season: June 1–August 26; Value Season: August 27–September 21 and April 24–June 8; Budget Season: September 22–April 23. Rooms: Traditional ($113/$86/$69); Lakeview ($133/$101/$81); Deluxe Lakeview ($154/$116/$94); Suite ($221/$199/$178). Children under eighteen years of age stay free.

Location: Lake Powell Resort is on US 89, 6 miles north of Page, Arizona.

Season: The lodge is open all year.

Food: A full-service restaurant offering panoramic vistas of the lake and countryside serves breakfast ($4.00–$10.00), lunch ($7.00–$13.00), and dinner ($13.00–$24.00). Alcoholic beverages are available in the restaurant and in an adjacent lounge that serves appetizers, salads, and sandwiches ($7.00-$10.00). A coffee bar in the lobby serves gourmet coffee and pastries. A pizzeria with indoor/outdoor dining at the end of the complex serves pizza, sandwiches, salads, and ice cream from Memorial Day weekend through Labor Day. Room service is available from both the restaurant and pizzeria. The *Canyon King* paddlewheeler offers dinner cruises April through October depending on demand. Advance reservations are required.

Transportation: Regularly scheduled flights to Page, Arizona, operate from Phoenix. Charter flights are available to other cities within the region. Rental cars are available at the airport. From mid-May through mid-October, the lodge operates scheduled bus service between the lodge and the airport, as well as other destinations in the town of Page. This service is offered "on request" in the off-season. A courtesy shuttle service to various locations around the Lake Powell area is offered year-round to lodge guests.

Facilities: A sport shop (with limited groceries), cocktail lounge, gift shop, gas station, restaurant, pizza parlor, Adventure Cove Beach area, and marina. Two swimming pools, an outdoor spa, and a fitness room with top-of-the-line equipment and a sauna are at the lodge. A coin-operated laundry is at the nearby RV park. Postal services and stamps are available at the marina. Fax service is available for a fee.

Activities: Swimming (two pools and a beach); walking and hiking; boat rentals (all sizes); waterskiing; fishing; float trips, half-day and all-day; many water tours of from one hour to all day; evening campfire programs at the campground presented by the National Park Service.

Pets: A fee of $10 per night per pet is charged in addition to a $75 deposit.

BULLFROG RESORT AND MARINA

Box 4055 • Lake Powell, UT 84533 • (435) 684–3000

BULLFROG RESORT AND MARINA OFFERS FORTY-eight lodge rooms at Defiance House Lodge plus eight housekeeping units. The lodge rooms are in a single stucco building that sits atop a high bluff overlooking Bullfrog Bay. Both the building, constructed in the early 1980s, and the rooms within are almost identical in looks and room rates to those in Lake Powell Resort. Eight freestanding prefabricated housekeeping units (peak $193; value $146; budget $118; for one to six persons per unit) each contain three bedrooms, two full baths, a living room, a full kitchen, microwave, dishes and utensils for eight people, linens, and a television but no telephone. Pay phones are available. All of the units have heat and air-conditioning. The interiors are attractive and nicely furnished.

The resort is located at Bullfrog Basin on Utah Highway 276 on the west side of Lake Powell. A toll ferry at Bullfrog crosses the lake. Bullfrog Resort and Marina offers a restaurant, cocktail lounge, gift shop, liquor store, and a gas station. Like the resort, the restaurant is open year-round. It offers cocktails and three meals a day (breakfast is seasonal). A fast-food restaurant at the marina is open from Memorial Day through Labor Day. The marina store sells basic food supplies and beverages. Ranger programs and a medical clinic operate during summer months.

A National Park Service visitor center adjacent to the resort contains exhibits concerning the Colorado Plateau and the evolution of Glen Canyon plant and animal life. A concessionaire offers half- and full-day boat tours during the summer. Boat rental is available.

Lake Powell was created by the Glen Canyon Dam, which is just south of Lake Powell Resort. The dam backs up the Colorado River for 200 miles and supplies water and electricity to California, Arizona, and Nevada. Concrete for the dam and power plant was poured around the clock for more than three years. Dam tours once offered have been discontinued indefinitely.

HALLS CROSSING AND MARINA

Box 5101 • Lake Powell, UT 84533 • (435) 684–7000

HALLS CROSSING AND MARINA IS LOCATED ON Utah Highway 276 between Blanding and Hanksville. It offers twenty freestanding housekeeping units identical to those at Bullfrog Resort and Marina. Halls Crossing and Marina has auto service, a marina, and a store with limited supplies. Boat rentals and tours are offered. A toll ferry provides continuation of UT 276. Transportation is available from a small airport 10 miles from Halls Crossing. Rates are the same as at Bullfrog Resort and Marina.

HITE MARINA

Box 501 • Lake Powell, UT 84533 • (435) 684–2278

HITE MARINA IS OFF UTAH HIGHWAY 95 ON THE north end of Lake Powell between Blanding and Hanksville. This is the smallest of the four lodging complexes at Lake Powell, offering only five housekeeping units that are identical to those at Bullfrog Resort and Marina and Halls Crossing. One housekeeping unit is totally wheelchair accessible. Hite offers a gas station, a ranger station, a supply store, and a marina where boats can be rented. Rates for housekeeping units are the same as at Bullfrog Resort and Marina.

Grand Canyon National Park

P.O. Box 129 • Grand Canyon, AZ 86023 • (928) 638–7888 • www.nps.gov/grca

Grand Canyon National Park, covering 1,904 square miles, is one of the most popular parks operated by the National Park Service, especially the South Rim section. The Grand Canyon itself is so spectacular that first-time visitors are likely to think they are viewing a painting. The canyon has been created by massive uplift and the cutting effect of the Colorado River, which originates in the Rocky Mountains. The river now flows nearly a mile below the South Rim and even farther below the higher North Rim. Although the developed areas of the North Rim and the South Rim are separated by only about 10 miles, the distance by road is 214 miles. An alternative is the 21-mile Kaibab Trail, which leads from Yaki Point on the South Rim to within 2 miles of Grand Canyon Lodge on the North Rim. A daily shuttle service (fee charged) is offered between the South Rim and the North Rim.

North Rim or South Rim? The two sides of the Grand Canyon are so different that they share little other than the same canyon and river. The more popular South Rim is open year-round and has easier canyon access, more facilities, and many more visitors. The South Rim offers more eating facilities, more stores, more places to walk, and more people to bump into. Vehicles and people are in constant motion. Things seem to move much more slowly at the North Rim, where services and visitors are limited. The higher elevation of the North Rim results in cooler temperatures and more trees. Vistas from the North Rim seem more intimate, and fewer people will be standing next to you straining for the same view. The North Rim is closed in winter. If you are lucky, you will be able to sample both rims, perhaps on the same trip. **Park Entrance Fee:** $20 per vehicle or $10 per person, good for seven days.

Lodging in Grand Canyon National Park: Grand Canyon National Park has eight lodges, six at the popular South Rim, one on the floor of the canyon, and one at the North Rim. Lodging alternatives range from small lodge rooms without a private bath, to historic cabins, to rooms in a classic historical hotel building. Rates also vary a great deal depending on where you decide to stay (or are able to locate a room). The wide variation in accommodations means that you should have a basic understanding of the alternatives when you make your reservations. All the lodges are operated by one concessioner, and reservations are made using the same address, telephone number, or Web site. The lodges are all very popular, and reservations should, if possible, be made many months in advance. Keep in mind that several motels are a short distance outside the south entrance, which is only 7 miles from Grand Canyon Village and the South Rim.

SOUTH RIM (Six Lodges)

www.grandcanyonlodges.com

Most visitors reach the South Rim of the Grand Canyon via Arizona Highways 180 and 64 from Flagstaff, Arizona. An alternative route via AZ 89 to AZ 64 and the east entrance is longer and slower but offers numerous views of the canyon. The center of activity for the South Rim is Grand Canyon Village, where you will find lodges, cabins, gift shops, restaurants, a large National Park Service visitor center, and the start of numerous tours.

Grand Canyon Village is generally very popular, and thus, crowded, partcularly in summer months. Parking is often difficult to find, so grab the first parking space you see and use the free shuttles to get around the South Rim developed area. Shuttles operate year-round in the Grand Canyon Village area and provide access to the visitor center at Canyon View Information Plaza. The shuttle to Hermits Rest, west of Grand Canyon Village, operates March through November. All shuttles run every fifteen to thirty minutes.

The South Rim has six lodging alternatives (actually, eight because two have two separate sections). The classic El Tovar, the most expensive, is directly on the rim and is the South Rim's top-of-the-line hotel. This historic hotel is in an ideal location and offers recently remodeled rooms, but nearby parking is scarce. Next door are Thunderbird and Kachina, two identical lodges with nice, recently remodeled rooms. North-facing rooms in both units have terrific canyon views. Bright Angel Lodge offers historic Grand Canyon cabins. Parking can be a problem, but we think Bright Angel's rim cabins with fireplaces may be among the best accommodations on the South Rim. Maswik is a large lodging complex with two very different sections. Both offer plentiful parking and a nearby cafeteria. Maswik North has nice motel-type rooms a moderate walk from the canyon rim. Maswik South has smaller, less expensive but less desirable rooms. Perhaps the best value is the recently remodeled Yavapai East, which offers nice rooms, plenty of parking, and proximity to Market Plaza, the South Rim's commercial center. Although Yavapai is about a half-mile from the rim and 1 mile from the South Rim's other hotels and restaurants, a free shuttle offers frequent service. Yavapai West is less desirable than Yavapai East, but probably superior to Maswik South.

Reservations: Grand Canyon National Park Lodges, Xanterra Parks and Resorts, 6312 S. Fiddlers Green Circle, Suite 600N, Greenwood Village, CO 80111. Phone (888) 297–2757; fax (303) 297–3175; www.xanterra.com or www.grandcanyonlodges.com. The cost of the first night's lodging is required as a deposit. Cancellation notice of forty-eight hours is required for a full refund. Reservations may be made up to thirteen months in advance. Try to make reservations six or more months in advance for the busy summer months. Space is often available on short notice because of cancellations. For same-day reservations phone (928) 638–2631.

Food: A variety of restaurants and snack bars are scattered around Grand Canyon Village. Inexpensive cafeterias are at Maswik and Yavapai Lodges, while an elegant and expensive restaurant is at El Tovar. Excellent steaks are served at the Arizona Room. A very nice restaurant and a coffee shop/lounge are located in Bright Angel Lodge. A deli/bakery and a full-service grocery store are located at Market Plaza.

Transportation: Commercial air service is available to Grand Canyon Airport at Tusayan, 6 miles south of Grand Canyon Village. Private taxi service is available from the airport to the South Rim (928–638–6563; $10 one-way for one or two passengers). Many visitors to the Grand Canyon fly to either Las Vegas or Flagstaff where rental vehicles are available. Open Road Tours (602–997–6476; www.openroadtours.com) provides daily shuttle service to Grand Canyon Village from both Flagstaff and Phoenix. Amtrak serves Flagstaff and Williams. The Grand Canyon Railroad (800–843–8724) operates between Williams and the historic Santa Fe station at Grand Canyon Village.

Facilities: Grand Canyon Village is truly a village. It includes a full-service grocery store, a post office, a full-service bank, a laundry, gift shops, emergency medical and dental services, bookstores, film processing, an ice cream shop, and an array of restaurants. An auto service garage is available, and gasoline is available in Tusayan and at Desert View, but not in Grand Canyon Village.

Activities: A variety of activities begin in the village. Narrated motor coach tours of various sites along the South Rim are offered. Additional activities, some of which begin outside the village, include river raft excursions, hiking, mule rides to Plateau Point and to the canyon floor, horseback riding, and helicopter and airplane trips over the canyon. The National Park Service offers programs on the history and geology of the park throughout the day and evening. A fall chamber music festival is offered annually in September. Make the Canyon View Information Plaza an early stop so you can plan your visit.

Grand Canyon National Park

Grand Canyon Village

BRIGHT ANGEL LODGE

*Historic Cabin at
Bright Angel Lodge*

Bright Angel Lodge is a complex consisting of a main registration building plus eighteen cabins and dormitory-style buildings that provide a total of eighty-nine rooms. The buildings with lodging are separate from but adjacent to the main registration building, which also houses a tour desk, gift shop, coffee shop/lounge, steak house, and restaurant. The complex is at the center of South Rim activity and handy to the other hotels, eating facilities, and gift shops. This area of Grand Canyon Village is very busy with people and traffic, which makes it a hectic setting for individuals and families intent on discovering nature. On the plus side, Bright Angel provides some of the least expensive rooms on the South Rim and the cabins retain a flavor of the South Rim's historic nature.

Bright Angel Lodge provides four types of rooms. All have heat but no air-conditioning. The least expensive "standard," or "lodge," rooms are in Powell Lodge and Bucky Lodge, two dormitory-style buildings. Thirty-eight rooms offer one double bed (one room has two double beds) and a telephone. Some also have a television. Some

of the rooms have a full bath, while others have a shower or tub. Likewise, some have a sink and a toilet, while some have only a sink. Common bath and shower facilities are in the hallway. These rooms are particularly popular with hikers who want a relatively inexpensive place to crash after returning from a trek through the canyon.

The oldest surviving structure on the South Rim is Bucky O'Neill's cabin, which was constructed in the early 1890s. O'Neill, a prospector-turned-tourism promoter, was killed in Cuba while serving as a member of Theodore Roosevelt's Rough Riders. The cabin was preserved by Mary Colter, architect of Bright Angel Lodge, who incorporated the structure into her design for one of the lodge buildings. Today the cabin is rented to guests as the "Bucky Suite."

The original Bright Angel Hotel was constructed in 1895 to serve stagecoach passengers passing through this area. In 1905 the hotel became Bright Angel Camp, which eventually included cabins and an adjoining tent village to serve tourists who were attracted by the canyon's spectacular scenery. In 1935 the Fred Harvey Company replaced the camp with today's Bright Angel Lodge.

\\/

One step up are thirty-five rooms in fifteen wooden or wood-and-stucco buildings with vaulted ceilings called historic cabins. Some of these buildings have a single cabin, while others have two, three, or four cabin-style rooms. Although the exteriors are rustic, the interiors are nicely furnished and comfortable. Each of the cabins has one queen bed, a ceiling fan, a television, and telephone. Some have a full bath, while others have a shower only. The most expensive rooms in Bright Angel are fifteen rim cabins that offer a view of the Grand Canyon. These rooms are situated in several buildings beside a paved walking trail along the rim. Rim cabins each have one queen-size bed, a full bath, a ceiling fan, a small refrigerator, a telephone, and a television. Four have gas fireplaces. Two rim cabins with fireplaces, 6151 and 6152, provide an outstanding view of the canyon. These are the most desirable rim cabins and are two of our favorite accommodations on the South Rim. They rent for slightly more than rim units without fireplaces.

The Bright Angel complex includes three suites. A two-room historic cabin has a living room and a bedroom with two queen beds. The Powell Semi-Suite has two double beds in one room, one double bed in the second room, and a bathroom with a clawfoot tub (no shower) in between. The Bucky Suite is the top of the line and sits on the rim of the canyon. It includes two large rooms, one bedroom with a king bed, and a living room with a large stone gas fireplace. This suite also includes a wet bar and two televisions. This is by far the nicest and most expensive lodging accommodation in Bright Angel and one of the most desirable lodging facilities on the South Rim.

Bright Angel Lodge is a handy location for all the activities and facilities the South Rim offers. The main registration building, which is a short walk from all of the Bright Angel lodging buildings, has a gift shop, coffee shop/lounge, fountain/ice cream shop, and restaurant. A wooden thunderbird hangs above a giant stone fireplace in the lobby. Although none of the rooms is directly on the rim and most don't offer a view of it, spectacular vistas of the canyon are only a few steps from any of the buildings. Other dining facilities, including a cafeteria, a steak house, and the most elegant dining room on the South Rim, are a reasonable walk from any of the rooms at Bright Angel. Parking can be a problem in the busy season, when a relatively large parking lot directly in front of the lodge is packed. Parking spaces scattered among the cabins can generally be counted on to yield a few empty slots, although they may not be directly outside your room.

Rooms: Singles and doubles. One two-room cabin can sleep up to four, and rollaways are available. All but rooms in the two lodge buildings have full private baths. The two lodge buildings with standard rooms have some rooms with private baths. Other rooms use common baths and showers located in the hallway.

Wheelchair Accessibility: No rooms in Bright Angel Lodge are wheelchair accessible. The registration building, gift shop, and restaurants in this complex are wheelchair accessible.

Rates: Standard rooms ($59–$77); historic cabins ($94); two-room historic cabin ($129); rim cabins ($115–$137); suite ($250). Each additional person is $7.00 per night.

Location: On the South Rim at the center of activity in Grand Canyon Village.

Season: Rooms at Bright Angel Lodge are open year-round.

Food: A full-service restaurant is inside the main registration building and convenient to all the rooms. The restaurant is open daily from 6:30 to 10:45 A.M. for breakfast ($5.00–$9.00), 11:15 A.M. to 4:00 P.M. for lunch ($7.00–$9.00), and 4:00 to 11:00 P.M. for dinner ($7.00–$16.00), and alcoholic beverages are available. The Bright Angel Fountain, open May through September (10:00 A.M.–6:00 P.M.), directly outside the registration building, offers sandwiches, soft drinks, and ice cream. The Arizona Room, offering steaks, poultry, and fish, is attached to the east end of the Bright Angel registration building. It is open for lunch ($8.00–$12.00) from 11:00 A.M. to 2:00 P.M. and dinner ($12.00–$26.00) from 4:30 P.M. to 10:00 P.M.

EL TOVAR HOTEL

EL TOVAR IS THE REGAL HOTEL OF THE GRAND Canyon's South Rim. Constructed in 1905 by the Santa Fe Railroad to promote the firm's transportation services, the hotel was named after Spanish explorer Pedro de Tovar, who led a 1540 expedition to this area. El Tovar is the type of hotel most people envision when they think about a national park lodge. It is a single large wood-and-stone four-story structure that commands a hilltop vista on the canyon rim. The two-story lobby area is complete with log beams, a large stone fireplace, and comfortable sofas and chairs for chatting with other guests. Several verandas and a large covered front porch have chairs for relaxing in the early morning or after dinner or an evening walk. A nice mezzanine with an overlook of the lobby area has tables, stuffed chairs, a television, a piano, and a fireplace. Complimentary coffee and tea are served here for guests each morning. No elevators are in the building, but bell service is available to assist with luggage. A

The El Tovar has welcomed many famous guests, including Paul McCartney, who visited the hotel in the fall of 2001. With his room booked under a company name, the former Beatle spent the first night on the third floor in room 6474. The hotel upgraded him to the El Tovar Suite for the second and last night of his stay. One evening McCartney began playing the piano on the mezzanine until other guests, unaware the famous singer/songwriter was staying at the hotel, complained to the front desk about the noise. Instructed not to reveal that Mr. McCartney was staying at the El Tovar, employees were forced to ask the famous musician to stop playing. If the other guests had only known.

circular drive directly in front of the hotel entrance can be used for registration and baggage drop-off, but parking near the hotel is very limited.

El Tovar offers seventy-eight rooms in five classifications. Like many historic hotels, rooms in the same classification have different sizes and shapes. An extensive 2005 renovation included new carpeting, furnishings, decorations, and bathroom fixtures. All of the rooms are attractively decorated and have heat, air-conditioning, a refrigerator, telephone, CD/radio, television, safe, iron and ironing board, and a hair dryer. Although a number of rooms provide good window views, the siting of the hotel results in only a few rooms having an excellent view of the Grand Canyon. The least expensive lodging at El Tovar is a standard double with one double bed in a relatively small room. Standard queen rooms are also generally small, but the bed type varies from one queen to two doubles to two queens. Deluxe rooms

El Tovar, built at a cost of $250,000, was to be a first-rate lodging facility, and at its completion, in 1905, many considered it to be the most elegant hotel west of the Mississippi. Designed as a cross between a Swiss chalet and a Norwegian villa, the hotel was constructed of stone and Oregon pine. The building was equipped with a coal-fired steam generator to provide electric lighting, and Santa Fe railroad tank cars brought fresh water from a distance of 120 miles. Water from the tank cars was pumped into a large metal container in the El Tovar's famous cupelo, where gravity feed brought it to the rooms. Hens raised here supplied fresh eggs, and a dairy herd provided milk. Fresh fruit and vegetables were grown in greenhouses on the premises.

are larger and offer either a king or two queen-size beds with a small sitting area. Two deluxe rooms, 6463 and 6465, have small balconies with chairs. Suites in the El Tovar are named and decorated to a particular theme. For example, the Zane Grey Suite is decorated western style with movie posters, several of the author's books, and framed first edition book jackets. All of the twelve suites have a bedroom with either a king or two queen beds, a sitting room with chairs and a couch (some convert into a bed), a full bath, and a dressing area with a wet bar. Four view suites each offer stunning canyon views and have a large porch with tables and chairs. The two third-floor view suites are smaller but offer more privacy from their porches than the two second-floor view suites. Eight nonview suites on the south end of the hotel rent for slightly less than view suites. Four nonview suites have a porch and two have a Jacuzzi (the Roof Garden Suite has both). Porches off the nonview suites offer some views of the canyon, but not on the same scale as the more expensive view suites.

El Tovar provides most of the things you will want or need during a trip to the Grand Canyon. The ground floor has gift shops, a lounge, and the elegant El Tovar dining room, which offers an extensive menu in a formal setting. The dining room looks like it belongs in a national park. Murals on the walls reflect different Indian tribes, and a number of tables offer diners a view of the rim. A small private dining room that holds up to ten persons is available at no charge with a seventy-two-hour advance reservation. The lounge has a bar and windows that overlook the canyon. Travel information is available, and tours can be booked at a small tour desk in the lobby across from the registration desk. Service at El Tovar is a cut above that found at other lodging facilities at the Grand Canyon. For example, room service is available from the El Tovar dining room, and mints are placed on your bed each evening.

Rooms: Singles, doubles, triples, and quads. Some suites can sleep up to six, and rollaways are available. All rooms have full baths.

Wheelchair Accessibility: Two rooms on the first floor, one standard queen and one deluxe, provide wheelchair accessibility that includes bathroom grab bars and a wide bathroom doorway. These units include a combination shower-tub. The El Tovar restaurant is also wheelchair accessible.

Rates: Standard double ($137); standard queen ($152); deluxe ($194); suites (nonview $246–$286); (view $315).

Rates quoted are for two adults. Each additional person is $11 per night.

Location: Center of Grand Canyon Village, directly east of Kachina Lodge and just up the hill from the historic train depot.

Season: El Tovar Hotel is open year-round.

Food: A first-class dining room off the hotel's lobby serves breakfast ($8.00–$11.00), lunch ($9.00–$16.00), and dinner ($18.00–$29.00). Alcoholic beverages are available, and reservations are recommended for dinner. A lounge is open from 11:00 A.M. to 11:00 P.M. Other less expensive food service is within easy walking distance.

KACHINA LODGE/THUNDERBIRD LODGE

Kachina Lodge

KACHINA LODGE AND THUNDERBIRD LODGE ARE two virtually identical facilities that sit side by side on the South Rim of Grand Canyon Village between El Tovar Hotel and Bright Angel Lodge. The two-story stone buildings house a total of 104 rooms that, other than the view they provide, are identical. Approximately half the rooms face the rim, while the remainder face the road and parking lot. No registration facilities are in either of the lodges. Registration for Kachina Lodge is at the registration desk of El Tovar Hotel, and registration for Thunderbird Lodge is at the registration desk in the main building of Bright Angel Lodge.

The exteriors of Kachina and Thunderbird resemble upscale college dormitories but the recently remodeled interiors with Southwestern decor have the appearance of fashionable hotel rooms. Each room has electric heat, a small refrigerator, coffeemaker, iron and ironing board, safe, hair dryer, CD/radio, television, and a full tiled bath. In addition, each building offers an evaporative cooling system with individual room controls. The rooms have two queen beds. Rollaways are available but result in a crowded room. Rim-view rooms in both buildings rent for an extra $10 per day and are worth the additional cost. Two medium-size conference rooms in Thunderbird can be reserved.

Thunderbird and Kachina Lodges are in a convenient location at the center of South Rim activity. The central location results in insufficient parking during the busy summer season. No information desk or commercial facilities are in either building, but food service, gift shops, and anything else offered at the South Rim is just a short walk from any of the rooms at these two lodges. If you plan to stay at one of these two lodges, our choice would be a second-floor rim-view room in Kachina.

Rooms: Singles, doubles, triples, and quads. All rooms have full baths.

Wheelchair Accessibility: Two rooms in Thunderbird have a bathroom with a wide doorway, a roll-in shower, a raised toilet, and grab bars. Two rooms in Kachina have similar facilities, with the exception of a combination shower-tub instead of a roll-in shower.

Rates: Nonview rooms ($130); view rooms ($140). There's an extra charge of $9.00 per person per night for more than two persons.

Location: On the Rim between El Tovar Hotel and Bright Angel Lodge.

Season: All rooms are available year-round.

Food: No eating facilities are available in either building. Restaurants and cafeterias are within easy walking distance.

MASWIK LODGE

Maswik North at Maswik Lodge

MASWIK LODGE (NAMED FOR A HOPI KACHINA who guards the Grand Canyon) is a lodging complex of modern apartment-type buildings and older cabins that provide 278 rooms in two large areas on each side of a centrally located registration building. Maswik buildings with accommodations are clustered around the main lodge building that houses the registration desk, cafeteria, gift shop, sports lounge, and tour desk. All of the rooms and cabins at Maswik have heat, a telephone, a television, and convenient parking.

Maswik North, the section of this complex nearest the canyon rim, underwent an extensive renovation in 2005. These units each have air-conditioning, a hair dryer, and a full bathroom with a combination shower-tub, and offer the largest, nicest, and most expensive rooms in Maswik. The rooms are in a cluster of twelve attractive wooden and stone buildings. Most of the structures are two-story buildings (no elevators) typical

Many visitors to the Grand Canyon try a mule ride to the bottom of the canyon, where the views are spectacular and the temperature is considerably warmer than on the rim. Those with limited time are likely to choose the 12-mile, seven-hour round-trip to Plateau Point, 3,200 feet below the rim and 1,300 feet above the Colorado River. A lunch is included. More adventurous souls may prefer the two-day round-trip to Phantom Ranch on the canyon's bottom. The 10-mile ride down Bright Angel Trail takes five and a half hours. After an overnight at Phantom Ranch, the four-and-a-half-hour return trip follows the South Kaibab Trail. Advance reservations are required for mule trips and stays at Phantom Ranch. For information and reservations call (303) 297–2757 or fax (303) 297–3175.

\|/

of an upscale apartment complex. Most rooms run the depth of the building with a front window and either a window or a sliding glass door in back. Those with a sliding door have either a balcony or a patio. Eight end rooms are considerably larger than average and have vaulted ceilings but rent for the same price as the other rooms in this section. The larger rooms include 6803 through 6806 and 6831 through 6834. Try for a larger room or, failing this, a room with a balcony or patio if you will be staying in Maswik North.

Maswik South comprises six two-story, motel-type buildings (no elevators) at the end of the complex most distant from the rim. These relatively small rooms, renovated in 2001–2002, have two queen-size beds, a wall fan, a full bathroom with a combination shower-tub, but no balcony or rear window. They rent for about $40 per night less than the more spacious rooms in Maswik North. The Maswik complex also includes seven quad-style cabin buildings that house a total of twenty-eight rooms, each with a vaulted ceiling, bathroom with a tiled shower, two double beds, and a ceiling fan. The cabin interiors were totally remodeled in 2004 and offer some of the least expensive housing on the South Rim.

The lodge's location on the west side of the village, across the main road from the rim, is relatively peaceful. Staying in Maswik allows you to avoid the hustle and bustle of vehicles and crowds that roam over the rim area and yet remain within easy walking distance of the rim and most facilities in Grand Canyon Village. Of course, you are unable to view the Grand Canyon from the window of your room, but the same disadvantage exists with many rooms in other complexes closer to the rim. Maswik offers plentiful parking, a considerable advantage if you are driving, because other areas of the village are often very crowded.

Grand Canyon Railway operates a vintage train that offers daily service between Williams, Arizona, and Grand Canyon Village year-round. The 62-mile trip (one-way) from Williams to the canyon takes two and a quarter hours, with departure in the morning. Live entertainment is provided on board. Tours from Grand Canyon Village allow visitors to travel one way in a motor-coach and return on the train. Three classes of service, from coach to a parlor car, are available. The railway offers package plans that include overnight accommodations and meals in the park and in Williams. For information or reservations, call (800) 843-8724.

\|/

Rooms: Singles, doubles, triples, and quads. Rollaways are available. All rooms have private baths, most with a combination shower-tub.

Wheelchair Accessibility: Wheelchair-accessible rooms are available in both Maswik North and Maswik South, but not the cabins. Access ramps lead to wheelchair-accessible rooms that have a wide bathroom door and grab bars in the bathroom. No roll-in showers are available. The registration building housing the cafeteria and gift shop is wheelchair accessible.

Rates: Rustic cabins ($77); South Unit ($83); North Unit ($127). Additional person: cabin, $7.00; North and South Units, $9.00. Children sixteen and under stay free with an adult.

Location: West side of Grand Canyon Village, approximately a quarter-mile from the canyon rim.

Season: All rooms except for cabins (closed in winter) are open year-round.

Food: An attractive full-service cafeteria in the registration building (6:00 A.M. to 10:00 P.M.) serves a full breakfast ($3.00–$7.50), while lunch and dinner ($4.00–$8.00) offerings include Mexican dishes, hot and cold sandwiches, home-style meals, soups, salads, beer, wine, and ice cream. The cafeteria is within easy walking distance of all Maswik rooms. Additional dining facilities on the rim are also within walking distance of Maswik.

YAVAPAI LODGE

Yavapai West at Yavapai Lodge

YAVAPAI LODGE IS A COMPLEX OF SIXTEEN BUILD-
ings a distance from a separate registration building that houses a gift shop and large cafeteria. Yavapai Lodge is located on the east side of Grand Canyon Village near Market Plaza. It is located about halfway between Yavapai Point and the rim hotels. It is a moderate walk from the rim of the Grand Canyon. Although the lodge is not in the center of Grand Canyon Village activity, free shuttle transportation to various points in the village is available.

Yavapai Lodge, with 358 rooms, is the largest lodging complex in Grand Canyon National Park. The facility is divided into two separate complexes containing very different styles of buildings. The newest (constructed in the mid-1970s) and slightly more expensive rooms are in Yavapai East. Six two-story wooden buildings (no elevators) each contain thirty-three spacious rooms that were renovated in 2003, have a king or two queen beds, a telephone, a television, a full bath, heat, air-conditioning, a small refrigerator, and a coffeemaker. The buildings have an outside staircase that leads to an inside corridor with access to the rooms. A large window in each room provides a nice view of the pine and juniper woodlands in which the buildings sit. None of the rooms has a balcony or patio. The buildings, which sit well back from large parking areas, have the appearance of a nice apartment complex.

At the bottom of Grand Canyon, Phantom Ranch provides food and overnight accommodations for hikers, rafters, and mule riders. Cabin accommodations are included with two-day mule tours, while dormitory-style lodging and a limited number of cabins are available to backpackers. The ranch was originally constructed in 1922, and dormitories were added in 1976. Space is limited, so plan to make reservations (phone 888–297–2757; fax 303–297–3175) well in advance for both lodging and food service. Reservations are accepted up to twenty-three months in advance.

Ten buildings in the slightly less expensive Yavapai West were constructed in the late 1960s and remodeled in 2002. These one-story brick buildings have the appearance of a motel, but the remodeled interiors are quite attractive. Each room has a full bath, heat, two queen beds, a telephone, a television, and a ceiling fan. The rooms are smaller than the rooms in Yavapai East. Plenty of parking is in front of each structure, and the buildings are widely spaced in two large circles and surrounded by woodlands. Rooms are accessed via a front door that faces the parking lot. Rooms in buildings 1 through 6 have front windows only, which seem to result in a darker interior. The rooms in buildings 7 through 10 have back windows that provide more light and a pleasant outside view.

Yavapai is convenient to the Canyon View Information Plaza and to Market Plaza, a large commercial complex with a post office, a bank, and a general store with a large grocery selection. Meals are available at a cafeteria connected to the registration building and at a deli/bakery in the general store.

Rooms: Doubles, triples, and quads. Rollaways are available. All rooms have a full bath.

Wheelchair Accessibility: Yavapai East has four first-floor rooms with wheelchair accessibility. Only one of the rooms has a roll-in shower. The cafeteria and store are wheelchair accessible.

Rates: Yavapai East ($115); Yavapai West ($97). Rates quoted are for two adults. Each additional person is $9.00 per night. Children sixteen and under stay free with an adult.

Location: On the east side of Grand Canyon Village, across from Market Plaza.

Season: Yavapai Lodge is open from mid-March through November. Rooms are also available seasonally at Thanksgiving and Christmas.

Food: A large and attractive cafeteria (6:00 A.M. to 10:00 P.M. with shorter hours in the off-season) connected to the registration building serves breakfast ($3.00–$7.50), lunch, and dinner ($4.00–$8.00). Food selections include salads, pasta, pizza, hamburgers, and chicken. Beer and wine are available. The general store has a deli/bakery that serves bakery items, soups, salads, pizza, and large sandwiches. A large selection of grocery items, beer, wine, and other alcoholic beverages is available in the general store.

Many visitors to Grand Canyon National Park decide to take an air tour of the canyon. Several airline and helicopter companies in the town of Tusayan and at the Grand Canyon Airport offer scenic flights over the canyon. The helicopter tours are generally shorter and somewhat more expensive than flights in fixed-wing aircraft but add extra excitement to the trip. Most firms offer several types of tours of various lengths. Any of the tours presents a very different perspective of the Grand Canyon. Prices begin at about $75 per person.

NORTH RIM

Visiting the North Rim of Grand Canyon National Park makes you feel you are in an entirely different park compared with a visit to the South Rim, except, of course, for the Grand Canyon itself, which is the common thread dividing these two areas. With fewer visitors, the North Rim provides fewer facilities and is much more relaxing to visit than the South Rim. Also, the North Rim offers only a single lodge in which to stay. The address, phone number, activities, and facilities for Grand Canyon Lodge are different from those for the six lodges on the South Rim discussed above, although the reservation system is the same.

GRAND CANYON LODGE

North Rim, AZ 86052 • (928) 638–2611 • www.grandcanyonnorthrim.com

Western Cabin at Grand Canyon Lodge (North Rim)

Grand Canyon Lodge is the only lodging facility at Grand Canyon National Park's North Rim. The lodge consists of a classic main lodge building that houses the registration desk, lobby, and dining room, and more than 100 cabin units scattered along a peninsula of the Kaibab Plateau. The peninsula is surrounded by two spectacular canyons that snake off the Grand Canyon, which can be viewed at the tip of the peninsula. All of the rooms are in buildings that are separate from but within walking distance of the main lodge, which itself has no overnight rooms. The lodge is at the end of Arizona Highway 67, which leads into the park from Jacob Lake.

The main lodge building at the North Rim was constructed in 1936, after the original lodge burned. It is what every national park lodge should look like. It was designed by Gilbert Stanley Underwood, who also served as architect for the Ahwahnee at Yosemite National Park and the lodge at Bryce Canyon National Park. The U-shaped building is constructed of massive limestone walls and timber beams and is situated on the canyon rim near Bright Angel Point. The spectacular high-ceilinged dining room provides wonderful vistas of the canyon. A large sunroom that provides canyon views through three huge windows is just off the registration area. A veranda off the sunroom provides an area where guests can enjoy equally spectacular views from wooden chairs and benches. The building has two huge stone fireplaces, one in the sunroom and the other outside on the veranda. The lodge also houses a tour desk, deli, gift shop, post office, and coffee shop/saloon.

More than a hundred rustic log cabins constructed

in the 1920s provide the majority of the 209 rooms for visitors to the North Rim. Forty rooms are in two motel-style buildings. Four basic types of rooms are offered. All the rooms on the North Rim have heat, a telephone, a private bath, and carpeted floors, but no air-conditioning (you don't need it) or television. Fifty-six Western Cabins offer by far the largest and nicest accommodations on the North Rim. The cabins are constructed either two or four to a building and were refurbished from 2000 to 2003. Each Western Cabin has a finished interior, a vaulted log-beam ceiling, and a private front porch with rocking chairs. These cabins have two queen beds, a full tiled bath with a combination shower-tub, a small dressing area, a small refrigerator, and a gas fireplace. Four of the Western Cabins sit directly on the North Rim and rent for about $10 extra per day. Western Cabins 310, 320, and 332 offer a nice view and rent for the regular rate.

Eighty-three Frontier Cabins are constructed two units to a building. Each Frontier Cabin has one double and one single bed and a bath with a shower only. These cabins have an unfinished log interior, including a vaulted log ceiling, and are relatively small, so that the beds consume most of the interior space. The bathroom is also quite small. Thirty Pioneer Cabins each have two bedrooms, one on each side of a central bathroom with a shower, toilet, and sink. One bedroom has two single beds and a sink and the other bedroom has a double and a single bed. The Pioneer Cabins farthest from the road (and parking) offer the best views. Choose units 98, 107, 117, 127, 135, or 142 if this is important. A disadvantage of Frontier and Pioneer Cabins is neither has a porch or chairs where you can sit outside and read, relax, or visit with other guests.

Two motel-type buildings with forty rooms sit farthest from the main lodge and dining room. The rooms in each building back up to one another and are entered from an outside door. The room has a small front window and an outside bench beside the door. Each motel room has a queen bed, a ceiling fan, a hair dryer, a sink

in the room, and a small bathroom with a toilet and shower. These rooms are of modest size and, because of the small front window, relatively dark. Rooms on the back side (410 through 420 and 431 through 440) provide the best view. Rooms 415, 416, 432, and 433 sit on the back side and are considerably larger than other rooms in these two buildings. Backside end rooms 410, 420, 431, and 440 have windows on two sides and provide for a brighter interior. Corresponding end rooms on the front of the building also each have an extra window. The corner rooms are also a little larger than most other rooms in these buildings. Rooms in the motel units are slightly larger than the Frontier Cabins.

The Western Cabins are by far the nicest and best value of all the rooms offered at Grand Canyon Lodge. They rent for only a little more than the Frontier Cabins and motel units but offer more room, more privacy, nicer furnishings, and a better location. They are also the units in greatest demand, so reservations for Western Cabins should be made early. The four Western Cabins on the rim are usually reserved one year in advance. The Pioneer Cabins offer two bedrooms and are priced for four people. Thus, these cabins may offer the best value for families with children.

Most of the lodging units are some distance from parking. Getting to the motel units involves descending forty-five steps from the parking lot to the building. In addition, visitors (other than handicapped) are not permitted to drive to the main lodge that houses the registration desk. You should park in any open spot, walk down the road to the main lodge, and check in at the registration desk before removing any luggage from your vehicle. Once you determine the location of your assigned unit you may want to move your vehicle to a different parking place closer to where you will be staying. Porters are available to help with luggage.

Grand Canyon Lodge offers everything you will need for an enjoyable vacation. The main lodge building houses a large gift shop, a coffee shop (morning)/saloon (afternoon and evening), a post office, and a deli. The

Construction of the original Grand Lodge using Mormon craftsmen from surrounding towns began in 1927. The two-story lodge was completed at a cost of $350,000 in June 1928 and dedicated three months later. One year later the rustic North Rim Inn was constructed one mile north to offer less expensive accommodations. The second inn is now utilized as the camp store. Grand Lodge burned in September 1932, and construction of the current one-story lodge commenced on the same site in June 1936. It was completed one year later. Pictures of the original Grand Lodge are in the lodge Sunroom. Only a couple of cabins were lost to the fire. The current motel units were built later in order to serve as employee housing. Interior corridors were later changed into small bathrooms when it was decided to convert employee housing into guest lodging.

\|/

beauty of the dining room is surpassed only by the dining room in Yosemite's Ahwahnee. A gas station and laundry facilities are near the campground, 1 mile north of the lodge. The campground also has a general store that sells a few groceries, camping supplies, and beverages. Several hiking trails originate near the lodge, and guests can enjoy mule rides and evening programs. Guided hikes are provided by the National Park Service.

Rooms: Doubles, triples, and quads in the Western Cabins. Doubles and triples in the Frontier Cabins. Pioneer Cabins can sleep up to five. Doubles only in the motel units. Rollaways are available for the Western Cabins and some motel units. All rooms have a private bath, although only Western Cabins offer a combination shower-tub.

Wheelchair Accessibility: Four Western Cabins offer ramp access, wide bathroom doorways, and bathroom grab bars. These units have a combination shower-tub. All four units

are some distance from disabled parking. One Frontier Cabin with one queen bed has ramp access and grab bars in a bathroom with a shower. The main lodge building and restaurant are wheelchair accessible with lifts that have been installed.

Reservations: See reservation information listed in the previous South Rim section.

Rates: Western Cabins ($115); Western Rim Cabins ($125); motel units ($94). Western Cabin and motel unit rates are quoted for two adults. Frontier Cabins for up to three people ($95); Pioneer Cabins for up to four people ($104). Each additional person is $7.00 per night. Children sixteen and under stay free. Rollaways in Western Cabins and some motel rooms are $10.

Location: Forty miles south on AZ 67 from the town of Jacob Lake, Arizona.

Season: The lodge is open from mid-May to mid-October.

Food: An excellent restaurant with spectacular views offers three meals a day. Breakfast ($5.00 to $9.00 with a buffet available most mornings) is from 6:30 to 10:00 A.M., lunch ($6.00 to $9.00) from 11:30 A.M. to 2:30 P.M., and dinner ($15.00 to $22.00) from 4:45 to 9:45 P.M. Mixed drinks, beer, and an extensive wine list are available. Reservations are required for dinner only and should be made as early as possible. The lodge begins accepting dinner reservations each year on May 1. The deli serves breakfast each day from 7:00 to 10:30 A.M. and salads, sandwiches, pasta, pizza, rice bowls, ice cream, and beverages the rest of the day until closing at 9:00 P.M. The saloon offers gourmet coffee and fresh-baked rolls each morning beginning at 5:30 A.M. Alcoholic beverages are served in the saloon beginning at 11:30 A.M. A limited selection of groceries, prepackaged sandwiches, and beverages are in the general store at the campground 1 mile away. A microwave is available for heating frozen and canned goods purchased in the store.

Transportation: Scheduled air service is available to Kanab, Utah, and Page, Arizona, where rental cars are available. A daily shuttle (fee charged) is offered between the North Rim and the South Rim.

Facilities: A gift shop, information desk, post office, full-service restaurant, coffee shop/saloon, and deli are at the main lodge. A general store, laundry facilities, and gas station are 1 mile north at the campground.

Activities: Hiking, mule rides, horse rides, evening interpretive program, and guided nature walks. Several short- and intermediate-length trails originate near the lodge.

ARKANSAS

State Tourist Information
(800) 628–8725 | www.arkansas.com

Buffalo National River

402 North Walnut, Suite 136 • Harrison, AR 72601 • (870) 741–5443 • www.nps.gov/buff

Buffalo National River is one of the most scenic, unpolluted, and undeveloped free-flowing rivers remaining in the lower forty-eight states. The 135-mile river flows eastward through forested hill country dominated by oaks and hickories. The river is especially popular for canoeing or floating. The park is located in northwestern Arkansas in the Ozarks, across a three-county area. The nearest sizable community is Harrison, Arkansas.

Lodging at Buffalo National River: A single lodging facility is inside the river boundaries operated by the National Park Service. Buffalo Point Concessions offers cabins and a restaurant at Buffalo Point, 20 miles south of Yellville via state Highway 14 and an access road. Additional lodging facilities are in the area surrounding Yellville.

Buffalo National River

BUFFALO POINT CONCESSIONS

2261 Highway 268 East • Yellville, AR 72687 • (870) 449–6206 • www.buffalopoint.com

Rustic Cabin number 2 at Buffalo Point Concessions

THE BUFFALO POINT LODGING COMPLEX CONSISTS of an office and registration building, eleven wooden structures offering a total of nineteen rental cabins, and a separate restaurant. The restaurant sits on a high bluff overlooking the Buffalo National River. The dining room has seating for forty and has large windows that offer great views of this scenic river. The cabins sit in clusters atop a bluff in a hilly and heavily wooded area. Adequate parking is near each cabin and beside the restaurant. Only a few of the cabins are within easy walking distance of the restaurant although all are only a short drive away. The complex is approximately a mile and a half from the Buffalo National River. A National Park Service visitor center is beside the access road to Buffalo Point.

Three types of cabins are available at Buffalo Point. Each of the air-conditioned cabins has a private bathroom with a shower but no tub. All units also offer a full kitchen with refrigerator, oven, stove, microwave, coffeemaker, and toaster. Cooking utensils, dishes, and

glasses are supplied. The units do not have a television or telephone. Outside each cabin is a grill and picnic table. The cabins are set up to sleep four to six people, although additional occupants can be accommodated with rollaway beds that are available. All of the cabins are nonsmoking.

Five freestanding rustic cabins with wooden floors and beamed ceilings were built by the Civilian Conservation Corps in the 1940s. Each of these cabins has a large screened porch with two single beds, a separate bedroom with a full bed, and a large living area with a full bed, table, and chairs. These are the only cabins at Buffalo Point with a fireplace (firewood provided without charge), which serves as the only source of heat. Cabins number 1 and 2 are preferred for the screened porches that face a wooded area. Porches on the three other rustic cabins face a road.

Eight modern cabins were constructed in the 1960s as duplex units in four wooden buildings. They have larger windows and are brighter and more spacious than

The last of the six rustic cabins at Buffalo Point constructed by the Civilian Conservation Corps (CCC) were completed in 1942 as part of Buffalo River State Park. CCC workers quarried the rock, finished the lumber, and crafted the furniture used in the construction. The cabins that retain their original design and most of the original material were placed on the National Register of Historic Places in 1988. Cabin 1, completed in 1940, is the only one of the six rustic cabins that was built using log construction. Cabin 6 is currently used as the lodging office.

\\\//

the rustic cabins. Each cabin has electric heat, a separate bedroom with a full bed and a rollaway, and a living area with a full bed, a futon, a table, chairs, and a large back deck. Especially popular are cabins 13 and 14, which provide a spectacular view of the Buffalo River and which are in walking distance from the restaurant.

The least expensive lodging at Buffalo is in four one-room cabins in a CCC-constructed building that sits on a bluff above the river. Each cabin has electric heat, a double bed, a futon, a table with chairs, and shares a large deck that spans the back of the building. The two end cabins are slightly larger and have a rollaway. These four cabins are also close to the restaurant.

Buffalo Point is a relatively small lodging complex in rural northern Arkansas that offers solitude, nature, a beautiful river, a good and inexpensive restaurant, and friendly people. Bring a book, some hiking shoes, and

a canoe. You can always rent a canoe if you don't have one of your own.

Rooms: Each cabin can accommodate four to six occupants without additional bedding. All cabins have a private bath with a shower but no tub. Each of the cabins also has a full kitchen with utensils supplied.

Wheelchair Accessibility: One modern cabin is fully wheelchair accessible with wide doorways and lowered counters. It has a bathroom that is also fully wheelchair accessible.

Reservations: Buffalo Point Concessions, 2261 Highway 268 E., Yellville, AR 72687. Phone (870) 449–6206. One night deposit required. Twenty days' cancellation notice required for a refund.

Rates: Rustic cabin ($81); modern cabin ($76); one-room cabin ($55–$60). Rates are quoted for two adults. Extra persons are $5.00 each. Children six years and younger are free. Rates are reduced during the winter season.

Location: Twenty miles south of Yellville, Arkansas, on Arkansas Highway 14 and a paved access road.

Season: Four modern cabins, including those with a river view, are open year-round. The other cabins are open from mid-March through November.

Food: A full-service restaurant serves breakfast ($3.00–$5.00), lunch ($3.00–$5.00), and dinner ($6.00–$12.00) from Memorial Day Weekend through Labor Day. Meals are inexpensive. Groceries and restaurants are available in Yellville. No alcoholic drinks are available at Buffalo Point.

Transportation: The nearest scheduled airline service is in Harrison, approximately 50 miles from Buffalo Point.

Facilities: Dining room, National Park Service visitor center, pay phone at NPS visitor center.

Activities: Hiking, canoeing, horseback riding, guided hunting and fishing trips. Ranger-led walks and programs are daily during the summer. The old mining town of Rush is nearby and can be accessed via automobile or via canoe on the Buffalo National River.

CALIFORNIA

State Tourist Information
(800) 862–2543 | www.gocalif.com

Death Valley National Park

P.O. Box 579 • Death Valley, CA 92328 • (760) 786–3200 • www.nps.gov/deva/

Death Valley National Park comprises 3.3 million acres of harsh desert environment that includes the lowest point in the Western Hemisphere. The park features a desert mansion, ruins of old mining towns, abandoned borax works, mountain peaks, volcanic craters, and some of the highest summer temperatures you have ever encountered. The visitor center is at Furnace Creek. The major part of Death Valley National Park is in southeastern California. The main road is California Highway 190, which provides access to many of the major features and activity areas. **Park Entrance Fee:** $10.00 per vehicle or $5.00 per person, good for seven days.

Lodging in Death Valley National Park: Four very different types of lodging facilities in Death Valley National Park provide accommodations that range from exquisite and expensive to quaint and moderately priced. Furnace Creek Inn and Furnace Creek Ranch near the park's visitor center are privately owned and operated by Xanterra Parks and Resorts. Stovepipe Wells is owned by the National Park Service but operated as a concession by Xanterra. On the park's west side, Panamint Springs Resort is privately owned and operated. We have stayed in all four locations, and each provides a different desert experience. Furnace Creek Inn allows you to experience the desert on your terms, with a very nice room plus great food and service. Nearby Furnace Creek Resort offers motel-type rooms in a desert oasis. This facility is less expensive and appeals to families and tours. Stovepipe Wells sits isolated, with little surrounding vegetation, and provides a true desert experience. Keep in mind that all three of these facilities are at sea level and experience sweltering summer temperatures. Panamint Springs is one of the most unique places we have visited. The rooms are relatively small, and there is little to do other than hike and enjoy the desert. On the other hand, spending the evening sitting on the front porch nursing a cold beer and viewing the desert valley and distant mountains is an experience worth remembering. Panamint Springs sits approximately 2,000 feet higher than the three other lodging facilities, allowing it to avoid some of the highest daytime temperatures.

DEATH VALLEY TEMPERATURE (°FAHRENHEIT) AND PRECIPITATION

	Jan.	Feb.	March	April	May	June	July	Aug.	Sept.	Oct.	Nov.	Dec.
Record high	89	97	102	111	122	128	134	127	123	113	97	88
Ave. daily high	65	72	80	90	99	109	115	113	106	92	76	65
Ave. daily low	39	46	53	62	71	80	88	85	75	62	48	39
Record low	15	25	30	35	42	49	52	64	41	32	24	19
Ave. precip.	.26"	.35"	.25"	.12"	.08"	.04"	.11"	.10"	.14"	.11"	.18"	.18"

Death Valley National Park

FURNACE CREEK INN

P.O. Box 1 • Death Valley, CA 92328 • (760) 786–2361 • www.furnacecreekresort.com

Furnace Creek Inn may be the most elegant hotel located in a National Park Service–administered area, and it is certainly one of the most unique lodging facilities in the United States. Located in the middle of one of the country's most inhospitable environments, the AAA-rated, four-diamond inn has retained its original grandeur. Pacific Coast Borax Company commenced construction of the hotel in the early 1920s to accommodate the increasing number of visitors to Death Valley. Improvements and additions continued into the mid-1930s. Furnace Creek Inn was purchased by Fred Harvey in 1969. The inn is built of stone and adobe in a Mission-style architecture. It sits on a hill overlooking a desolate but starkly beautiful desert that encompasses both the lowest point in the Western Hemisphere (282 feet below sea level) and the Panamint Mountain Range, which soars to more than 11,000 feet. Furnace Creek Inn is situated on the back side of an oasis of green grass and palm trees complete with stone walkways, a stream, and ponds on a terraced hillside. Services include shuttle service to Furnace Creek Ranch or the nearby airstrip, room service, and massage therapy. A large conference room with stone walls, beamed ceiling, and large windows that face the swimming pool has stone fireplaces at each end. A bar at the end of the pool serves beverages and snacks.

Furnace Creek Inn offers a total of sixty-six luxurious rooms on four floors. An elevator is located in the main building. Each room has heat, air-conditioning, a ceiling fan, a refrigerator, a television, a coffeemaker, an iron and ironing board, a hair dryer, and a telephone with data port and voice mail. The rooms are rented in five categories according to size, view, and amenities.

Eight relatively small hillside rooms on the back side of the hotel offer no view and are the least expensive accommodations at Furnace Creek Inn. Five of these rooms have one king bed and the other three have two twins. Thirty-four standard view rooms, slightly larger than hillside rooms, offer varying views depending upon location. Most of fourteen standards

The rumor is that room 199 at Furnace Creek Inn, the Pool Bungalow is haunted by a ghost, most probably the former chef. The inn's maids claim to have made up the room, closed the curtains, and turned off the lights, only to find the curtains open and the lights on again soon after they had left. Despite the ghost story, this room remains much in demand, so you will need to make an early reservation in order to check if the rumor is really fact.

\|/

in the main lodge building have a king bed, and those on the first or second floors have a terrace or deck. Twenty of the standards are on a U-shaped terrace above the pool. These rooms have either a king bed or a double bed plus a twin bed. Several of these rooms have connecting doors. Sixteen deluxe view rooms with either a deck or terrace are larger than standards, and most have a king bed. Five large luxury rooms have a spa tub and either two double beds or one king bed. These are the largest rooms other than suites, and each has a deck or terrace. Two two-room suites each have a living room with a sofa bed plus a bedroom with a king bed. The suites have access to a very large deck.

One of the unique rooms at Furnace Creek Inn is the pool bungalow, which is isolated from other rooms and requires descending several staircases. It is located on the second floor of a separate building with a private outside staircase to the swimming pool. The room has stone walls and a beamed ceiling.

Furnace Creek Inn has about anything you will need for a first-class vacation. The attractive, spring-fed swimming pool, four lighted tennis courts, an exercise room, a men's and a women's sauna, a nearby eighteen-hole golf course, horseback riding, and hiking are available for sports-minded visitors. A first-class

hotel dining room serves three meals a day. Two other restaurants at nearby Furnace Creek Ranch can be reached by hotel shuttle. A lounge is located off the lobby at the inn. The Death Valley National Park Service visitor center, with exhibits and naturalist talks, is about 2 miles from the inn.

Rooms: Doubles, plus a limited number of triples and quads. All rooms have a private bath, many with a combination shower-tub.

Wheelchair Accessibility: One standard view room with a king bed is wheelchair accessible. The room has a wide entrance door and grab bars around a combination tub/shower. An elevator operates from the hotel's first floor to the third floor, where the room is located. The registration area, gift shop, and restaurant are also on the third floor.

Reservations: Furnace Creek Inn & Ranch Resort, P.O. Box 1, Death Valley, CA 92328. Phone central reservations (800) 236–7916 or on site (760) 786–2345; fax (760) 786–2514; www.furnacecreekresort.com. Cost of the first night's lodging is required as a deposit. Cancellation of forty-eight hours required for full refund.

Rates: Hillside—no view ($250); standard view ($275); deluxe view ($310); luxury view ($345); suite ($360). Two- and three-night minimums and higher rates apply during holidays and blackout periods. Rates are for two persons. Additional person is $20; cribs and rollaways, $20. Children seventeen and under stay free. Senior discounts are available.

Location: Furnace Creek Inn is 120 miles northwest of Las Vegas and 300 miles northeast of Los Angeles.

Season: The inn is open mid-October to Mother's Day (May).

Food: Diners are treated to a scenic view of the Panamint Mountains from the elegant Inn Dining Room, which offers a complete menu for breakfast, lunch, and dinner. Entree prices range from $21 to $30. Afternoon tea ($15) is served in the lobby from 4:00 to 5:30 P.M. The Lobby Bar, open from 3:30 to 11:00 P.M. daily, serves espresso, liquor, wine, and light hors d'oeuvres. Two less expensive restaurants at nearby Furnace Creek Ranch are described in the write-up of that facility.

Transportation: The nearest major airport is in Las Vegas, where rental cars are available. The resort has a concrete airstrip with lights for private planes. Transportation from the airstrip is available (contact the inn in advance).

Facilities: The inn has a large, spring-fed swimming pool (constant 82° Fahrenheit), a men's and a women's sauna, massage therapy, four lighted tennis courts, a restaurant, a lobby-bar, a gift shop, and four meeting rooms, two of

which can be used as banquet rooms. A gas station and general store are at Furnace Creek Ranch.

Activities: Swimming, tennis, and golf (year-round); horse-back riding, group hay rides, and carriage rides. The National Park Service offers interpretive programs throughout the park.

Furnace Creek Ranch

P.O. Box 1 • Death Valley, CA 92328 • (760) 786–2345 • www.furnacecreekresort.com

Deluxe Units at Furnace Creek Ranch

FURNACE CREEK RANCH IS THE FAMILY ALTERNA-tive to the more expensive and elegant Furnace Creek Inn. Located in an oasis area of Furnace Creek, about 1.5 miles from the inn, Furnace Creek Ranch offers a total of 224 rooms in three classifications of accommodations. The buildings sit amid tall palm and tamarisk trees, with an eighteen-hole golf course at one end. The ranch offers more activities and eating places than the more famous inn. A building just to the right of the stone entrance gate houses the registration desk. Inside the gate and to the left in a western-style wooden building are a general store, a saloon, and two restaurants. Lodging rooms are in six one- and two-story motel-type buildings behind the restaurant building, plus fourteen freestanding wood cabins beside the registration building. All of the buildings with overnight rooms are within easy walking distance of

the registration building and restaurants. Plentiful parking is available near each of the buildings.

All of the rooms at Furnace Creek Ranch have heat, air-conditioning, television, coffeemakers, hair dryers, and telephone. One hundred and sixty-four deluxe rooms are in four two-story wooden buildings constructed in the 1960s. These buildings do not have elevators. An entrance is at each end of the building, with access to the rooms through an interior corridor. Second-floor rooms each have a balcony, and rooms on the bottom floor have a patio. Each deluxe room has two double beds, a refrigerator, and a ceiling fan. Half the 164 rooms face either the golf course or a grassy area surrounding the swimming pool. Rooms on the opposite side of each building face one another. All these rooms rent for the same price, so try for one with a view toward the golf course.

Furnace Creek Golf Course, at Furnace Creek Ranch, is situated 214 feet below sea level, which qualifies it as the lowest grass golf course in the world. The course was opened in 1931 and, during the early years, closed each summer when it was leased to a cattle rancher. A small flock of sheep kept the course mowed during winter months. The 6,215-foot course was renovated in 1997 by Peter Dye. Even though the course lies in the middle of a desert, nine of its eighteen holes have water hazards.

Two one-story wood buildings contain thirty-two parkside rooms, which each have a sliding glass patio door on the back side that opens to a large grassy area near the swimming pool. These rooms each have either two double beds or one queen, a small refrigerator, and a ceiling fan, and rent for about $20 per night above the rate for rooms in the two-story units. Parkside rooms are priced higher because they are larger than the deluxe rooms, have parking directly in front of each room, and offer closer access to the swimming area.

Twenty-eight cabin units are constructed two to a building. Each has either one queen or two double beds and a bath with a shower but no bathtub. The cabin units are nicely done but quite a bit smaller than the deluxe or parkside rooms.

Furnace Creek Ranch provides all the facilities you will need for a comfortable stay in Death Valley National Park. Best of all, the facilities are near the rooms. The golf course, the Borax Museum with interesting displays, and the National Park Service visitor center are within walking distance. If you desire a special dinner, take the free shuttle or drive a little more than a mile to the Furnace Creek Inn (mid-October to Mother's Day). You can play golf in the morning, swim in the afternoon in a spring-fed pool, have a beer in the saloon, take a nap, and walk to a restaurant without ever getting in your vehicle. Keep in mind that some of these things are easier to handle in the spring, winter, and fall than in the heat of the summer. On the other hand, this is a great place to spend a spring weekend, when daytime temperatures are more reasonable.

Rooms: Doubles, triples, and quads. All rooms have a private bath with a combination shower-tub except the cabins, which have only a shower.

Wheelchair Accessibility: Two parkside rooms are each fully wheelchair accessible, with a ramp and a roll-in shower. Four deluxe rooms each have a ramp and a bathroom with grab bars and a combination shower-tub. The main office, general store, and restaurants are wheelchair accessible.

Reservations: Furnace Creek Inn & Ranch Resort, P.O. Box 1, Death Valley, CA 92328. Phone central reservations (800) 236-7916 or on site (760) 786-2345; fax (760) 786-2514. Cost of the first night's lodging is required as a deposit. Cancellation of forty-eight hours required for full refund.

Rates: High season (mid-October to mid-May)/low season (mid-May to mid-October): Cabin ($105/$88); deluxe

Water, the lifeblood for development in the Furnace Creek area, flows from two nearby hot water springs. The springs caused the 49ers to camp here during their rush for riches and even resulted in ranchers giving this area a try. The water now flows from the springs to a holding tank that supplies Furnace Creek Inn, and eventually, Furnace Creek Ranch and the Furnace Creek Golf Course. The National Park Service sells the water to the lodging facilities for irrigation and drinking water, as well as for the two swimming pools. Take a swim and enjoy the warm water.

($137/$120); parkside ($159/$152). Rates are $5.00 per night higher during some holidays and special events and $15.00 per night higher during Thanksgiving, Christmas, and New Year's. A three-night minimum stay is required during New Year's. Rates quoted are for two adults. Children under eighteen stay free when accompanied by an adult. Each additional person is $20 per night.

Location: Furnace Creek Ranch is 120 miles northwest of Las Vegas and 300 miles northeast of Los Angeles. The ranch is approximately 1.5 miles north of Furnace Creek Inn.

Season: The ranch is open all year. The busiest seasons are mid-July through August, spring, and all holidays, when the hotel is frequently full.

Food: The Wrangler Steakhouse offers a buffet for breakfast ($9.00) and lunch ($11.00). Dinner (seasonally) is ordered from a menu that includes steaks, seafood, and poultry ($18–$28). The 49er Cafe offers breakfast (seasonally), lunch ($7.00–$12.00), and dinner ($10.00–$18.00). The

Saloon offers hot dogs, pizza, and snacks. Beer, wine, other beverages, and limited groceries are sold in the general store.

Transportation: The nearest major airport is in Las Vegas, where rental cars are available. The resort has a concrete airstrip with lights for private planes. Transportation from the airstrip is available (contact the ranch in advance).

Facilities: The ranch has a large, spring-fed swimming pool (constant 82° Fahrenheit), two lighted tennis courts, a basketball court, a children's playground, a horseshoe area, a volleyball court, an eighteen-hole golf course, the Borax Museum, a coin-operated laundry, two restaurants, a saloon, a gas station, and a general store.

Activities: Swimming, tennis, golf, basketball, volleyball, horseshoes, and hiking. Horseback riding, group hay rides, and carriage rides are offered from mid-October to mid-May. The National Park Service offers interpretive programs throughout the park except during summer.

PANAMINT SPRINGS RESORT

P.O. Box 395 • Ridgecrest, CA 93556 • (775) 482–7680 • www.deathvalley.com

PANAMINT SPRINGS RESORT IS A SMALL FACILITY that, if not for the surrounding landscape, causes you to wonder if you are in Key West, Florida. In fact, walk in the front door of the main building that houses the registration area and dining room and you might expect to see Ernest Hemingway sitting on one of the stools at a bar made from a large slab of walnut supported by

redwood roots. Most likely, he would be sampling one of many varieties of beer they offer at the resort. A large porch wraps around the building, with the front and east sides serving as an outside dining area. A small grassy area east of the building has chairs for relaxing. Four wooden buildings with shake roofs sit directly behind the main building and house fourteen motel rooms.

Panamint Springs offers fourteen motel-type rooms and one two-bedroom cottage. The motel rooms are of varying size, but all are relatively small. Room rates are based on the number of beds in a room, not the number of occupants. Rooms with one bed generally have a queen, although one has a king. Rooms with more than one bed have either two or three double beds. Each room has heat, air-conditioning, a ceiling fan, and a private bathroom with a shower but no tub. Only the cottage has a television, and the only pay telephone is a cellular unit in the registration building.

The one cottage unit with a covered front porch sits behind the motel units and has a living room with a sofa, a television with satellite hookup, a refrigerator, a table and four chairs, but no cooking facilities. One large bedroom has a queen bed, and a second, smaller bedroom has a bunk bed with a double bottom and single top. The cottage has a full bathroom with a combination shower-tub.

Panamint Springs Resort is a small, quaint motel-type facility in a desert setting. The resort generates its own electricity, and water is piped from a spring 5 miles away. Panamint Springs isn't fancy, but it is a fun and unique place that you will remember. The dining room holds about twenty-five persons, and additional seating is outside on a covered patio. The homemade food is very good, and the steaks are exceptional. The bar is terrific, and the atmosphere of the whole place can't be beat. Stay here and you will think you are a thousand miles from civilization, which isn't too far from the truth.

Rooms: Two people in one double bed to six people in three double beds. All rooms have private baths with a shower but no tub.

Wheelchair Accessibility: No wheelchair-accessible rooms are available at Panamint Springs Resort. A ramp provides wheelchair access to the restaurant.

Reservations: Panamint Springs Resort, P.O. Box 395, Ridgecrest, CA 93556. Phone (775) 482–7680; fax (775) 482–7682; www.deathvalley.com. A credit card is required to guarantee a room. A cancellation notice of forty-eight hours is required.

The best-known man-made structure in Death Valley National Park is Scotty's Castle, which lies just inside the park's north entrance. This unique rock building, which cost nearly $2 million, was constructed in the 1920s as a vacation retreat for Albert Johnson, a partner and lifelong friend of Walter Scott, alias Death Valley Scotty, for whom the castle is named. Today you can take a fifty-minute tour conducted by Park Service rangers in period clothing. The tours are offered daily from 9:00 A.M. to 5:00 P.M., and waits of an hour or two can be expected during busy times of the year. The castle also includes a bookstore, a gift shop, an exhibit room, and a snack bar.

Rates: One bed ($65); two beds ($79); three beds ($94); cottage ($139). Rollaway ($5.00). A 10 percent discount is given for AAA and AARP.

Location: The resort is on the western edge of Death Valley on California Highway 190, 48 miles east of Lone Pine.

Season: The resort is open all year. The busiest season is mid-July through August.

Food: The attractive dining room serves breakfast ($6.00–$12.00), lunch ($6.00–$12.00), and dinner ($13.00–$24.00) from 6:30 A.M. to 10:00 P.M. Beer, wine, cocktails, and soft drinks are available from the bar or coolers just off the registration area. The bar remains open until the registration desk closes at midnight.

Transportation: The nearest airports are in Bakersfield, California (168 miles), and Las Vegas (174 miles), where rental cars are available.

Facilities: Dining room, bar, and gift shop area. Gasoline, diesel fuel, and propane are available. A campground with full hook-ups is across the road.

Activities: Hiking, four-wheel off-road vehicles, birdwatching, sightseeing.

Pets: Pet fee is $5.00 per night per pet.

STOVEPIPE WELLS VILLAGE

Death Valley, CA 92328 • (760) 786–2387 • www.stovepipewells.com

Standard Units at Stovepipe Wells Village

STOVEPIPE WELLS VILLAGE IS A COMPLEX OF ELEVEN wooden buildings that provide eighty-three overnight rooms and supporting services. A general store, a small gas station, and a National Park Service ranger station are directly across the road. The village has the appearance of a small western town, which in some respects it is. Six separate one-story buildings each contain from eight to twenty-three rooms. The guest registration area is in a building that also houses an auditorium/meeting room, a gift shop, and a small TV/game lobby. Employee housing is scattered around the back of the complex. Stovepipe Wells Village is situated in the middle of Death Valley National Park, on California Highway 190, approximately 25 miles northwest of Furnace Creek. It is about 33 miles southwest of Beatty, Nevada.

Stovepipe Wells offers three categories of rooms that range from a limited number of small, inexpensive patio rooms to deluxe rooms similar to those at Furnace Creek Ranch. All the rooms have heat, air-conditioning, and a private bath but no telephone. Be aware that only three of the buildings (Roadrunner, Tucki, and Patio) have potable water in the rooms. Guests in other rooms

Although not covered with sand, Death Valley does have a few areas where large amounts of sand have collected to form dunes. The best known and easiest to visit are near Stovepipe Wells. These can be accessed from CA 190. Dunes can also be viewed north of CA 190 on the west side of the park at Panamint Dunes. Other dunes are in both the extreme north and south ends of the park. Dunes require a source of sand, a wind to move the sand, and a place for the sand to collect. Death Valley has an abundance of the first two but only a few of the latter.

will find drinkable water in several locations outside the buildings. Water at Stovepipe Wells has a high mineral content and is treated for drinking purposes. Forty-seven deluxe rooms in three buildings each have either two double beds or one king bed. These rooms offer a full bathroom, television, refrigerator, and a ceiling fan. Rooms in the Roadrunner and 49er buildings facing toward the east provide good views of the valley and distant mountains. Rooms on the west side have views obscured by other buildings. Less expensive and smaller standard rooms were recently renovated, and each has two double beds, a double plus a single, or two single beds. These rooms have a full bathroom but no television. Standard rooms rent for about $20 less per night than deluxe rooms. Eight even smaller patio rooms, constructed in 1927 as part of the original building, were renovated in 1999. Each room has one double or two single beds, and a bath with shower but no tub. These rooms are attached to the front of the registration building near the highway. All of the buildings with rooms are a short walk from the registration building.

Stovepipe Wells is particularly appealing to someone seeking the solitude of the desert. Being located on Highway 190, which passes through Death Valley, makes it a convenient stop for travelers crossing the park. Stovepipe Wells Village offers an attractive restaurant and saloon with a real western atmosphere. The dining room and saloon have vaulted ceilings and were built with timbers from an old Death Valley mining operation. In fact, staying at Stovepipe Wells is itself a bit of the Old West, even though the rooms are quite comfortable and modern. A general store across the road offers supplies, souvenirs, limited groceries, soft drinks, beer, and wine. A pool with heated mineral water is available for guests.

Rooms: Doubles, triples, and quads. All rooms have private baths, although the patio rooms have showers but no tubs.

Wheelchair Accessibility: Two standard rooms are fully wheelchair accessible, with a ramp and roll-in shower. Two deluxe rooms in the Tucki building each have a ramp and bathroom grab bars with a combination shower-tub. The restaurant and saloon are both wheelchair accessible.

Reservations: Stovepipe Wells Village, Death Valley, CA 92328. Phone (760) 786-2387; fax (760) 786-2389. The first night's lodging is required as a deposit. Cancellation of forty-eight hours is required for full refund.

Rates: Patio ($63), standard ($83), and deluxe ($103). Rates quoted are for two adults. Children twelve and under stay free when accompanied by an adult. Each additional person is $10 per night. A crib is $5.00 and a rollaway (deluxe rooms only) is $10.00.

Location: Stovepipe Wells Village is on CA 190, near the middle of Death Valley National Park. It is approximately 25 miles northwest of the Furnace Creek Ranch and about 33 miles southwest of Beatty, Nevada.

Season: The facility is open all year. The busiest season is mid-July through August, when it is frequently full.

Food: The Toll Road Restaurant offers a buffet for breakfast ($8.00) and dinner ($17.00) during summer. From mid-October to mid-May, breakfast ($4.00-$7.00), lunch ($6.00-$8.00), and dinner ($10.00-$23.00) are ordered from a complete menu. A children's menu is available. The Badwater Saloon just off the restaurant offers draft beer, cocktails, and appetizers. Beer, wine, other beverages, and limited groceries are sold in the general store.

Transportation: The nearest major airport is in Las Vegas, where rental cars are available. A concrete airstrip with lights for private planes is near Furnace Creek Ranch. Another airstrip is next to Stovepipe Wells.

Facilities: Stovepipe has a heated mineral water swimming pool, restaurant, saloon, lobby with TV and board games, auditorium/meeting room (fee), gift shop (seasonal), gas station (regular only), and general store.

Activities: Swimming, walking, and hiking. The National Park Service offers interpretive programs throughout the park except during summer.

Pets: Pets are permitted with a $20 deposit.

Lassen Volcanic National Park

P.O. Box 100 • Mineral, CA 96063 • (530) 595–4444 • www.nps.gov/lavo

Lassen Volcanic National Park comprises 106,000 acres of a beautiful and relatively uncrowded mountainous area centered on Lassen Peak, a 10,457-foot plug-dome volcano that last erupted during a seven-year period beginning in 1914. The park has other evidence of geothermal activity, including boiling springs, mud pots, fumaroles, and sulfurous vents. A paved road connecting the southwest entrance station with the north entrance station provides scenic views and access to many features of this beautiful area. Road guides are sold at the information center. Lassen Volcanic National Park is located in north-central California, 42 miles east of Redding and 55 miles east of Red Bluff. **Park Entrance Fee:** $10.00 per vehicle or $5.00 per person, good for seven days.

Lodging in Lassen Volcanic National Park: Lassen Volcanic has only one lodging facility, and it is an out-of-the-way location for most visitors who will drive along the single paved road through the park. Drakesbad Guest Ranch is in the southeast part of the park, 17 miles north of the small town of Chester. Private accommodations are available in Chester, Mineral, Mill Creek, Shingletown, Old Station, and Hat Creek.

DRAKESBAD GUEST RANCH

End of Warner Valley Road • Lassen Volcanic National Park
Chester, CA 96020 • (See below for phone information) • www.drakesbad.com

Lodge Building at Drakesbad Guest Ranch

Lassen Volcanic National Park

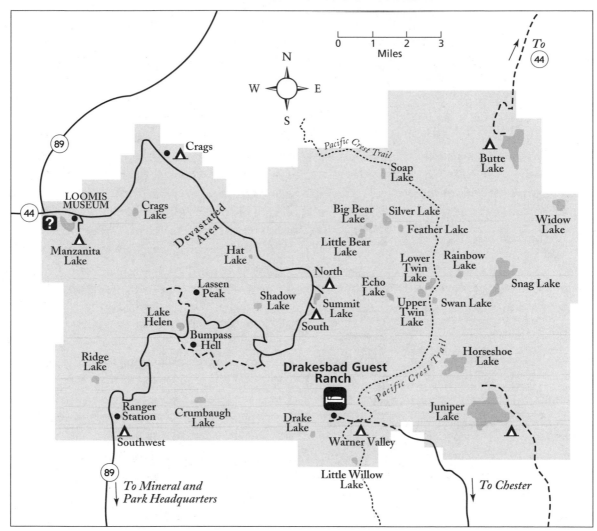

RAKESBAD GUEST RANCH PROVIDES A TOTAL OF nineteen rooms in a relatively isolated complex of cabins, bungalows, and a two-story lodge. The ranch also has a central dining hall, a thermal heated swimming pool, and several service buildings. The complex lies beside a meadow in the southeast portion of Lassen Volcanic National Park. It is at an altitude of 5,700 feet and surrounded by trees, hills, and mountains. Drakesbad Guest Ranch is reached via a 17-mile road from the town of Chester, California. The first 14 miles are a winding but well-maintained paved road. The last 3 miles, through national park land, are on a relatively rough gravel road. Drakesbad can be called directly by asking the long-distance phone operator to connect you with Drakesbad Toll Station No. 2 at area code 530 (in season) or call (530) 529–1512, ext. 120, and leave a message.

Drakesbad Guest Ranch offers several types of ac-

The valley in which Drakesbad Guest Ranch is located was first settled by Edward Drake, a trapper and guide who may have arrived here as early as 1875. Drake hosted occasional campers during summers but moved down the valley to Prattville during the harsh winters. In 1900 the seventy-year-old Drake sold his 400 acres to Alexander Sifford, a school teacher from Susanville who had traveled here to drink the healing soda water. Sifford later purchased an additional forty acres and in 1908 renamed the valley Drakesbad, the original owner's name in combination with the German term for warm-water bath. Sifford and his family spent sixty years improving the property and providing visitor services and in 1958 deeded the property to the National Park Service.

commodations, although all rent for approximately the same rate. All the rooms are relatively small and nicely finished with pine paneling. All rooms have propane heat but no telephone, air-conditioning, television, or electrical outlets. The two-story rustic wooden lodge building has six rooms, all on the second floor. Rooms are on each side of an inside corridor that is accessed via an inside stairway from the first-floor recreation room. No elevator is in the building. The three even-numbered lodge rooms each have one double bed and one single bed. Odd-numbered rooms on the opposite side of the building are somewhat smaller and have only one double bed. Each of the lodge rooms has electric lights and a private bath with a sink and toilet, but no tub or shower. Showers and bathtubs are in the swimming pool bathhouse, a short walk from the lodge building.

The northeast annex, directly behind the dining hall, is the only other accommodation with electric lights. The one-story wooden annex has two rooms, each with two double beds and a bathroom with a sink, a toilet, and a shower but no tub. A porch runs across the front of the building. These rooms are somewhat larger and rent for a little more than rooms in the main lodge building.

The remaining rooms at Drakesbad have no electricity, and light is by means of kerosene lanterns. Four freestanding wooden cabins sit at the base of a hill across from the parking lot and the stable. Each cabin has a double bed plus a single bed and a bathroom with a sink and toilet. Cabin guests must shower at the swimming pool bathhouse. Parking is directly in front of each cabin. The cabins rent for the same price and are somewhat larger than rooms in the lodge.

Six one-story bungalows are constructed two to a building. Each bungalow has two double beds, a full bath with a shower, and a back porch that overlooks a large meadow. Parking is directly in front of each building. These are probably the nicest rooms at Drakesbad.

A single one-story wooden duplex has two rooms on each side of a central full bathroom. One room has two double beds; the other has a double bed plus a single bed. The duplex is rented only as a single unit and is particularly desirable for families with two or more children.

For most travelers, even frequent visitors to national parks, staying at Drakesbad will be a very different experience. Drakesbad is not for people who expect a fancy lodge with room service; it is a place for individuals who want to get away from it all and experience nature, but without giving up good food and friendship. The facilities at Drakesbad are comfortable but basic. A dinner bell rings three times a day to announce that food is being served in a pine-paneled dining room. The entire bottom floor of the lodge building, filled with chairs, tables, and sofas, serves as a meeting place to read and chat with other guests. A wood stove is near the middle of the room, and a large stone fireplace occupies one end wall. Chairs are also on the outside porch, which wraps around the lodge. Short to all-day horseback rides are offered. The swimming pool has naturally heated spring water.

Equipment is provided for a variety of activities, including table tennis, volleyball, badminton, croquet, and horseshoes. Fly-fishing for trout is excellent for anglers. A fly-fishing instructor is available with advance notice. Several trails, both short and long, lead from the lodge to some of Lassen's best spots. Massage therapy and yoga classes are available. Campfires are held each evening, and programs are frequently presented by the National Park Service. Best of all, both employees and guests seem to be family members who have found a good thing few other people have even heard about. The ease with which you will make friends with other guests is one of the great pleasures of staying at Drakesbad. Everyone eats together in the dining hall and guests sit with one another around the evening campfire or on the porch of the recreation hall of the main lodge building. Likewise, most children have an easy time making friends with the children of other guests. Best of all, Drakesbad is a place where you can wind down and push your worries to another day.

Rooms: Singles, doubles, triples, and quads. A single duplex holds up to seven individuals. Cabins and lodge rooms have half-baths. Other rooms have a full bath with shower.

Wheelchair Accessibility: One bungalow is wheelchair accessible, with an entry ramp to the back porch and double doors. A large bathroom has a combination shower-tub with grab bars.

Reservations: California Guest Services, 2150 North Main Street, Suite 5, Red Bluffs, CA 96080. Phone (530) 529–1512, ext. 120; fax (530) 529–4511. Reservations can be made up to two years in advance and should be made no later than the end of February to ensure a choice of rooms and dates. Two nights' deposit is required, and a thirty-day cancellation is required for a full refund, less a 10 percent fee.

Rates: Rates quoted are per person and include three meals per day. Lodge and cabins (single, $155; double, $134; extra adult, $114; child, $77); bungalows and northeast annex (single, $185; double, $153; extra adult, $128; child, $77); duplex (double, $163; extra adult, $125; child, $77). Weekly rate is approximately six times the daily rate. Children age two and under are free; for ages three to eleven there is a child rate; twelve and over pay an adult rate.

Location: Seventeen miles north of Chester, California, at the end of Warner Valley Road.

Season: Open from the first Friday in June to the second Monday in October, depending on the weather.

Food: Three meals are served daily in an attractive dining room that is a short walk from all the lodging units. Breakfast includes fresh fruits, hot and cold cereals, and a hot entree. Lunch is buffet-style (sack lunches are available upon request), while dinner with your choice of two entrees is served at the table. An outdoor cookout is scheduled each Wednesday evening. Beer and wine are available for purchase.

Transportation: Scheduled airline service is available to Redding and Chico, California, and Reno, Nevada, where rental cars are available. Private planes may land at a small lighted airport at Chester, where rental cars are available. The lodge will pick up guests in Chester if prior arrangements are made. Amtrak serves Redding and Chico.

Facilities: Hot-spring-fed swimming pool, dining hall, and stables.

Activities: Horseback riding (fee), fishing, swimming, hiking, canoeing, and a variety of games, including volleyball, croquet, Ping-Pong, horseshoes, and badminton. Massage therapy (fee). Yoga classes (fee). Fly-fishing lessons are by reservation only (fee).

Lassen Volcanic National Park once housed a lodging facility other than Drakesbad, this one near Manzanita Lake in the northwest corner of the park. Manzanita Lake Lodge and nine cabins were built by Lassen National Park Camp, Ltd. (which later became Lassen National Park Company) in 1933. A dining room and ten wooden double housekeeping cabins were added in 1935. The lodging facility expanded yet again in 1940 when forty tent cabins and a cafeteria, grocery store/gift shop, and gas station were added. The entire area was closed in 1974 when this area of the park was declared hazardous because of a potential rock avalanche. The lodge, cabins, store, and service station were removed in 1977. Photos of the lodge are available in a loose-leaf binder kept at the Loomis Museum near the park's northwest entrance station.

Sequoia National Park/Kings Canyon National Park

47050 Generals Highway • Three Rivers, CA 93271 • (559) 565–3341 • www.nps.gov/seki

Sequoia and Kings Canyon are separate parks that adjoin one another. The parks are administered jointly and nearly always visited together, so they are discussed here as one unit. The two parks have more than 865,000 acres combined, including groves of giant sequoias on plateaus surrounded by the scenic High Sierra. The parks are located in central California, between Yosemite National Park and Death Valley National Park. Access from the west is via California Highway 180 from Fresno, which leads through the Grant Grove section of Kings Canyon to Cedar Grove. From the south California Highway 198 leads to the Giant Forest area of Sequoia National Park, then connects with CA 180 at Grant Grove. **Park Entrance Fee:** $10.00 per vehicle or $5.00 per person, good for seven days.

Lodging in Sequoia and Kings Canyon National Parks Three locations within Kings Canyon and Sequoia National Parks offer overnight accommodations that range from very rustic cabins to two relatively new lodges. Wuksachi Village and Lodge is just north of Lodgepole and the only lodging facility in Sequoia National Park. Two lodging facilities in Kings Canyon National Park include rustic cabins and a new lodge building at Grant Grove, as well as a nice motel unit at Cedar Grove. Although not included in this book, private lodging facilities are at Mineral King in the southern end of Sequoia National Park and in Sequoia National Forest on the road to Cedar Grove from Grant Grove.

The lodging facilities at Grant Grove and Cedar Grove in Kings Canyon National Park are operated by Kings Canyon Park Services. The same address, phone number, and deposit and cancellation regulations apply to reservations at both facilities. Wuksachi Village and Lodge is operated by Delaware-North, the same firm that serves as the concessionaire for lodging, food, and gift facilities in Yosemite National Park.

Cedar Grove Lodge

P.O. Box 909 • Kings Canyon National Park, CA 93633 • (559) 565–0100
www.sequoia-kingscanyon.com

Sequoia National Park/Kings Canyon National Park

McClure Meadow

Le Conte Canyon

John Muir Trail and Pacific Crest Trail

Copper Creek Trail

Woods Creek Trail

Cedar Grove

Grant Grove Village

Hume Lake

Kings Canyon Scenic Byway

Rae Lakes

Charlotte Lake

180

Road open in summer only

Cedar Grove Lodge

Roaring River

KINGS CANYON NATIONAL PARK

Tyndall Creek

180

Wuksachi Village and Lodge

198

Lodgepole

To Lone Pine

Crystal Cave

Wolverton

Giant Forest

Bearpaw Meadow

SEQUOIA NATIONAL PARK

John Muir Trail

Crabtree

Potwisha

Buckeye Flat

Rock Creek

Foothills

Atwell Mill

Mineral King Cold Springs

To Visalia

198

Three Rivers

Lookout Point

Hockett Meadow

South Fork

Kern Canyon

N
W E
S

0   5   10
Miles

CEDAR GROVE LODGE IS A MODERN TWO-STORY wooden building in the isolated Cedar Grove area of Kings Canyon National Park. The lodge has the appearance of a ski chalet, with eighteen rooms on the second floor and three rooms on the ground level. The first floor houses a combination market/gift shop, a cafe, and a small guest registration desk just inside the entrance to the market. The lodge sits among giant cedar and pine trees beside the South Fork of the Kings River. Picnic tables are scattered about the grounds, many near the river. A large, covered second-floor balcony provides a restful place to read and relax while viewing the surrounding tree-covered mountains and listening to the river roar. Another large deck area, one floor below on the same side of the building, has picnic tables just outside the snack bar. Cedar Grove Lodge is 35 miles east of Grant Grove Village, 6 miles from the terminus of Kings Canyon Highway. The drive to Cedar Grove is probably the most scenic in either Sequoia or Kings Canyon and worth the time and effort even if you don't plan to stay at the lodge.

All of the rooms at the lodge have heat, air-conditioning, and telephones, but no television. The second-story rooms are identical in size and furnishings, with two queen-size beds and a private bath that includes a shower but no tub. One handicap-accessible room has a bathtub. Each room has a modest back window but no balcony. The rooms have plenty of space for two people and adequate room for a family of four. The rooms on the second floor are entered through a relatively narrow inside corridor that runs the length of the building between a ramp at one end and a wide stairway at the opposite end. The three ground-level Patio rooms are smaller, with one queen-size bed, a full bath with a shower only, and a kitchen area with a sink, microwave, coffeemaker, and small refrigerator. These rooms have a private patio with a table and chairs a short distance from the river. Plentiful parking is in front of and beside the lodge.

The Sequoia Field Institute, a department of the Sequoia Natural History Association, offers a variety of educational programs throughout the year in Sequoia and Kings Canyon National Parks. Programs include indoor and outdoor seminars, school programs, nature hikes, backpacking, cross-country skiing, and environmental education. For example, you can take snowshoe treks or enhance your ski skills in winter months, or learn about birding, backpacking, and photography in the spring and summer months. The Institute offers guided mountain treks of several days and programs for children. Instructors include park naturalists, college professors, and professional photographers. Participants are charged a fee that is reduced for members of the Sequoia Natural History Association. For a current catalog containing a program listing and registration form write: Sequoia Natural History Association, HCR 89, Box 10, Three Rivers, CA 93271. Similar institutes operate in other national park areas.

Cedar Grove is a very pleasant place to spend several days. The lodge is 2,000 feet lower and about ten degrees warmer than Wuksachi and Grant Grove. It's also somewhat out of the way, near the end of a 30-mile road that leads into Cedar Grove. The remoteness reduces visitation to this area of the park so that Cedar Grove is not nearly as crowded as other, more popular locations. The cafe serves the usual sandwiches, hamburgers, fries, and soft drinks. It also offers other selections, including breakfast items, and dinner specials that might include fried chicken, trout, steak, and pasta. The market carries grocery items, such as milk, sandwiches, ice cream treats, beer, wine, fresh vegetables and fruits, and drugstore items. A small National

Park Service visitor center is a short walk down the road and across the bridge. Park rangers conduct evening programs at the campground amphitheater.

Rooms: Doubles, triples, and quads. All rooms have private baths with showers. One wheelchair-accessible room has a bathtub.

Wheelchair Accessibility: One second-floor room is wheelchair accessible, with a wide bathroom door and grab bars around the toilet and combination shower-tub. Access to the room is via a relatively long outside ramp. The registration area, cafe, and market are also wheelchair accessible.

Reservations: Kings Canyon Park Services, 5755 E. Kings Canyon Road, Suite 101, Fresno, CA 93727. Telephone toll free (866) 522–6966; (559) 452–1081; www.sequoia-kingscanyon.com.

Rates: Doubles ($109); Patio rooms ($125). Rates quoted are for two adults. Children twelve and under stay free unless an extra bed is requested. Each additional person is $12 per night.

Location: Cedar Grove Lodge is located just beyond the terminus of CA 180, Kings Canyon Highway. It is 35 miles east of Grant Grove Village.

Season: The lodge is open from mid-May to early October, depending on the weather.

Food: The cafe serves breakfast ($4.00–$6.00), lunch ($4.00-$8.00) (seasonal), and dinner ($10.00–$17.00). Food items can be purchased in the market.

Transportation: Scheduled air, bus, and train service are available to Fresno, where rental cars are available.

Facilities: Laundry. Gift items are available in the market. A small National Park Service visitor center is a quarter mile away.

Activities: Hiking, fishing, evening campfire programs, horseback riding.

Grant Grove Village

P.O. Box 907 • Kings Canyon National Park, CA 93633 • (559) 335–5505, ext. 1603
www.sequoia-kingscanyon.com

John Muir Lodge at Grant Grove Village

GRANT GROVE VILLAGE, ONE OF TWO MAJOR LODG-ing facilities in Kings Canyon National Park, includes fifty older wood cabins and a new two-story cedar lodge building. Both the cabins and the lodge are located behind a small commercial center that houses the registration desk, restaurant, post office, market, gift shop, and a National Park Service visitor center. No guest rooms are in the registration building, although the lodge and cabins are within walking distance. Guests for both the cabins and lodge register in the restaurant/gift shop building. Cabins sit in two separate but adjacent areas a short distance behind the commercial center just off of Generals Highway. One cabin area, called Village Cabins, is on a hillside overlooking a meadow that separates the cabins from the restaurant and registration building. The hillside is dotted with numerous big trees. The remainder of the cabins sit in an adjacent area called Meadow Camp, a more heavily wooded area across the road from the meadow and a little farther from the visitor center. The lodge is on a hillside a short distance behind and above the cabins. A nice National Park Service visitor center is across the road from the commercial center. The Grant Grove area can be quite busy in summer, so expect heavy traffic. Grant Grove Village is 3 miles from the Kings Canyon entrance on California Highway 180 from Fresno, California. It is 24 miles north of Lodgepole on a small peninsula of Kings Canyon National Park that juts from the northwest corner of Sequoia National Park.

Grant Grove offers four types of cabin accommodations and two types of lodge rooms. Nine cabins have a private bathroom, while occupants of the other forty-one cabins must use one of two central bathhouses. All cabins have sheets, towels, and daily maid service. The least expensive rooms at Grant Grove are rustic tent cabins with wooden walls and canvas roofs. These cabins sit on a hillside above the meadow, and each has two double beds in a dark and stark unfinished interior with a wooden floor. There is no heat or electricity, although a battery operated lamp is provided. Parking at the bottom of the hill is some distance from these cabins. One step up and about $15 more expensive are the somewhat larger standard rustic cabins without a bathroom. Most standard rustics have two double beds (a few have three doubles), propane heat, and electricity. Each unit has an unfinished interior and a covered patio with a wood stove and picnic table. Grant Grove also offers deluxe rustic cabins that have a similar exterior but a much nicer interior than standard rustics. Deluxe rustics have finished paneled interiors with carpeting and rent for about $10 per night more than standard rustics. Parking is directly beside most of the standard and deluxe rustic cabins, but keep in mind that some of the cabins are a long walk from the bathroom. Deluxe rustic cabin 510 is surrounded by tall shrubs and near the bathroom, which makes it a good choice. Deluxe rustic 508

If you want something to tax your brain, think about this: The complex at Grant Grove spans two California counties. Tulare County on the south side levies a 10 percent hotel/motel tax, while Fresno County on the north side does not. Stay in a cabin on the south side of the complex and you will be charged the tax. Stay in an identical cabin on the north side of the complex and you will not be required to pay it. Occupants of the lodge are fortunate because the building sits in Fresno County, which does not levy the tax. Even the concessionaire was confused by this bizarre situation and was at one time charging tax on all the rooms. Guests in both the cabins and the lodge are charged a National Park Service impact fee of $2.50 per night. How can life on vacation become so complicated?

is the only cabin to have an inside wood stove. The top cabin accommodations at Grant Grove are nine cabins with private bathrooms. These units have interiors similar in size to the deluxe rustics, and are constructed two to a building with a shared front porch. Of the nine cabins with a private bath, cabin 9 is freestanding and classified as deluxe. It has one queen-size bed, a sofa bed, a refrigerator, and a front porch. Cabins 1 through 4 are in two buildings that sit just up the hill from the parking area, while cabins 5 through 9 are farther up the hill and require more walking.

John Muir Lodge, which opened in May 1999, offers thirty rooms in an attractive two-story cedar building. Each floor has a large balcony with chairs on the west end of the building. The lodge contains an impressive lobby area with a vaulted beamed ceiling and a large stone fireplace. Furnishings were especially created for the lodge. Twenty-four regular rooms have heat, two queen-size beds or a king with a sofa bed, a full bath, a coffeemaker, and a telephone. No air-conditioning is in any of the rooms. Six suites have two rooms, each identical in size to a regular room. One room in each suite has two queen-size beds, and the other has a king and sofa bed. The suites have two full bathrooms. The even-numbered rooms, which are on the south side of the building, offer a better view and less noise because they are on the opposite side of the building from the parking lot.

Grant Grove has a wide range of accommodations at different prices. Cabin 9 with a bath (also called the honeymoon cabin) is our favorite accommodation at Grant Grove. We consider it superior to even the more expensive lodge rooms. If you don't mind using a community bathroom, deluxe rustics are the best value in the Grant Grove complex. These are especially desirable for the outside wood stove that can be used for cooking. If you want modern accommodations, choose the lodge, which offers upscale rooms in an attractive cedar building. Staying here offers a convenient location for day trips to both

Cedar Grove and Giant Forest. You will also find horseback riding, guided hikes, and evening programs. Winter activities include cross-country skiing and snowshoeing. Equipment is available for rental at the market.

Rooms: Doubles, triples, and quads. Several of the cabins will accommodate six. Six to eight people will fit in a lodge suite. Only nine of the cabins have a private bathroom.

Wheelchair Accessibility: Two first-floor rooms in the John Muir Lodge are wheelchair accessible. These rooms offer a wide bathroom doorway and grab bars for the toilet and a combination shower-tub. None of the cabins is wheelchair accessible. The restaurant, registration area, and gift shop are wheelchair accessible, as is the National Park Service visitor center.

Reservations: Kings Canyon Park Services, 5755 E. Kings Canyon Road, Suite 101, Fresno, CA 93727. Telephone toll free (866) 522–6966; (559) 452–1081; www.sequoia-kingscanyon.com.

Rates: Rustic tent cabin ($58); standard rustic cabin ($69); deluxe rustic cabin ($79); cabin with private bath ($115); deluxe cabin with private bath ($125); lodge rooms ($159); suites ($260). Rates quoted are for two adults. Children twelve and under stay free. Each additional person is $12 per night. Rollaways are $12. A deposit of two nights' lodging is required. Cancellation of forty-eight hours is required for a refund. Rates are lowered from January to May.

Location: Three miles inside the entrance to Kings Canyon National Park on Highway 180 from Fresno.

Season: Grant Grove Village is open all year, although the three types of rustic cabins close for winter.

Food: A nice restaurant offers family dining with breakfast ($5.00–$8.00), lunch ($7.00–$10.00), and dinner ($11.00–$22.00). A children's menu is available. A market offers groceries. Both are within easy walking distance of the cabins and lodge.

Transportation: Scheduled air, bus, and train service from Fresno, California, where rental cars are available.

Facilities: Restaurant, market, gift shop, post office, and National Park Service visitor center.

Activities: Horseback riding, hiking, and interpretive programs. During winter months snowshoeing and cross-country skiing are popular.

WUKSACHI VILLAGE AND LODGE

P.O. Box 89 • Sequoia National Park, CA 93262 • (559) 565–4070 • www.visitsequoia.com

Lodge Rooms, Wuksachi Village and Lodge

WUKSACHI VILLAGE AND LODGE, NAMED FOR A Native American tribe that once lived in Sequoia, consists of an attractive registration/dining building and three nearby buildings that provide a total of 102 overnight rooms. The four cedar buildings of the lodge first opened in May 1999, and plans call for several additional lodging units and an expansion of the registration/dining building. The complex is on a hillside amid large cedar, sugar pine, and fir trees. Excellent mountain views are available from the windows of many of the rooms. Parking is down a hill from the buildings, and transporting luggage may require more exercise than you desire. Luggage carts are in each of the lodge buildings, and bellstaff are at the registration building to assist with luggage.

The registration building has a beamed vaulted ceiling and a handsome lobby area that includes comfortable chairs and a couch in front of a wood-burning stove. A small gift shop just off the registration area sells the usual assortment of T-shirts, sweatshirts, jewelry, and souvenirs, along with some fine pieces of pottery.

The dining room around the corner from the registration area has a large stone fireplace and features a wall of windows that provide an outstanding view of this beautiful area of the park. A lounge is situated just outside the dining room. Public telephones and conference rooms are downstairs. The entire complex is attractively done with first-class furnishings.

Paved walkways lead from a central parking lot to each of the three lodge buildings, which are virtually identical, with three floors in a split-level design. Rooms on each floor are accessed from central corridors that can be entered from either end of the three buildings. Rooms on the bottom floor of each building face the mountains to the east, while rooms on the third floor face the forest to the west. The second floor of each building has rooms on both sides of the corridor. There are no elevators in the three lodge buildings. Two of the buildings, Stewart and Silliman, are each entered on the second floor, which means you don't have to climb more than one flight of steps. The third and largest building, Sequoia, is entered on the first

Although Wuksachi Village and Lodge opened in May 1999, the planning for this facility had been in the works for well over a decade. The major activity and lodging center of Sequoia National Park was for many years at Giant Forest, 6 miles south of Wuksachi. Here there were cabins, motel-type units, and two two-story lodge buildings. The area also had a restaurant, market, gift shop, and pizza pub. For a variety of reasons, including an antiquated sewage system, danger from falling trees, high maintenance costs, and harm to reproduction of the area's sequoias, the National Park Service closed all commercial activities here in October 1998 and subsequently began removing most of the structures.

floor; you will have to climb two flights of steps if your room is on the third floor. If stairs will be a problem, ask for a room on the entry floor of the building to which you are assigned.

All of the 102 rooms have heat, a ceiling fan, a full bathroom with combination shower-tub, hair dryer, refrigerator, television, telephone with data port, coffeemaker, and very attractive furnishings. The rooms are not air-conditioned, but this is seldom needed. None of the rooms has a balcony. Each of the three lodge building offers rooms in three classifications. Twenty-four standard rooms, the lowest-priced alternative, and sixty deluxe rooms are similar except for a slight difference in room size and furnishings. Standard rooms are at least as large as, if not larger than, most nice motel rooms. These all have two queen beds. Deluxe rooms have about three feet of extra depth and come with two queen beds plus an overstuffed chair or a king plus a sofa bed. Eighteen superior rooms with either two queen-size beds or one king-size bed and a

sofa bed also have a side room with a sofa bed and chair. The extra room can be closed off with two sliding wood doors. We suggest a standard room and request a mountain view. Rooms within each classification rent for the same price, so obtaining a room with a view doesn't cost extra.

Wuksachi Village and Lodge is a great place to spend a restful weekend or to serve as a base to explore the Kings Canyon/Sequoia area. The location makes it convenient to visit most of the park's features. Lodgepole, a major activity area with a large visitor center, market, laundry facilities, mountain shop, deli, and nature center, is only 2 miles away. Giant Forest, with an outstanding museum and trails that give access to the park's namesake sequoias, is 4 miles south of Lodgepole.

Rooms: Doubles, triples, and quads. Superior rooms can sleep up to six. All rooms have private baths with combination shower-tub.

Sequoia and Kings Canyon winter activities include cross-country skiing and snowshoeing during winter months when the area is typically buried in snowfall. Both Wuksachi in Sequoia National Park and Grant Grove Lodge in Kings Canyon National Park are open all year. Cedar Grove Lodge is closed during the winter. Keep in mind that Generals Highway is sometimes closed by snow during the winter, so access to Wuksachi may be limited to the south entrance from Ash Mountain and access to Grant Grove Lodge may be only via California Highway 180 from Fresno. Call the National Park Service or the lodge where you will be staying prior to leaving home to determine which road to take. Also keep in mind that chains may be required on your vehicle even though a road is open.

Wheelchair Accessibility: Eight rooms, several in each of the three price categories, are each fully wheelchair accessible, with one queen bed and a large bathroom that includes a roll-in shower. Ramp access is provided to each of the three lodge buildings. Keep in mind that rooms are up a hill and some distance from parking. The registration area, restaurant, and gift shop are also wheelchair accessible. A porter with an electric cart is available to assist with luggage and transportation.

Reservations: Delaware North Park Services, P.O. Box 89, Sequoia National Park, CA 93262. Phone (888) 252–5757 or (559) 253–2199; www.visitsequoia.com. One night's deposit required. Cancellation requires seventy-two hours' notice.

Rates: Peak season rates apply from mid-May to mid-October and during holidays. Off-season rates are applicable the remainder of the year: standard (peak $160/off-peak $99); deluxe ($187/$119); superior ($229/$149). Rates quoted are for two adults. Each additional person is $10 per night. Children twelve and under stay free unless an extra bed is required. Rollaways and cribs are $10 per night.

Location: Wuksachi Village and Lodge is just off Generals Highway in the northern section of Sequoia National Park. The lodge is approximately 2 miles west of Lodgepole.

Season: The lodge is open all year.

Food: The restaurant serves breakfast (Continental, $6.25 or full buffet, $10.00), lunch ($8.00–$15.00), and dinner ($14.00–$27.00) daily. Two miles away, Lodgepole has a market and deli, as well as a snack bar that serves breakfast, sandwiches, and pizza. On Wednesday through Sunday during summer, the lodge offers an all-you-can-eat barbecue dinner ($20) at Wolverton Recreation Area.

Transportation: Scheduled air service is available to Fresno, California, where cars may be rented.

Facilities: Restaurant, lounge, gift shop, conference rooms. Two miles away, Lodgepole offers a mountain shop, post office, laundry facilities, deli, market, snack bar, and a National Park Service visitor center. Most services at Lodgepole are seasonal.

Activities: Hiking and fishing. Horseback riding offered at a stable near Wolverton. Cave tours are at Crystal Cave, about 20 miles from Wuksachi. Buy tickets at Lodgepole or Foothills visitor center. Winter activities include cross-country skiing, sledding, snowshoeing, and guided walks.

Yosemite National Park

P.O. Box 577 • Yosemite National Park, CA 95389 • (209) 372–0200 • www.nps.gov/yose

Yosemite National Park comprises 761,000 acres of scenic valleys, high-country meadows, and granite peaks and domes in one of America's most spectacular and popular national parks. The three major features of the park are beautiful Yosemite Valley, groves of giant sequoias at Crane Flat and Mariposa Grove, and the alpine wilderness reached via Tioga Road. The park's main activity area is in Yosemite Valley. Tioga Road is a beautiful paved road that cuts through the High Sierra and connects on the east side of the park with U.S. Highway 395 at Lee Vining, California. Yosemite National Park is in east-central California, approximately 190 miles due east of San Francisco. The southern edge of the park is approximately 60 miles north of Fresno via California Highway 41. **Park Entrance Fee:** $20 per vehicle or $10 per person, good for seven days.

Lodging in Yosemite National Park: Yosemite has seven lodging facilities, four of which are in Yosemite Valley. These include the Ahwahnee, Yosemite Lodge at the Falls, Curry Village, and Housekeeping Camp. Accommodations in the valley range from the upscale and expensive Ahwahnee (probably the most elegant hotel in any national park) to downscale and relatively inexpensive tent cabins. A free shuttle stops at each facility as well as other major points of interest in the valley. The valley can be congested in the summer, so park your vehicle and use the shuttle.

Three very different Yosemite National Park lodging facilities are outside Yosemite Valley. Probably the oldest lodging facility in any national park, the Wawona Hotel comprises six white frame buildings situated in a peaceful setting a few miles inside the park's south entrance.

Yosemite National Park

STANISLAUS
NATIONAL
FOREST

TOIYABE
NATIONAL
FOREST

N
W · E
S

Lake
Eleanor

Pacific Crest Trail

Hetch Hetchy
Reservoir

White Wolf Lodge

May
Lake

TIOGA PASS
ENTRANCE

Tioga Rd.

**Tuolumne
Meadows Lodge**

Hetch Hetchy Rd.

HETCH HETCHY
ENTRANCE

120

BIG OAK FLAT
ENTRANCE

120

Hodgdon
Meadow

Tioga Rd.

Yosemite
Creek

Porcupine
Flat

Merced
Lake

120

Big Oak Flat Rd.

Tamarack
Flat

Crane
Flat

YOSEMITE VALLEY

ARCH ROCK
ENTRANCE

Glacier Point

140

Badger
Pass Ski Area

Bridalveil Creek

Yosemite
West

Wawona

Wawona Hotel

SIERRA
NATIONAL
FOREST

SOUTH
ENTRANCE

SIERRA
NATIONAL
FOREST

41

0   5   10
Miles

Yosemite National Park—Yosemite Valley

Tuolumne Meadows Lodge and White Wolf Lodge offer canvas tent cabins and a few wood cabins on Tioga Pass for an experience in Yosemite's high country. Although in the same park, these two facilities seem worlds apart from one another as well as from Yosemite Valley lodging.

Yosemite is very popular during summer months, so make reservations at the earliest possible date. Accommodations with private bath are often booked ten to twelve months in advance.

Reservations: A central reservation office services all the lodging facilities in Yosemite National Park. For reservations write or call Yosemite Reservations, 6771 North Palm Avenue, Fresno, CA 93704. Phone (559) 252–4848. Reservations can be made online at www.yosemitepark.com. Cancellation with a full refund requires a ten-day notice. Reservations for all Yosemite lodging can be made up to 366 days prior to your planned arrival date. If the hotel is fully booked and you are not flexible with regard to dates, try again thirty, fifteen, or seven days prior to your intended arrival, when previous reservations by others are most likely to be canceled.

Food in the Valley: Food service is available at many Yosemite Valley locations, including all of the lodging facilities other than Housekeeping. The free shuttle system makes all of the food service easily accessible, so you can choose to have pizza at Curry Village even though you are staying at the Ahwahnee. Likewise, you can enjoy a memorable evening by dining at the Ahwahnee when you have a room at Yosemite Lodge. Nearly every type of food is available somewhere in Yosemite Valley. Beer and wine are available at most of these locations. Yosemite Village offers a pizza loft, a deli, a cafe, and a grill. Yosemite Lodge and Curry Village each offer several different dining experiences. The Ahwahnee's formal dining room is one of the most beautiful you will find anywhere. Markets selling cold sandwiches, alcoholic beverages, soft drinks, snacks, and groceries are at several locations.

Transportation: Scheduled air service is available to Fresno, where rental cars are available. Amtrak serves Yosemite Valley through a combination train-bus service. Yosemite Area Regional Transportation System (YARTS) buses serve Yosemite Valley on a year-round basis from Mariposa, El Portal, and Merced (an Amtrak stop). Seasonal bus service to Yosemite Valley is available from the towns of Mammoth Lakes and Lee Vining. For information check www.yarts.com, or call (877) 989–2787. A free shuttle bus system within Yosemite Valley serves all the lodges and other popular points of interest.

YOSEMITE VALLEY

THE AHWAHNEE

Yosemite National Park, CA 95389 • (209) 372–1407 • www.yosemitepark.com

MANY TRAVELERS CLAIM THAT THE AHWAHNEE IN Yosemite Valley is the finest lodging facility at any national park. This is difficult to dispute. The Ahwahnee, built in the late 1920s with a name that Native Americans gave to what is now Yosemite Valley, is both a National Historic Landmark and a world-class facility. Everything about this six-story hotel makes you want to stay, except perhaps the cost, which is rivaled only by Death Valley's Furnace Creek Inn and Grand Teton's Jenny Lake Lodge. The Great Lounge, with a 24-foot-high beamed ceiling, stained glass windows, and two of the largest stone fireplaces you will ever see, is a jewel. The spectacular dining room, with its 34-foot-high vaulted beamed ceiling and floor-to-ceiling windows, is one of the most beautiful you will ever enter. Pottery, baskets, paintings, and rugs are placed throughout the public rooms. The Ahwahnee offers a total of 123 rooms in both the main hotel building and several nearby secluded cottages. The Ahwahnee is located in the northeast section of Yosemite Valley, at the base of the Royal Arches. The location is remote enough to avoid most of the congestion that typifies much of the valley. Adequate parking is nearby, and valet parking is available. Bellstaff will assist with luggage.

The Ahwahnee offers two types of lodging. The main hotel has ninety-nine rooms on six floors. Most rooms have one king-size bed, while a few have two double beds. The rooms are stylishly furnished and include

Guests who have enjoyed staying in the Ahwahnee since its opening in 1927 can thank Stephen Mather, first superintendent of the National Park Service. Mather facilitated the merger of Yosemite's first concessionaires—Curry Company and the Yosemite Park Company—on the condition the new firm construct an upscale fireproof hotel with the capability of year-round operation. The luxurious hotel was expected to increase tourism (and the park's budget) and attract important people who would provide political and financial support for the National Park Service. The Ahwahnee's architect, Gilbert Stanley Underwood, had previously designed impressive lodges at Zion National Park and Bryce Canyon National Park, and would subsequently design Grand Canyon Lodge on the North Rim and Oregon's Timberline Lodge.

television, telephone, guest bathrobes, iron and ironing board, coffeemaker, hair dryer, and full tiled bath. One or more large windows in each hotel room offer differing views depending on room location. Vistas range from excellent views of Yosemite Falls or Glacier Point to rooms that look out at a loading dock or under a porch roof. The best views are from corner rooms, which each have windows on two sides. The hotel has two junior suites with extra large rooms. One has a sunken sitting area and offers the only Jacuzzi in Yosemite. The other has a four-poster bed that was used by Queen Elizabeth II when she stayed in this room during a 1983 visit. The top-of-the-line rooms are four suites that each have one bedroom plus a large, luxuriously furnished parlor with spectacular views. The suites offer varying amenities that can include a fireplace, library, large flat-screen television, and balcony. Each offers an option of adding a second adjoining bedroom.

The Ahwahnee has eight separate but nearby single-story frame buildings that house a total of twenty-four cottages. These cottages sit in a secluded and quiet wooded area near the hotel but away from the hotel traffic. They are in a natural setting, but most provide minimal views. Each cottage has a patio with table and chairs. Cottages 720 and 721 and cottages 722 and 723 share common patio areas and are probably less desirable. The cottages are larger than most of the hotel rooms and are decorated to highlight Yosemite's Native American heritage. Cottages 714 and 719 are the only two with wood-burning fireplaces (wood provided) and are slightly larger than average. Cottage 716 has a mountain view, and cottages 707 and 718 are more private and offer a view of the Merced River. Most cottages have one king-size bed, while five have two double beds. Amenities are the same as the hotel rooms plus a small refrigerator.

The hotel rooms and cottages rent for the same price, and choosing between the two isn't easy. Our suggestion is that first-time visitors who plan to stay a day or two should choose a room in the hotel to appreciate

The Ahwahnee has hosted many famous guests since the hotel's opening on July 14, 1927. President John F. Kennedy stayed here in August 1962, and Presidents Eisenhower and Reagan also stayed overnight, although not during their presidential terms. Winston Churchill, Will Rogers, and Eleanor Roosevelt were guests at the Ahwahnee. Among the numerous Hollywood stars who have stayed here are Shirley Temple, Ginger Rogers, Judy Garland, Clint Eastwood, Jack Benny, Greta Garbo, Red Skelton, and Humphrey Bogart. Among the hotel's most famous guests were Queen Elizabeth II and her husband, Prince Philip, who stayed three nights in March 1983.

the delight of staying overnight in such a wonderful place. If you plan on staying for a week or so and desire some quiet, you may be happier in one of the cottages.

The Ahwahnee offers fine lodging in a beautiful setting. If you can afford it, it is a wonderful place to stay while exploring the beauty and enjoying the many activities offered by Yosemite National Park. If you can't, try to schedule at least one night's lodging in this unique hotel. Walk through the lobby into the Great Lounge, where afternoon tea accompanied by background piano music is a tradition. On through the lounge past the second fireplace provides entry to the Solarium, whose massive windows furnish a sweeping view of a grassy area surrounded by trees with a background of granite cliffs. The hotel also offers a cocktail lounge, a sweetshop, a swimming pool, tennis courts, and a very nice gift shop. A free shuttle bus operates throughout Yosemite Valley, so that activities and facilities in other locations are only a few minutes away.

Rooms: Singles, doubles, triples, and quads. All rooms have a full tiled bath.

Wheelchair Accessibility: Two rooms in the main hotel are wheelchair accessible, with a wide bathroom door, an extra large bathroom, and a roll-in shower. Several other hotel rooms offer bathrooms with a combination shower-tub with grab bars. Two cottages have a bathroom with wide doorways and a roll-in shower. Keep in mind that the cottages are some distance from parking, although bell service is available.

Rates: Hotel rooms and cottages ($379); junior suites ($480); suites ($835-$936). Children twelve and under stay free in the same room with an adult. Each additional person is $21 per night. A variety of packages are offered in the off season.

Location: North section of Yosemite Valley, at the end of a dead-end road.

Season: The Ahwahnee is open year-round. It is often fully booked a year ahead for busy periods such as holidays and summer months.

Food: An elegant dining room serves breakfast ($8–$18), lunch ($11–$15), and dinner ($22–$39) until 10:00 P.M. A children's menu is available. Dinner reservations are highly recommended, and appropriate attire is required; athletic clothing is not allowed. A Sunday brunch ($32) is served from 7:00 A.M. to 3:00 P.M. The cocktail lounge serves light meals from 11:00 A.M. to 10:00 P.M. Room service is available. The famous Bracebridge Dinner, a three-hour Christmas pageant and feast, is presented over the eight days around Christmas.

Facilities: Outdoor heated swimming pool, tennis courts, gift shop, tour desk, cocktail lounge, sweetshop, and full-time concierge service. Wireless Internet access is available in the guest rooms, meeting rooms, and some public spaces.

Activities: Hiking, swimming, tennis, evening programs, guided hotel tours. Winter activities listed under Curry Village.

CURRY VILLAGE

Yosemite National Park, CA 95389 • (209) 372–8333 • www.yosemitepark.com

Cabins without Baths at Curry Village

CURRY VILLAGE IS THE LARGEST LODGING COMplex in Yosemite Valley, with a total of 628 rooms, mostly in canvas tents. The term *village* is certainly appropriate for this facility, because Curry is much like a small town, with tents, cabins, buffet, fast-food restaurants, bar, camp store, "sitting lodge building" (a cabin used as a lounge), post office (summer only), shower building, and rest rooms. The location, in the southeast section of Yosemite Valley, is near several campgrounds and a convenient place for campers to roam and eat.

Curry Village offers four types of accommodations. The least expensive lodging is 427 canvas tent cabins with a wooden platform and canvas walls and roof. These units are available in different sizes, with a variety of bedding options that range from two singles to a double and three singles. The bedding consists of metal cots, with linens, towels, soap, and maid service provided. A padlock is available for the front door. A light is in each tent, although there are no electrical outlets, heat, or plumbing. Rest room and shower facilities are centrally located. A few heated tent cabins are available in the winter.

Curry Village also has 183 wood-frame cabins, most of which are constructed as duplexes, although a few are quads and some are freestanding. Each cabin has carpeting, heat, and some have a front porch with a bench. Approximately a hundred of the cabins have private baths, mostly with showers but some with a combination shower-tub. The remaining cabins have no bath or running water. Excluding the bathrooms, both types of cabins have approximately the same amount of living space. Cabins with a bath rent for approximately $25 per night extra and are spaced better than cabins without a bath, which literally sit on top of one another. Most cabins have two double beds, but a few cabins with bath have a double and a single. Curry Village also has three deluxe cabins, 819, 90A, and 90B, which have a living room, a bathroom, and one or two bedrooms. Two also have fireplaces. These deluxe cabins sleep from two to four persons; they are by far the nicest lodging facilities at Curry Village. A single motel-type building, Stoneman House,

has eighteen standard rooms with private bath and shower but no tub. These units have heat and a ceiling fan. Beds range from one to three doubles; the three double beds are in units with a loft. The motel units with a loft are an especially desirable accommodation for families, as the loft can be used to separate children from parents, at least temporarily. In addition, they are a good value and rent for the same price as the other motel units.

Lodging facilities at Curry Village are tightly packed and most of the units are some distance from parking. Basically, this is a low-cost alternative to the Ahwahnee and Yosemite Lodge. The many tent cabins are among the cheapest of Yosemite's overnight offerings outside the campgrounds. Curry also includes a variety of eating facilities. Food options include a dining pavilion that serves an all-you-can-eat-style buffet for breakfast and dinner, a taco stand, a pizza deck, and an ice cream/coffee corner. Evening programs are presented at an outside amphitheater. A free shuttle service can transport you to other valley areas. The decision on whether to stay here depends on how much you are willing to spend, what lodging facilities are available when your reservation is made, and, because this area can be very busy in the summer, how well you tolerate crowds.

One of Yosemite's best-known activities was the evening Firefall, during which a massive pile of glowing red fir bark embers was pushed over the cliff at Glacier Point near Camp Curry. The practice was begun in the 1870s, abandoned several years later, then revived in 1899 by David Curry, proprietor of Camp Curry. The evening activity became so popular that everything in the valley would come to a halt when the time came for embers to be pushed over the side. The Firefall continued until 1968, when it was permanently halted by park management.

Rooms: Doubles, triples, and quads; a few units will hold five or six persons. Most rooms, including all the tent cabins, do not have private baths.

Wheelchair Accessibility: Two cabins with a bath, one motel room with a bath, and six cabins without a bath are ADA compliant. A paved path leads from cabins without a bath to the community bathroom, which has ramp access and a roll-in shower.

Rates: Canvas tent cabins ($69); cabins without bath ($85); cabins with bath ($108); deluxe cabins ($150–$195); standard motel-type rooms ($113). Children twelve and under stay free except in the tent cabins, where an additional child is $4.00 per night. Rates for an additional person are from $9.00 to $11.00. Prices are slightly lower from November through March, excluding holidays. Further reductions are available for midweek stays from November through March.

Location: Southeast side of Yosemite Valley.

Season: All of the lodging facilities in Curry Village are open spring through fall. Some of them are also open during the winter.

Food: A dining pavilion serves a buffet breakfast and a buffet dinner from spring through fall. Mexican food and pizza are served on the patio as fast-food items. An inside coffee corner has specialty coffees, bakery items, and ice cream. A bar serves alcoholic beverages beginning at noon along with hamburgers and a few other items. A small market sells beer, wine, cold sandwiches, and limited grocery items.

Facilities: Gift shop, mountain shop, bicycle rental and river raft rental stands, camp store, outdoor swimming pool, and post office (summer only). In winter an outside ice-skating rink is available and equipment for cross-country skiing can be rented.

Activities: River rafting, hiking, bicycling, swimming, and evening programs. Winter activities include cross-country skiing and ice-skating. Badger Pass, 23 miles from Yosemite Valley, usually receives substantial snowfall and has four chair lifts and one cable tow to serve nine ski runs. Ninety miles of marked cross-country ski trails begin here.

HOUSEKEEPING CAMP

Yosemite National Park, CA 95389 • (209) 372–8338 • www.yosemitepark.com

HOUSEKEEPING CAMP IS A COMPLEX OF 266 concrete and canvas guest rooms surrounding several larger wooden structures that provide support facilities, such as a registration desk, a laundry facility, and common bathrooms and showers. Rooms are built two to a unit, with the back of each room sharing a concrete wall with another identical room. The rooms are constructed of cement on three sides (each two-room unit has concrete walls constructed in an H pattern), with a canvas entry and a canvas roof that extends over a concrete floor and a front concrete patio area that has a picnic table and a cooking shelf. A large food storage box is located next to each patio. A privacy fence surrounds the front of each patio. The canvas entry door cannot be secured, which means that you must leave valuables locked in your vehicle.

Each room has one double bed and two single, fold-down bunk beds. The interior also has a mirror, an electric light, and electrical outlets. None of the rooms has a private bathroom, so guests are required to use centrally located bathhouses. Guests must supply their own sheets, blankets, and pillows, although blankets and pillows can be rented at the registration building. Soap and towels for bathing are supplied without charge in the common bathhouses. The housekeeping units on the bank of the Merced River are the best choice. Most units sit close together and have little in the way of privacy or a view.

Housekeeping Camp rooms represent national park lodging at its most basic. These relatively inexpensive rooms are preferable in Yosemite Valley only to the tightly packed tent cabins in Curry Village. No eating facilities are available here, although this is the only facility where guests may cook their own food. Housekeeping Camp does have showers and a laundry facility. This is a stop on the free shuttle so that guests can ride to other valley locations for food and frolic.

Rooms: The rooms are identical, with beds for four persons. Two additional cots can be rented. None of the rooms has a private bath.

Wheelchair Accessibility: Four housekeeping units near a parking area have access to a wheelchair-accessible bathroom with a roll-in shower. A paved walkway is between the living units and the bathroom.

Rates: One to four persons pay the same price ($67.00); each additional person is $5.00 per night.

Location: On the bank of the Merced River in the southeast section of Yosemite Valley, a short distance west of Curry Village.

Season: Spring to mid-October.

Food: No restaurant or snack bar is at Housekeeping Camp. A small market has limited groceries. A variety of restaurants and snack facilities can be reached via the free valley shuttle.

Facilities: Small market, shower, and laundry.

Activities: River rafting, swimming, and hiking.

YOSEMITE LODGE AT THE FALLS

Yosemite National Park, CA 95389 • (209) 372–1274 • www.yosemitepark.com

*Lodge Rooms
at Yosemite Lodge
at the Falls*

A variety of tours are offered to Yosemite visitors. These include the two-hour Valley Floor Tour, the four-hour Glacier Point Tour, the Mariposa Grove Tour, the Big Trees Tram Tour, the Tuolumne Meadows Hikers' Bus, and the full-day Grand Tour, which combines the Glacier Point and Mariposa Grove Tours with a lunch at the Wawona Hotel. Most tours depart from Yosemite Lodge at the Falls. Tickets can be purchased at several locations in the valley. Call (209) 372–1240 for information.

Yosemite Lodge at the Falls is a large complex of wooden buildings with two categories of overnight guest facilities, including one two-story motel unit and several one- and two-story lodge units. In all, the lodge provides a total of 245 rooms. The units are scattered about a service area that includes the registration building, located just south of Northside Drive in front of scenic Yosemite Falls. A variety of other stores and restaurants are near the registration building and within easy walking distance of any of the guest rooms. Registration parking is directly in front of the registration building, but overnight guest parking is a considerable distance from some of the rooms. Bellstaff are available to assist with luggage. Yosemite Lodge at the Falls is located in the northwest section of Yosemite Valley.

Nearly all of the 245 rooms at Yosemite Lodge at the Falls are in fourteen one- and two-story frame buildings constructed in the mid- to late-1960s. All of these lodge rooms are virtually identical, with a dressing area, hair dryers, iron, ironing board, television, a telephone, heat, a ceiling fan, and a full bathroom with a combination shower-tub. Beds are either a king or two doubles. Each room has a patio or balcony with a table and two chairs. These buildings do not have air-conditioning or elevators. Rooms in the two one-story buildings and top-floor rooms in the two-story buildings have vaulted beamed ceilings. Bottom-floor rooms have flat ceilings, making the rooms appear less spacious even though they are the same size. Lodge rooms are similar to large upscale motel rooms. Unfortunately, surrounding trees obstruct mountain and waterfall views from nearly all the rooms.

Yosemite Lodge at the Falls also offers nineteen smaller and less expensive standard rooms in a single two-story building constructed in the late 1950s adjacent to the registration building. All these rooms, which rent for about $50 less per night than the larger lodge rooms, have the same amenities as the lodge rooms. These rooms do not have a patio or balcony. Bedding in the standard rooms varies from one double bed to two queen beds. Four extra-large rooms on the second floor of this building are classified as "family" rooms although they rent for the same price as other standard rooms. These rooms each have a shower (no tub), a separate toilet, two sinks, and a double bed and from two to four single beds.

Yosemite Lodge at the Falls was a substantially larger complex prior to the disastrous flood of January 1997. Three days of rain flooded much of Yosemite Valley, including the Yosemite Lodge complex. The flood was actually similar in intensity to previous floods that occurred in Yosemite Valley during the previous one hundred years. The history of damaging floods caused the National Park Service to order the removal of more than 150 cabins and two lodge buildings that were in service prior to January 1997. In all, Yosemite Lodge lost approximately 200 rooms.

Our choice at Yosemite Lodge at the Falls is a second-floor lodge room on the back side of the Juniper or Laurel buildings. These rooms offer convenient parking but face away from the road and are relatively quiet. They also face away from Yosemite Falls, but few rooms in Yosemite Lodge at the Falls offer a view of this picturesque attraction. Our second choice would be any of the rooms in one-story Cottonwood. One disadvantage here is the distance from parking. Aspen, Dogwood, and Tamarack, three newer buildings with lodge rooms, are squeezed together on a corner between two parking lots. Rooms in these buildings are near parking but offer little privacy. With two or more children you will probably want to try for one of the four family rooms in the Cedar building.

Yosemite Lodge at the Falls is located in the center of facilities and activities. Food service includes a food court and an upscale restaurant. You will also find an ice cream stand, an environmental shop, a gift shop, and a cocktail lounge with wireless Internet access. A tour desk is inside the registration building. The free shuttle stops across the street from the registration building and provides access to all the facilities and activities in the valley.

Rooms: Doubles, triples, and quads, with six persons in a limited number of rooms. All rooms have private baths.

Wheelchair Accessibility: Yosemite Lodge at the Falls has four rooms that are ADA compliant, which includes three lodge rooms and one standard room.

Rates: Standard rooms ($113); lodge rooms ($161). Rates quoted are for two adults. Each additional person is $11 per night for standard rooms, $12 for lodge rooms. Children twelve and under stay free. Prices are slightly lower from November through March, excluding holidays. Further reductions are available for midweek stays from November through March.

Location: In the northwest section of Yosemite Valley, near the double waterfall.

Season: Yosemite Lodge at the Falls is open year-round.

Food: A food court offers breakfast, lunch, and dinner at moderate prices. Breakfast includes pancakes, French toast, eggs, oatmeal, cold cereals, and bakery items. Lunch and dinner items include pizza, pasta, chicken, fish, salads, and desserts. Lunch and dinner prices range from $4.00 to $14.00. Beer and wine are available. In the same complex, the Mountain Room offers an excellent view of Yosemite Falls in a dining room that serves upscale dinners including steaks, seafood, and chicken ($16 to $30) from 5:30 to 9:00 P.M. Dinner reservations are recommended. Beer, wine, and other alcoholic beverages are available. The nearby Mountain Room Lounge serves sandwiches and salads from 4:30 P.M. (noon on weekends) to 10:30 P.M. A market behind the registration building sells limited groceries including beer, wine, and snacks.

Facilities: Gift shops, food court, restaurant, cocktail lounge, branch post office, bicycle rental, tour desk, swimming pool, outdoor amphitheater. Wireless Internet is available in the lounge, meeting spaces, and the outdoor amphitheater.

Activities: Evening programs, swimming, biking, hiking. Winter activities are listed under Curry Village.

OUTSIDE YOSEMITE VALLEY

WAWONA HOTEL

P.O. Box 2005 • Wawona, CA 95389 • (209) 375–6556 • www.yosemitepark.com

Main Building at the Wawona Hotel

THE WAWONA (AN INDIAN TERM MEANING "big tree") Hotel is the grande dame of the national parks. While some would argue that Death Valley's Furnace Creek Inn and Yosemite's own Ahwahnee are more elegant, the Wawona is without doubt one of the grandest. The Wawona Hotel is a complex of six white frame, shake-roofed buildings, the oldest of which was constructed in 1876. The newest of the buildings was built in 1918. The complex is similar in appearance to a late-1800s western military post. The Wawona Hotel is 4 miles inside the south entrance to Yosemite National Park and 25 miles south of popular Yosemite Valley. No public transportation operates between the hotel and Yosemite Valley.

The six buildings at Wawona offer a total of 104 rooms. Each of the buildings contains overnight lodging rooms, although the size of the buildings and the rooms within them vary considerably. The main building, which houses registration, a large dining room, and an attractive lounge area, has twenty-nine rooms, all but one on the second floor. Each floor of this large, two-story building has an impressive wraparound veranda with white railings and posts. Wicker benches,

chairs, and tables on the lower veranda offer a place for guests to relax while viewing the grassy front lawn that surrounds a stone fountain. Beverages are served here during the late afternoon and early evening. The other five buildings are smaller but have a similar architectural style, including verandas with tables and chairs.

Although rooms vary by size, view, and building, only two price categories are used: with or without private bath. Fifty of the 104 rooms have a private bath

President Teddy Roosevelt came to the Wawona Hotel on May 3, 1903. Assigned to room 215, the president dropped off his bags and went off to the Big Trees area to meet with conservationist John Muir. This meeting gave Muir an opportunity to convince Roosevelt to expand the park to include Yosemite Valley. Mariposa Grove and Yosemite Valley were at the time owned by the state of California.

The Wawona Hotel has been in continuous operation for 130 years, longer than any other lodging unit in the national park system. The Wawona had already served travelers for more than a decade before Yosemite National Park was established. In the early days guests enjoyed meals featuring vegetables gathered from a local garden and freshly prepared fish and venison from the nearby streams and woods. The hotel even had its own dairy so guests could enjoy fresh milk and cream. The Wawona, a National Historic Landmark, has its own golf course, which opened for business in June 1918 as the first course in the Sierra Nevada.

and rent for about $55 per night more than rooms without a private bath. Guests in rooms without private bath must use community shower and bathroom facilities located in three of the buildings. Community bathrooms, accessed from the outside porches, can require a walk past up to eight rooms, depending on the location of your room. All but two of the rooms in the main building are relatively small and without a private bathroom or in-room sink. Rooms 223 and 224 each have a bathroom with a claw-foot tub. Views vary, with some rooms providing a scenic view toward the front lawn and others in an inside hallway having no view at all. Since the view is not considered in the rate, request a room in the front with a view of the lawn.

If staying in the main building isn't important, request a room in one-story Clark Cottage or Washburn Cottage, but be aware that both cottages have a limit of two persons per room. Clark Cottage sits directly beside the main hotel building and offers attractive rooms. The four front rooms in Clark Cottage probably offer the best views. Corner rooms have an extra

window that provides additional outside light. All rooms have a king-size bed, a ceiling fan, and a private bath. Two-story Washburn Cottage has a total of sixteen rooms, all with private baths. First-floor rooms are of nice size with a king bed. Upstairs rooms are smaller, have a queen bed, do not have a veranda, and require climbing a flight of stairs. Request a first-floor room.

Moore Cottage with nine rooms sits on a hill directly behind the main hotel building and offers the most convenient parking at Wawona. Only two rooms, both on the first floor, offer a private bath. The four upstairs rooms are small, with a single dormer window, and no veranda. In addition guests with an upstairs room must use a long, steep stairway to carry luggage or use the community bath that is on the first floor. We like room 87, which is quite large and has a private bath, and corner room 89, which has a sink but not a private bath. Try to avoid an upstairs room in Moore. Little White House is a small cottage with only three rooms, two of which have a private bath. The third room has connecting doorways to both the other rooms, and the entire building is an excellent choice for large family gatherings. The room without a bath (51) is large but requires guests to use bathroom facilities in another building if the room is not rented in conjunction with an adjoining room that has a bath. The two-story Annex has thirty-nine rooms, most of which have a double bed plus a single bed. Half the rooms each have a private bath with a claw-foot tub and shower. The other rooms, with in-room sinks only, have connecting doors for families that wish to rent two rooms. Room 137 with a private bathroom is quite large and includes a double bed plus two single beds. All of the buildings are clustered closely together, so there should be no concern about the walking distance to the restaurant or lounge.

The Wawona Hotel is a peaceful alternative to lodging facilities in busy Yosemite Valley. The dining room retains its Victorian flavor, with tall windows offering views out the front and side of the main building. Outside tables are also available. Although named a hotel, the Wawona is actually more of a resort. The hotel has a swimming pool (the tank), a tennis court, and a nine-hole golf course. A practice putting green is on the hotel's front lawn. The hotel is adjacent to Pioneer Village, a collection of historic buildings that introduce visitors to some of the events shaping Yosemite's history. Included are a covered bridge, horse-drawn coaches, a homestead, and numerous other historic buildings. A free shuttle bus operates between the hotel and Mariposa Grove, the site of many giant sequoia trees.

Rooms: Mostly doubles, with a few triples and quads. About half the rooms have private baths. Rooms with private bath are often fully booked a year ahead during peak season. Previous guests often request particular rooms, so be as specific as possible about the type and location of the room you want.

Wheelchair Accessibility: Two first-floor rooms in the Annex have limited wheelchair accessibility, with a ramp and sidewalk from the main lodge building. The bathrooms have a combination shower-tub, and the hotel staff can install grab bars. The hotel dining room is wheelchair accessible from the back of the main lodge building.

Rates: Rooms with private bath ($170); rooms without private bath ($115). Rates quoted are for two adults. Each additional person is $10 per night without a bath and $16 per night with a bath. Children twelve and under stay free. Rates are slightly lower from mid-November to mid-March, excluding holidays. Several packages are offered for fall and winter.

Location: Twenty miles north of the town of Oakhurst and 4 miles north of the south entrance to Yosemite National Park. The hotel is approximately 25 miles from Yosemite Valley.

Season: Open mid-April through Thanksgiving and most weekends and holidays through the winter. Closed most of January.

Food: An attractive dining room, with a wall of windows to the west overlooking the front lawn and to the north providing a view of a wooded area, serves breakfast ($7.00–$14.00) including a buffet, lunch ($10.00–$12.00), and dinner ($20.00–$25.00). Reservations are not accepted for dinner, which begins at 5:30 P.M. A children's menu is available. Alcoholic beverages are served on the front porch, in the lobby, and in the dining room. During summer months an old-fashioned barbecue is served Saturday nights on the front lawn. A snack shop at the golf shop in the bottom floor of the Annex offers sandwiches, chili, and beverages from spring to fall. A market with beer, wine, soft drinks, cold sandwiches, and limited groceries is a short walk from the hotel.

Facilities: Swimming pool, tennis court, nine-hole golf course, putting green, market, gift shop, post office, gas station, historic Pioneer Village.

Activities: Golf, tennis, horse rides, stagecoach rides, swimming, fishing, and hiking.

TUOLUMNE MEADOWS LODGE

Yosemite National Park, CA 95389 • (209) 372–8413 • www.yosemitepark.com

*Tent Cabin at
Tuolumne Meadows Lodge*

TUOLUMNE MEADOWS LODGE IS A GROUP OF SIXTY-nine canvas tent cabins situated at 8,775 feet in the Sierras. The lodge offers stays of up to seven days and is an attractive location for visitors who plan to hike to other camps in the High Sierra Loop. Tuolumne Meadows also attracts people who enjoy the crisp air of an alpine environment. The tents are on a hill to the east of a canvas lodge that houses the registration area and a dining room. The lodge is located about a mile off Tioga Road (California Highway 120), 9 miles from the Tioga Pass Entrance on the east side of Yosemite National Park. It is 52 miles from Yosemite Valley.

The sixty-nine tents at Tuolumne Meadows are virtually identical to those at Curry Village in the valley. Tents are on a cement slab, and each unit has an inside wood stove for heat. Each canvas tent is equipped with either four single beds or one double bed plus two single beds. Sheets, pillows, and blankets are provided. The lodge also has maid service. The tents have no electricity or plumbing, so guests must use a common bathhouse with showers. Guests are also provided with candles for light, wood for the stove, and towels for the bathhouse. A large central parking lot is a moderate walk from many of the tent cabins.

Tuolumne Meadows Lodge is in a lovely area of Yosemite National Park and is appropriate for those

Conservationist John Muir first visited Yosemite in 1868. Muir recruited Robert Underwood Johnson, editor of Century *magazine, to use Johnson's influence to protect this area, especially in the high meadows that were being used to graze sheep. Muir and Johnson camped together in Tuolumne Meadows as they planned a strategy to gain national park status for the high country around Yosemite Valley.*

At an elevation of 8,700 feet, Tuolumne Meadows is a center of summer activity in Yosemite National Park. It is also the main access point for the High Sierra camps—Merced Lake, Vogelsang, Glen Aulin, May Lake, and Sunrise Camp—that offer dormitory-style accommodations. These hike-in (or ride in on saddle) camps offer canvas cabins with concrete floors and single and double beds. Blankets are provided but not linens. Breakfast and dinner at each camp are served in a central dining tent. The High Sierra camps are very popular, and reservations are made by lottery applications available by calling (559) 252-4848 or visiting www.yosemitepark.com. Applications are accepted November 1 to December 15, with the drawing held in mid-December.

who don't mind roughing it a little. The tent cabins are near the Tuolumne River's Dana Fork, which runs through the largest subalpine meadow in the Sierra Nevada. No cooking or picnicking is permitted in or near the tent cabins. The nearby restaurant serves regular breakfast items and five or six dinner entrees at reasonable prices. Beer and wine are also available. Other facilities are available at Tuolumne Meadows Store, about 2 miles away on Tioga Road.

Rooms: Doubles, triples, and quads. No rooms have private baths. There are no wheelchair-accessible cabins.

Rates: All tent cabins ($75). Rate quoted is for two adults. Each additional adult is $9.00; each additional child, $4.00.

Location: One mile south of Tioga Road, 9 miles west of the Tioga Pass entrance.

Season: Late spring to early fall. Season depends on the weather.

Food: A dining room in the registration/dining tent serves breakfast ($4.00–$8.00) and dinner ($8.00–$19.00). Reservations are required for dinner. Box lunches ($8.00) are available when ordered by 8:00 the previous evening. Fast food is available at Tuolumne Meadows Grill from 7:30 A.M. to 6:00 P.M. The grill is 2 miles away on Tioga Road.

Transportation: A hiker's bus runs between Yosemite Valley and Tuolumne Meadows Lodge (fee). A free shuttle operates between the lodge and the store.

Facilities: Minimal gifts and necessities are sold near the registration desk. Tuolumne Meadows Store has a post office, market, gas station, climbing school, and stable.

Activities: Hiking, fishing, horseback riding, and rock climbing.

WHITE WOLF LODGE

Yosemite National Park 95389 • (209) 372–8416 • www.yosemitepark.com

Wooden Cabins at White Wolf Lodge

WHITE WOLF LODGE COMPRISES A WOODEN registration/dining building, four wood cabins, and twenty-four canvas tent cabins. A central bathhouse with showers is located near the tent cabins. The lodge appeals primarily to people who want to get away from it all, especially the congestion of Yosemite Valley. White Wolf Lodge, at an altitude of 8,000 feet, is in an isolated part of the High Sierra just off Tioga Road. The lodge is approximately 30 miles east of Yosemite Valley.

The lodge has four wood cabins, each with two double beds, propane heat, electricity, and a full bath. The cabins have a small front porch and are built as duplexes. The tent cabins at White Wolf Lodge are identical to the cabins described for Tuolumne Meadows Lodge. Each tent has a wood stove, with wood provided, candles for light, and either four single beds

Tioga Road (California Highway 120), which accesses both White Wolf Lodge and Tuolumne Meadows Lodge, was originally built as a mining road in 1882–1883. It was modernized in 1961. The two-lane paved road climbs to an elevation of 9,945 feet as it winds 75 miles across the Sierra high country from Yosemite Valley to Lee Vining, California. The road closes in winter and, depending on the weather, generally reopens in May. Road and weather information is available from a National Park Service recording at (209) 372–0200.

Yosemite's mountain meadows were once used for sheep grazing. According to legend, a sheepherder in this area claimed he had seen a "white wolf"— thus, the name for this area. It's not certain that wolves ever inhabited this area of the Sierra Nevada, so the sheepherder may actually have spotted a coyote.

\\//

fireplace and serves breakfast and dinner in small inside and outside dining areas.

Rooms: Doubles, triples, and quads. Full bathrooms are only in the four wood cabins. A community bathhouse is available for guests in the tent cabins. No handicap-accessible rooms are available.

Rates: Tent cabins ($71). Rate quoted is for two adults. Each additional adult is $9.00 per night; each additional child, $4.00. Wood cabins with private bath ($105). Rate quoted is for one to four persons.

Location: Just north of Tioga Road, 30 miles east of Yosemite Valley.

Season: Late spring to early fall, depending on the weather.

Food: A small dining room serves regular breakfast items ($5.00–$8.50) and four to five dinner entrees ($7.00–$17.00). Reservations are advised for dinner.

Transportation: A hiker's bus runs between Yosemite Valley and Tuolumne Meadows. It stops at White Wolf Lodge.

Facilities: Small store and restaurant. Central bathhouse with showers.

Activities: Hiking.

or one double and two single beds. Linens with maid service are provided. The tents have no electricity or plumbing. This area is known to have bears, so food must be stored in metal "bear boxes" located behind the tent cabins.

White Wolf Lodge provides solitude in an attractive outdoor environment. This is a good place to meet other guests, because there are not many activities to divert their attention. The cozy restaurant has a stone

COLORADO

State Tourist Information
(800) 265–6723 | www.colorado.com

Mesa Verde National Park
P.O. Box 8 • Mesa Verde, CO 81330 • (970) 529–4465 • www.nps.gov/meve

Mesa Verde (Spanish for "green table") is our country's outstanding archaeological national park that preserves sites built by ancient Native Americans who are claimed as ancestors by twenty-four current Native American nations. The park's magnificent cliff dwellings, abandoned in the late 1200s, represent the last 75 to 100 years of the 700 years of the Ancestral Puebloans who lived here on the mesa tops and sheltered alcoves of the canyon walls. Mesa Verde offers a variety of visitor activities, but most people come here to tour one or more of the park's impressive ruins. Tour tickets can be purchased 15 miles from the entrance station at Far View Visitor Center (open from mid-April to mid-October), which should be your first stop. The visitor center has an information station and exhibits of prehistoric and historic Indian arts and crafts. Chapin Mesa Archeological Museum offers exhibits and a twenty-five-minute video presentation. The park's entrance road from U.S. Highway 160 is narrow with steep grades and sharp curves. Trailers must be dropped off 4 miles inside the entrance, near the campground. The 12-mile mountain road to Wetherill Mesa (open summer only) is not open to vehicles over 8,000 GVW and/or longer than 25 feet. Mesa Verde National Park is in the southwestern corner of Colorado, 36 miles west of Durango on US 160. **Park Entrance Fee:** $10.00 per vehicle or $5.00 per person, good for seven days.

Lodging in Mesa Verde National Park: Mesa Verde has only a single lodging facility, which provides a total of 150 rooms in seventeen older, motel-style buildings. Far View Lodge is 15 miles from the park entrance station, near Far View Visitor Center and Far View Terrace. None of the park ruins is within walking distance of the lodge.

FAR VIEW LODGE

P.O. Box 277 • Mancos, CO 81328 • (970) 529–4421 • www.visitmesaverde.com

A Four–Unit Building at Far View Lodge

FAR VIEW LODGE FEATURES AN ATTRACTIVE ADOBE building housing the registration desk, a small lobby, a dining room, a gift shop, and a cocktail lounge, with seventeen separate but nearby motel-type wooden buildings, each with from four to twenty rooms that generally offer exceptional views. The lodge is 15 miles inside the park entrance, near the Far View Visitor Center. Paved roads near the lodge lead to the park ruins.

Far View Lodge is situated at an altitude of 8,250 feet on a shoulder of the Mesa Verde. It provides an outstanding view of up to 100 miles and three states: Colorado, New Mexico, and Arizona (hence the name). The lodge offers 150 rooms in three categories: standard, deluxe, and kiva. Each room in all three categories has electric heat, a private bath with either a shower or a combination shower-tub, and a telephone, but no air-conditioning or television. Deluxe and kiva rooms have been refurbished and provide a coffee-maker, hair dryer, and an iron and ironing board. Most also have a small refrigerator. These rooms are slightly more expensive than standard rooms. Kiva rooms also feature a CD player/radio and authentic Native Amer-

ican and Southwestern artwork and handcrafted furnishings made by local artisans. Kiva rooms are available with either a king or two queen beds. Deluxe and standard rooms are furnished with one queen, two queens, or two double beds.

All of the seventeen lodge buildings are one level except for two units on each side of the registration building, which are two-story. Each room has a large window and a private balcony with two chairs. The buildings are situated on a hillside so that all the rooms offer a view of mesas and canyons. All rooms have at least a good view, but some are better than others. The best views are in rooms 131 through 140 and 111 through 120. All these rooms are on the second floor of a two-story building. Adequate parking is available directly outside each building.

Far View Lodge is ideally situated for visitors to Mesa Verde National Park. It is a short distance off the main road to Wetherill and Chapin Mesas, a quiet but handy location because most guests plan to visit both these areas. A quarter-mile paved trail from the lodge leads to the park's main visitor center, which has ex-

Mesa Verde National Park

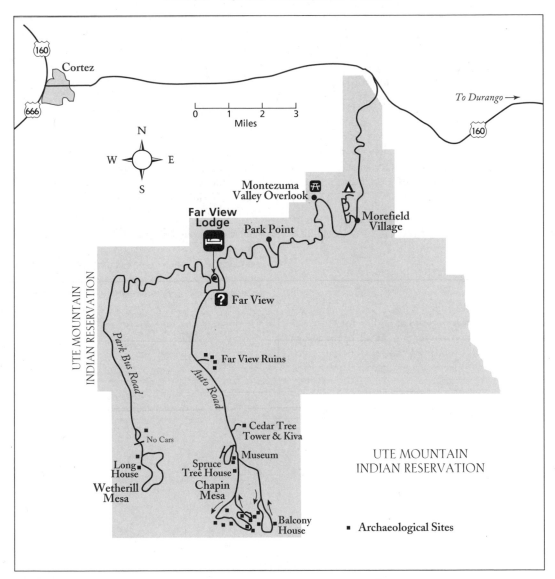

hibits of both prehistoric and historic tribes of the region, including native jewelry and pottery. Tickets for ranger-guided tours of Cliff Palace, Balcony House, Long House, and other guided tours can be purchased in the visitor center. Another quarter mile along the same trail brings visitors to the Far View Terrace, which offers a cafeteria and a large gift shop. Guided bus tours of the park begin at the lodge, where reservations can be made and tickets purchased. A small gift shop, a very nice restaurant (dinner only), and a lounge are located in the main registration building.

Rooms: Doubles, triples, and quads. Rates quoted are for two adults. All rooms have private baths with shower or a combination tub-shower.

Wheelchair Accessibility: Ten rooms, some in each category, have ramp access, wide doorways, grab bars, and a roll-in shower. Each of these rooms has one queen bed.

Reservations: Far View Lodge, P.O. Box 277, Mancos, CO 81328. Phone (800) 449–2288; fax (970) 533–7831. Deposit required for one night's lodging. Cancellation notice of twenty-four hours is required for refund of deposit.

Rates: Standard ($110); deluxe ($117); kiva ($127). Rates quoted are for two adults. Each additional person is $10 per night. Children twelve and under with adults stay free. A $10 fee per night is charged for a rollaway or a baby bed. Special packages (room plus tour and/or food) are available. AAA and AARP discounts are offered, based on availability.

Location: Fifteen miles inside the entrance to Mesa Verde National Park. The nearest major town is Cortez, Colorado, 10 miles west of the park entrance.

Season: Far View Lodge is open from mid-April to late October.

Food: The registration building houses one of the most attractive dining rooms in any national park lodge. The decorations, vistas, and menu are unique. Many of the tables are situated to take advantage of the outstanding views. Dinner only ($14–$30) is served, although rolls and coffee are sometimes available for breakfast. Alcoholic beverages including an extensive wine list are offered in the dining room and in a lounge on the second floor. A quarter-mile away, Far View Terrace offers a full breakfast from 7:00 to 11:00 A.M., and lunch and dinner ($6.00–$12.00) until 8:00 P.M. Beer and wine are available. Specialty coffees and homemade fudge are also offered in the cafeteria.

Transportation: Scheduled air service serves Cortez and Durango, where rental cars are available. The nearest train service is in Grand Junction, Colorado.

Facilities: Dining room, gift shop, cocktail lounge. Eleven-miles away Morefield Village has laundry facilities, a gift shop, and store with groceries, beer, wine, and camping supplies. A gift shop and cafeteria are at Far View Terrace and Spruce Tree Terrace.

Activities: Guided tours of Mesa Verde Puebloan ruins originate from Far View Lodge. Chapin Mesa Museum has exhibits on native tribes. Evening campground programs are presented at Morefield Campground. Trails of from 1.5 to nearly 8 miles are available for hikers. Special events, such as Hopi dances and pottery demonstrations, are scheduled from May through October.

Pets: Small pets are permitted.

FLORIDA

State Tourist Information
(888) 246–8728 | www.flausa.com

Everglades National Park

40001 State Road 9336 • Homestead, FL 33034 • (305) 242–7700 • www.nps.gov/ever

Everglades National Park comprises more than 1.5 million acres of subtropical wilderness, including extensive freshwater and saltwater areas, open prairies, and mangrove forests. A large portion of the park is covered by a giant river only a few inches deep and 50 miles wide. The park's main visitor center is near the main entrance, west of Florida City. A 38-mile paved road that leads from the visitor center to Flamingo provides access to many trails, both long and short, through the park. These trails offer the best chance to see wildlife close-up. Many of the trails are only one-fourth- to one-half-mile long. Longer trails near Flamingo lead deeper into the Everglades. The park also has many miles of canoe trails. Wildlife in the park, both varied and abundant, includes the endangered American crocodile, alligators, bobcats, deer, dolphins, and a variety of fish. More than 300 species of birds winter in Everglades National Park. The park is located across the southern tip of Florida, with main access from Florida Highway 9336. The entrance is 11 miles south of Florida City. **Park Entrance Fee:** $10.00 per vehicle or $5.00 per person, good for seven days.

Lodging in Everglades National Park: The park's lodging consists of a motel-style facility and cottages at Flamingo, near the terminus of the main park road. A restaurant and marina are nearby. No other accommodations or eating facilities are in the park. A variety of lodging and eating establishments are outside the park at Florida City and Homestead. Flamingo is approximately 83 miles southwest of Miami International Airport.

FLAMINGO LODGE, MARINA, AND OUTPOST RESORT

1 Flamingo Lodge Highway • Flamingo, FL 33034 • (941) 695–3101
www.flamingolodge.com

Everglades National Park

FLAMINGO LODGE IS PART OF A RESORT COMPLEX consisting of motel buildings, multiple cottage units, a full-service marina with a store, the National Park visitor center, and a main building with a restaurant, bar, cafe, and gift shop. The lodge provides a total of 98 rooms, most of which are in the motel buildings. The motel buildings and the cottages are separate from but only a short walk to the restaurant and marina. The resort is on Florida Bay at the southern tip of Everglades National Park.

Accommodations at the lodge consist of 74 rooms in five cement motel buildings and twenty-four rooms in twelve wood duplex cottages. Rooms in the four one-story and one two-story motel buildings each have a telephone with voice mail and data port, heat, air-conditioning, and television. The rooms, which were refurbished in 2004, are carpeted and have two double beds and a private bathroom with a combination shower-tub. The forty-two rooms in the one-story buildings each have a back sliding-glass door. The rooms in the two-story building have a large back window. One suite has one bedroom with two double beds, two baths, a fully-equipped kitchen, and a sitting/dining area with a sofa bed. Most of the motel rooms offer a view.

Twelve cottage buildings are constructed as duplex units to offer twenty-four rooms. Each has a living area with a kitchenette, a bath with a shower, and one bedroom with two double beds. Two cottage units that are wheelchair accessible have one double bed. The kitchenette is fully equipped for cooking, and the attached sitting area has a table with chairs and a sofa bed. All but the bathroom and kitchenette are carpeted. The cottages do not have televisions.

Flamingo Lodge is a good place to stay while you explore one of America's most unique national parks. The lodge enjoys a scenic location on Florida Bay and is close to a restaurant, cafe, and cocktail lounge, although these facilities are limited April through October. A National Park Service visitor center is also nearby. This is a pleasant place to walk, jog, or bike. Motorboats, kayaks, canoes, and bicycles are available for rent at the marina. Narrated boat tours are available at the marina. Be warned that mosquitoes can get nasty in the wet season, which begins in late spring and continues through summer. The best time to visit is in winter, when the weather is mild and mosquitoes are less numerous.

Rooms: Doubles, triples, and quads. The suite and cottages can hold up to six. All rooms have a private bathroom.

Wheelchair Accessibility: Two cottages are wheelchair accessible with wide doorways; one has a roll-in shower and the other has a tub with grab bars.

Reservations: Flamingo Lodge, 1 Flamingo Lodge Highway, Flamingo, FL 33034. Phone (800) 600–3813; fax (941) 695–3921. One night's deposit is required within two weeks of making a reservation. Cancellation requires at least forty-eight hours' notice for refund of deposit.

Rates: High season (December 15–March 31); swing season (April 1–April 30 and November 1–December 14); low season (May 1–October 31). Lodge room ($98/$85/$68); Cottage ($138/$105/$92); Lodge suite ($148/$116/$102). Rates quoted are for two adults in lodge units and for four adults in suites and cottages. Each additional adult is $10 per night. Children seventeen and under stay free with an adult. Rollaways are $10 per night.

Flamingo Lodge derives its name from several hundred flamingos that once wintered in Florida Bay following migration from their summer breeding grounds in the Bahamas. In the late 1800s a small fishing village here selected the name for its post office. Habitat destruction and the killing of the birds for their meat caused an end of the migration around the turn of the twentieth century. Although it is uncertain where the birds come from, flamingos are still occasionally sighted in the Florida Bay area.

Location: Directly on Florida Bay at the southern tip of Everglades National Park. Flamingo is 38 miles southwest of the park's main visitor center.

Season: Flamingo Lodge is open year-round. Services offered vary seasonally and are limited during the summer. Peak season is during winter.

Food: A full-service restaurant serves three meals a day during winter months but may be closed in spring, summer, and fall. A cafe in the same building is open seasonally. Food service April through October is limited. Limited groceries are sold at the marina year-round.

Transportation: Scheduled air, train, and bus service is available at Miami, about 85 miles northeast of Flamingo and 45 miles northeast of the park's main visitor center. *Note:* No public transportation serves the park.

Facilities: Restaurant, cocktail lounge, cafe, store, rentals of canoes, kayaks, boats, and bicycles, gift shop, full-service marina, guest laundry.

Activities: Fishing, bird-watching, hiking, biking, boating, charter fishing, sightseeing boat tours, guided hikes.

Pets: Pets that weigh forty pounds or less are allowed in both the lodge rooms and the cottages. Please note that pets cannot be left unattended in the rooms, are not allowed on the boat tours, and are not allowed on most of the trails in the park.

GEORGIA

Cumberland Island National Seashore

P.O. Box 806 • St. Marys, GA 31558-0806 • (912) 882–4336, ext. 224 • www.nps.gov/cuis

Cumberland Island National Seashore comprises more than 36,000 acres of freshwater lakes, magnificent beaches and dunes, and saltwater marshes on Georgia's southernmost coastal barrier island. The island is 18 miles long and, at its widest, 3 miles wide. The National Park Service limit of 300 visitors per day results in a visit to Cumberland Island National Seashore being one of life's great pleasures. The seashore is in southeast Georgia, approximately 30 miles north of Jacksonville, Florida, via Interstate 95 and Georgia Highway 40. Main access to the national seashore is only by a concessioner-operated boat (fee charged) from the small coastal town of St. Marys, Georgia. Access to the island's only public lodging facility is via an inn-operated boat from Fernandina Beach, Florida. No bridges provide vehicular access from the mainland to the island.

Lodging on Cumberland Island National Seashore: The only public accommodations on Cumberland Island National Seashore are at Greyfield Inn, a privately owned and operated, turn-of-the-twentieth-century mansion situated in the southern portion of the island. Access to the inn is via a private ferry that makes three trips daily from Dock 3 at the waterfront in Fernandina Beach, Florida. Fernandina Beach is on Amelia Island, situated at the extreme northeast corner of Florida. No vehicular access is available to the island or the inn.

GREYFIELD INN

8 North Second Street • P.O. Box 900 • Fernandina Beach, Florida 32035
(904) 261–6408 • www.greyfieldinn.com

Cumberland Island National Seashore

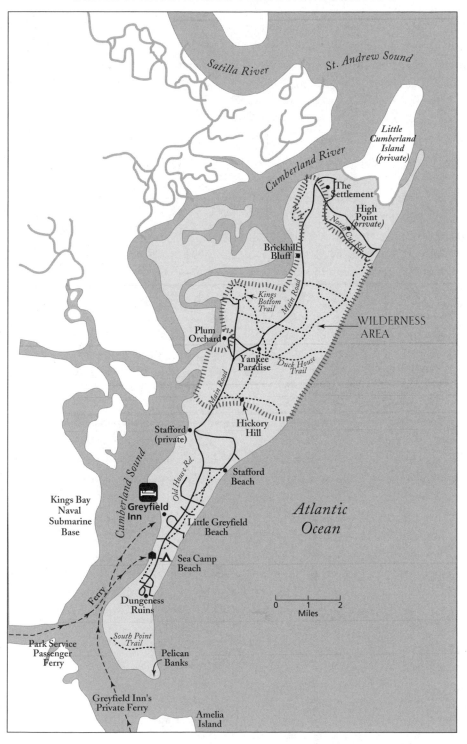

Greyfield Inn is a turn-of-the-twentieth-century, four-story wooden mansion, constructed in 1901 for Margaret Ricketson, daughter of business tycoon Thomas Carnegie (brother to steel magnate Andrew). Margaret Ricketson's daughter, Lucy Ferguson, and her family opened the home to the public in 1962 as an inn. The inn provides ten rooms in the main house and six rooms in two separate but nearby cottage buildings. Both the main house and the two cottages are on the western side of the island near the dock area, where employees meet the ferry from Fernandina Beach. Other nearby buildings include a maintenance barn, where bicycles are stored, a bathhouse, and several private homes. The inn and its surrounding buildings sit in a large, cleared area surrounded by forests on three sides and the Intercoastal Waterway on the western side. The Greyfield Inn is accessible only via the inn's private boat that leaves from Fernandina Beach, Florida, and docks adjacent to the inn. Guests of the inn who arrive by private boat may also utilize the dock. Greyfield Inn offers day trips for $75 per person that include boat transportation, a picnic lunch, and use of the inn's facilities.

Greyfield Inn is entered via stairs on the south side that lead to an impressive second-floor veranda with rocking chairs and a large porch swing. The second floor of the house contains a large living room with fireplace, library, self-serve bar, and one bedroom. The dining room, kitchen, breakfast room, offices, and a small gift shop are on the first floor. Bedrooms and bathrooms occupy all of the third and fourth floors. No elevator is available.

Ten of the sixteen rooms available at the Greyfield Inn are in the main house. Of these, only one bedroom, the Library Suite, is on the second floor of the house. Seven rooms are on the third floor, and two are on the fourth floor. The rooms differ in size, furniture, and bath facilities. The bedrooms have either a double, a queen, a king, or two twin beds, depending on the size

Pittsburgh residents Thomas and Lucy Carnegie first came to Cumberland Island in 1881. After purchasing 4,000 acres on the island, the couple set about building an impressive plantation home, which they named Dungeness, that would rival homes constructed by other millionaires on neighboring Jekyll Island. Thomas died in 1886, prior to completion of the home. Widow Lucy stayed on and expanded the family holdings until she had acquired nearly 90 percent of the island. The mansion that is now Greyfield Inn, given as a wedding gift to daughter Margaret and her husband Oliver Ricketson, is one of four homes that Lucy Carnegie had built on Cumberland Island for her children. The uninhabited Dungeness was destroyed by fire in 1959. The ruins at the south end of the island continue to attract tourists.

of the room. Price is determined by the size of the room and its accompanying bath facilities. All of the rooms have heating and air-conditioning, but not all rooms have a private bathroom. Six of the seven bedrooms on the third floor share two bathrooms. The seventh room, the two-room Porch Suite, accommodates three people and has a private bathroom. The Stafford and Dungeness Suites on the fourth floor and the Library Suite on the second floor each have a private bathroom. All bedrooms in the two one-story cottage units have private bathrooms. The larger cottage building has four bedrooms that share a common living area and a covered porch. The smaller cottage building has two bedrooms, with a common living area and a small, covered front porch. All the bedrooms are comfortable and nicely decorated with family heirlooms and antiques. Our choice would be the Stafford Suite on the fourth floor of the main house, if you don't mind climbing stairs. If stairs are a problem, choose the Library Suite on the second floor.

Greyfield Inn is a perfect place to relax and get away from it all. You don't need to cook, make the bed, or worry about meeting a deadline. There are no televisions to watch, cars to drive, or telephones to answer. In fact, the inn has just one telephone that it reserves for emergency use only. As a guest you will be treated to a full Southern breakfast with fresh-squeezed orange juice, a very nice picnic lunch, and a gourmet dinner at which guests are expected to dress appropriately (dinner jackets are available for those who left theirs behind). Your stay will include a half-day naturalist-guided tour to the north end of the island and the church where John Kennedy Jr. was married in 1996 to Carolyn Bessette. One of the country's most beautiful and uncrowded beaches is a short hike from the inn. Here you can jump in the waves, fish in the surf, or just stroll the pristine beach as far as you like. Perhaps you would like to hop on a bicycle and peddle down the dirt road to view the remains of Dungeness, Thomas Carnegie's burned mansion. A National Park Service visitor center is nearby. Stay alert and you may see some of the island wildlife, including the famous wild horses. Maybe you would prefer to curl up by the living room fireplace and read a book or sit in the porch swing on the veranda. Regardless, you should return home rested and ready for battle.

Rooms: All rooms except the Porch Suite accommodate only two people. The Porch Suite with a king and a daybed can accommodate three people. The six cottage rooms and four suites in the main house each have a private bathroom. A shower house (single shower) is located just behind the inn.

Wheelchair Accessibility: No rooms at Greyfield Inn are wheelchair accessible.

Reservations: Greyfield Inn, 8 North 2nd Street, P.O. Box 900, Fernandina Beach, Florida 32035-0900. Phone (866) 410–8051 or (904) 261–6408. A two-night minimum is required for all stays with the exception of holidays, which have a three-night minimum. A deposit equal to half the stay is required. A full refund requires thirty days' notice except for holidays, when no refunds are granted. Check-in is 1:00 P.M. and checkout is 11:00 A.M.

Rates: Rates range from $395 (marsh rooms and south porch) to $575 (Library and Porch Suites with private bath) per night. The majority of rooms are $495 per night. Taxes and gratuities add approximately 25 percent to the quoted room charge. Rates are for single or double occupancy and include three meals per day. Also included in the rates are unlimited snacks and nonalcoholic beverages, canapés at the evening cocktail hour, a three- to four-hour guided nature tour, the boat trip to and from Fernandina Beach, and use of bicycles, beach equipment, and fishing gear. Midweek rate reductions are given during the off-season. Check the Web site for special packages.

Location: The inn is located on Cumberland Island, the southernmost barrier island off the coast of Georgia. Access is from the boat dock in downtown Fernandina Beach, north of Jacksonville.

Season: Greyfield Inn is open all year.

Food: Three meals a day are included in the price of the room. Meals include a full breakfast, a picnic lunch, and a gourmet dinner of regional specialties. Canapés are served during the cocktail hour. Complimentary coffee, tea, soft drinks, and snacks are available throughout the day. A full bar and wine service are available to guests. With advance notice, special dietary needs can be met.

Transportation: Scheduled airlines and Amtrak serve Jacksonville, Florida, where rental vehicles are available. The inn offers free boat transportation from Dock 3 in downtown Fernandina Beach to the inn, three times a day, at 9:30 A.M., 12:15 P.M., and 5:30 P.M. The boat leaves Cumberland Island for Fernandina Beach at 8:00 A.M., 10:45 A.M., and 3:30 P.M. The boat ride takes about forty-five minutes.

Facilities: Dining room, bar, library, shower house, gift shop, bicycles, beach equipment, and fishing gear.

Activities: Guided nature tour, beach walking, hiking, swimming in the ocean, bird-watching, bicycling, and fishing. Massage therapy (fee) with advance reservation.

HAWAII

Hawaii Volcanoes National Park

P.O. Box 52 • Hawaii Volcanoes N.P., HI 96718 • (808) 985–6000 • www.nps.gov/havo

Hawaii Volcanoes National Park comprises 333,000 acres of active volcanism, including 13,677-foot Mauna Loa and famous Kilauea, near where most of the park's activity is centered. An 11-mile paved road that circles the Kilauea Caldera provides access to scenic stops and nature walks. Hawaii Volcanoes National Park is located in the southeastern corner of the island of Hawaii. The visitor center and museum are approximately 29 miles southwest of Hilo, on Hawaii Highway 11, which bisects the park. **Park Entrance Fee:** $10.00 per vehicle or $5.00 per person, good for seven days.

Lodging in Hawaii Volcanoes National Park: Volcano House, with forty-two rooms, is the only hotel facility in the park. It is located just off HI 11 on the north end of Crater Rim Drive, which circles Kilauea Crater. Ten camper cabins operated by the same firm are at Namakani Paio Campground, 3 miles west of the park entrance, on Highway 11. Additional lodging is available in nearby communities and in Hilo. Members of the military may find accommodations at Kilauea Military Camp, 1 mile west of Park Headquarters. Phone (800) 438–6707 from Oahu and (808) 967–7321 from out of state.

VOLCANO HOUSE

Crater Rim Drive • Hawaii Volcanoes National Park, HI 96718 • (808) 967–7321
www.volcanohousehotel.com

Hawaii Volcanoes National Park

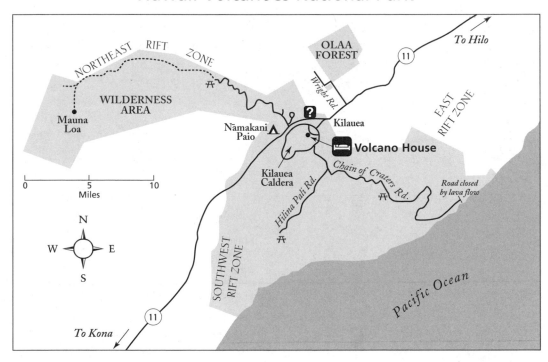

VOLCANO HOUSE IS A RUSTIC, TWO-STORY WOOD-
and-stone hotel constructed in 1941 and expanded in 1962. The hotel has since been completely
renovated. It is the oldest continuously operated hotel
in Hawaii. The dining room, gift shops, cocktail
lounge, snack bar, lobby, and most of the accommodations are all in a single building on the edge of Kilauea
Crater. A separate two-story building, which was originally the rangers' station, houses ten rooms. Ten less
expensive wood cabins without private baths are 3
miles from the hotel, in the Namakani Paio Campground. Volcano House is located just off HI 11, on
Crater Rim Drive, which circles Kilauea Caldera.

The hotel offers a total of forty-two rooms, all of
which have been refurbished with an island decor.
Each room is furnished with koa wood furniture, carpeting, heat, telephone, and a private bath, most with a
shower. Three hotel rooms have bathtubs. The rooms
are divided into five classifications, distinguished pri-

marily by size and view. Six crater-view deluxe rooms
in the newer wing of the hotel are the largest offered.
Five of these rooms have a king bed, and the other
room has two doubles. Fourteen crater-view rooms in
the original sections of the hotel have either a king, a
queen with two twin beds, or two double beds. The
twenty rooms in these first two classifications offer
outstanding views of Kilauea Crater. The other twelve
rooms in the original section of the hotel offer views of
the ohia and fern forests and have either a king or two
double beds.

Ten somewhat smaller rooms in a separate building called the Ohia Wing rent for substantially less
than rooms in the main hotel. This former ranger station has a small lobby with a fireplace and is surrounded by ohia trees. Eight of these rooms have
garden views while the remaining two are classified as
standard rooms. Bedding in the Ohia Wing varies
from two twins to a queen plus two twins.

The original Volcano House was constructed in 1866 of grass and ohia poles. The first wooden hotel was built here eleven years later. This structure is across the road from the hotel and now serves as the Volcano Art Center. The main building of the hotel burned in 1940 and was replaced by the current Volcano House, which opened in November 1941. (Embers from the fireplace were saved in order to keep the fire burning.)

\\/

The ten single-room wood cabins, which look like tiny A-frames, are located at Namakani Paio Campground, 3 miles from Volcano House. Each cabin has one double bed and one bunk bed, an electric light (no outlets), and an outdoor grill and picnic table. Linens, which include one pillow, sheets, a towel, and one blanket per bed, are provided when you check in at the Volcano House registration desk. You may wish to bring additional blankets as the nights can be quite cold at that altitude and the cabins do not have heat. Cabin guests must use community bathroom facilities, which are situated among the cluster of cabins.

Volcano House is a convenient and interesting place to stay when you will be spending several days touring the Big Island, including a day in this unique national park. The location on the edge of the huge caldera is spectacular. The large lobby includes a famous fireplace that has been burning continuously for 125 years. The Ka Ohelo restaurant serves a breakfast and lunch buffet, while the dinner menu includes entrees from Continental, American, and Pacific Rim cuisines. A snack bar is open from 9:00 A.M. to 5:00 P.M. for a quick food stop. The historic Uncle George's

Lounge is open from 4:30 to 9:00 P.M. for specialty drinks such as Pele's Fire. The hotel has two gift shops including one that specializes in Hawaiian arts and crafts created by local artisans. Many visitors like to experience this national park by hiking on over 150 miles of trails.

Rooms: Doubles, triples, and quads. All forty-two rooms in the hotel have a private bath. Cabins at Namakani Paio do not have private baths.

Wheelchair Accessibility: Two rooms are wheelchair accessible, one in the main hotel and one in the Ohia Wing. Both rooms have wide doorways, and the bathrooms have grab bars with a combination shower-tub.

Reservations: Volcano House, Crater Rim Drive, Hawaii Volcanoes National Park, HI 96718. Phone (808) 967–7321; fax (808) 967–8429; or online at www.volcanohousehotel.com. One night's deposit is required. Cancellation required seventy-two hours ahead of scheduled arrival.

Rates: Crater view deluxe ($225); crater view ($200); non-crater view ($170); Ohia garden view ($125); Ohia standard ($95). Namakani Paio cabins ($50). Rates quoted are for two adults. Each additional person is $15.00 per night in Volcano House and $8.00 in the cabins. Children twelve and under stay free with adults.

Location: Just off HI 11 on the north section of Crater Rim Drive. Volcano House is 30 miles from Hilo.

Season: Both Volcano House and Namakani Paio cabins are open year-round.

Food: Ka Ohelo Dining Room serves daily breakfast ($11.50) and lunch buffets ($14.00). Dinner ($15.00–$26.00) is ordered from a menu. A less expensive snack bar serves chili, salads, sandwiches, and beverages. Limited groceries are available in nearby Volcano Village.

Transportation: The nearest scheduled airline service is in Hilo, where rental cars are available. A city bus operates between Hilo and the park's visitor center, which is across the road from the hotel.

Facilities: Restaurant, snack bar, cocktail lounge, gift shop, craft gallery, National Park Service visitor center, art center, golf course (1 mile away).

Activities: Hiking, interpretive programs, golf.

K E N T U C K Y

State Tourist Information
(800) 225–8747 | Kentuckytourism.com

Mammoth Cave National Park

P.O. Box 7 • Mammoth Cave, KY 42259 • (270) 758–2180 • www.nps.gov/maca

Mammoth Cave National Park covers 52,830 acres, including the longest recorded cave system in the world. The park features rugged hillsides and beautiful rivers. A variety of guided cave tours are offered throughout the day. The park also has 70 miles of hiking trails, a gravel bicycle trail, and scenic boat rides. Mammoth Cave National Park is located in central Kentucky, approximately 90 miles south of Louisville via Interstate 65. **Park Entrance Fee:** No charge.

Lodging in Mammoth Cave National Park: A single lodging complex in the park, managed by Forever Resorts, offers a wide variety of accommodations that are all close to the visitor center and ticket sales area for cave tours. Buses near the visitor center provide transportation to the cave entrance.

Mammoth Cave National Park

MAMMOTH CAVE HOTEL

P.O. Box 27 • Mammoth Cave, KY 42259-0027 • (270) 758–2225
www.mammothcavehotel.com

*Woodland Cottage at
Mammoth Cave Hotel*

MAMMOTH CAVE HOTEL IS ACTUALLY MUCH more than a hotel. It is a lodging complex consisting of thirty cottages, four one-story buildings, and a two-story brick hotel. In all, the complex provides ninety-two lodging units at reasonable rates. Registration for all lodging is just inside the front entrance to the main hotel, which also houses a wonderful craft store, a gift shop, meeting rooms, and three dining facilities. The lodging complex sits in expansive grassy areas near the National Park Service visitor center, where tickets are sold for tours of this world-famous cave. A paved walkway connects the hotel with the NPS visitor center, where buses leave for scheduled cave tours. A large parking area is in front of the hotel. Mammoth Cave Hotel is located just off Kentucky Highway 70, in the southeastern section of Mammoth Cave National Park. The park is just off I–65 at either the Park City exit for northbound vehicles or the Cave City exit for those traveling south.

Four types of accommodations are available at Mammoth Cave Hotel. The least expensive lodging is the twenty Woodland Cottages, clustered on the north side of the visitor center. These rustic but pleasant wooden structures were constructed in the 1930s and are available mostly in two-bedroom units but also include four one-bedroom units, one three-bedroom unit, and one four-bedroom unit. Beds vary, but the four-bedroom unit can accommodate up to twenty individuals when rollaways are added. All the Woodland Cottages have hardwood floors, ceiling fans, and a small private bath with hot water, a sink, a shower, and a toilet. The two-bedroom units also have a sink in each bedroom. The three-bedroom and four-bedroom units each have two bathrooms. None of these units has heat, air-conditioning, phones, or televisions. Windows and doors are screened to allow ventilation, but consider the lack of air-conditioning if you will be staying when the weather is likely to be hot and humid. Two-bedroom units 204/205, 206/207, and 208/209 are at the back of the complex next to a wooded area and offer the most privacy.

Ten Hotel Cottages across the parking lot from

The current Mammoth Cave Hotel sits near the sites of two earlier hotels, one of which commenced operations in the early 1800s. This hotel, which was located just to the east of the current hotel, burned in 1916 and was replaced in the 1930s by a large wooden hotel situated across the parking lot from the current hotel building. The second hotel had thirty-eight rooms and a dining room that would seat 125 guests. It was near the current Hotel Cottages, hence their name. This hotel received several additions over the years and was torn down in 1977 after being removed from the National Register of Historic Places. A picture of the second hotel can be viewed in the Travertine Restaurant.

the main hotel sit in a semicircle in a large grassy area adjacent to a wooded ravine. The small wood cabins, constructed in the 1930s, sit along the top of a wooded hillside. Each cabin has electric heat, air-conditioning, a television, carpeting, a coffeemaker, and a small private bath with a shower but no tub. The Hotel Cottages were refurbished in 1999. Each cottage has one double bed. The cottages face a wooded ravine, and two lawn chairs sit outside the front entrance to each cottage. The Hotel Cottages are situated some distance from the parking lot and, if needed, assistance is available to move luggage between your vehicle and the cottages. Still, consider the walk when you are booking a room.

The Sunset Terrace Units consist of four single-story buildings constructed in the 1960s. These fairly large units were refurbished in 2001 and are designed for families. Each unit offers electric heat, air-conditioning, a telephone, a television, and a full bath with a combination shower-tub. The units are identical, with two double beds, and each could easily accommodate a roll-away. Windows across the back side of each face out on a wooded area. Cement patios between the buildings have lawn chairs and tables. A large grassy area in front of the four buildings is a good place for kids to play.

The main hotel, constructed in 1964, has thirty-eight Heritage Trail Rooms in a two-story brick building adjacent to the registration/restaurant building. This building does not have an elevator, so access to second-floor rooms requires climbing a flight of stairs. Heritage Trail Rooms each have a full bath with a combination shower-tub, heat, air-conditioning, telephone, coffeemaker, and television. Each room has a private balcony or patio with chairs and a small table. The rooms are small but nicely furnished and have either one king, one queen, or two double beds. Ten of the first-floor rooms on the ravine side of the building have a small refrigerator and have been totally refurbished with new furniture and carpet. These rooms rent for slightly more than other Heritage Trail Rooms. Rooms on both floors are entered through an interior corridor that runs the length of the building. This building is the most convenient to the lobby and dining facilities. We suggest you choose a back room overlooking a wooded ravine.

Mammoth Cave National Park offers more than the cave tours for which it is so famous. In fact, this is one of our favorite parks, both for camping and overnight stays in the lodging units. The area in which the lodging facilities are located is very pleasant, with lots of trees and open grassy spaces. Most park visitors have completed their cave tours by the late afternoon, so evenings are perfect for a quiet walk. Inexpensive one-hour scenic boat rides on the Green River are operated several times each day, and canoes are available for rent. Hiking trails and ranger-led walks are also available, and an amphitheater with evening programs is a short walk from any of the lodging facilities.

If you plan to take a ranger-led cave tour, be certain to check in at the visitor center behind the hotel as

Cave tours are the most popular activity at Mammoth Cave National Park. Approximately a dozen different types of tours are offered, depending on the season and demand. Some tours are easy and last about an hour. Others are strenuous and last from three to six hours. A schedule of each day's cave tours is posted in the visitor center. Cave temperatures are in the fifties, and the paths can be slick, with many steps, so it is important to dress properly. Most tours fill rapidly, so, if possible, make a reservation prior to arrival by mail or phone (800–967–2283) or online at reservations.nps.gov. Reservations may be made up to five months in advance of the tour date you desire. If you arrive at the park without a reservation, be sure to head for the visitor center, where reservations can be made and tickets purchased. You will also be able to obtain information about the various tours that are offered.

\|/

soon as possible after your arrival so you that can reserve a tour time if you have not already done so prior to your arrival.

Rooms: Singles, doubles, triples, and quads. Some units can accommodate more than four persons. All rooms and cabins have private baths.

Wheelchair Accessibility: Four rooms near the lobby of the main hotel are fully wheelchair accessible with two rooms having roll-in showers and two with a combination shower-tub. These rooms are large and each has two double beds. They enjoy all of the amenities of the other Heritage Trail Rooms, with the exception of a patio. Two fully wheelchair-accessible rooms are also available in Sunset Terrace Units.

Reservations: Mammoth Cave Hotel, P.O. Box 27, Mammoth Cave, KY 42259-0027. Phone (270) 758–2225; fax (270) 758–2301. One night's deposit required. Refund of deposit requires forty-eight-hour cancellation notice.

Rates: Woodland Cottages ($36 one person; $45 two persons in one-room cottages; $52 for up to four persons in two-room cottages). Hotel Cottages ($55 one person; $62 two persons). Sunset Terrace Units ($83 for up to three persons). Heritage Trail Rooms: Basic ($71 for two persons); Upgraded ($78 for two persons). Each extra adult is $7.00 per night. Rollaway beds are $8.00 per night, and cribs are $5.00 per night. The hotel offers packages and seasonal discounts. Call for information.

Location: The lodging complex is near the National Park Service visitor center in the eastern section of Mammoth Cave National Park. From I–65, take exit 53 at Cave City when traveling south and exit 48 at Park City when traveling north. The hotel is approximately 7 miles inside the park entrance.

Season: The hotel and motel units are open all year. The Hotel Cottages are open from early spring to late fall, and the Woodland Cottages are open from late spring to early fall. Call for information on exact opening and closing dates.

Food: The Travertine Restaurant serves breakfast, lunch, and dinner ($6.00–$16.00). A breakfast buffet may be offered depending on the number of people staying at the hotel. The adjacent Crystal Lake Coffee Shop serves breakfast and lunch ($3.50–$8.00) and is open until 4:30 P.M. A fast-food restaurant is open from 10:30 A.M. to 5:00 P.M. from late spring to early fall. Mammoth Cave Hotel is in a dry county, and no alcoholic beverages are served. Limited groceries and snacks are available at the gas station.

Transportation: The nearest major airports are in Louisville, Kentucky, and Nashville, Tennessee, where rental vehicles are available. Scheduled bus service is in nearby Cave City, Kentucky.

Facilities: Gas station, pet kennels (free to hotel guests), restaurant, coffee shop, fast-food restaurant (summer only), gift shop, craft shop, nature trails, laundry, post office, canoe rentals.

Activities: Hiking, cave tours, boat tours, fishing (no license required), canoeing, evening campfire programs (in season), ranger talks.

Pets: Pets are allowed only in the Woodland Cottages. A kennel is available without charge for hotel guests.

MICHIGAN

State Tourist Information
(800) 543–2937 | www.michigan.org

Isle Royale National Park

800 East Lakeshore Drive • Houghton, MI 49931 • (906) 482–0984 • www.nps.gov/isro

Isle Royale National Park comprises almost 572,000 acres, including the largest island in Lake Superior. Eighty percent of the park is under water. Isle Royale, approximately 45 miles long and 9 miles wide, is a roadless island of forests, lakes, and rugged shores. There are 166 miles of foot trails and numerous inland lakes on the island, where travel is via foot, boat, canoe, or kayak. Isle Royale is located in northwestern Lake Superior, 22 miles southeast of Grand Portage, Minnesota. No roads or bridges provide access to the island. **Park Entrance Fee:** A user fee of $4.00 per person per day.

Lodging in Isle Royale National Park: The only overnight accommodations inside the park are at Rock Harbor, on the south shore of the northeastern tip of the island. Rock Harbor Lodge features motel-type buildings and duplex housekeeping cabins, for a total of eighty rooms. Access to Rock Harbor is via seaplane or scheduled passenger boats from Houghton and Copper Harbor in Michigan's Upper Peninsula and from Grand Portage on Minnesota's north shore.

Isle Royale National Park

ROCK HARBOR LODGE

P.O. Box 605 • Houghton, MI 49931-0405 • (906) 337–4993 • www.rockharborlodge.com

ROCK HARBOR LODGE IS A COMPLEX OF FOUR motel-type lodge buildings, twenty housekeeping cabins, a dining room, a meeting hall, a gift shop, a store, and a marina, all located on or near the shore of Lake Superior. The four two-story lodge buildings sit side by side on each side of a meeting hall (actually, an old lodge building) used as a gathering place for guests. All these buildings are directly on the shoreline. The dining room is a short distance behind the lodge buildings. The housekeeping cottages are nearby and convenient to the dining room and store.

The four identical lodge buildings house a total of sixty rooms, each with a private bath with combination shower-tub. The buildings have a stone-and-wood exterior and cement block interior walls. Lodge rooms have steam heat but no television or telephone. Beds vary from one double, to two twins, to two doubles. Rooms on the first floor each have a balcony. Second-floor rooms have a better window view but no balcony. Lodge guests can choose between the American plan in which three meals a day are included in the room rate, or the European plan in which meals may be purchased individually. The lodge also offers a grill with light meals and casual dining.

Ten stone-and-wood duplexes offer twenty housekeeping cottages, which each have an electric stove, a refrigerator, dishes, and utensils. These units have a double bed and two bunk beds, with linens, blankets, and electric heat but no maid service. The cottages are located near Tobin Harbor, a short distance from the four lodge buildings. An asphalt walkway connects the cottages with the dining room and lodge buildings. Units 1–12 have a view of the harbor, while units 13–20 are deeper in the woods. Meals are not included in cottage units, but guests may choose to purchase meals in the lodge restaurant and charge expenses to their room.

Isle Royale appeals to visitors who want to try something different. There are no roads, no vehicles, and few people. You won't pass through this park on your way to some other destination, and neither will anyone else. The lodge allows you to experience nature while enjoying nice accommodations and good food. The dining room serves three meals daily; the grill is open from 7:00 A.M. to 7:30 P.M. or later depending on business. A marina store sells a variety of groceries, fishing equipment, day fishing licenses, and personal

Isle Royale has a rich history to share with present-day visitors. Native tribes had mined copper here thousands of years before the French claimed possession of Isle Royale in 1671. The island became a possession of the United States in 1783 and was identified as Chippewa Territory until the mid-1800s. Copper mining continued during the latter half of the 1800s, when large areas were burned and logged.

\|/

supplies. The nearby marina offers gasoline and diesel fuel and will accommodate boats of up to 65 feet. Motorboats, kayaks, and canoes are available for rent. (A canoe is included with the American plan rate.) Charter fishing boats and sightseeing boats are also available at Rock Harbor. The lodge operates a water taxi service daily, dropping off and picking up campers, canoers, and kayakers at numerous points on the island.

Rooms: Doubles, triples, and quads. Housekeeping cottages can accommodate up to six people. All rooms in the lodge buildings and housekeeping cottages have private baths.

Wheelchair Accessibility: Three lodge rooms and one housekeeping cottage are ADA compliant. These units have wide doorways, the bathrooms have grab bars, and the combination shower-tub has a seat. (*Note:* No trails are wheelchair accessible.)

Reservations: From May through September, Rock Harbor Lodge, Isle Royale National Park, P.O. Box 605, Houghton, MI 49931-0405. Phone (906) 337–4993. From October through April, Rock Harbor Lodge, P.O. Box 27, Mammoth Cave, KY 42259. Phone (270) 773–2191 or visit www.rock harborlodge.com. A deposit of the first night's lodging is required to guarantee a reservation. A refund of 90 percent of the deposit is made for cancellations at least five days prior to scheduled arrival.

Rates: All rates are quoted for two adults. Peak season (July 15 through August 15)/low season (rest of the season): Lodge rooms on American plan ($319/$276), additional adult ($106/$96), additional child under twelve ($51/$47); American plan guests also get use of a canoe. Lodge rooms on European plan ($212/$170), additional adult ($49/$40), additional child under twelve ($15/$11); Cottages ($206/$165), additional adult or child ($43/$34). Prices include taxes and a National Park Service utility pass-through fee.

Location: South shore on the northeastern tip of Isle Royale.

Season: The lodge is open from the second week in June through the first week in September. Housekeeping units are available from Memorial Day weekend through early September.

Food: A dining room serves breakfast ($12), lunch ($15), and dinner ($27) and is open to guests staying on the European plan and the public. Children eat for about 33 percent less. Meals are included for lodge guests on the American plan. A grill serves pizza, burgers, sandwiches, late-night snacks, beer, and wine.

Transportation: Passenger boats to Rock Harbor Lodge are available from Houghton and Copper Harbor, Michigan, and from Grand Portage, Minnesota. The Houghton trip takes six hours one-way and operates two days a week in each direction. Call (906) 482–0984. The trip from Copper Harbor takes three hours and frequency varies depending on the season. Daily service is offered during high season from July 15 to August 15. Call (906) 289–4437. The boat from Grand Portage stops at Windigo and takes approximately seven hours one-way. Frequency of service varies with the season although this boat generally operates three times per week from late May to early September. Call (888) 746–2305 for information. Check the current schedule for each of the boats on the Internet at www.rockharborlodge.com. Transportation information for Isle Royale is posted on the National Park Service Web site at www.nps.gov/isro/getthere.htm.

A seaplane leaves from Houghton. The boat from Grand Portage, Minnesota, circumnavigates the island and will drop off and pick up passengers at various points. The lodge's water taxi will drop off and pick up campers, canoers, and kayakers at numerous places on the island.

Facilities: Dining room, grill, store, gift shop, laundry facilities, marina with motorboat, kayak, and canoe rentals. Also available are slips, gasoline and diesel fuel, and pump-out services.

Activities: Hiking, fishing, kayaking, canoeing, charter fishing, sightseeing, and diving.

MINNESOTA

State Tourist Information
(800) 657–3700 | www.exploreminnesota.com

Voyageurs National Park

3131 Highway 53 South • International Falls, MN 56649-8904 • (218) 283–9821• www.nps.gov/voya

Voyageurs National Park preserves 218,000 acres of beautiful forested lake country that was once inhabited by French-Canadian fur traders, who used canoes to transport animal pelts and other trade goods through this area during the late eighteenth and early nineteenth centuries. A 1783 treaty established the U.S.–Canadian boundary along the waterway used by the voyageurs. The south side of the Kabetogama Peninsula is dotted with numerous islands, while the north shore is broken with many coves and small bays. One of the park's visitor centers is in its southwest corner, on Minnesota Country Road 123. Voyageurs National Park stretches 55 miles along the U.S.–Canadian border, east of International Falls in northern Minnesota. Summer travel within the park is confined to watercraft or floatplane. **Park Entrance Fee:** No charge.

Lodging in Voyageurs National Park: Overnight accommodations within Voyageurs National Park are available only at the Kettle Falls Hotel and Resort. Kettle Falls, in the northeast corner of the park, is reached via private boat or by private water taxi. Accommodations are available outside the park in Ash River, Crane Lake, Kabetogama Lake, and International Falls.

KETTLE FALLS HOTEL AND RESORT

10502 Gamma Road • Kabetogama, MN 56669 • (218) 240–1724
www.kettlefallshotel.com

Voyageurs National Park

KETTLE FALLS HOTEL AND RESORT IS A RELA-tively small lodging complex consisting of a historic two-story frame hotel plus three newer nearby wooden villas that each contain from two to four lodging units, for a total of twenty-two rooms. The hotel is part of a National Register of Historic Places District that also includes the historic dam, a dam tenders cabin, and other sites and features. The first floor of the main building has a lobby, a dining room where they serve homemade soups, desserts, and the best walleye dinners we have eaten, and a saloon with a pool table and walls covered by antiques. The twelve guest rooms are on the second floor. The hotel sits in a small clearing surrounded by woods, and the villas overlook the rocky shore of Rainy Lake. A quarter-mile gravel road leads from the dock to the hotel. Transportation from dockside to the lodging complex is available. Kettle Falls Hotel and Resort is in the northeast corner of Voyageurs National Park and is reached only by boat or seaplane.

Transportation to the Kettle Falls via a hotel-operated boat is available (fee charged) on a daily basis from the Frontier Resort dock at the end of Ash River Trail (CR 129). There is no charge for parking at the resort. Call the Kettle Falls Hotel and Resort for information. A free docking area is available for those who arrive via their own boats.

Several types of rooms are available. None of the rooms has a telephone or television, although a telephone is in the lobby and televisions are in the lobby and in the saloon. The least expensive rooms, all without private bath, are in the hotel, which was constructed from 1910 through 1913 to house construction workers on the nearby dam. The twelve hotel rooms are furnished with antiques and have either one double bed or two single beds. All these rooms are approximately the same size. The twelve hotel rooms and three centrally located modern community bathrooms with showers are on the second floor of the hotel. Coffee and rolls are served free to hotel guests in the dining room each morning.

Kettle Falls also offers ten villas in three separate buildings on the Rainy Lake side of the Kettle Falls Dam. These buildings, constructed in the early 1990s, are finished with a pine and oak decor. Each villa has a screened porch, air-conditioning, and a private ceramic-tiled bathroom with a shower. One single-story building with two villas is wheelchair accessible (as is the first floor of the hotel). The other two buildings each have two first-floor villas and two second-floor villas. Five of the villas have a fully equipped kitchen, including utensils. Beds in these units range from bunk beds to full-size beds. The villas can sleep up to ten persons when an adjoining door is used to convert two units to a suite. A three-night minimum stay is required when renting any of the villas. While the villas are newer and larger than rooms in the hotel, you will save some money and probably enjoy a more intimate lodging experience by choosing to stay in the hotel. Keep in mind that guests who stay in the hotel must use community bathrooms.

Staying at Kettle Falls Hotel and Resort is a restful and refreshing experience in a historic location where fur traders and trappers once portaged canoes and goods around the falls. If you want to get away

The Kettle Falls Hotel was built in 1910 by W. E. Rose, reputedly with money from famous madam Nellie Bly. According to legend, "fancy ladies" practiced their trade at the hotel. Other buildings predated the hotel, but little is known about them, and only traces of these structures remain. The hotel that once served as a relatively luxurious refuge for lumberjacks and construction workers for the Kettle Falls Dam now provides food and lodging to modern-day voyagers.

from it all, and do so in the great outdoors, this may be just the place. The hotel has a large screened veranda, where guests can sit and drink coffee or have a meal. Most activities center on the water, where fishing and canoeing are the most popular activities. Guide service is available when arrangements have been made ahead of time, and boats, kayaks, and canoes can be rented.

Rooms: Singles, doubles, triples, and quads. Villas with connecting doors can be converted to suites that accommodate up to ten people. All villas have private baths. Guests at the main hotel have access to community bathrooms.

Wheelchair Accessibility: Two villas, one with kitchen and one without, have wide doorways and a shower with grab bars and a seat. The toilet also has grab bars. The trail between the hotel and the villas is not paved, but a golf cart is available for transportation. The first floor of the hotel, with a dining room, saloon, and lobby, is wheelchair accessible.

Reservations: Kettle Falls Hotel and Resort, 10502 Gamma Road, Kabetogama, MN 56669. Phone (218) 240–1724 or (218) 240–1726 in the summer; (218) 875–2070 during the off-season. A deposit of one night's rental is required for stays of one or two nights. Stays of more than two nights require a deposit equal to 30 percent of the total reservation cost. Cancellation required in writing at least thirty days prior to scheduled arrival to receive a full refund.

Rates: Hotel rooms (single, $50; double, $70); villas per unit (night, $160; week, $750); villas with kitchenette per unit (night, $190; week $950); suite per unit (night, $290; week, $1,500). A three-night minimum stay is required in any of the villas.

Location: Kettle Falls Hotel and Resort is in the northeast corner of Voyageurs National Park.

Season: May through mid-October.

Food: A hotel dining room serves meals from 7:00 A.M. to 9:00 P.M. daily (dinner $12–$18). Morning coffee and rolls are free to guests staying in the hotel. An American plan is available. Check with the hotel for details. Limited groceries are available at the trading post.

Transportation: The nearest scheduled air service is 50 miles from Kettle Falls, in International Falls, Minnesota, where rental cars are available. With advance notice the hotel will arrange for pickup at the airport. Daily boat service, $40 per person, round-trip, is available to Kettle Falls from Ash River.

Facilities: Dining room, saloon, motorboat, canoe, and kayak rental, trading post with souvenirs, gifts, and groceries.

Activities: Hiking, bird-watching, fishing, canoeing, and kayaking.

Pets: Pets are allowed in the villas only at $10 per night, or $50 per week.

MISSOURI

State Tourist Information
(800) 877–1234 | www.missouritourism.org

Ozark National Scenic Riverways

P.O. Box 490 • Van Buren, MO 63965 • (573) 323–4236 • www.nps.gov/ozar

Ozark National Scenic Riverways covers 80,000 acres of forested hills and mountains along 134 miles of the beautiful Current and Jacks Fork Rivers. The rivers are especially popular for fishing and for float trips in canoes, rafts, kayaks, and inner tubes, all of which can be rented. The park includes large freshwater springs and caverns. Ozark National Scenic Riverways is located in south-eastern Missouri, 150 miles south of St. Louis. **Park Entrance Fee:** No charge.

Lodging in Ozark National Scenic Riverways: The riverways has a single lodging facility at Big Spring, 4 miles south of the town of Van Buren. Other accommodations are available outside park boundaries in Eminence, Mountain View, Salem, and Van Buren.

BIG SPRING LODGE AND CABINS

HCR 1, Box 169 • Van Buren, MO 63965 • (573) 323–4423

*Cabin at Big Spring
Lodge and Cabins*

Bıg Spring Lodge and Cabins consists of a main lodge plus fourteen freestanding cabins. The timber-and-stone lodge building houses the registra-

tion desk, an attractive dining room, and a small gift area on a bluff overlooking the confluence of Big Spring and the Current River. The cozy dining room

Ozark National Scenic Riverways

includes a small wing with windows that overlook the river. The rustic wood-and-stone and frame cabins on a hill above the main lodge building provide the only overnight accommodations at Big Spring. A paved road winds up the hill from the lodge to the cabins. Parking is available for each cabin, but access from parking to a cabin may involve climbing or descending numerous uneven stairs. The entire complex sits amid a thick forest of hardwood trees. Big Spring Lodge and Cabins is in southeastern Missouri, 4 miles south of the small town of Van Buren on Missouri Highway 103.

The fourteen cabins at Big Spring are available in four sizes that sleep two, four, six, or eight persons. The rate charged includes two, four, or six occupants depending upon the particular cabin that is rented. An additional fee is charged for guests that exceed the number included in the rate.

All the cabins have a private bath with shower but no tub. The cabins are roomy, with hardwood floors, stained wood walls, updated furniture, and a private screened porch. They also have fans but no air-conditioning, telephone, or television. They each have kitchen facilities that include a two-burner cooktop,

Big Spring Lodge and Cabins was built from 1934 to 1938, initially by the Civilian Conservation Corps (CCC) and, later, the Works Progress Administration (WPA), in what was then Big Spring State Park. The entrance station, lodge building, and initial cabins were constructed of local oak timbers and cut stone. Later cabins were of frame construction. Local employees started first on tourist cabin 403, classified as a "Type A" cabin. Next were cabin 402, similar in style to the first cabin, and the considerably larger Type B cabin 403, with two large stone chimneys and fireplaces. Nine additional Type E frame cabins with large stone chimneys were constructed, first by the CCC, and later by the WPA. Frame cabin 413, the only unit overlooking the Current River, was built as a residence for the fire-tower keeper. The main lodge building, on a hill overlooking the confluence of the Current River and Big Spring branch, and the entrance building were both completed in 1936. The Missouri State Parks Board signed over the state park to the National Park Service in 1969, and the big Spring Historic District was placed on the National Register of Historic Places in 1976.

small refrigerator, microwave, toaster, and coffeemaker. They do not include an oven or utensils. Four cabins do not have a kitchen sink, and two cabins (413 and 414) do not have a fireplace. Be certain to discuss the size, bedding, and amenities of the cabin you will be renting when making a reservation. Outside each cabin is a grill and picnic table. The cabins are widely spaced along both sides of a paved road to provide relative privacy.

Big Spring Lodge and Cabins, a small lodging complex in a quiet rural area of Missouri, is a good place to get away from the hustle and bustle. Plan to read a few books, play some cards, and do a little hiking. Many of the visitors to Ozark National Scenic Riverways come to float on one or both of the Class II rivers that include 134 miles of clear, spring-fed streams. Nineteen National Park Service–authorized concessionaires rent canoes at or near Alley Spring, Big Spring, Paullotite, Round Spring, Two Rivers, and Watercress. Inner tubes are available for rent at several locations. A list of concessionaires is available from the National Park Service. On a rainy day you can sit in front of the stone fireplace in the small lobby area of the lodge building. Another stone fireplace is in the dining room.

Rooms: From doubles to eight persons per unit. All cabins have a private bath with a shower but no tub.

Wheelchair Accessibility: No cabins are wheelchair-accessible.

Reservations: Big Spring Lodge and Cabins, HCR 1, Box 169, Van Buren, MO 63965. Phone (573) 323–4423. A one-night deposit is required and a two-night minimum stay is mandatory on weekends. Ten days' cancellation is necessary for a refund.

Rates: The three smallest cabins for two persons rent for $55 per night while one large cabin for six guests rents for $110 per night. Most of the remaining cabins that accommodate two to four persons rent for $70 per night. Each cabin rental includes a maximum number of occupants. Additional guests are $5.00 each per night.

Location: In southeast Missouri, 4 miles south of the town of Van Buren on MO 103.

Season: Mid-March through November.

Food: A cozy dining room serves breakfast, lunch, and dinner ($4.00–$14.00). Groceries are available in Van Buren.

Transportation: The nearest scheduled airline service is in St. Louis and Springfield, Missouri.

Facilities: Dining room.

Activities: Hiking, fishing, canoeing, tubing, swimming.

Pets: Pets require a $10 per night fee.

MONTANA

State Tourist Information
(800) 541–1447 | visitmt.com

Glacier National Park

P.O. Box 128 • West Glacier, MT 59936 • (406) 888–7800 • www.nps.gov/glac

Glacier National Park, covering more than one million acres, features towering mountains, glacial valleys, sparkling lakes, and more than thirty glaciers. Visitor centers are on the west side at Apgar, on the east side at St. Mary, and in the high country at Logan Pass. The high country is best seen by driving Going-to-the-Sun Road, a 50-mile paved road that bisects the park via the Continental Divide at 6,646-foot Logan Pass. If time permits, drive the Chief Mountain International Highway to Canada's Waterton Lakes National Park and the quaint town of Waterton Park. The 12-mile paved road to Many Glacier also offers beautiful views. The park is in northwestern Montana. The west entrance is 32 miles east of Kalispell, Montana. **Park Entrance Fee:** $20.00 per vehicle or $5.00 per person, good for seven days.

Lodging in Glacier National Park: Six lodging facilities are in four locations inside the borders of Glacier National Park. Two lodges sit just inside the park's west entrance from Kalispell in the village of Apgar. Apgar Village Lodge is privately owned and offers accommodations in historic cabins and two motel-type buildings. Nearby, Village Inn is directly on Lake McDonald and offers great views from a two-story motel building. A short distance east on Going-to-the-Sun Road, Lake McDonald Lodge has numerous cabins and two two-story motel buildings in addition to rooms in what was once a private hunting lodge. On the east side of the mountain pass on Going-to-the-Sun Road, Rising Sun Motor Inn has motel units and numerous duplex cabins in the park's scenic high country. This is a beautiful and uncrowded area of Glacier. The picturesque Many Glacier area in the park's interior has two lodging facilities, famous Many Glacier Hotel, one of the great old national park lodges, and nearby Swift Current Motor Inn, with inexpensive rustic cabins and motel units. We have also included two additional lodges that sit a short distance outside the park border but are closely associated with Glacier National Park. Glacier Park Lodge on the east side of the park in the small town of East Glacier is a classic lodge with an outstanding lobby. North of the border in Canada, Glacier's sister national park of Waterton Lakes is the home of the Prince of Wales Hotel, one of North America's most picturesque lodges.

Reservations: All the lodges (except for Apgar Village Lodge) are operated by Glacier Park, Inc., P.O. Box 2025, 774 Railroad Street, Columbia Falls, MT 59912. Phone (406) 892–2525. A deposit of one night's stay is required. The deposit is forfeited for cancellations within three days of scheduled arrival. Cancellations prior to three days of arrival generally incur a $10 administrative fee. No administrative fee is charged for cancellations within thirty days from the date a reservation is made unless it is within thirty days of scheduled arrival. Apgar Village Lodge reservation information is listed separately, in the lodge write-up that follows.

Glacier National Park

Transportation: Commercial airline service and rental vehicles are available in Kalispell on the park's west side and Great Falls on the east side. Amtrak stops on the park's east side directly across from Glacier Park Lodge and on the west side in the town of Belton/West Glacier where a shuttle operates between the train station and Apgar Village and Lake McDonald Lodge. A hiker's shuttle operates within the park during July and August between West Glacier and Many Glacier Hotel. This connects at Many Glacier Hotel and the St. Mary Visitor Center with an east-side shuttle that operates between Glacier Park Lodge and the Prince of Wales Hotel. A variety of scenic interpretive tours in historic red "Jammer" buses are offered from each of the hotels.

APGAR VILLAGE LODGE

P.O. Box 410 • West Glacier, MT 59936 • (406) 888–5484 • www.westglacier.com

Cabin at Apgar Village Lodge

APGAR VILLAGE LODGE IS A CLUSTER OF RUSTIC wooden buildings including two small motel units, twenty-eight cabins, a registration building, and a gift shop. The entire complex is in a wooded area between McDonald Creek and the road through Apgar Village, a small commercial district on the west side of the park. The small registration building, the gift shop, and one motel unit are on Apgar Road, and another motel unit and several cabins are on McDonald Creek. The majority of the cabins are in a wooded area between these two boundaries. None of the buildings sits directly on Lake McDonald, although the complex is no more than a half block from the shoreline of the lake. Apgar Village Lodge is also near a restaurant and a National Park Service visitor center. The lodge is located in Apgar Village, 2 miles inside the west entrance to Glacier National Park.

Apgar Village Lodge offers a wide variety of accommodations. All the rooms have electric heat and private baths with showers but no air-conditioning or telephone. All rooms, with the exception of the McDonald Creek motel unit, have a television. Picnic tables are scattered about the complex. The least expensive rooms are in the motel building on the creek. These units do not have balconies, but the back window offers a good view of the creek. These small rooms have either one double bed, one queen-size bed, or one double bed and a single. The beds pretty much fill the room. The front motel building, with eleven rooms, is directly beside the registration building on Apgar Road. Each of the eleven units has two rooms, one with a queen bed and the other with a queen, a double, or two twins. These units are larger than those in the other motel building, but they do not offer any views and are directly on Apgar Road, which receives considerable vehicle traffic. Parking is directly in front of the building.

Most of the lodging at Apgar Village Lodge is in rustic cabins. The majority of the cabins are wood-frame, although several of the older units are of log construction. The cabins are fairly old but well maintained, with

Milo Apgar, an early homesteader in the area where Apgar Village now stands, arrived soon after the Great Northern Railway reached Belton (now called West Glacier) in the early 1890s. Unable to make it as a farmer, Apgar started offering overnight accommodations for miners and visitors to this beautiful area. Some of Apgar's original cabins are still standing as part of Apgar Village Lodge. Cabin 21 was part of Apgar's first home.

\|/

interiors that have carpeting, knotty pine walls, and many with impressive beamed ceilings. The cabins do not have porches, although a picnic table is near each unit. Bigger cabins have both front and back doors. Parking is directly in front of or beside each of the cabins. All but two of the twenty-eight cabins have a kitchen with refrigerator, stove, oven, sink, toaster, coffeemaker, and utensils including pots, pans, silverware, and glasses. Cabin sizes vary from a small unit with one double bed and no kitchen to a large unit that can sleep ten and has a bath and a half. The majority of the cabins have a kitchen and either one or two queen beds. Cabins 6, 7, and 8 have kitchens and are situated directly beside McDonald Creek. Each of the three cabins can sleep four, and they offer the most desirable location in the complex, with cabin 6 being the most desirable of the three. Four other cabins with kitchens (cabins 10, 11, 12, and 22) face the creek from across a small parking area. Unfortunately parked cars directly in front of the cabins often block views of the creek. Each of these cabins sleeps four.

Apgar Village Lodge offers rustic buildings in a relatively quiet setting. The complex tends to be quiet and is suited for people who like this type of environment. Walks, viewing and wading in the lake, fishing and boating are several of the activities that are available here. The National Park Service visitor center is about a half block away. Although the lodge doesn't have its own eating facility, a restaurant flanks the building. Gift shops and a grocery are a short walk away.

Rooms: Singles, doubles, triples, and quads. A few large cabins can hold six or more persons. All rooms have private baths with showers but no tubs.

Wheelchair Accessibility: No rooms at Apgar Village Lodge are wheelchair accessible.

Reservations: Apgar Village Lodge, P.O. Box 410, West Glacier, MT 59936. Phone (406) 888–5484; fax (406) 888–5273. A deposit of one night's stay or 50 percent of the total cost, whichever is larger, is required. Reservations made prior to April 15 must be changed or canceled thirty days in advance of the arrival date for a deposit refund. Cancellation for reservations made on or after April 15 requires seventy-two-hour notice for a refund. A $10 administration fee is charged for any cancellation.

Rates: McDonald Creek motel units ($72); Front motel units ($95–$107); one-bed cabin units ($87–$106); cabins with two or three beds ($120–$137); three-room cabin ($145–$220). Rates for motel units and small cabins quoted are for two adults. Rates on medium and large cabins are for four adults. Rates are reduced from May 1 to mid-June and from mid-September to the end of the season.

Location: In the village of Apgar, Montana, 2 miles from the West Glacier entrance station.

Season: Early May through early October.

Food: A restaurant next to the Apgar Road motel offers breakfast, lunch, and dinner from mid-May through most of September. Very limited groceries are sold at a gift shop next to the restaurant. The lodge is 2½ miles from a full-service grocery store and several restaurants in the town of West Glacier.

Facilities: The village of Apgar has gift shops, a restaurant, an ice cream shop, boat rentals, a National Park Service visitor center, and an ATM.

Activities: Nightly ranger/naturalist talks at the Apgar campground, boating, swimming (very cool water), fishing, hiking. Sightseeing tours of the park leave from Apgar.

GLACIER PARK LODGE

East Glacier, MT 59434 • (406) 226–5600 • www.glacierparkinc.com • www.bigtreehotel.com

GLACIER PARK LODGE IS ONE OF THE CLASSIC PARK hotels built in the early 1900s by the transcontinental railroads to entice people to ride their trains. This majestic lodge was constructed in 1912 and 1913 by the Great Northern Railway, which was also responsible for sister lodges Many Glacier and Prince of Wales. Freight and passenger trains continue to operate a little more than a stone's throw from the impressive hotel entry, which is connected to the railway station by a wide corridor of beautiful flowers. The main lodge building was constructed in 1912 and the adjacent West Wing annex building a year later. The two buildings have a similar outside appearance and are connected by a covered walkway beginning at the south end of the giant lobby. The massive three-story lobby, with 40-inch-diameter fir and cedar pillars and surrounded by two interior balconies, consumes nearly all of the first floor of the main building. The West Wing is without a lobby and has more than twice as many guest rooms as the main building. A wide swath of flowers separates a large front lawn. A large parking area is near the hotel, but you will want to register and drop off luggage at the front door of whichever building you will be staying in. No elevators are in either building, but bell service is available. The lodge is just outside the southeast corner of Glacier National Park in East Glacier, Montana. It is at the inter-section of U.S. Highway 2 and Montana Highway 49.

Glacier Park Lodge has 162 guest rooms that fall into a number of classifications plus a two-bedroom chalet that is located next to the golf course. Rates are set by room size and not by view. Rooms on the west side of both buildings have a view of the Rocky Mountains, while rooms on the east view the front lawn and distant rolling hills. All the rooms have heat, telephone, and private bath with a shower or shower-tub combination. None of the rooms has air-conditioning or television. Beds in nearly all the rooms vary from two twins to two double beds. Some of the rooms have balconies.

All of the forty-eight rooms in the main building are on the second and third floors, which surround the massive lobby behind wide balconies. All overnight rooms in this building are carpeted. Thirty-four of these are the hotel's least expensive value rooms, which tend to be quite small, most with one double bed. This building also has ten larger main lodge rooms with two double beds that rent for about $20 per night more than the value rooms. Main lodge rooms have approximately 50 percent more space than value rooms. Six of the lodge's seven suites are in the main lodge building. Two on the second floor are "top of the line" suites, each with a king bed, a sofa bed, stuffed chairs, and a remodeled bathroom. Suite 264 also has a private balcony and a table with four

Glacier National Park is famous for the red "Jammer" motor coaches that transport people between the park hotels and sites. The coaches, built by the White Motor Company between 1933 and 1939, have black canvas tops that can be rolled back for greater visibility by occupants. The coaches derive their name from the drivers who at one time had to "jam" the gears to get up the mountain roads of Glacier. Structural problems caused the Jammer fleet to be temporarily retired from service in August 1999. Following a collaborative effort among the National Park Service, Ford Motor Company, and the concessionaire, Glacier Park, Inc., the popular red buses returned to service with propane-fueled engines and new chassis in the summer of 2002.

\|/

chairs. Four third-floor corner suites (354 and 368 on the mountain side; 355 and 369 on the lawn side) each provide one very large room with either three or four queen beds (one of these has a king plus two twins) below a sloped ceiling. These suites rent for about $40 more and have well over twice the space of a main lodge room. The windows are low, so you must squat to gain any view.

The 111 West Wing rooms in the adjoining building are a little bigger and rent for slightly more than the main lodge rooms. These rooms have hardwood floors, and the majority have two double beds. Most West Wing rooms on the first and second floors have balconies. Three family rooms on the third floor are quite large and can sleep up to six in three double beds. Five corner suites each have one king bed, over-stuffed chairs, a decorative fireplace, and a balcony. One first-floor two-room suite with decorative fireplace, two bathrooms, and a private balcony has a king bed in the bedroom and a sofa bed and chairs in the living room. This suite is on the northwest corner of the West

Wing and offers a mountain view. Situated on the ninth hole of the golf course is a one-story wooden house, called the golf chalet. It has a living room, a dining area, a full kitchen (utensils and dishes supplied), two bathrooms with a combination tub/shower, and two bedrooms, each with two queen-size beds. The chalet has an outside deck with a gas grill, flower beds, and a rustic fence. A telephone and satellite television with a VCR/DVD player are included. The chalet was renovated in 2005.

When choosing a room consider the ambience of walking out your doorway onto a wide balcony that overlooks the main lobby. This is part of the experience of staying in the main lodge building. On the other hand, no elevator is available, so you must climb at least one flight of stairs (twenty-four steps) each time you go to or leave your room. Rooms on the third floor require climbing two flights of stairs (another nineteen steps). The advantage of staying in the West Wing is that you can request a room on the first floor at lobby level. In other words, no climbing steps unless you leave the hotel; and the rooms in the West Wing are larger. In the main lodge we would choose a Main Lodge room on the mountain side, which offers considerably more space than a value room. Two good choices would be rooms 252 or 260, which are large and have balconies. Both rooms have a combination shower-tub. Main lodge rooms on the ends of the building tend to offer marginal views, so you should shy away from these. In the West Wing, rooms 526 on the garden level (one flight down from the first floor; don't ask us why these rooms have 500 numbers) and 226 on the second floor are very large rooms and have balconies on the mountain side of the building. Any of the even-numbered rooms on the first floor (104 through 124) of the West Wing offer a balcony and a mountain view.

Glacier Park Lodge is a handy place to spend a night or more on the east side of Glacier National Park. It's perfect if you travel on the train, because the station is only a short walk from the hotel entrance. It is also a good place to stay if you plan to take a day trip across the park's Going-to-the-Sun Road. The hotel has a nine-hole golf course and a nine-hole pitch and putt. It also has a swimming pool and a day spa. Horseback riding and hayrides are also available. The hotel restaurant serves a buffet breakfast and a la carte lunch and dinner, with the specialty of the house being steak and ribs. If food in the hotel restaurant isn't to your liking or you consider it too expensive, a short walk takes you to several restaurants and a grocery in the town of East Glacier.

Rooms: Singles, doubles, triples, and quads. Three family rooms hold up to six persons. All rooms have a private bath.

Wheelchair Accessibility: Two rooms on the first floor of the West Wing each have a wide entry door and wide entry to a large bathroom. The bathroom has a raised toilet and a combination shower-tub with grab bars. A bathroom at the south end of the lobby and the lodge restaurant are both wheelchair accessible.

Rates: Value room ($140); main lodge ($165); annex ($165); family room ($199); Big Sky room ($199); mini-suite ($199);

suite ($299); golf chalet ($499). Rates quoted are for two adults with the exception of the family room, which is quoted for four, and the golf chalet, which is a flat rate. Children eleven and under stay free. Each additional person is $10 per night. Rates are reduced from mid-May to mid-June.

Location: In East Glacier, Montana, at the intersection of US 2 and MT 49. The lodge is at the southeast corner of the park.

Season: Mid-May to mid-September.

Food: The dining rooms offer a buffet breakfast ($9.00), lunch ($7.00–$9.00), and dinner ($15.00–$22.00) until 10:00 P.M. Alcoholic beverages are served. The lounge serves snacks and sandwiches. A snack shop in the lobby sells cold sandwiches, ice cream, and drinks. Additional restaurants and a grocery are nearby in the town of East Glacier.

Facilities: Restaurant, cocktail lounge, gift shop, swimming pool, golf course, ATM. Restaurants, gas stations, and a grocery store are across the road in the town of East Glacier.

Activities: Hiking, horseback riding, swimming, golf, evening entertainment by employees.

LAKE MCDONALD LODGE

P.O. Box 210052 • Lake McDonald, MT 59921-0052 • (406) 888–5431
www.glacierparkinc.com • www.lakemcdonaldlodge.com

LAKE MCDONALD LODGE IS A COMPLEX CONSISTING of a historic lodge building, fourteen structures with cabin accommodations, two two-story motel units, a restaurant, several support buildings for employee housing, and a store. The main hotel is a rustic Swiss

chalet–style lodge with a spacious, open lobby surrounded on three sides by upper-floor balconies. The lobby, restaurant, gift shop, lounge, and a few guest rooms are on the main floor, while the second and third floors are devoted to guest rooms. The lodge sits on a small hill facing Lake

McDonald, which was used by visitors who arrived by boat until 1920, when the road was built. A huge fireplace with Indian designs in the masonry above the opening dominates the lobby with its large cedar columns in each corner. The mezzanines, supported by log beams and brackets, provide public areas with tables and chairs where guests can write letters, play cards, or read a book. A covered back patio has chairs and benches for relaxing while viewing Glacier National Park's largest lake.

Lake McDonald Lodge offers rooms of various sizes and beds in the main lodge, cabins, and motel-type buildings. All the rooms have heat, a telephone, and a private bath with a shower (no tub) but no television or air-conditioning. The main lodge has thirty-two rooms, nearly all of which are on the second and third floors. Two wheelchair-accessible rooms are on the first floor. The building has no elevator. Bell service is available. Rooms in the lodge are priced the same regardless of size, beds, and view. Beds range from one to two double beds. Rooms 202, 212, 302, and 312 are lakeside corner rooms with two windows. Rooms 201, 213, 301, and 313 are the largest in the lodge and have windows toward the lake. The latter two also have balconies.

Fourteen separate buildings, some log and some frame, house a total of thirty-eight cabins that begin beside the main lodge and stretch along Lake McDonald. Most of these buildings comprise two, three, or four cabin rooms, although one particularly large building has six units. All of the cabins have finished interiors and are on the lake, but views tend to be obscured by trees and bushes along the bank of the lake. Parking is directly behind or beside the cabins. Cabins are rented and priced in two classifications, small and large, even though units within each class vary in size and beds. Twenty small cabins, which rent for about $50 less per day than the large cabins, have beds ranging from two twin beds to two double beds. Eighteen large cabins have beds ranging from a double plus a twin to two double beds plus a twin. Most of the large cabins offer significantly more floor space than the small cabins.

Lake McDonald Lodge is on the site of the earlier and smaller Glacier Hotel, which was built in 1895 by homesteader George Snyder. The property was sold in 1906 to land speculator John Lewis, who built cabins and operated a fishing and tourist camp. In 1913 Snyder hired an architectural firm to design a hotel that would compete with the hotels and backcountry chalets being constructed by the Great Northern Railroad. Concrete and stone foundations were completed just prior to the winter of 1913, and in June 1914 the hotel opened for business. In 1930 the hotel was acquired by a subsidiary of the Great Northern Railroad, and in 1957 the name was changed from Lewis Glacier Hotel to Lake McDonald Lodge. The lodge was included in the National Register of Historic Places in 1978 and partially renovated in 1988.

Two two-story wooden motel buildings near the store and some distance from the main lodge building offer a total of thirty rooms. Parking is between the two buildings that are parallel to one another. Neither building has an elevator. The relatively small rooms do not have balconies or offer a view. The larger motel building has twenty relatively small paneled rooms that are entered from outside walkways. The smaller motel building, with ten rooms, has interior hallways that can be entered from either end of the building. We prefer rooms in the larger unit (rooms 1 through 20) to rooms in the smaller unit.

Our first choice at Lake McDonald is one of the larger lakeside rooms (noted above) in the main lodge building. These rooms are off the often noisy lobby area. Third-floor rooms are quieter than second floor rooms but require climbing an additional flight of stairs. Free-standing cabin 8, with a large covered porch facing the lake, is our favorite large cabin. Cabin 12-B, with a nice covered porch facing the lake, is our favorite small cabin. Our least favorite lodging is the motel units, but if this is where you end up, ask for room 20 with two windows, one of which faces the lake.

Lake McDonald Lodge is a great place to spend a vacation in Glacier National Park. It is a beautiful lodge with attractive rooms in both the main lodge and the cabins. The lake offers boating and fishing, although the water is a little cool for swimming. Boat tours of the lake leave from the back of the lodge. The complex also includes a general store with gifts, supplies, and limited groceries, as well as a gas station (regular unleaded only) and post office. A classic national park lodge restaurant with a large fireplace and a wall of windows offering a view of the lake serves three meals a day, including evening specialties of wild game and fish. A restaurant across the road offers pizza, pasta, and salads in a casual atmosphere. Take-out items are also available here.

Rooms: Singles, doubles, triples, and quads. All rooms have a private bath with shower but no tub, with the exception of the two first-floor rooms.

Wheelchair Accessibility: The only two first-floor lodge rooms each have a wheelchair-accessible bathroom with a wide doorway and grab bars by the toilet and the combination shower-tub. Two cabins each have ramp access and a wheelchair-accessible bathroom with grab bars and a shower with a seat. The restaurant and lounge are also accessible.

Rates: Main lodge ($147); small cabins ($96); large cabins ($147); motor inn ($110). Room rates are quoted for two adults. Each additional person is $10 per night. Children eleven and under stay free.

Location: Ten miles inside the west entrance to Glacier National Park. The lodge is on Lake McDonald, just off the Going-to-the-Sun Road.

Season: End of May through September.

Food: A relatively small but attractive restaurant in the main lodge serves a breakfast buffet ($9.00), lunch ($6.50–$10.00), and dinner ($14.00–$29.00) until 10:00 P.M. Alcoholic beverages are served here and in the adjacent lounge. No reservations are taken. The lounge offers food items from the restaurant's lunch menu all afternoon and evening. Across the road, a "Jammer-themed" pizzeria is open from 11:00 A.M. to 10:00 P.M. for pizza, pasta, salads, and hamburgers ($7.00–$18.00). Beer, wine, and ice cream are available.

Facilities: Restaurants, gift shop, post office, ATM, cocktail lounge, boat rental, riding stable.

Activities: Boating, hiking, fishing (no license required), boat tours of Lake McDonald, sightseeing tours, horseback riding, evening ranger programs.

MANY GLACIER HOTEL

P.O. Box 147 • East Glacier, MT 59434 • (406) 732–4411
www.glacierparkinc.com • www.manyglacierhotel.com

MANY GLACIER HOTEL IS A CLASSIC NATIONAL park lodge. The five-story Swiss-themed wooden structure with shake roof and numerous gables and balconies is situated on the edge of Swiftcurrent Lake. Although it appears as a single structure, the hotel is actually two separate buildings connected by an enclosed walkway. The main floor is highlighted by an outstanding three-story lobby with log beams, interior balconies, and a huge conical metal fireplace suspended from the roof. The lobby also has a traditional stone fireplace. Many guest rooms in both the main hotel and the annex have an outstanding view of Swiftcurrent Lake and the surrounding mountains. Parking is on a steep hill above the hotel, so register and drop off luggage before parking your vehicle. A small elevator is near the lounge, and bell service is available to assist with luggage. Many Glacier Hotel is in the northeastern section of Glacier National Park, 11 miles west of Babb on Many Glacier Road.

The hotel offers a total of 211 rooms of varying size, beds, and view. All of the rooms have heat, telephone, and a private bath but no television. All but eleven rooms fall into three categories: lakeside, standard, and value. The remaining rooms are two suites and eight family rooms. The largest category, lakeside rooms, rent at a premium price and include all but a few of the rooms facing Swiftcurrent Lake. Most of these rooms have balconies, but room size and beds vary, with the largest lakeside rooms being in the annex. Standard rooms are similar in size and beds to lakeside rooms but do not offer a lake view and fewer standard rooms have balconies. Value rooms are the least expensive rooms in the lodge and are generally quite small with two twins or one double bed. Rooms in this category may also offer an obscured view or be located on a main hallway in a heavy-traffic area. All rooms in a category rent for the same price regardless of size, view, or whether a balcony is available. Small rooms above the lobby in the main lodge with excellent lakeside views and balconies are 224, 226, 228, and 230, and corresponding rooms on the third floor. Larger lakeside rooms without balconies in the main lodge

Construction on Many Glacier Hotel commenced in 1914, and the first guests were welcomed on July 4 of the following year. The annex next door was completed two years later. The Great Northern Railroad, which built the hotel, erected a sawmill and drying kiln near the site to process timber used in the construction. Trees for the lobby columns were harvested from the upper end of nearby Lake Josephine. Even though most of the timber and rocks came from the local area, the high cost of fixtures, glass, and boilers resulted in construction costs of $500,000. A swimming pool that sat beside the dining room and a stone fountain near the current St. Moritz Room have both been removed. The hotel once had its own hydroelectric plant at Swift Current Falls, but the unit was put permanently out of operation by a 1964 flood.

include rooms 222, 322, and 332, although these are not as large as bigger rooms in the annex. Larger lakeside rooms in the annex with balconies include rooms 102, 104, 112, 114, and corresponding rooms on the second and third floors. Larger mountainside rooms in the annex include rooms 105, 205, and 305.

Six family rooms that are located on the fourth floor of the annex each consist of two bedrooms on each side of a bathroom. One bedroom has a double plus a twin bed, and the other bedroom has a double bed. Four of these rooms provide a lake view (rooms 400, 404, 408, and 414), and two do not, even though all six rooms rent for the same rate. Keep in mind that these are fourth-floor rooms and no elevator is available. In addition, a sloping roof results in reduced headroom. None of the family rooms has a balcony. Two family rooms on the first floor each have two small bedrooms, one with a double bed plus a twin bed and the other with one twin bed. These units have one bathroom with a shower only and sit on the side of the building opposite Swiftcurrent Lake. Two suites on the second floor each consist of two bedrooms and two bathrooms. One bedroom has a king bed and the other has a double bed. The suites are corner rooms, with balconies that provide excellent lake views. Each suite has a nonworking stone fireplace and rents for approximately 50 percent more than a regular lakeside room.

Many Glacier Lodge is a wonderful historic hotel. An inviting restaurant at one end of the building has a large stone fireplace and big windows that allow diners to look out over Swiftcurrent Lake. The lounge is located just outside the restaurant. Soup, sandwiches, and snacks are available in the lounge. Evening entertainment (fee charged) is offered Monday through Saturday. Take a few steps outside the hotel and you can canoe, fish, or enjoy a boat tour accompanied by a park naturalist. Or perhaps you would rather relax in one of the chairs or benches on the large porch that wraps around two sides of the first floor. A stable next to the parking area offers horseback riding. Evening natural history programs are presented in the hotel basement by National Park Service rangers. All in all, this is a great place to spend several days or a week.

Rooms: Singles, doubles, triples, and quads. Eight family rooms hold four to five persons. All the hotel rooms have private baths.

Wheelchair Accessibility: The lodge offers three first-floor wheelchair-accessible rooms, two in the lakeside category and one in the value category. Each room has a bathroom shower with a seat and grab bars for both the shower and toilet.

Rates: Value rooms ($114); standard ($140); lakeside ($147); family rooms ($190); suites ($225). Room rates quoted are for two adults with the exception of the family room, which is quoted for four adults. Each additional person is $10 per night. Children eleven and under stay free.

Location: In the northeast section of the park, at the end of Many Glacier Road, 11 miles east of Babb, Montana.

Season: Mid-June to mid-September.

Food: A restaurant offers a breakfast buffet ($9.00), lunch ($8.00–$10.00), and dinner ($14.00–$29.00). Alcoholic beverages are available. Soup, sandwiches, and snacks are available in the lounge. A small store sells hot dogs, ice cream, yogurt, snacks, drinks, beer, and wine from 6:30 A.M. to 10:30 P.M. Limited groceries are available in a general store 1 mile up the road at Swiftcurrent Motor Inn. The motor inn also has a less expensive restaurant.

Facilities: Restaurant, cocktail lounge, snack bar, gift shop, tour desk in lobby, horse stable, boat rentals, ATM.

Activities: Hiking, fishing, boating, horseback riding, evening naturalist programs, entertainment, boat tours of Swiftcurrent Lake and Lake Josephine.

PRINCE OF WALES HOTEL

Box 33, Waterton, Alberta, Canada T0K 2M0 • (403) 859–2231
www.princeofwaleswaterton.com • www.glacierparkinc.com

The Prince of Wales Hotel, named after Prince Edward, who later became King Edward VIII, is a single seven-story alpine chalet that may be the most picturesque of all the national park lodging facilities. The only Canadian park lodge constructed by the Great Northern Railroad, the hotel sits high on a bluff overlooking Waterton Lake and the quaint town of Waterton. Built in 1927, the hotel features two-story windows across one end of a six-story lobby. Interior balconies on each floor and huge timbers near the roof highlight the attractive lobby filled with chairs, tables, and sofas. The hotel is about 48 miles northwest of the town of St. Mary, Montana, via U.S. Highway 89 and the Chief Mountain International Highway, which turns off 4 miles north of Babb, Montana. You must pass through a Canadian port of entry and pay a Canadian park fee to enter Waterton Lakes National Park, where the hotel is located.

The hotel has eighty-six rooms on the five floors above the main floor lobby. Although an elevator stops at floors 1 through 4, it is ancient (the oldest in Alberta) and can only be operated by a hotel employee, who must be summoned. This means you will likely be climbing steps during your stay. Consider this when reserving a room because you may want to request a second- or third-floor room and save some steps during your stay. Also keep in mind that the elevator does not go to the fifth and sixth floors, where rooms are offered at a lower rate. Sixteen steps are between the fourth and fifth floors, and another sixteen steps are required to climb from the fifth to the sixth floor. Bell service is available to assist with luggage.

Each of the rooms in the hotel has electric heat, a telephone, and a private bathroom but no television or air-conditioning. Most rooms in the Prince of Wales fall into two classifications: lakeside or mountainside. Lakeside rooms offer a view of Waterton Lake, while mountainside rooms, which rent for about $50 less per night, do not. Rooms in both classifications are of nice size, with beds ranging from two twins to two doubles. Bath-

While standing in the lobby, look up at the ceiling and notice a dark panel. This trap door hides a pulley that was once used to lower a rope to an employee who was hoisted to change burned-out lightbulbs in the massive chandelier that hangs between the second and fourth floors. This was a prized job by bellmen. Today, a crank is used to lower the chandelier.

rooms have a combination shower-tub. Along with three suites, lakeside and mountainside rooms comprise all of the accommodations on the second, third, and fourth floors. All third-floor rooms, but only a few second- and fourth-floor rooms, have balconies. The wind is generally strong enough, especially on the southern side of the hotel, that you won't want to spend much time on a balcony, so having one of these shouldn't be a major consideration in choosing a room. You may prefer a corner room with windows on two sides. Lakeside corner rooms include 201 and 225 on the second floor, and the corresponding numbered rooms on the third and fourth floors, plus 409 and 417. Mountainside corner rooms include 200, 208, 214, and 222 on the second floor, and corresponding numbered rooms on the third and fourth floors.

The hotel offers twenty fifth-floor value rooms that are smaller, with variable views. About half face Waterton Lake. These rooms require climbing an additional flight of stairs, and the hotel's sloping roofline reduces headspace in some of these rooms, which rent for about $30 to $70 less than the mountainside and lakeside rooms, respectively. Value rooms have one double or two single beds. Bathrooms have a shower but no tub. Again, keep in mind that the lobby elevator does not provide access to the fifth floor. On the positive side, rooms on the fifth floor tend to be quieter, with the exception of 505, which is located near the elevator motor and can be noisy. Lakeside value rooms 509 and 517 each have one double bed and are slightly larger than most other value rooms.

The sixth floor (yet another flight of sixteen stairs to climb) has four rooms: two value rooms plus two two-room units. The two-room units have a double bed in each room and one bathroom with a shower but no tub. These two-room units have balconies and rent at the lakeside rate or the mountainside rate, depending on the side of the hotel on which the room is located.

The hotel offers one fourth-floor lakeside mini-suite with a king-size bed and two wing-back chairs. This is the most requested room in the hotel. Two upscale suites on the third floor, the Prince and Princess,

Great Northern Railroad president Louis Hill originally envisioned the Prince of Wales as a long three-story building similar to the hotel his firm had built a decade earlier at Many Glacier. Hill changed his mind several times and finally settled on the current seven-story rectangular building that was designed to resemble a Swiss chalet. Construction of the hotel was complicated by high winds and the need to bring all of the materials and supplies the last 25 miles by mules. The winds blew the building off center twice during construction and almost caused the project to be abandoned. The structure is anchored with large cables that run from the loft into the ground. The hotel opened during the summer of 1927, one year after construction commenced and fourteen years after the site was selected. It was closed for three years during the Depression and five years during World War II.

were completely renovated in 1999. Each suite has a living room, with a wet bar and refrigerator, coffeemaker, and a separate bedroom with a king-size bed. The bathroom in each suite has a large bathtub and a separate shower. These suites are expensive and exquisite, with custom-designed furniture.

The Prince of Wales Hotel offers a touch of English tradition. Tea is served each afternoon in the lobby, where you can relax and look out over Waterton Lake. The hotel's main floor has a restaurant and a lounge, both of which provide great views of the lake and surrounding mountains. The lounge serves the restaurant's full lunch and dinner menus and has the hotel's only fireplace. A large gift shop is also on the main floor. The town of Waterton, with additional restaurants, clothing stores, and gift shops, is a short distance down the hill. Keep in mind that lodging rates are quoted in Canadian dollars. If you pay with a credit card, you won't have to worry about obtaining Canadian currency or getting an unfavorable exchange rate.

Rooms: Singles, doubles, triples, and quads. All rooms have private baths.

Wheelchair Accessibility: The hotel has no wheelchair-accessible rooms. The dining room, lounge, and a first-floor bathroom are wheelchair accessible.

Rates: Value room with mountain view ($259); value room with lake view ($269); mountainside room ($286); lakeside room ($339); sixth-floor two room (mountainside–$286, lakeside–$339); mini-suite ($339); suite ($799). Rates quoted in Canadian dollars are for two adults. Each additional person is $10 per night. Children eleven and under stay free with an adult. Rates are 20 to 30 percent less during the weeks prior to mid-June.

Location: In Canada's Waterton Lakes National Park, about 48 miles northwest of St. Mary, Montana.

Season: June to mid-September.

Food: An attractive restaurant with a wall of windows offering a view of Waterton Lake serves three meals a day including a continental breakfast ($7.00) and a hot breakfast buffet ($15.00), lunch ($11.00–$16.00), and dinner ($20.00–$36.00). The lounge serves the full lunch and dinner menus from the restaurant. A traditional British tea with sandwiches, pastries, scones, cookies, and other sweets is served in the lobby each afternoon from 2:00 to 4:00 ($30). Several restaurants and a small grocery store are in the town of Waterton.

Facilities: Gift shop, restaurant, cocktail lounge. Additional facilities are in the town of Waterton, a short distance away.

Activities: Hiking, golf, tennis, horseback riding, boat rentals, fishing, lake cruises, and national park programs are offered in Waterton.

RISING SUN MOTOR INN

P.O. Box 147 • East Glacier, MT 59434 • (406) 732–5523
www.glacierparkinc.com • www.risingsunmotorinn.com

Cabin at Rising Sun Motor Inn

RISING SUN MOTOR INN, INITIALLY KNOWN AS East Glacier Auto Camp, is a complex of wooden buildings, including a main registration/restaurant building without guest rooms, a separate general store with attached lodging rooms, nineteen duplex cabin buildings, and two motel-type structures. Rising Sun offers seventy-two rooms, approximately half of which are wooden cabins dating from 1941. Registration for all guest rooms is in the main building, which houses a restaurant and a small gift shop. The general store is across the parking lot, and the cabins and motel buildings are up a small hill but within easy walking distance of both buildings. Rising Sun is in a scenic area overlooking St. Mary Lake and surrounded by tall mountains. Rising Sun Motor Inn is located on the east side of the park on the Going-to-the-Sun Road, 6 miles from the park entrance at St. Mary.

Rising Sun Motor Inn offers three types of rooms, all of which rent for approximately the same price. Rooms in all three classifications have heat and a private bathroom with a shower but no tub. No television, telephone, or air-conditioning is in any of the rooms. The majority of the rooms at Rising Sun are in thirty-five rustic cabins built as duplex units. The cabins are clustered on a hill behind the store with a few offering a view of the mountains. Parking is directly in front of or beside each of the cabins. Interiors are finished with varnished plywood. The small bathroom has a toilet and shower; the sink is in the bedroom. The cabins have small windows, no porch, and beds that range from two twins to two doubles, although most of the units have a double plus a twin. Cabins 2 through 7 are larger and rent for the same price as the smaller cabins.

We would choose cabins 4, 5, or 6, which are larger, offer a good mountain view, and receive morning sun.

The wooden structure that includes the general store also houses nine rooms that are accessed from an interior hallway entered from either the front or end of the building. A large covered porch with chairs and tables runs across the front of the building, which faces south toward the mountains. Plentiful parking is directly in front of the building in a large lot that separates the store from the restaurant. The rooms vary in size and beds, which range from one double to two doubles. Room 31, with two double beds, is very large. Room 37 on the corner of the building has windows on two sides and is the most desirable of the store motel rooms. Rooms 33 through 37 are on the front and offer the best views, although the porch roof partially obstructs mountain views for all but room 37.

Two identical wooden motel-type buildings are up the hill from the restaurant. Each building houses fourteen rooms, seven on each side. A covered walkway runs across each side of the two buildings. Rooms on the south side (rooms 8 through 14 in one building and rooms 22 through 28 in the other building) offer good views of the mountains and a fair view of St. Mary Lake. Parking is directly in front of each room.

Rising Sun Motor Inn is in a very scenic location, where the blue waters of St. Mary Lake glimmer from down a hill. The lake is mostly out of direct view of the lodging units, and the surrounding mountains are only partially visible from some of the units. Still, this is a quiet place to relax in a natural setting. Walk a short distance from your room and gaze at some of the prettiest landscape in the United States. Rising Sun certainly isn't a busy or congested area, since most people on the Going-to-the-Sun Road drive right by. The restaurant, with a vaulted ceiling and large windows facing the lake and mountains, offers meals at reasonable prices. The general store has limited groceries, camping supplies, fishing supplies, and souvenirs. You can hike, fish, or just experience nature without bumping into hundreds of

The 52-mile Going-to-the-Sun Road, one of the country's most scenic drives, is the product of more than a decade of work that commenced in 1921. Although several routes were considered, 6,664-foot Logan Pass was chosen, partially because greater exposure to the sun would help clear the road of snow. It takes up to two months each spring to clear the road of snow, which can reach a depth of 80 feet in places. The road provides spectacular views of mountains, lakes, waterfalls, and glacial valleys in the heart of Glacier National Park. The road is winding and quite narrow. Vehicles longer than 21 feet or wider than 8 feet are prohibited from travel between Avalanche Campground and the Sun Point parking area.

other vacationers. You can also take a boat tour of St. Mary Lake.

Rooms: Singles, doubles, triples, and quads. All rooms have a private bath with a shower but no tub.

Wheelchair Accessibility: Four wheelchair-accessible rooms are in one of the two motel buildings. These rooms include ramp access and bathrooms with wide doorways and a grab bar for the toilet. The shower has a seat and an adjustable showerhead but does not have roll-in access. Two wheelchair-accessible rooms have two double beds, while the other two rooms have two twin beds. The restaurant, gift shop, and general store are also accessible.

Rates: Cottages ($96); store motel rooms ($94); motel-type units ($110). Rates quoted are for two adults. Children eleven years and under stay free. Each additional person is $10 per night.

Location: East side of Glacier National Park, 6 miles west of the park entrance station at St. Mary.

Season: Mid-June to mid-September.

Food: A coffee shop/grill in the main building serves breakfast ($5.00–$7.00), lunch ($7.00–$11.00), and dinner ($8.00–$13.00). Beer and wine are served. Limited groceries, beer, and wine are sold in the general store.

Facilities: Restaurant, gift shop, general store with camp-

ing and fishing supplies and limited groceries.

Activities: Hiking, fishing, boating, boat tour of St. Mary Lake, National Park Service evening naturalist program in campground amphitheater.

SWIFT CURRENT MOTOR INN

P.O. Box 147 • East Glacier Park, MT 59434 • (406) 732–5531
www.glacierparkinc.com • www.swiftcurrentmotorinn.com

One Bedroom Cabin without Bath at Swift Current Motor Inn

SWIFT CURRENT MOTOR INN OFFERS EIGHTY-EIGHT lodging rooms in a complex that has twenty-six cabins, four motel buildings, a central bathhouse, and a registration building that also houses a store and restaurant. The cabins and motel units sit behind and to the side of the registration building, which offers a small lobby and a large covered porch with chairs. Plentiful parking is outside the registration building and directly beside the cabins and motel units. A large National Park Service campground is across the road.

Swift Current Motor Inn is in the northeast section of Glacier National Park, at the end of Many Glacier Road, 12 miles west of the town of Babb.

Two types of accommodations are available at Swift Current. Both types have electric heat but no air-conditioning, television, or telephone. The least expen-

sive lodging is in cabins without bath. A community bathroom has toilets and showers. The cabins are rustic and plain, with painted wooden floors, but clean. They are nicely spaced, and all are single units (no duplex units, common among other lodges). Eighteen small one-bedroom cabins each have a double bed in one room and a sink (cold water only) and small picnic table in a separate room. Two one-bedroom cabins with a private bath rent for about $30 per night more than the one-bedroom units without a bath. Six two-bedroom cabins have a small bedroom with a double bed on each side of a small room, with a sink and picnic table. These cabins do not have a private bathroom. The two-bedroom units rent for about $10 per night more than the one-bedroom units without bath. Cabins in Loop C are closest to the community bathhouse.

The cabins were constructed in 1937 after a fire destroyed cabins built several years earlier.

Four one-story wooden motel buildings house a total of sixty-two rooms in two price categories. Rooms in all four buildings have carpeted floors, two double beds, and a private bath with a shower but no tub. Three of the buildings near the back of the complex each have fourteen rooms, seven on a side, that are entered from walkways that run across both sides of each building. The rooms are average size, with walls that are partially paneled. The fourth motor inn unit, Pinetop, sits toward the front of the complex and has twenty rooms that are entered from an interior corridor. These rooms have no porch or balcony and are smaller and a little less expensive than the rooms in the other three motel buildings.

Swift Current Motor Inn offers inexpensive lodging in a scenic area of this magnificent national park. In fact, the one-bedroom cabins without bath are about the cheapest lodging offered in any national park. Trees surround all of the lodging buildings, so you won't enjoy great vistas from your room. On a positive note, the area is relatively quiet and a pleasant 1-mile walk down the road leads to the fancier and more expensive Many Glacier Hotel. The registration building has a small lobby area and a large covered porch with chairs. The Swift Current restaurant serves three meals a day with lunches and dinners featuring hamburgers plus pasta and pizza specialties. Meals and snacks are also available at Many Glacier Hotel. Swift Current is especially popular with hikers. Trails lead to Iceberg Lake and Ptarmigan Lake through an unusual 180-foot tunnel constructed for horseback riders and hikers.

Rooms: Singles, doubles, triples, and quads. All the motel rooms have private baths. Most cabin guests must use a community bathroom.

Wheelchair Accessibility: Four wheelchair-accessible rooms in one of the motel buildings near the rear of the complex

Swift Current Motor Inn is on the site of what was once a tepee camp established in 1911 by the Great Northern Railroad. Here guests slept on army cots in replicas of Blackfoot Indian tepees. By 1933 the tepees had been replaced by twenty-seven cabins and the area was called "Many Glacier Auto Tourist Camp." The current camp store was built two years later, and in 1940 a central comfort station with showers was added. Three motel-type buildings were constructed in 1955.

include ramp access and bathrooms with wide doorways and a grab bar for the toilet. The shower has a seat and an adjustable showerhead, but it does not have roll-in access. Two of the rooms have two double beds, while the other two rooms have two twin beds.

Rates: One-bedroom cabin without bath ($43); two-bed cabin without bath ($53); one-bedroom cabin with bath ($73); Pinetop ($94); Motor Inn ($110). Room rates quoted are for two adults. Each additional person is $10 per night. Children eleven and under stay free with an adult.

Location: In the northeast section of the Glacier National Park at the end of Many Glacier Road, 12 miles east of Babb, Montana.

Season: Mid-June to mid-September.

Food: A restaurant in the registration building offers breakfast ($5.00–$7.00), lunch, and dinner ($6.00–$17.00). Lunch and dinner have the same menu. Beer and wine are served. Limited groceries, beer, and wine are available in the general store.

Facilities: Restaurant, laundry, and camp store with gifts, groceries, and supplies.

Activities: Hiking, fishing, horseback riding, evening campfire programs, boat tours of Swiftcurrent Lake and Lake Josephine.

VILLAGE INN

1038 Apgar Street • Apgar, MT 59936 • (406) 888–5632
www.glacierparkinc.com • www.villageinnatapgar.com

VILLAGE INN IS A LONG, TWO-STORY MOTEL-STYLE building with thirty-six rooms. The inn is at the end of the road, directly on the shore of scenic Lake McDonald. The building, constructed in 1956, was flooded and remodeled in the mid-1960s. Each room enjoys an excellent view of the lake and the mountains beyond. A small registration area is located at the street-end of the building. The inn also has no restaurant, although a restaurant is a short walk up the street. Village Inn is located in Apgar, Montana, 3 miles inside the west entrance to Glacier National Park.

The inn offers four types of rooms. All the rooms are nicely furnished and have coffeemakers, heat and a full bath but no air-conditioning, telephone, or television. All are wood paneled, and each room has a large window and an outside balcony or patio that offer excellent views of Lake McDonald. The rooms all have doors that open to the balcony or patio. Larger rooms on the first floor can also be entered from the parking lot behind the building. Unless you specifically desire one of the kitchen units, we recommend a second-floor room for increased privacy and a better view of the lake. The twelve least expensive rooms sit at one end of the building, six on the second floor and six on the ground floor. Half the rooms have one double bed, and the other half have two twin beds, which almost fill these small rooms.

Ten two-bedroom family units, all on the second floor, have a double bed in one bedroom and either a double and twin bed or a double bed and a sofa bed.

Famous western artist Charles Russell had a home built beside Lake McDonald in 1908 by Dimon Apgar. Russell's studio, which still stands, was constructed eight years later.

These rooms cost $16 more per night and are quite a bit larger than the least expensive rooms described above. On the first floor eleven rooms have a bedroom and a kitchen with a refrigerator, sink, oven, stove, and all cooking and eating utensils. These are the same size as the two-bedroom units on the second floor and have a kitchen in place of the second bedroom. The Inn has three suites. Two suites on the second floor each have a living room and two back bedrooms, each with a double bed. A sofa bed is in the living room. One first-floor suite has two bedrooms and a kitchen. This suite is wheelchair accessible.

Village Inn is a quiet place to spend a night or two on the west side of Glacier National Park. The inn's location at the end of a short road allows you to avoid the crowds while enjoying a view of Lake McDonald and some of the park's scenic mountains. A gravel beach just outside the rooms leads to the cool waters of the lake. The inn is located less than a block from a restaurant that serves good food at reasonable prices. It is also a short walk from a National Park Service visitor center. Park Service rangers are at the visitor center to answer questions about the park. You will also find three gift shops and an ice cream shop nearby. A store offers limited groceries, beer, and wine.

Rooms: Singles, doubles, triples, and quads. Some of the family units and two suites can hold up to six persons. All rooms have private baths.

Wheelchair Accessibility: A one-bedroom kitchen unit and the first-floor suite are wheelchair accessible, with a wide bathroom door and grab bars by the toilet and combination shower-tub.

Rates: One bedroom ($108); two bedroom ($124); one-bedroom kitchen units ($145); three-room suites ($145–$170). Rates quoted are for two adults with the exception of the suites, which are for four adults. Children eleven and under stay free with an adult. Additional adults are $10.

Location: In the village of Apgar, Montana, 3 miles from the West Glacier entrance station.

Season: May to October.

Food: A restaurant one block away on Apgar Road offers breakfast, lunch, and dinner from mid-May through most of September. Very limited groceries are sold at a gift shop next to the restaurant. The lodge is 2½ miles from a full-service grocery store and several restaurants in the town of West Glacier.

Facilities: The village of Apgar has gift shops, a restaurant, an ice cream shop, boat rentals, and a National Park Service visitor center.

Activities: Nightly ranger/naturalist talks at the Apgar campground, boating, swimming (very cool water), fishing (no license required), hiking. Sightseeing tours of the park leave from Apgar.

NEVADA

Lake Mead National Recreation Area

601 Nevada Highway • Boulder City, NV 89005 • (702) 293–8906 • www.nps.gov/lame

Lake Mead National Recreation Area comprises nearly 1.5 million acres of desert landscape surrounding Lake Mead and Lake Mohave. The 290 square miles of clear water in the two lakes is supplied by the Colorado River. Lake Mead is 110 miles long and results from the famous Hoover Dam near Boulder City, Nevada. Farther south, 67-mile-long Lake Mohave is formed by Davis Dam near Bullhead City, Arizona. The recreation area is particularly popular for water-related activities such as boating, fishing, and waterskiing. Areas near the lake are often five to ten degrees warmer than Las Vegas, which means that summer temperatures frequently rise to 110° Fahrenheit and above. The recreation area is located in southern Nevada and northwestern Arizona. Main access is via U.S. Highway 93, which connects Las Vegas, Nevada, and Kingman, Arizona. **Recreation Area Entrance Fee:** $5.00 per vehicle or $3.00 per person, good for five days.

Lodging in Lake Mead National Recreation Area: Five lodging facilities are scattered throughout Lake Mead National Recreation Area. Echo Bay Resort, Lake Mead Resort at Boulder Beach, and Temple Bar Resort are each on Lake Mead in the northern half of the recreation area. Cottonwood Cove Resort and Lake Mohave Resort at Katherine Landing are on Lake Mohave in the southern half of the recreation area. The three facilities on Lake Mead and Lake Mohave Resort on Lake Mohave are operated by Seven Crown Resorts of Irvine, California. Cottonwood Cove is operated by Forever Resorts. All five facilities are geared to visitors interested in water-based activities, in particular boating and fishing.

Lake Mead National Recreation Area

COTTONWOOD COVE RESORT

10000 Cottonwood Cove Road • Searchlight, NV 89046 • (702) 297–1464
www.cottonwoodcoveresort.com

COTTONWOOD COVE IS A FAMILY RESORT WITH overnight accommodations, a cafe, and a large marina, all on the Nevada shoreline of Lake Mohave. The attractive single-story brick building with a red tile roof houses twenty-four guest rooms. Grass on both the front and back sides adds to the attractiveness of the building. A small restaurant is a short walk from all the rooms. Cottonwood Cove Resort is on the west side of Lake Mohave, 14 miles east of the intersection of Nevada Highway 164 and U.S. Highway 95. It is 70 miles southeast of Las Vegas, Nevada, via US 95.

Entry to the guest rooms is in the front, with sliding glass doors in the back. Parking is to the side and is a moderate distance from the end rooms. All of the rooms are the same size and are quite large. They each have heat, air conditioning, carpet, cable TV, telephone, and a full bathroom with a combination shower-tub. Twenty-one of the rooms have two double beds, and the other three rooms have a king-size bed plus a queen-size sofa bed. Each guest room includes tables and chairs on a covered patio that overlooks the lake. There are barbecue grills in a grassy area that spreads across the back of the building.

The cafe serves three meals a day. A store/gift shop sells supplies, groceries, beer, and wine. A separate meeting room with a capacity of forty people is available for rental. The room includes a microwave, sink, tables, and chairs.

Rooms: Doubles, triples, and quads. All rooms have a full bath.

Wheelchair Accessibility: One room is ADA compliant.

Reservations: Cottonwood Cove Marina, 10000 Cottonwood Cove Road, Searchlight, NV 89046. Phone (702) 297–1464. A deposit of one night's stay is required. A seventy-two-hour cancellation notice is required for a full refund.

Rates: All rooms ($108) from May through October; ($65) during Value Season, from November through April. Value Season rates not applicable during national holidays. Rates

Cottonwood was the site of an automobile engine-powered aerial ferry that connected Chloride, Arizona, and Searchlight, Nevada. The aerial tramway, which operated until the 1930s, was located about 1 mile north of Cottonwood Cove. In 1946 the National Park Service issued a permit to Murl Emery to establish a landing at Cottonwood. He soon put in a dock and several tent cabins, one serving as a store.

\\/

quoted are for two adults. Each additional person is $10 per night. Rollaway beds are $6.00 extra. Children five and under stay free. Check the Web site for special packages.

Location: Fourteen miles east of Searchlight, Nevada, on NV 164. The resort is approximately 70 miles southeast of Las Vegas, Nevada.

Season: The resort is open year-round.

Food: A cafe serves breakfast ($3.00–$9.00), lunch ($5.00–$9.00), and dinner ($5.00–$14.00). A store sells groceries, beer, wine, and supplies.

Transportation: No public transportation serves Cottonwood Cove. The nearest major airport is in Las Vegas, where rental cars are available. An airport is also in Laughlin, Nevada. The town of Searchlight has an airstrip where private planes may land.

Facilities: Cafe, convenience store/gift shop, meeting room, laundry in the nearby RV park, full-service marina that rents a variety of boats including houseboats, powerboats, fishing boats, and personal watercraft.

Activities: Volleyball, shuffleboard, horseshoes, fishing, boating, and waterskiing. Park ranger programs are offered in the nearby campground. Numerous casinos are about forty-five minutes away in Laughlin, Nevada.

ECHO BAY RESORT

Overton, NV 89040 • (702) 394–4000 • www.sevencrown.com

A MARINA COMPLEX, ECHO BAY RESORT INCLUDES a 1970s two-story cement block motel that sits on a hill overlooking the west side of the Overton Arm of Lake Mead. Approximately half of the resort's fifty-two rooms face the water; a marina is in front. The motel, with several nearby palm trees, has an appearance

NEVADA

Many people who visit Lake Mead National Recreation Area are interested in houseboat rentals, which are available at the marinas. Most houseboats are about 14 feet wide, with lengths that range from 40 to nearly 60 feet. The smaller units sleep six or eight persons, while the larger units can sleep a dozen or more. Be forewarned that houseboats aren't cheap to rent. Smaller houseboats often cost $200 to $300 per night for weeklong rentals and more for shorter rentals. Larger houseboats that hold up to ten or twelve persons rent for $400 to $500 per night for weeklong rentals and even more for two- or three-night rentals. Rental fees are often reduced during the off-season of mid-September to mid-June (excluding Memorial Day weekend). Houseboats are available at 7:00 A.M. on the first day and need to be returned by 4:00 P.M. on the last day. Reservations and deposits are required.

\|/

similar to what you might expect near the Florida coast. A large wooden deck on the lake side is accessed from the second floor. Plentiful parking is directly behind the building and close to the main entrance to the registration area. Pets are permitted with a deposit and an additional daily charge. The resort is 60 miles northeast of Las Vegas, Nevada, and the farthest north of the five lodging facilities in Lake Mead National Recreation Area. It is located at the end of a paved road, 5 miles east of Northshore Drive.

All of the rooms at Echo Bay have a telephone, air-conditioning, heat, carpet, television, a coffee pot, and a hair dryer. Nearly all of the rooms have two chairs on a private balcony or patio. Rooms on both sides of the building are accessed through a central corridor that can be entered at either end of the building or near the registration area on the main floor. Three categories of rooms are offered. The least expensive rooms have two double beds and face west, toward the parking lot. A few face a cement block wall and have no balcony or patio—try to avoid these. Twenty-five rooms face the water and have a single king-size bed; these cost $15 more than rooms on the opposite side of the building. Four extra-large rooms have two double beds, a sofa bed, and a small refrigerator.

Echo Bay is a water-based resort that appeals primarily to visitors who boat and fish. A National Park Service ranger station and campground are nearby, but most facilities are some distance away. A marina rents boats of all types, from personal watercraft to large houseboats. The main resort building has a 2,500-square-foot conference room on the second floor. A restaurant, Tail O' The Whale, has a nautical decor, with a wall of large windows that provides a view of the lake. A cocktail lounge located next to the restaurant is accessed through the same outside door. A snack bar/store with supplies and limited groceries is at the marina.

Rooms: Doubles, triples, and quads. All rooms have a full bath.

Wheelchair Accessibility: Two non-waterside rooms are wheelchair accessible. These are large rooms that have wide doorways, grab bars, and a low sink in the bathroom. Only one of the rooms has a roll-in-shower; the other shower has a lip.

Reservations: Seven Crown Resorts, P.O. Box 16247, Irvine, CA 92623-0068. Phone (800) 752–9669. A deposit of one night's stay is required. A seventy-two-hour cancellation notice is required for a full refund.

Rates: High season (April 1–October 31)/low season (November 1–March 31): Non-waterside ($90/$60); waterside ($105/$65); extra large room ($115/$65). Rates are quoted for two adults per room. Each extra person is $10. Children under five stay free. There is a one-time $7.50 fee for a rollaway bed.

Location: Sixty miles northeast of Las Vegas via Nevada Highway 147 and Northshore Drive. The resort is at the end of a paved road, 5 miles east of Northshore Drive.

Season: The resort is open year-round except Christmas Day. High season is during summer months, when the resort often fills on weekends.

Food: A full-service restaurant serves breakfast ($4.00–$7.00), lunch ($5.00–$9.00), and dinner ($8.00–$20.00), and a children's menu is available. The restaurant is open from 7:00 A.M. to 9:00 P.M. in-season. Hours can change during the off-season. The cocktail lounge is open from 4:00 P.M. to midnight. A snack bar/store at the marina is open from 7:00 A.M. to 8:00 P.M.

Transportation: The nearest major airport is in Las Vegas, where rental cars are available. An asphalt landing strip 3 miles from Echo Bay provides access for private planes. The resort has a free pickup service when called ahead.

Facilities: A restaurant, cocktail lounge, and conference room are in the main building. An adjacent gas station sells unleaded gasoline, diesel fuel, and propane. A laundry facility is in the nearby RV park. A full-service marina rents a variety of boats, including houseboats, ski boats, patio boats, fishing boats, and personal watercraft.

Activities: Fishing, waterskiing, boating.

Pets: Pets are permitted with a $50 deposit and an additional daily charge of $10 per pet.

LAKE MEAD RESORT

322 Lake Shore Road • Boulder City, NV 89005 • (702) 293–2074 • www.sevencrown.com

*Registration building
with rooms*

LAKE MEAD RESORT IS A COMPLEX OF FOUR ONE-story cement block buildings overlooking the Boulder Basin section of Lake Mead, with a marina and floating restaurant and lounge situated a quarter mile down the road. The lodging buildings are in a grassy area a short distance back from the lakeshore. Lake Mead Resort is located at Boulder Beach, 6 miles north of Boulder City, Nevada. Of the five lodging facilities in Lake Mead National Recreation Area, this is the nearest to Las Vegas (30 miles).

Thirty-four of the resort's forty-four rooms are in two U-shaped block buildings positioned on each side of the central registration building. These buildings are situated parallel to the shoreline of Boulder Basin. All

Lake Mead, with 550 miles of shoreline, is formed by famous Hoover Dam. The dam, completed in 1935, tamed this portion of the often wild Colorado River. The giant concrete structure required more than 5,000 men to work around the clock for five years. Downstream, Davis Dam was completed in 1953. Dam tours once offered have been discontinued indefinitely.

the rooms in both buildings are relatively small and have one queen-size bed. Each room has a small private bathroom with a combination shower-tub. The two corner rooms in each building have an extra window that allows for a brighter interior. A separate but nearby annex has eight larger rooms with two queen beds. The central registration building houses a conference room and two nice suites. Each suite has a living room, a bedroom with one queen bed, and a kitchenette with a stove, microwave, a refrigerator, coffeemaker, pots, pans, and eating utensils. The smaller of the two suites can sleep up to four with a twin sofa sleeper and a rollaway in the living room. It has one television and one bathroom. The Super Suite can sleep a maximum of six with a queen sofa sleeper and a rollaway in the living room. It has two televisions, two bathrooms, and a fireplace. All the rooms at Lake Mead Resort have air-conditioning, heat, and television with cable.

Lake Mead Resort is in a good location for water-related activities punctuated with occasional trips to nearby Las Vegas. A nice swimming pool near the front of the lodge buildings has a large patio area with tables and lounge chairs. A marina near the restaurant rents boats, including houseboats, and sells fishing licenses.

Rooms: Mostly doubles, with some triples, and quads. The large suite will hold six. All rooms have a private bath.

Wheelchair Accessibility: One room in the annex has a wide bathroom doorway and a combination shower-tub with grab bars.

Reservations: Seven Crown Resorts, P.O. Box 16247, Irvine, CA 92623-0068. Phone (800) 752–9669. Reservations require a one-night deposit. A seventy-two-hour cancellation is required for a full refund.

Rates: High season (April 1–October 31)/low season (November 1–March 31): one queen ($75/$55); two queens ($85/$70); kitchen suite ($130/$100); kitchen super suite ($175/$130). Rates quoted are for two adults per room and four adults for the suite. Each additional person is $10. There is a one-time fee of $7.50 for a rollaway bed. Children five and under stay free.

Location: Six miles north of Boulder City, Nevada, on Lakeshore Scenic Drive. The resort is 30 miles southeast of Las Vegas.

Season: The resort is open year-round except Christmas Day. High season is during summer months, when the resort often fills on weekends.

Food: A full-service restaurant, Tail O'The Whale, at the marina serves breakfast ($4.00–$7.00), lunch ($5.00–$9.00), and dinner ($8.00–$20.00). A children's menu is available. The cocktail lounge, Pelican's Perch, and store are also at the marina.

Transportation: The nearest major airport is in Las Vegas, where rental cars are available.

Facilities: Swimming pool with a propane barbecue grill. A restaurant, cocktail lounge, waterside store, and a tackle and bait shop are at the full-service marina. Ski boats, patio boats, fishing boats, and personal watercraft are available for rent (1–800–752–9669 or www.sevencrown.com).

Activities: Fishing, waterskiing, boating, and swimming. No lifeguards.

Pets: Pets are permitted with a $50 deposit and an additional daily charge of $10 per pet.

LAKE MOHAVE RESORT AT KATHERINE LANDING

Bullhead City, AZ 86430 • (520) 754–3245 • www.sevencrown.com

L ake Mohave Resort is a marina complex situated on a hill above Lake Mohave. The two motel buildings, constructed of cement block in the early 1970s, provide a total of fifty rooms in a large grassy area landscaped with palm trees. The resort is located at the south end of Lake Mohave, just off Nevada Highway 68, north of Davis Dam. It is the southernmost lodging facility in Lake Mead National Recreation Area. Lake Mohave Resort is 32 miles west of Kingman, Arizona.

The resort offers five types of accommodations. All of the rooms have air-conditioning, heat, a telephone, a television, and a bathroom. Six rooms have a private balcony or patio. Eleven of the resort's least expensive rooms have one king-size bed. Thirty-one rooms have two double beds. Six of these rooms include a kitchen and rent for an additional $10 per night. Eight rooms classified as kitchen suites have two queen-size beds. Each building has a covered walkway with chairs in front of each room. A single deluxe rental house, which sleeps up to ten persons, includes three bedrooms, two baths, and a full kitchen. The rental house is across the street from the main building.

Activities at Lake Mohave Resort primarily appeal to visitors who enjoy fishing, waterskiing, and boating. A full marina provides slips, moorage, a gas dock, and

Lake Mead and Lake Mohave offer excellent fishing and have open season on all species of fish year-round. Largemouth bass, rainbow trout, channel catfish, black crappie, and bluegill are in both lakes. Lake Mead is noted for an abundance of striped bass, some weighing fifty pounds and more. Rainbow trout are the most popular catch in Lake Mohave. Fishing from shore requires an appropriate state fishing license. Fishing from a boat requires a fishing license from either Nevada or Arizona and a special use stamp from the other state. Licenses and stamps are sold at most of the marinas.

repair facilities. The marina has a full-service Tail O' The Whale Restaurant and lounge. Laundry facilities are at the nearby RV park, and a convenience store and tackle shop are adjacent to the restaurant. The booming town of Laughlin, Nevada, and its many casinos is a short drive from the resort.

Rooms: Doubles, triples, and quads. All rooms have a bath. The house sleeps up to ten.

Wheelchair Accessibility: Two rooms are wheelchair accessible with wide bathroom doors and a combination shower-tub with an adjustable shower head, a seat, and grab bars.

Reservations: Seven Crown Resorts, P.O. Box 16247, Irvine, CA 92623-0068. Phone (800) 752–9669. A deposit of one night's stay is required. A seventy-two-hour cancellation notice is required for a full refund.

Rates: High season (April 16–September 7)/low season (September 8–April 15): Room with one king bed ($85/$35); room with two double beds ($95/$45); kitchen with two double beds ($105/$55); kitchen suite with two queen-size beds ($115/$65); house ($240/$240). Rates for the regular rooms and the kitchen with two double beds are for two adults; rates for the kitchen suite are for three adults; rates for the house are for six people. Each additional person is $10. There is a one-time fee of $7.50 for a rollaway bed. Children five and under stay free.

Location: The resort is located on the shore of Lake Mohave, 32 miles west of Kingman, Arizona. It is 3 miles off NV 68.

Season: The resort is open year-round except for Christmas Day. High season is during summer, and the resort often fills on summer weekends.

Food: A full-service restaurant serves breakfast ($4.00–$8.00), lunch ($5.00–$9.00), and dinner ($8.00–$20.00). A children's menu is available. A snack bar is open during the summer with the same menu and take-out service. A store adjacent to the restaurant sells groceries and supplies.

Transportation: Kingman, Arizona, and Las Vegas both have airports with rental car service.

Facilities: A restaurant, cocktail lounge, store, and tackle shop are at the marina. Laundry facilitiers are at the nearby RV park. A full-service marina located in front of the lodge buildings rents houseboats, ski boats, patio boats, fishing boats, and personal watercraft (1–800–752–9669 or www.sevencrown.com).

Activities: Fishing, boating, swimming (no lifeguards), and waterskiing. Numerous casinos are a short distance away in Laughlin, Nevada.

Pets: Pets are permitted with a $50 deposit and an additional daily charge of $10 per pet.

TEMPLE BAR RESORT

Temple Bar, AZ 86443 • (520) 767–3211 • www.sevencrown.com

Temple Bar Resort comprises two concrete-block motel-type buildings with eighteen rooms, four freestanding shake-sided cabins, a restaurant, an adjacent store, and a tackle and bait shop. The complex also includes a full-service marina. The resort is on the south shoreline of Lake Mead within view of a large monolith called The Temple. Temple Bar Resort is located on a paved road 28 miles northeast of U.S. Highway 93, which connects Las Vegas, Nevada, with Kingman, Arizona. It is 78 miles east of Las Vegas and 85 miles from Kingman.

All of the eighteen motel rooms at Temple Bar have heat, air-conditioning, television, and a private bathroom. There are no telephones in the rooms; pay phones are available. The larger motel building houses twelve large rooms, six on each side. Each room has two double beds and a patio with table and chairs. Half of these units are desert view rooms and the other half are lakeview rooms. A separate building has six rooms in three classes. Two traditional rooms offer a double bed and double sofa bed. Two kitchen units have one double bed and a sofa bed in one room. The kitchen area includes a stove with an oven, microwave oven, full-size refrigerator, dishes, and basic cooking utensils. Two kitchen suites feature two double beds in a separate bedroom with a sofa bed in the livingroom/ kitchen. The four cabins have two double beds, a stove with an oven, a sink with hot water, and a refrigerator but no bath. The bathhouse is adjacent to the cabins. There are no dishes or cooking utensils provided in the cabins.

Rooms: Doubles, triples, and quads. Suites hold up to six adults. All rooms except cabins have a full bath.

Wheelchair Accessibility: One room is wheelchair accessible. It has ramp access and wide doorways; the bathroom has grab bars, and the tub has an adjustable showerhead and a seat.

Reservations: Seven Crown Resorts, P.O. Box 16247, Irvine, CA 92623-0068. Phone (800) 752–9669. A deposit of one night's stay is required. A seventy-two-hour cancellation notice is required for a full refund.

Rates: High season (April 1–October 31)/low season (November 1–March 31): Traditional rooms ($80/$65); desert view rooms ($90/$75); lakeview rooms ($100/$80); kitchen units ($100/$80); kitchen suites $115/$90); cabins ($55/$45). Rates quoted are for two adults in regular units and three adults in the kitchen suites. Each additional person is $10. Children five and under stay free. There is a one-time $7.50 fee for a rollaway bed.

Location: The resort is 78 miles east of Las Vegas, Nevada. It is at the end of a paved road 28 miles northeast of US 93.

Season: The resort is open year-round except for Christmas Day. High season is during summer, and the resort often fills on summer weekends.

Food: A full-service restaurant serves breakfast ($4.00–$7.00), lunch ($5.00–$9.00), and dinner ($8.00–$20.00). A children's menu is available. A convenience store sells groceries and supplies.

Transportation: Kingman, Arizona, and Las Vegas both have airports with rental car service.

Facilities: Restaurant, cocktail lounge, store, and tackle and bait shop. The Marina rents ski boats, patio boats, fishing boats, and personal watercraft (1–800–752–9669 or www.sevencrown.com). Laundry facilities are at the nearby RV park.

Activities: Fishing, boating, swimming (no lifeguards), and waterskiing.

Pets: Pets are permitted with a $50 deposit and an additional daily charge of $10 per pet.

NORTH CAROLINA

State Tourist Information
(800) 847–4862 | www.visitnc.com

Blue Ridge Parkway

199 Hemphill Knob Road • Asheville, NC 28803 • (828) 271–4779• www.nps.gov/blri

The Blue Ridge Parkway comprises 93,000 acres in a narrow strip along 469 miles of winding road that follows the crest of the Blue Ridge Mountains. The parkway provides access to craft centers, campgrounds, scenic overlooks, log cabins, rail fences, and beautiful mountain vistas. Lodges, overlooks, restaurants, and other major points of interest along the Blue Ridge Parkway can be located according to milepost markers alongside the road. Mile marker 0 is at Rockfish Gap near Waynesboro, Virginia, the northern entrance to the parkway. Each mile is numbered progressively southward. Be certain to stop at a visitor center and pick up a copy of the parkway folder that provides a map along with the locations of points of interest on the parkway. The parkway is located in western North Carolina and western Virginia. The north end of the parkway connects with Shenandoah National Park, and the south end leads to Great Smoky Mountains National Park. **Parkway Entrance Fee:** No charge.

Lodging along the Blue Ridge Parkway: Four lodging facilities are within the boundaries of the Blue Ridge Parkway. Accommodations range from very nice two-story lodges to very rustic cabins without private bath. The facilities are scattered along the parkway from mile marker 86 in the north to very near the south entrance, near Great Smoky Mountains National Park.

BLUFFS LODGE

45356 Blue Ridge Parkway • Laurel Springs, NC 28644-9716 • (336) 372–4499
www.blueridgeresort.com

Blue Ridge Parkway

Bluffs Lodge consists of two identical two-story lodge buildings built into a grassy hillside overlooking a meadow and surrounding hills. No other buildings are connected to the lodge, although a coffee shop and gas station are a quarter mile away on the parkway. Each lodge building contains twelve rooms, four on each floor of the back side facing the meadow and rolling hills and four rooms on the front facing the parking lot. A spacious, covered second-floor balcony runs across the back of each building. Chairs are on the balcony and on the rock walkways on the ground level, as well as the front of the building. A nice rock patio area between the two buildings has a large outdoor stone fireplace and many chairs and tables for viewing the scenery or visiting. The buildings, which opened in 1949, are well maintained. Bluffs Lodge is located in northern North Carolina in the Doughton Park area of the Blue Ridge Parkway. It is at milepost 241, about midway between the north and south entrances to the parkway.

All twenty-four rooms at Bluffs Lodge are nearly identical except for the views and beds. Each room has heat, a coffeemaker, a hair dryer, and a tiled bathroom with a combination shower-tub, but no telephone, television, or air-conditioning. Fans are available from the office. The rooms are not particularly spacious but are clean and comfortable, and each has an amazingly large closet to store suitcases, coolers, clothes, and other gear you bring in. Several rooms have a queen bed, and one has a king bed, but the majority of rooms have two double beds. The best views are from rooms on the back side facing the southwest. Rooms in the front face the northeast, which may be an advantage on particularly hot days when you may not want to deal with the afternoon sun. Remember, there is no air-conditioning. We would choose a second-floor room on the back side, preferably either 203A or 203B, which are end rooms

Linn Cove Viaduct at mile marker 305 on the Blue Ridge Parkway is considered one of the most complicated concrete bridges ever built. It is one of America's most scenic bridges and has received half a dozen national design awards. The S-shaped viaduct was designed and constructed to minimize environmental damage. Skirting the perimeter of North Carolina's Grandfather Mountain, the viaduct is 1,243 feet long and contains 153 concrete segments, only one of which is straight. Although nearly all of the Blue Ridge Parkway had been completed and open to travelers by 1967, the viaduct was not finished until 1983. A trail leading underneath the viaduct begins at a visitor contact station at the south end of the viaduct.

with an added side window and brighter interior. In addition, other guests will not be walking by when they enter or exit their own rooms. The lodge is built on a hillside, so second-floor rooms do not require climbing stairs. All rooms rent for the same price.

Bluffs Lodge is as peaceful a place to stay as you will find in any national park or, for that matter, anywhere at all. It is a quarter mile off the Blue Ridge Parkway, so you won't be bothered by traffic noise, and since no restaurant or visitor center is at the site, there is no congestion of people and vehicles. With only twenty-three rooms (the manager lives in the twenty-fourth room), you are likely to meet up with others who are seeking a similar experience. Without televisions to consume attention, you will almost surely find yourself striking up a conversation with other guests as you spend the late afternoon or early

Although the Blue Ridge Parkway was completed into the Doughton Park (then called Bluff Park) area in 1937, it was not until 1948 that construction commenced on a gasoline station and coffee shop. Doughton Park was also designated for the first of three inns to be constructed on the parkway. The National Park Service office drew up initial plans for the inn that, according to one person, looked "like a two story army barracks." The original plans were changed by new architects, who separated the structure with a patio and bent the two sections in the middle to conform to the contours of the land on which the lodge would be built. The gas station across the road opened on May 28, 1949, and the first unit of Bluffs Lodge opened on September 1 of the same year. Excluding campgrounds, this was the first overnight lodging for visitors on the Blue Ridge Parkway.

\\/

evening relaxing on the wooden balcony or rock walkway outside your room. In the evening guests mingle in front of the large stone fireplace between the two buildings. A short walk up a nearby hillside provides an outstanding view of a valley and the surrounding mountains. One of the greatest experiences of staying here is eating a meal in the nearby old-fashioned coffee shop, which still offers counter service. Both the interior and exterior of the coffee shop are virtually identical to when it opened in June 1949. Ellen, the server who waited on us during our August 2005 visit, had worked in the coffee shop for fifty-five years! Who says employee loyalty has gone

out of style? The coffee shop serves regional specialties including pinto beans and cornbread, biscuits and gravy, and country ham. Where else can you get barbecued pork with melted cheese served between two golden brown corn cakes topped with cole slaw?

Rooms: Doubles, triples, and quads. All rooms have a private bath with a combination shower-tub.

Wheelchair Accessibility: No rooms at Bluffs Lodge are specifically labeled as wheelchair accessible. Rooms can be accessed without steps, but the rooms do not have wide doorways or wheelchair-accessible bathrooms.

Reservations: Bluffs Lodge, 45356 Blue Ridge Parkway, Laurel Springs, NC 28644-9716. Phone (336) 372–4499. During the off-season write Bluffs Lodge, P.O. Box 397, Jefferson, NC 28640. A deposit of one night's stay is required. A forty-eight-hour cancellation notice is required for a full refund.

Rates: All rooms ($80). Rates quoted are for two adults. Each additional person is $9.00 per night. Children twelve and under stay free. Rollaway is $9.00 per night.

Location: In northern North Carolina, near the midpoint of the Blue Ridge Parkway at milepost 241. The lodge is a quarter mile off the parkway.

Season: May through the end of October.

Food: A 1950s-era coffee shop a quarter mile from the lodge serves breakfast ($4.00–$8.00), lunch ($4.00–$10.00), and dinner ($4.00–$12.00). Regional specialties are offered and a children's menu is available. Hours are 7:30 A.M. to 7:30 P.M. daily. Snacks are sold at a gas station/gift shop next to the coffee shop.

Transportation: The nearest scheduled airline service is in Charlotte and Greensboro, North Carolina. Both cities are about two hours from the lodge.

Facilities: No facilities are at the lodge. A coffee shop, gift shop, and gas station are a quarter mile away on the Blue Ridge Parkway.

Activities: Hiking. Park Service rangers present programs on the lodge patio each Thursday and Sunday evening. Programs are presented on Friday and Saturday nights at the nearby campground.

PEAKS OF OTTER LODGE

P.O. Box 489 • Bedford, VA 24523 • (540) 586–1081 • www.peaksotter.com

PEAKS OF OTTER LODGE CONSISTS OF A MAIN REGistration and dining building and three adjacent two-story lodging buildings that provide a total of sixty-three overnight rooms. All four of the attractive wood-and-cement block buildings were constructed in the mid-1960s and have a similar appearance. The three buildings with rooms are on the grassy bank of Abbott Lake, and all the rooms provide an excellent view of this small but pretty body of water. Peaks of Otter Lodge is located about 25 miles north of Roanoke, Virginia, at mile marker 86 on the Blue Ridge Parkway. It is the farthest north of the four lodging facilities on the parkway.

All but three wheelchair-accessible rooms are in three two-story buildings connected end-to-end by covered walkways. Each of the three buildings sit on a grassy hillside below the parking lot. Because the buildings are built into a hillside, a half flight of stairs gains entry to a walkway that runs in front of the front doors of either first- or second-floor rooms. Unit One, with rooms numbered in the 100s, is closest to the main lodge building,

although the buildings are close together, so no room is far from the dining room and lounge. The rooms are bright and airy, with a large back window that provides a view of Abbott Lake backed by a wooded hillside. Scenic Sharp Top Mountain peaks over the southwest corner of the lake. All but two rooms have either a patio or balcony with two chairs. Each room has air-conditioning, electric heat, carpeting, and a tiled bathroom with a combination shower-tub. The rooms do not have a television or a telephone. Two satellite televisions are in the main lodge, one in the lounge and the other in the ground floor lobby, and pay telephones and ice machines are scattered about the complex. The majority of rooms have two double beds, while several have one king bed. We generally prefer second-floor rooms, but at this lodge you might want to choose a room on the first floor, where you can move your patio chairs onto a large grassy hillside leading to the nearby lake. In addition, you can use the lakeside doorway for a nice walk to the main lodge building.

Peaks of Otter Lodge is a quiet and relaxing place to spend several nights. The rooms are comfortable,

A lodging facility served the Peaks of Otter area as early as 1834, when Polly Woods operated a combination tavern/lodge for nearly a decade. This was followed by several hotels built in this locale prior to the construction of the parkway through the Peaks of Otter area beginning in 1939. The initial development plan for the Peaks of Otter area envisioned a picnic area and aquatic center at the present lodge site in addition to twenty-two cabins on the hillside behind the current visitor center. Several proposals followed, including one that called for a lodge and a small lake to replace the aquatic center. The present lodge site was confirmed in 1951 with a plan calling for one large lodging structure. This plan underwent several changes, and construction of the present lodge got underway in 1962. Two years later work commenced on the lake. The lodge began operating year-round in 1973.

and the view from a back balcony is similar to what an armchair traveler might see on a picture postcard. Plan to do a lot of hiking during your visit. A 1-mile paved trail behind the lodge circles Abbott Lake. This is as pleasant a stroll as you will find anywhere. Many other trails are nearby. Or maybe you would rather walk out your back door and fish in the lake (artificial lures only). Daily bus trips to Sharp Top Mountain (fee charged) leave hourly from the nearby camp store when weather permits. The country-style dining room, with its vaulted, beamed ceiling and large windows overlooking Lake Abbott, serves three meals a day, including a Friday night seafood buffet and a Sunday country buffet. Beverages are served in an adjacent lounge, which has a large stone fireplace

and offers great lake views. Two conference rooms are located on the ground floor. The main lodge also has a gift shop off the lobby.

Rooms: Singles, doubles, triples, and quads. All rooms have a private bath with a combination shower-tub.

Wheelchair Accessibility: Three rooms on the ground floor (one floor below the main entrance) of the main lodge building are ADA compliant. Access to the rooms is via an elevator from the main lobby. The rooms have either two doubles or a king bed plus a sofa bed. Depending on the room, the bathroom has either a roll-in shower or a combination shower-tub. Each room has a small refrigerator.

Reservations: Peaks of Otter Lodge, P.O. Box 489, Bedford, VA 24523. Phone (800) 542–5927. One night's deposit is required. A twenty-four-hour cancellation notice is required for full refund.

Rates: November 1–April 30 weekdays ($66); November 1–April 30 weekends ($72); May 1–September 30 ($89); some holiday weekends and the month of October ($93). Rates are quoted for singles or doubles. Each additional person is $8.00 per night. Children under twelve stay free. Rollaway beds are $8.00 per night. Call or check the Web site for special packages.

Location: Twenty-five miles north of Roanoke, Virginia, at mileposts 84/87 of the Blue Ridge Parkway.

Season: Open year-round.

Food: A dining room serves breakfast ($4.00–$8.00), lunch ($5.00–$11.00), and dinner ($8.00–$29.00), including a special seafood buffet on Fridays ($22.00) and a country buffet on Sundays ($14.00). A children's menu is available.

Transportation: Nearby Roanoke and Lynchburg, Virginia, each provide scheduled airline service. Rental cars are available in each town.

Facilities: Restaurant, cocktail lounge, gift shop, conference rooms, nature center, country store, National Park Service visitor center.

Activities: Hiking, fishing, interpretive programs, bus trip to Sharp Top Mountain, National Park Service campfire programs on weekend evenings.

THE PISGAH INN

P.O. Box 749 • Waynesville, NC 28786 • (828) 235–8228 • www.pisgahinn.com

THE PISGAH INN CONSISTS OF THREE BUILDINGS with accommodations, a separate building with a restaurant and gift shop, and a camp store. All of the buildings are of wood and masonry construction. The registration desk is at the end of the lodging building nearest the restaurant. The three two-story buildings with lodging provide a total of fifty-one rooms, including one suite. All of the rooms are a short walk from the dining room. Each of the rooms offers an excellent view of the distant mountains. The three lodge buildings and the restaurant are situated at 5,000 feet on the side of 5,749-foot Mt. Pisgah. The camp store with a laundry is nearby. The inn, constructed in the mid-1960s, is in southwestern North Carolina, approximately 25 miles south of Asheville, North Carolina. It is the farthest south of the four lodging facilities on the Blue Ridge Parkway, at milepost 408.

Two types of rooms and one suite are offered. All of the rooms have heat, a tiled bathroom with a combination shower-tub, and a color television but no air-conditioning or telephone. Each room has a private balcony with rocking chairs. Most of the rooms have two double beds, and some have one queen-size bed. The back balcony and windows of each room generally offer excellent views of the distant mountains, although some of the first-floor rooms have views that are partially obstructed by nearby trees and plants. Choose a second-floor room if you don't mind climbing a flight of stairs. Rooms are entered from an outside door facing the parking lot. More than enough parking is available and close to each building. Thirty rooms labeled "deluxe" are larger, have ceiling fans, coffeemakers, refrigerators, and were remodeled in 2001. Twenty rooms rent as "standard" at a slightly reduced rate. The single suite located above the office

The Biltmore Estate near Asheville, North Carolina, is one of this region's major visitor attractions. The 250-room mansion was constructed in the late 1800s by George Washington Vanderbilt, grandson of railroad tycoon Cornelius Vanderbilt. Allow at least a half-day for the full self-guided tour (fee charged) of the home, winery, gardens, and greenhouse. The Biltmore Estate is 3 blocks north of Interstate 40 (exit 50) on U.S. Highway 25.

is twice as large as, and rents for approximately $45 per night more than, a deluxe room. The suite is one large room with a king bed, two televisions, a sitting area with a sofa, a table and chairs, and the only fireplace in a room in the inn. Sufficient firewood is provided for an evening fire. Additional wood can be purchased at the store.

Pisgah Inn is a place to get away from the heat while enjoying mountain views and good food. Views from the rooms are the best of any lodging facility on the parkway. At an altitude of 5,000 feet, temperatures are generally cool, even during summer months when the surrounding valleys are hot and humid. Weekends can be busy, so you might want to reserve a weekday night or two if you have the flexibility. The restaurant, with its vaulted ceiling and ceiling-high windows on three walls, offers diners good views from nearly any table. Best of all, the restaurant has excellent food, with nearly a dozen specials each day for lunch and dinner. On the evening we ate here the menu included Walnut Crusted Trout with Raspberry Sauce and Apple Raisin Stuffed Pork Chop with Cider Glaze. We can assure you these are not meals we frequently fix at home. Guests of the inn receive preference in the event there is a waiting list for seating. This is an excellent area for hiking, and good fishing is about 10 miles away. National Park Service rangers conduct evening weekend programs across the road at the campground amphitheater.

Rooms: Singles, doubles, triples, and quads. All rooms have a private bath with a combination shower-tub.

Wheelchair Accessibility: Three first-floor deluxe rooms each have nearby parking and ramp access to the room. The bathroom has a wide doorway, a high toilet, and a combination shower-tub with grab bars. No wheelchair-accessible standard rooms are available, so the inn rents these deluxe rooms to individuals with accessibility needs for the standard room price.

Reservations: The Pisgah Inn, P.O. Box 749, Waynesville, NC 28786. Phone (828) 235–8228. One night's deposit is required. A fee of $15 is charged for cancellations made two weeks or less from the arrival date. One night's deposit is charged for cancellations made forty-eight hours or less from the arrival date.

Rates: Standard ($84); deluxe ($94); suite ($140). Rates quoted are for two adults. Each additional person is $9.00. Rollaways are $9.00 per night. Children twelve and under stay free.

Location: Southwest North Carolina, 25 miles south of Asheville on the Blue Ridge Parkway.

Season: April 1 through October 31.

Food: An attractive restaurant serves breakfast ($4.00–$12.00), lunch ($6.00–$12.00), and dinner ($7.00–$25.00). A children's menu is available. A nearby camp store sells limited groceries.

Transportation: The nearest scheduled airline service is in Asheville, where rental cars are available. No public transportation services the inn.

Facilities: Restaurant, gift shop, laundry, camp store.

Activities: Hiking, evening weekend programs at the nearby campground amphitheater.

ROCKY KNOB CABINS

266 Mabry Mill Road • Meadows of Dan, VA 24120-9603 • (540) 593–3503
www.blueridgeresort.com

Rocky Knob Cabins is a small complex consisting of one registration office/manager's cabin, a central bathhouse, and five older wooden buildings in a semicircle behind the bathhouse. Two of the buildings are constructed as duplex units, for a total of seven rental cabins. The cabins are in a meadow surrounded by heavily wooded hills. The complex has no lobby, dining room, or recreation hall. The buildings are in one of the most remote settings of any national park. The buildings are from the 1930s, erected during construction of the parkway. Rocky Knob Cabins is in southern Virginia, at milepost 174 on the Blue Ridge Parkway. It is 54 miles south of Roanoke, Virginia.

The seven cabins at Rocky Knob Cabins are virtually identical except for the one wheelchair-accessible unit. The cabins have a vaulted ceiling, two double beds, a refrigerator, stove top, window fans, small electric space heater, and sink with cold water only. Each cabin has a kitchen table with chairs plus an outside grill. Except for the wheelchair-accessible unit, the cabins do not have a private bathroom, so guests must utilize a nearby central bathhouse that has sinks, toilets, and showers. The cabins also do not have air-conditioning, a telephone, or a television. One unit in

Mabry Mill, at milepost 176, is a favorite stop for travelers on the Blue Ridge Parkway. The mill, operated by E. B. Mabry from 1910 to 1935, today serves country ham, barbecue, homemade biscuits, and corn and buckwheat pancakes. Native handicrafts, including pottery, woodcraft, and metalcraft, are available for purchase. A trail takes you to the original gristmill, sawmill, blacksmith shop, and other outdoor exhibits. Demonstrations are presented in summer and fall.

\\\/

The cabins at Rocky Knob were constructed in 1941 as the first of a planned series of "trail lodges" along the parkway. The complex was intended to accommodate Boy Scouts, Girl Scouts, and other youth groups. These were to be "rough-it" camps that would provide built-in bunks, benches, toilets, showers, and a picnic-type table. At the same time authorities planned a conventional lodge, coffee shop, and gas station. The lodge and coffee shop were never built, and the gas station, completed in 1949, was converted to a visitor contact station in 1978. The cabins were never used as intended. Rather, they were remodeled for use as family housekeeping units and made available to the public in 1950.

\\\/

each of the two duplex cabins (22 and wheelchair-accessible unit 18) has a stone fireplace but no front porch. Firewood is sold in the office. Each of the remaining five cabins, including three freestanding units, has a front porch but no fireplace. If you don't care about having a fireplace, choose one of the three freestanding cabins. Our choice is cabin 21, which is close to the bathroom and offers the best view from the front porch. If having a fireplace is important, request cabin 22, or, if available, wheelchair-accessible cabin 18, which has a fireplace plus a private bathroom.

Rocky Knob Cabins is certainly one of the more unusual lodging units in the national park system. Staying there is like returning to Appalachia in years past—many years past. The cabins are old but clean and comfortable. The deciding factor for many travelers is whether a community bath is a viable alternative. If you don't mind this inconvenience and you want to stay overnight in a very rural setting, Rocky Knob may be your place. Also, Rocky Knob has no planned activities or other facilities; you are on your own for something to do. You will also enjoy a sense of solitude that many seek in a vacation. If you don't want to cook, a restaurant is a mile down the road. In addition, Mabry Mill, a famous stop on the Blue Ridge Parkway, is 2 miles south.

Rooms: Doubles, triples, and quads. Only the wheelchair-accessible cabin has a private bath.

Wheelchair Accessibility: One cabin in a duplex unit is ADA accessible and has a large private bathroom with a high toilet, roll-in shower, and grab bars.

Reservations: Rocky Knob Cabins, 266 Mabry Mill Road, Meadows of Dan, VA 24120-9603. Phone (540) 593–3503; during the off-season write Rocky Knob Cabins, P.O. Box 27, Mammoth Cave, KY 42259. Phone (270) 773–2191. One night's deposit is required. Cancellation notice of forty-eight hours is required for a full refund.

Rates: All cabins ($59). Rates quoted are for two adults. Each additional person is $8.00 per night. Rollaways are $8.00 per night. Cabins are $49 per night Sunday through Thursday when staying two or more nights.

Location: Southern Virginia, 1 mile off the Blue Ridge Parkway at milepost 174. The cabins are approximately 55 miles south of Roanoke, Virginia.

Season: Last week of May through the end of October.

Food: No dining facilities are available. A restaurant is about a mile up the road near the Blue Ridge Parkway. The Mabry Mill Restaurant is 2 miles south on the Blue Ridge Parkway.

Transportation: Scheduled airlines serve Roanoke, Virginia, where rental cars are available.

Facilities: Community bathhouse with showers.

Activities: Hiking, horseshoes, a swing (porch type).

Pets: Pets are permitted for $5.00 per night per pet, but they must be kept on a leash.

OHIO

Cuyahoga Valley National Park

15610 Vaughn Road • Brecksville, OH 44141 • (216) 524–1497
www.dayinthevalley.com • www.nps.gov/cuva

Cuyahoga Valley National Park encompasses 33,000 acres of a rural river valley that links the two urban centers of Cleveland and Akron. The national park offers a place to enjoy a stroll, hike, or bike along the 19-mile Ohio & Erie Canal Towpath Trail, a primary park attraction. Cuyahoga Valley National Park includes a restored 1800s farm and village, hiking and biking trails, several visitor centers, and the remnants of a company town built in 1906. Throughout the year, the Cuyahoga Valley Scenic Railroad operates the full length of the park and beyond. **Park Entrance Fee**: No charge. Fee for some special events.

Lodging in Cuyahoga Valley National Park: A bed-and-breakfast inn with six accommodations sits within the boundaries of the national park. The Inn at Brandywine Falls is midway between the north and south ends of the park, approximately 4 miles northeast of the crossing of Interstates 80 and 271. A large number and variety of accommodations are available just outside the border of the national park.

THE INN AT BRANDYWINE FALLS

8230 Brandywine Road • Sagamore Hills, OH 44067-2810 • (330) 467–1812
www.innatbrandywinefalls.com

Cuyahoga Valley National Park

THE INN AT BRANDYWINE FALLS IS A CIVIL War–era farmstead renovated in 1988 by an enterprising couple who operate it as a bed-and-breakfast under a fifty-year lease from the U.S. government. The property includes the main house, an adjacent carriage barn, and a nearby stable. Cats, chickens, goats, and an affable dog add to the country atmosphere of the inn, which is located on the east rim of the valley, approximately 3 miles north of I–80. From downtown Cleveland (forty minutes) take Interstate 77 south to Ohio Highway 82. Drive east about 6 miles to Brandywine Road, then 2.5 miles south.

The inn offers six overnight rooms, four in the main house and two in the carriage barn. All the rooms have heat, air-conditioning, a telephone, and a private bathroom. The main house has three rooms on the second floor, one of which has one double bed. The other second-floor accommodations include the "Simon Perkins Room" with two double four-poster beds, and "Anna Hale's Garret Suite," which comprises a small bedroom with two double beds plus a small sitting room that can be used as a second bedroom. The single first-floor accommodation has a double sleigh bed and is wheelchair accessible. The more expensive suites in the carriage house each have plank floors, a table and chairs, either a double futon or daybeds, a Franklin stove, a microwave, and a refrigerator, all on the first floor, plus a king bed in the loft. Each suite has a Jacuzzi plus a wall of windows that offers guests a feel of the outdoors. The bathroom in one suite is on the second floor while the bathroom in the other suite is on the first floor.

Located in a rural area of Ohio, the Inn at Brandywine Falls is a place to relax and use as a base from which to explore this diverse national park. You can ride a train, drive to Cleveland and take in the Rock and Roll Hall of Fame, or sit on the front porch and sip tea. Sixty-seven-foot Brandywine Falls is a short walk from the inn, or you can hike the 1.7-mile-long Brandywine Gorge Trail. Guests are encouraged

The James Wallace family, who came to this area in the early 1800s, built the farmhouse that is now The Inn at Brandywine Falls. Although difficult to visualize from today's serene setting, this was once the thriving community of Brandywine Mills. Wallace built a mill powered by the nearby waterfall and used money earned from the business to purchase 600 acres and build a farmhouse. The farmhouse passed through five owners before being purchased by the National Park Service. The property was renovated by innkeepers Katie and George Hoy under an agreement with the NPS.

to use the inn's living room, library, dining room, and porch. A full breakfast of fresh-squeezed juice, fruit-filled oatmeal, homemade bread, and an entree is served each morning from 7:00 to 10:00 A.M. (from 8:45 A.M. on weekends).

Rooms: Doubles, triples, and quads. All rooms have private baths.

Wheelchair Accessibility: One room on the first floor has wide doorways, the bathroom has grab bars, and the combination shower-tub has a stool.

Reservations: The Inn at Brandywine Falls, 8230 Brandywine Road, Sagamore Hills, Ohio 44067-2810. Phone (888) 306–3381, (330) 467–1812 or 650–4965. A 65 percent deposit is required with a reservation. A two-week cancellation is required for a full refund unless the accommodation is subsequently booked by another party. The innkeepers recommend that reservations be made at least two months in advance.

Arrival/Departure: Check-in between 4:01 and 6:45 P.M. and after 8:30 P.M. Checkout at 11:00 A.M.

Rates: Sunday through Thursday non-holiday prices: Main house rooms ($119); main house suite ($139); Carriage barn suites ($198); Fridays are $25 to $35 higher. Saturdays and holidays are $50 to $100 higher. Prices are for two persons and include a full breakfast. Additional persons are $10 to $35 per night, depending on age. A 10 percent discount is offered for stays of three days or more, except holidays, and two-day stays on Sunday through Thursday from January 15 through May. Holidays are excluded.

Location: In northeast Ohio, midway between Cleveland and Akron.

Season: Open year-round.

Food: Breakfast is included. Refreshments are provided at 4:30 P.M. Alcoholic beverages may be brought by guests. Over a dozen restaurants are within 6 miles of the inn.

Transportation: Scheduled airline service is in Cleveland and Akron/Canton, where rental cars are available.

Facilities: Dining room for breakfast.

Activities: Hiking and biking. Historic attractions, scenic railroad, museums, golf, and waterpark nearby. Cross-country and downhill skiing in the winter.

OREGON

Crater Lake National Park

P.O. Box 7 • Crater Lake, OR 97604 • (541) 594–2211 • www.nps.gov/crla

Crater Lake National Park encompasses 183,000 acres, including a deep blue lake that resulted from the collapse of Mt. Mazama, an ancient 12,000-foot volcano. A 33-mile paved road circles the lake. The summer days can be cool and the nights quite chilly. Heavy winter snowfall that averages 533 inches can keep portions of the Rim Road closed until July. Crater Lake is located in southern Oregon, 57 miles north of Klamath Falls. The major road into the park is Oregon Highway 62, which enters through the southwest corner. **Park Entrance Fee:** $10.00 per vehicle or $5.00 per person, good for seven days.

Lodging in Crater Lake National Park: The park has two very different facilities that provide overnight accommodations. Crater Lake Lodge offers seventy-one rooms in an old but newly remodeled four-story wooden lodge on the rim of Crater Lake. Mazama Village Motor Inn offers forty basic and less expensive rooms 7 miles south of the rim. While Crater Lake Lodge is one of the classic national park lodges, with a back patio, a large lobby, a cozy dining room, and two fireplaces, Mazama Village Motor Inn is more of a motel unit. Both locations have eating facilities.

CRATER LAKE LODGE

Crater Lake National Park, OR 97604 • (541) 830-8700 • www.craterlakelodges.com

Crater Lake National Park

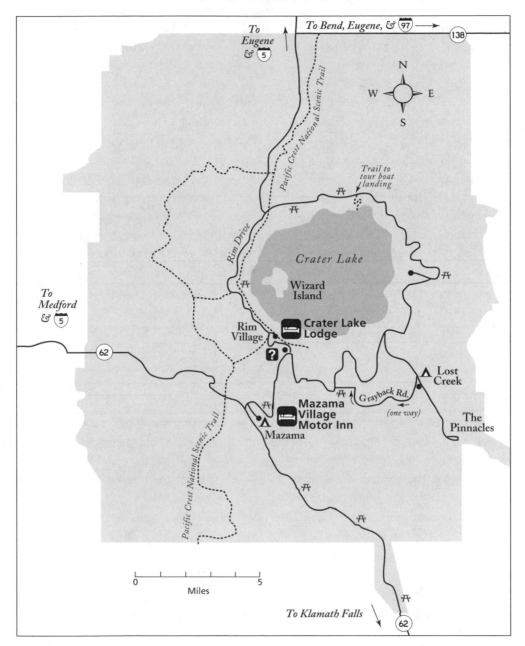

CRATER LAKE LODGE OFFERS A TOTAL OF SEVENTY-one rooms in a restored national park hotel. The four-story stone-and-wood building was originally completed in 1915 and reopened in 1995 after a six-year renovation. The building is on the rim of Crater Lake, allowing guests to view what many consider to be America's most beautiful lake from the window of some rooms. The lodge building has a cozy dining

Construction on Crater Lake Lodge commenced about a decade after Crater Lake became a national park in 1900. The building, while impressive from the outside, had many structural faults. Over the years major maintenance, including the installation of columns to support the ceiling and walls in the Great Hall, was required to keep the lodge in operation. The National Park Service assumed ownership of the lodge in 1967 and in the early 1980s started considering its demolition. The lodge was closed to visitors in 1989, but public and political pressure resulted in congressional support for a $15 million rehabilitation that included everything from a new foundation to a new roof frame. Essentially, the lodge was torn down and completely rebuilt from the ground up for a reopening in May 1995.

\|/

room on the first floor, which also has the registration desk, lobby, and Great Hall with its massive stone fireplace. Another stone fireplace is in the registration lobby. Two elevators are near the registration area on the first floor. Parking may involve a short walk, so it is best to unload your luggage from a loading zone in front of the entrance, then locate a parking spot. Bell service is available. Crater Lake Lodge is at the east end of Rim Village. The lodge is 15 miles from the north entrance to the park and 7 miles from the south entrance.

Rooms at Crater Lake Lodge are grouped into five price classifications depending on size, view, and beds. Four smaller rooms without a view, on the first floor, are cheapest, and four two-story loft rooms on floors three and four are most expensive. The remaining sixty-three rooms offer lake views, excellent lake views, or valley views. The remodeled rooms look

much newer than the exterior of the lodge would lead you to expect. All are nicely furnished and have heat but no air-conditioning, telephone, or television. Most rooms have full bathrooms with a combination shower-tub. A few rooms have bathtubs only. Rooms are entered from a center corridor that is accessed from elevators or a stairway near the registration desk. Beds vary from one to two queen-size beds. Rooms at the back look out on the lake; those at the front look across the parking lot toward the mountains. Prices depend on view and room size. Second-floor rooms have the largest windows and may be the best choice on the lake side. Third-floor windows in most rooms are high (your chin may rest on the windowsill), and fourth-floor windows are smaller but have window seats. The few first-floor rooms have virtually no view. Room 401, with one queen-size bed, offers a lake view from the claw-foot bathtub. Room 410 is quite large and has two window seats that provide a lake view. Room 213 allows guests to lie in bed and look out the window at Crater Lake. Room 221, a large corner room with two queen-size beds, offers good views of both Crater Lake and Garfield Peak. The four two-level loft rooms have a queen bed on each floor. Loft rooms are entered from the third floor, where guests can view the valley. Lake views are available from the bedroom on the fourth floor. Two loft rooms have the bathroom (claw-foot tub) on the third-floor entry level, while the other two loft rooms require guests to climb to the fourth-floor bedroom to reach the bathroom. Rooms on both floors are comparatively large.

Crater Lake Lodge is one of our favorite national park lodges. Situated in an outstanding location, the lodge provides travelers with a modern facility that radiates the rustic charm appropriate to one of our country's oldest national parks. The large back porch that spans the length of the original hotel has rocking chairs and offers a relaxing (and, often, chilly) place to view Crater Lake's deep blue water. Guests often spend much of their time in the Great Hall talking, playing cards and board games, reading, or just sitting in rocking chairs enjoying the flames and warmth of the huge gas log fireplace. Here is a place to make new friends on a lazy afternoon or after a meal in the cozy dining room. The dining room is quite small, and it is wise to make dinner reservations at the same time you book a lodge room.

Rooms: Doubles, triples, and quads. All rooms have a private bath, most with a shower-tub combination.

Wheelchair Accessibility: Six rooms on the first floor are ADA compliant. The front door to the lodge has a ramp access, and the side door nearest the wheelchair-accessible rooms is at ground level.

Reservations: Crater Lake Lodge, Crater Lake National Park, 1211 Avenue C, White City, OR 97503. Phone (541) 830–8700; fax (541) 830–8514. A deposit of one night's stay is required. A cancellation notice of forty-eight hours is required for a full refund less a $10 fee.

Rates: Ground floor ($129—4 rooms only); most rooms ($168-$180); two-level loft rooms ($248). Rates quoted are for two adults except the loft rooms, which are for four adults. Children eleven and under stay free in the same

room with an adult. Each additional person is $25. Weekend packages are offered in early spring and late fall.

Location: On the south rim of Crater Lake, 15 miles from the north entrance and 7 miles from the south entrance to Crater Lake National Park.

Season: Late May to mid-October. The lodge generally sells out from mid-June to the end of September.

Food: A dining room offers breakfast ($5.00–$10.00), lunch ($9.00–$13.00), and dinner ($18.00–$26.00). A children's menu is available. Alcoholic beverages are served. Reservations are only required for the dinner meal. Lodge guests get priority making dinner reservations. Nonguests may make only early or late reservations. A deli-style restaurant at Rim Village is scheduled to open in 2007. A family-style restaurant at Mazama Village offers pizza, pasta, and salads.

Transportation: Scheduled airline service is available to Klamath Falls, Medford, and Eugene, Oregon, where rental cars are available.

Facilities: A dining room. Rim Village, a short walk from the lodge, has a deli-style restaurant (opening in 2007).

Activities: Boat tours of Crater Lake, hiking, fishing, and ranger-guided walks.

Mazama Village Motor Inn

Crater Lake National Park, OR 97604 • (541) 594–2255 • www.craterlakelodges.com

Mazama Village Motor Inn offers a total of forty rooms in ten modern chalet-style wooden buildings. The one-story buildings, constructed in 1983, each contain four guest rooms and are situated around the outside of a paved one-way loop drive. Ample parking is directly in front of each building. The lodging complex is in a heavily wooded area a short distance from facilities in Mazama Village that include a market and a new family-style restaurant. Mazama Village Motor Inn is in the southern part of the park, at the intersection of Highway 62 and the road to Rim Drive. It is 7 miles from the rim and 22 miles from the north entrance of Crater Lake National Park. At an altitude of 6,000 feet, the complex offers warmer conditions than at the higher rim area.

All of the rooms at Mazama Village Motor Inn are identical in size, beds, and layout except for two that are wheelchair accessible. The rooms are nice, but this is basic motel-style lodging. Each room is relatively small and has two queen-size beds. The bath has a shower but no tub. There's also a coffeemaker. Each room has an entrance door in the front and a medium-size window in the back. No particularly good views are available from any of the rooms, and so no one room or building is preferable to any other. Each building has a picnic table in front. The wheelchair-accessible rooms have one queen-size bed and a somewhat larger bathroom.

The motor inn is a convenient place to stay on a one- or two-day visit to Crater Lake National Park. The rooms are basic but relatively close to places in the park you are likely to want to visit—in particular, the rim. The motor inn is within walking distance of Mazama Village, which includes a gas station, a market, a family-style restaurant, and laundry facilities. Evening programs are presented by National Park Service rangers at the nearby campground amphitheater, which is within easy walking distance. The motor inn is only a 7-mile drive from Rim Village, which has several restaurants and attractive Crater Lake Lodge.

Rooms: Doubles, triples, and quads. All rooms have private baths with showers only.

Mazama Village derives its name from the ancient volcano that formed what is now Crater Lake. This dormant volcano is a member of the Cascade Range, a string of volcanoes that extend from Lassen Peak in the south to Mt. Garibaldi near Vancouver, British Columbia. Mt. Mazama may once have towered to 12,000 feet above sea level before a violent eruption occurred about 7,700 years ago. After the chamber inside the mountain was emptied, the walls of the volcano collapsed to form a caldera that filled with water from rain and snow and resulted in the nation's deepest lake, at 1,932 feet.

Wheelchair Accessibility: Two rooms are ADA compliant.

Reservations: Crater Lake National Park, 1211 Avenue C, White City, OR 97503. Phone (541) 830–8700; fax (541) 830–8514. A deposit of one night's stay is required. A cancellation notice of forty-eight hours is required for a full refund less a $10 fee.

Rates: For all rooms ($110). Rate quoted is for two adults. Each additional person is $9.00 per night. Children eleven and under stay free with an adult. Rollaway or crib is $9.00 per night.

Location: On the south side of Crater Lake National Park, 8 miles from the west entrance.

Season: Early June to early October.

Food: A new family-style restaurant offers pizza, pasta, and salads. A deli-style restaurant at Rim Village will open in 2007.

Transportation: Scheduled airline service is available to Medford, Klamath Falls, and Eugene, Oregon, where rental cars are available.

Facilities: Restaurant, gift shop, market, laundry, public showers, gas station.

Activities: Hiking and evening naturalist programs, depending on snowmelt.

Oregon Caves National Monument

19000 Caves Highway • Cave Junction, OR 97523 • (541) 592–2100 • www.nps.gov/orca

Oregon Caves National Monument was established in 1909 to protect eleven small caves and a 3-mile-long cave that has endangered bats and all of the earth's six main rock types. The area covers 480 acres of old-growth forest, including part of the most diverse conifer forest in the world. The monument is located in southwestern Oregon, 20 miles east of Cave Junction via Oregon Highway 46. Although Oregon Highway 46 is paved, the last 8 miles are crooked and steep. Drivers should be cautious due to icy conditions in late fall or early spring. Parking at the monument is limited, especially for motorhomes and vehicles pulling trailers. Trailers can be dropped off at the Illinois Valley Visitor Center in Cave Junction or at Grayback Campground on OR 46.

Guided cave tours operate daily from mid-March through late November. Tour times and frequency vary by season, with summer tours beginning at 10:00 A.M. and ending at 6:00 P.M. The last tour of the day is usually a flashlight or candle tour. The cave temperature is 42° Fahrenheit year-round, so be sure to dress properly and wear shoes suitable for walking and hiking. Children must be at least 42 inches tall and pass a step test in order to qualify for a tour, but special tours are available for families with children who are too small to go on the regular tour. Canes, staffs, walking aids, and tripods are not permitted in the cave. **Monument Entrance Fee:** No charge.

Lodging in Oregon Caves National Monument: A classic six-story chateau with twenty-three guest rooms is the only lodging facility in this relatively small national monument. The chateau is at the end of the road near the entrance to the main cave. Motels and restaurants are in the town of Cave Junction.

Oregon Caves National Monument

THE CHATEAU AT THE OREGON CAVES

P.O. Box 1824 • Cave Junction, OR 97523 • (877) 245–9022 • www.oregoncavesoutfitters.com

THE CHATEAU AT THE OREGON CAVES REMAINS an undiscovered national park lodge for many seasoned travelers. Unlike numerous facilities that call themselves a lodge, but are not, at least in the traditional sense, the chateau is a classic lodging facility. The registration area, lobby, dining room, coffee shop, and all the overnight rooms are in the same alpine-style wooden building that was constructed in 1934 and became a National Historic Landmark in 1987. The lobby is entered on the building's fourth floor (which the chateau calls the first floor), and overnight rooms are on that floor and the two floors above. A restaurant and coffee shop are one floor below. The Chateau at the Oregon Caves is located at the end of Oregon Highway 46, 20 miles east of Cave Junction, Oregon.

The six-story chateau retains a coziness and warmth that modern hotels lack. It is completely covered with cedar bark sheathing, and wood shakes top the roof with its many gables. The large lobby area, with huge log supports and giant beams across the ceiling, is dominated by a double-hearth marble fireplace. Some of the original furnishings, including, chairs, card tables, writing desks, and a piano, remain in the lobby. Original furnishings are also in a few guest rooms. Parking is adjacent to the building. The chateau fills on summer weekends, but rooms are likely to be available on most weekdays.

All of the twenty-three guest rooms offer heat and a private bathroom, but no air-conditioning, telephone,

The first wooden buildings, including the original chalet, were constructed here in 1923 by a group of businessmen who hoped to profit from curious tourists attracted to the caves. The original building was expanded in 1941–1942 and currently serves as the visitor center and cave ticket office. The lower story is the original lodge, while the added story now houses employees. The current Chateau at the Oregon Caves was finished at a total cost of $50,000 in 1934 and remains relatively unchanged since its construction. A local nonprofit organization assumed management of the chateau in 2002.

The Chateau at the Oregon Caves served as the meeting place for two men, who together would alter the way people viewed nature . . . and other things. Harold Graves, a businessman and photographer from Portland, Oregon, was taking photographs in the park one day when he encountered another visitor, William Gruber. Gruber was carrying a tripod on which he had mounted two cameras side by side. The two men met later that evening in Graves's room at the chateau, where Gruber described his idea for a viewing device that would place the viewer in the middle of the scene. That meeting led to the development of the viewmaster, a viewing device familiar to nearly every child.

The Chateau at the Oregon Caves is a great place to spend several peaceful days. Spend the first afternoon taking one of the cave tours and the next day walking along the trails. The ticket office for the cave tour is directly across from the chateau. Arrive early enough and you may be able to do the cave tour and some hiking in the same day. On the other hand, maybe you would prefer sitting in the lobby and reading a good mystery. The chateau offers all the facilities you will need for a pleasant stay. The attractive dining room has large windows that look out over the ravine. A coffee shop is on the same floor.

Rooms: Doubles, triples, and quads. One family suite holds up to seven persons. All rooms have a private bath, although some on the third floor have only a tub or a shower. There are no wheelchair-accessible rooms.

Reservations: Oregon Caves Outfitters, P.O. Box 1824, Cave Junction, OR 97523. Phone (541) 592–3400 or (877) 245–9022. A deposit of one night's stay is required. A cancellation notice of forty-eight hours is required for a full refund less a $10 fee.

Rates: Economy ($80); standard ($90); deluxe ($105); suites ($125–$135). Rates are for two adults, and four adults in family suites. Children six and under stay free with an adult. Each additional person is $10 each per night. Special packages are offered throughout the season.

Location: Twenty miles south of Cave Junction, Oregon, at the end of OR 46.

Season: The lodge is open from May through mid-October. Cave tours are offered mid-March through late November.

Food: An attractive dining room is open for dinner only ($14–$22). Reservations are recommended but not required. A coffee shop on the same floor serves breakfast ($5.00–$11.00), lunch ($8.00–$12.00), real milk shakes, and snacks. The gift shop sells ice cream and beverages.

Transportation: The nearest scheduled air service is in Medford, Oregon, about 50 miles away. A shuttle (fee charged) operates from the lodge to Cave Junction visitor center and the Cave Junction airport.

Facilities: Gift shop with crafts made by local artisans, restaurant, and coffee shop.

Activities: Cave tours, ranger programs and nature walks, and hiking. Three major trails begin at the lodge.

or television. The rooms differ with respect to size, layout, view, and beds, which range from one double (economy room) to a queen plus two doubles (family suite). Most rooms are classified as standard or deluxe with one queen or two double beds. Some rooms offer a view of a tree-covered ravine while others overlook the parking lot or entrance road. Several rooms on the top floor are snuggled under gables. Five suites on the second and third floors each have two bedrooms and one bath. The chateau has no elevator, and second-floor rooms require climbing twenty-three steps while third-floor rooms require an additional fifteen steps. (Top-floor rooms are the quietest.) We like first-floor corner room 105 with two double beds, which is convenient to the lobby and offers a good view of the ravine. Room 205 directly above offers the same good view. Room 201 is quite large, has one queen bed, and offers a view and the pleasant sound of the waterfall. Room 312 has a unique toilet location. When arriving we suggest you ask to view several available rooms. You may find a room that is larger and/or offers a better view than your assigned room.

SOUTH DAKOTA

State Tourist Information
(800) 732–5682 | www.travelsd.com

Badlands National Park

P.O. Box 6 • Interior, SD 57750 • (605) 433–5361 • www.nps.gov/badl

Badlands National Park comprises 244,000 acres of prairie grasslands and scenic eroded landscape created millions of years ago by slow-moving streams. An ancient sea once covered this region, which contains a variety of fossilized remains including crabs, clams, and snails. When traveling east on Interstate 90, use exit 110 at Wall to access the Badlands Loop Road and its numerous exhibits, scenic overlooks, and self-guiding trails. Travelers driving west on I–90 access this road by using exit 131. The Ben Reifel Visitor Center in the park's eastern section has exhibits and a video presentation that help interpret the history and geology of the Badlands. Three other National Park Service units—Jewel Cave National Monument, Wind Cave National Park, and world-famous Mount Rushmore National Memorial—are a short distance west of Badlands National Park. Information on these and other nearby attractions is available at the visitor center in Badlands National Park. **Park Entrance Fee:** $10.00 per vehicle or $5.00 per person, good for seven days.

Lodging in Badlands National Park: Cedar Pass Lodge, with twenty-one small cabins and a large cottage, provides the only overnight accommodations in Badlands National Park. The lodge has a dining room and nice gift shop selling specialized items related to the plains and America's westward expansion. Additional accommodations are along the interstate. A two-story motel is just outside the park's boundary and within sight of Cedar Pass Lodge. Cedar Pass Lodge is 8 miles south of I–90 on Badlands Loop Road.

CEDAR PASS LODGE

20681 SD Hwy 240 • P.O. Box 5 • Interior, SD 57750 • (605) 433–5460
www.cedarpasslodge.com

One-bedroom Cabin
at Cedar Pass Lodge

Badlands National Park

To Kadoka

240

90

To Rapid City & Wall

Buffalo Gap National Grassland

240

590

502

Pinnacles

240

SAGE CREEK UNIT

Buffalo Gap National Grassland

? Ben Reifel Visitor Center

Cedar Pass Lodge

377

Interior

44

White River

N
W — E
S

10
5
Miles
0

To Wounded Knee

44

2

PINE RIDGE INDIAN RESERVATION

PALMER CREEK UNIT

589

27

White River ?

STRONGHOLD UNIT

2

Scenic

44

Buffalo Gap National Grassland

Cheyenne River

To Rapid City

To Rapid City

40

CEDAR PASS LODGE IS A COMPLEX OF SMALL, MOSTLY freestanding stucco cabins situated on each side of a U-shaped drive in a grassy area behind a wood-and-stucco registration building. The registration building also houses a restaurant and a large gift shop. No accommodations are in the main building, but all the cabins are a short walk from the registration desk and restaurant. A large parking lot is in front of the main building and adequate parking is directly beside or in front of each cabin. Cedar Pass Lodge sits in an area of grass and small trees at the east end of Badlands National Park, within view of the Badlands. It is 8 miles south of I–90 and just south of the park's main visitor center.

The lodge offers twenty-one cabins plus a large cottage unit. The cabins are similar, but each is a little different. They are small but nicely spaced and well-maintained both inside and out. Each cabin has carpeting, wood-paneled walls, and a private bathroom. Three one-bedroom cabins (3, 14, and 15), the three two-bedroom cabins (1, 2, and 16), and the cottage each have a combination shower-tub. The remaining cottages have showers only. The dark wall paneling and small windows result in relatively dark interiors, although adequate lighting is provided by a combination of lamps and ceiling lights. Picnic tables are scattered about the complex, and each cabin has a small front porch with a bench or two chairs. The cabins vary in size but most are freestanding one-bedroom units with two double beds or a double bed plus a single bed. Three two-room cabins have two doubles plus one queen or three doubles plus a single bed. Cabins 10, 11, and 12, each with one bedroom and two double beds, are fairly large and can accommodate a rollaway. These are at the end of a row of cabins and have front doors and porches that face east, away from the afternoon sun. On the same side of the road, cabin 3 has two double beds and an attractive exterior style. Across the road with no other unit nearby, cabin 33 with one queen bed has a similar exterior and is sometimes called "The Dollhouse." This is the smallest cabin at

Cedar Pass Camp was opened here in 1928 to provide refreshments to the growing number of sightseers to this area. By the 1930s the facility had become an important stop for Badlands travelers. The owner, Ben Millard, died here in 1956, and Cedar Pass Lodge was purchased by the National Park Service in 1964. Cedar Pass Lodge was operated by the Oglala Sioux Tribe of the Pine Ridge Indian Reservation from 1971 to 2002.

Cedar Pass Lodge. One large cottage (actually, a complete house with a fenced back yard) near the registration building has two bedrooms, one with a queen and the other with two doubles. It also has a living room/dining room and a full-size kitchen with a refrigerator, gas range, and washer and dryer. Pots, pans, and eating utensils are included. Try for the cottage if your party includes four or more people.

Cedar Pass Lodge is a convenient location from which to explore Badlands National Park. It is also a quiet and restful place to stay the night before or after a visit to nearby attractions Mount Rushmore National Memorial, Jewel Cave National Monument, Wind Cave National Park, and Custer State Park. The lodge is a short walk from the park's Ben Reifel Visitor Center, which includes exhibits to explain the geology and history of this rugged section of South Dakota. It is also near the park campground, where evening programs are presented in summer by National Park Service rangers. Guided walks and other programs are scheduled daily from various points in the park. An 80-mile loop drive through the park to the small town of Scenic and back through Buffalo Gap National Grassland on South Dakota Highway 44 offers an interesting day of sightseeing and hiking. Take a side trip to the town of Wall (north of the Pinnacles entrance to the park), where famous Wall Drug gives away ice water and sells coffee for a nickel.

Rooms: Singles, doubles, triples, and quads. Three cabins with two bedrooms and the cottage hold up to six adults. All units have a private bathroom, some with a shower and others with a combination shower-tub.

Wheelchair Accessibility: None of the cabins at Cedar Pass Lodge is ADA compliant. Cabin 1 is "wheelchair friendly."

Reservations: Cedar Pass Lodge, Box 5, Interior, SD 57750. Phone (605) 433–5460; fax (605) 433–5560. A credit card guarantee is required. Cancellation requires a twenty-four hours' notice.

Rates: One-bedroom cabin ($65); two-bedroom cabin ($80); cottage ($90). Rates quoted are for two people. Additional persons are $5.00. Children ten and under stay free. Prices are reduced from early to mid-May and from mid-September to closing in mid-October. AAA and AARP members receive a 10 percent discount.

Location: At the eastern end of Badlands National Park, 8 miles south of I–90 at exit 131. Guests who will be approaching on I–90 from Rapid City should take exit 110 and drive the Badlands Loop Road (South Dakota Highway 240), which passes by the lodge.

Season: April 15 to mid-October.

Food: A cafe-type restaurant serves breakfast ($4.00–$8.50), lunch ($5.00–$7.00), and dinner ($7.50–$16.00). Menu items include buffalo burgers, trout, and Sioux Indian tacos. A children's menu is available.

Transportation: The nearest commercial airport is in Rapid City, South Dakota, where airline service and rental vehicles are available.

Facilities: Restaurant, gift shop with a large selection of silver jewelry and crafts made by local artisans, National Park Service visitor center.

Activities: Hiking, evening interpretive programs.

Pets: Pets are permitted for an extra charge of $10 per pet, per night.

TEXAS

Big Bend National Park

P.O. Box 129 • Big Bend N.P., TX 79834 • (432) 477-2251 • www.nps.gov/bibe

Big Bend National Park covers 801,000 acres of wild and scenic desert, mountain ranges, steep-walled canyons, and ribbons of green plant life along the fabled Rio Grande. Because of its remote location, the park is not as crowded as some of the other national parks. Popular activities at Big Bend include bird-watching, hiking, and rafting on the Rio Grande. The park is located on the Mexican border in southwestern Texas. **Park Entrance Fee:** $10.00 per vehicle or $5.00 per person, good for seven days.

Lodging in Big Bend National Park: Chisos Mountains Lodge in the park's Basin area offers the only lodging in Big Bend National Park. The road to the Basin is not recommended for trailers exceeding 20 feet and RVs exceeding 24 feet. A trailer village at Rio Grande Village is available for visitors with trailers and motor homes.

CHISOS MOUNTAINS LODGE

Basin Rural Branch • Big Bend National Park, TX 79834-9999 • (432) 477–2291
www.bigbendresorts.com

*Casa Grande Motor Lodge
at Chisos Mountains Lodge*

TEXAS

Big Bend National Park

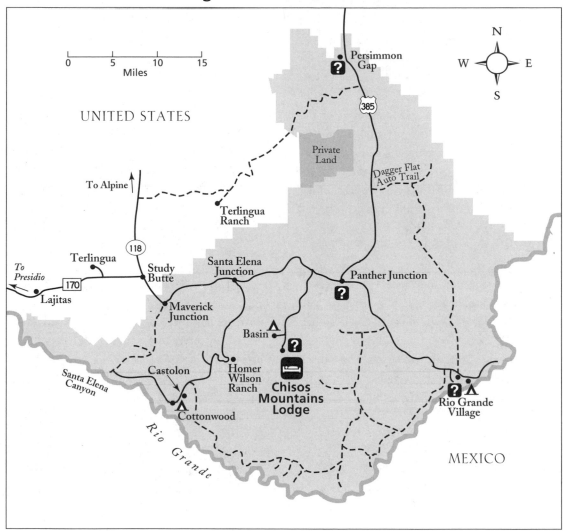

CHISOS MOUNTAINS LODGE IS A GROUP OF MOD-
ern motel-type units and older stone and adobe
cabins and lodge units in the scenic Basin area of Big
Bend National Park. All the lodging units rent for
about the same price and are open year-round. The
Basin area of Big Bend is approximately 40 miles inside the north park entrance, which itself is 40 miles
south of U.S. Highway 90. In other words, this is a
pretty remote lodge in a very remote national park.

The good news is the Basin area of the park provides
breathtaking scenery along with the outdoor experience you are probably seeking in a national park visit.
The lodge is at an altitude of 5,400 feet, which results
in moderate summer temperatures when much of the
rest of the park swelters in the desert heat. Scenery is
provided by the Chisos Mountains, which surround
and tower 2,000 to 3,000 feet above the Basin and are
fully contained within Big Bend's boundary.

Chisos Mountains Lodge is actually a combination of a main registration and food service building and four types of separate lodging units for a total of seventy-two rooms. All rooms have heat, a small refrigerator, a microwave, and a coffeemaker. About half the rooms are in three two-story motor-lodge-type buildings (called Casa Grande units) that offer private rear balconies with an excellent view of the surrounding mountains. Most of these units, built in 1989, have two double beds, although a limited number of rooms offer one queen or one double bed. Each room has a full tiled bath and air-conditioning.

Two one-story motel-type buildings constructed in the late 1970s each have ten rooms. That is, five rooms are located on each side of the building. As a result, these units do not have balconies and views are not as good as those in the Casa Grande section. Rooms have two double beds, a full tiled bath and air-conditioning. They are somewhat smaller than the rooms in Casa Grande.

The stone lodge units and adobe cottages offer a quieter setting a short distance away from the previously mentioned lodging units. One duplex and four

Bird-watching is a major activity at Big Bend National Park, where more than 450 species of birds have been identified. Although most are migrants that pass through on their way from wintering in Latin America, occasional rare species end up in Big Bend after wandering off-course. The Chisos Mountains of Big Bend are the only location in the United States where the rare Colima warbler can be observed. Multiday seminars on birding are regularly sponsored by the Big Bend Natural History Association.

Although the Rio Grande is one of the major natural features of Big Bend National Park, by the time the river forms the southern boundary of the park, most of the water is supplied by the Rio Conchos, which flows out of Mexico, rather than the headwaters of the Rio Grande. Much of the water of the Rio Grande has evaporated or been diverted for irrigation by the time the river reaches the western border of the park. Abrasive particles carried in the water give the river its impressive power to carve the canyons that have formed along its path.

freestanding stone cottages, constructed in the late 1930s, have three double beds and a bath with a shower but no tub. They also lack air-conditioning but do have ceiling fans. The thick construction and cross-ventilation generally result in a comfortable inside temperature. Most popular with frequent visitors to Big Bend are cottages 102 and 103, which offer the best mountain views of any of the park's lodging facilities. Cottage 100 is isolated and makes a nice honeymoon cottage. Eight 1950s-era stone lodge units situated near the cottages each have one single and one double bed, a full tiled bath, and ceiling fans. These units are in two buildings, each with four rooms. Access to one of the buildings involves climbing about thirty-two steps.

None of the rooms have a television or telephone, although a number of pay phones are scattered throughout the Basin area. Ice machines are scattered throughout the lodging area. Although you will probably be pleased with any of the lodging facilities, we recommend the Casa Grande units in buildings A, B, and C. Rooms in all three buildings are large, offer great views, and cost about the same as rooms in the other units. Rooms on the second floor have a better view and more privacy.

Other than the cottages and stone lodge units that are located a short distance from the main Basin area, the units are arranged in a circular fashion near the lodge building that houses registration, a small gift shop, and eating facilities. Adequate parking is available near each of the buildings, although a couple of the Casa Grande units require a climb of approximately thirty steps to reach the second floor. If stairs are a problem, you should note this in your reservation request. The stone cottages and lodge units are about a quarter mile away from the other units, but everything in the Basin is within walking distance. Also in the Basin is a small store, with a limited selection of groceries and camping supplies, and a post office substation. A National Park Service visitor center is next to the store. A variety of hikes and nature programs are offered in-season. A self-guided trail and access to several other trails originate near the lodge.

The Chisos Mountains Basin is only a small part of a very large national park that offers much to attract visitors, especially during the spring and fall, when temperatures are mild. The main National Park Service visitor facilities are at Panther Junction. Here you will find the main visitor center and a host of facilities, including a post office and gas station. Other major activity areas of the park center on Rio Grande Village, 20 miles southeast of park headquarters, which offers hiking, camping, a trailer park, a coin laundry, showers, groceries, general merchandise, gasoline, propane, and a visitor center. Castolon, a historic district 35 miles southwest of the visitor center, offers a campground, a ranger station, historic exhibits, and a frontier store that sells picnic supplies, groceries, and general merchandise.

Rooms: Doubles, triples, and quads. A few units sleep up to six. All rooms have private baths.

Wheelchair Accessibility: Four Casa Grande units are equipped with wheelchair-accessible features, although there are six steps leading into these units.

Reservations: Forever Resorts, Chisos Mountains Lodge, Basin Rural Branch, Big Bend National Park, TX 79834-9999. Phone (432) 477–2291; fax (432) 477–2352. A deposit of one night's stay is required. A cancellation notice of forty-eight hours is required for a refund; a $10 cancellation fee applies to all canceled reservations. Failure to arrive on the designated date means automatic forfeit of the deposit and cancels the reservation. Reservations in any calendar year may be made at the beginning of the previous year.

Rates: Casa Grande ($88); motel units ($88); cottage ($100); lodge units ($85). Rates quoted are for two adults. Each additional person is $10 per night. Children under twelve stay free with two paying adults.

Location: About 40 miles south of the north park entrance station and 30 miles east of the west entrance station.

Season: All of the lodging units are open year-round. Heaviest season is in the spring up to Memorial Day and in the fall following Labor Day. The lodge is heavily booked during Thanksgiving and Christmas holidays.

Food: A full-service restaurant serves three meals a day. Breakfast is served from 7:00 to 10:30 A.M., lunch from 11:30 A.M. to 4:30 P.M., and dinner from 5:30 to 8:00 P.M. Dinner prices range from $7.00 to $19.00. The restaurant is located in the main lodge building and is within walking distance of all the rooms.

Transportation: No public transportation is available to or through the park. Train and bus service is provided in the town of Alpine, about 110 miles north of the park. Airlines serve Del Rio, Midland-Odessa, and El Paso, where rental cars are available.

Facilities: The Chisos Basin has a store with a post office substation, visitor center, restaurant, and gift shop. A gas station, post office, and grocery are at Panther Junction. A variety of supplies and services are at Rio Grande Village, 20 miles southeast of the visitor center.

Activities: Hiking, bird-watching, guided walks, and National Park Service programs. Float trips on the Rio Grande are available with your own equipment (permit required) or through one of four local services approved by the Park Service.

U.S. VIRGIN ISLANDS

State Tourist Information
(800) 372–8784 | USVI-info.com

Virgin Islands National Park

1300 Cruz Bay Creek • St. Thomas, VI 00830 • (340) 776–6201 • www.nps.gov/viis

Virgin Islands National Park, encompassing nearly 14,700 acres, features quiet coves, blue-green waters, and white sandy beaches fringed by lush green hills. The park is located on St. John Island and can be reached via hourly ferry service across Pillsbury Sound from Red Hook, St. Thomas. Ferry service also operates from Charlotte Amalie. Major airlines fly from the U.S. mainland to St. Thomas and St. Croix. **Park Entrance Fee:** No charge.

Lodging in Virgin Islands National Park: Although a variety of lodging is available on the island, Cinnamon Bay Campground, with tents and cottages, offers the only accommodations within the national park. Cinnamon Bay is on St. John Island's north shore, midway across the island via North Shore Road. The campground is a fifteen-minute taxi ride from the town of Cruz Bay, where the ferries dock.

CINNAMON BAY CAMPGROUND

P.O. Box 720 • Cruz Bay, St. John • U.S. Virgin Islands 00831 • (340) 776–6330
www.cinnamonbay.com

Cottages at Cinnamon Bay Campground

Virgin Islands National Park

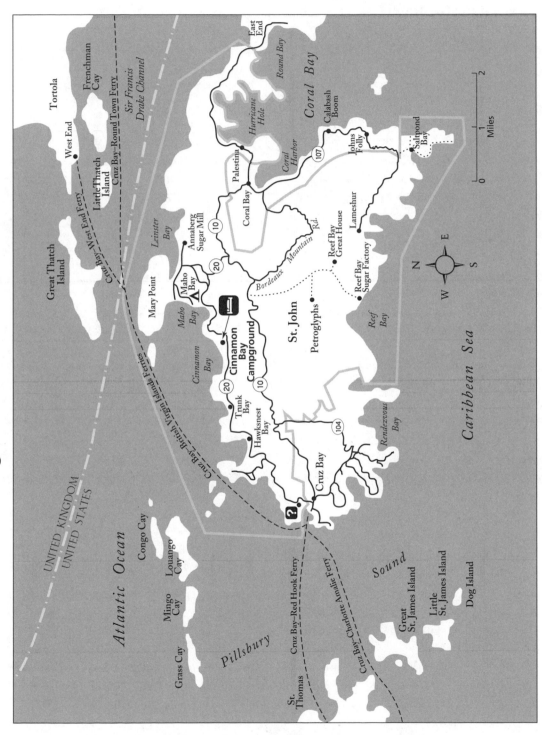

Cinnamon Bay Campground is a complex of cottages, tents, separate bathhouses, and a separate main building that houses a registration area, restaurant, and general store. The cottages and tents are grouped separately, with bathhouses available in each grouping. All the buildings are located in a natural area of trees a short walk from half-mile-long Cinnamon Bay Beach. The campground does not have a lodge with accommodations or the wood cabins you might expect to find at a Park Service lodging facility.

The forty cottages are 15 by 15 feet and constructed of cement sides and floor with front and back screening to allow breezes from the trade winds and have an outside terrace. Each cottage is equipped with electric lights, table and chairs, ceiling fan, picnic table, charcoal grill, propane stove, ice chest, water container, and eating and cooking utensils. Each has four twin beds that are made by the guest on the day of arrival. Additional linens can be obtained twice a week at the front desk. The central bathhouse has cool-water showers. The cost of the cottages varies, because those that are closer to the beach cost more than those farther away.

Forty-four tents have a wood floor and are 10 by 14 feet. Each tent includes four cots with a 3-inch mattress, propane stove, charcoal grill, gas lantern, ice chest, water container, and utensils. A picnic table is under a large canvas flap that extends from the front roof. As with the cottages, beds are made on the day of arrival, and fresh linens are available at the front desk twice a week. Three bathhouses scattered throughout the tenting area also have cool-water showers.

Staying at Cinnamon Bay Campground offers a different national park experience, one in which the accommodations permit a full appreciation of the natural surroundings. Both the cottages and the tents are a short walk from Cinnamon Bay Beach. Phones, safe-deposit boxes, and storage lockers are near the lodging facilities. A general store carries grocery items if you are interested in cooking some or all of your own

Rosewood Hotels & Resorts, the firm that manages Cinnamon Bay Campground, also operates exclusive Caneel Bay on the same island. Although separated by two bays and only a few miles, in cost and accommodations these two facilities are a world apart. For example, rooms at Caneel Bay run from $650 to $1400 daily, depending on season and type of accommodation. The 171 rooms include wall safes, personal bars, and handcrafted furniture. Three restaurants provide a choice of formal, eclectic, and casual dining.

meals. A restaurant is available when you choose to eat out. No laundry facilities are in the campground. Not surprisingly, water-based activities such as snorkeling are popular, and sailboards, sea kayaks, and sailboats are available for rent at a water sports center. Park rangers offer daily activities, which include walks, talks, and snorkeling. Reservations are required for most of the activities with park rangers (340–776–6201).

Rooms: Doubles, triples, and quads. None of the cottages or tents have a private bathroom.

Wheelchair Accessibility: One cottage and one tent are wheelchair accessible. The community bathrooms also have wheelchair-accessible facilities.

Reservations: Cinnamon Bay Campground, P.O. Box 720, Cruz Bay, St. John, U.S. Virgin Islands 00831. Phone (800) 539–9998; (340) 776–6330; fax (340) 776–6458. Reservations can be guaranteed with a credit card. A 50 percent deposit is required. Payment must be made in full at the time of check-in (personal checks are not accepted). Cancellations are required at least thirty days prior to arrival for a full refund. Later cancellations will be charged the equivalent of a three-night stay. Reservations for the winter months should be made at least four to six months in advance.

Rates: Cottages ($70–$90) from May 1 through December 14, ($110–$140) from December 15 through April 30; tents ($58) from May 1 through December 14, ($80) from December 15 through April 30. Rates quoted are for two adults. Children under three stay free with an adult. Each additional person is $17 per night. Meal packages are available.

Location: On the north shore of St. John Island, approximately 4 miles (fifteen minutes) from the town of Cruz Bay on the island's west end.

Season: Open year-round. Peak season is January through June.

Food: A restaurant serves three meals daily. Breakfast ($4.00–$8.00) is served from 7:30 to 10:30 A.M. Lunch ($6.00–$10.00) is served from 11:30 A.M. to 3:00 P.M., and dinner ($5.00–$20.00) is served from 5:30 to 8:30 P.M. Meal times vary in the off-season. Groceries are available at a general store.

Transportation: Ferries for Cruz Bay, St. John, leave from Red Hook ($3.00 per person) and Charlotte Amalie ($7.00 per person) on St. Thomas. Taxis (about $3.00 per person) provide transportation from Cruz Bay to the campground. For more information check the Web site at www .cinnamonbay.com or call (800) 539–9998.

Facilities: Restaurant, general store, beach shop, water sports center with boat rentals.

Activities: Swimming, snorkeling, fishing, hiking, National Park Service activities, and commercial guided tours.

UTAH

Bryce Canyon National Park

P.O. Box 170001 • Bryce Canyon, UT 84717 • (435) 834–5322 • www.nps.gov/brca

Bryce Canyon National Park comprises nearly 36,000 acres highlighted by numerous alcoves cut into cliffs along the eastern edge of the Paunsaugunt Plateau. The cliffs are bordered by badlands of vivid colors and strange shapes called hoodoos for which this park is most famous. A paved road with numerous scenic pullouts leads 18 miles south from the entrance to Rainbow Point. Trailers are not permitted beyond Sunrise Point, which lies about 3 miles inside the park entrance. The park is in southwestern Utah and most easily reached via U.S. Highway 89 to Utah Highways 12 and 63.

A free shuttle service that begins outside the park serves the lodge and the northern portion of the park. Lodge guests and other park visitors can hop on and off the shuttle at the lodge and ten additional stops including the NPS visitor center, Inspiration Point, and Bryce Point. The shuttle operates from late May until early September. **Park Entrance Fee:** $20 per vehicle, good for seven days.

Lodging in Bryce Canyon: Bryce Canyon Lodge, with several types of accommodations, offers the only lodging in Bryce Canyon National Park. All of the rooms are comfortable and within easy walking distance of both the main lodge and spectacular Bryce Canyon. The lodge is in the northern section of the park, about 1.5 miles south of the park entrance and the visitor center. Privately operated motels are just outside the park entrance.

BRYCE CANYON LODGE

1 Bryce Canyon Lodge • Bryce Canyon National Park, UT 84717 • (435) 834–5361
www.brycecanyonlodge.com

Main Lodge at
Bryce Canyon Lodge

Bryce Canyon National Park

Bryce Canyon Lodge offers a total of 114 rooms in a complex of two motor lodge units, fifteen multiunit cabin buildings with forty rooms, and an impressive wood-and-stone main lodge building that houses the restaurant, registration area, and three suites and a studio. The main lodge was constructed in the 1920s and has been completely renovated. The lodge was designed by Gilbert Stanley Underwood, the same architect who designed the Ahwahnee in Yosemite, Zion Lodge, and Grand Canyon Lodge on the North Rim. The attractive lobby area has a huge stone fireplace surrounded by chairs. A large brick porch with chairs and benches stretches across the entire front of the building and offers guests a pleasant place to spend idle time. The porch faces a wooded area that separates the lodge from the canyon rim. Bryce Canyon Lodge is located near the rim of the canyon, about 1.5 miles south of the park visitor center and entrance station.

Construction on Bryce Canyon Lodge began in 1923, and the foundation and skeletal work were completed the following year. The original building, with upstairs accommodations and an office, lobby, dining room, kitchen, showers, and toilets on the main floor, was completed by May 1925. Wings and a rock facade were added the following year, when the lodge was opened for operation. In September 1927, the recreation hall was added, and sixty-seven standard and economy cabins were grouped around the lodge. The few original cabins that remain are currently used as employee housing. The other economy cabins were sold and moved. By September 1927, five deluxe cabins (the current Western Cabins) had been constructed. The remaining ten deluxe cabins were completed by 1929.

Each of the three types of lodging facilities at Bryce Canyon Lodge is attractive. All of the rooms have heat, carpeting, a fan, and a telephone, but no air-conditioning or television. Forty Western Cabins are built from two to four to a building. Most of these cabins have two queen-size beds, a gas fireplace, and a dressing room with a sink. The full tiled bathrooms were totally refurbished in 2004–2005. The log and limestone cabins, constructed in the 1920s, are roomy and nicely finished. Most of the Western Cabins have log-beamed vaulted ceilings and shake roofs. Each has a private covered front porch with a bench. Cabins 506, 517, 525, 533, and 537 have windows and porches that face a large wooded area but are a walk from the parking area. Two two-story motor lodge buildings have a total of 70 rooms that were renovated in 2004. Each room has two queen-size beds (a few have one queen), and a full tiled bath. These units each have a private covered balcony with a table and two chairs. Rooms are on either side of the building and are entered through a central corridor that can be accessed at either end or in the middle. Although the lodge classifies these as "motel" units, they are actually larger and the buildings are more attractive than most motels. Rooms on the second floor and in the back of the building provide the most privacy and best view.

The main lodge building houses three second-floor suites and one studio. These are the only sleeping rooms in the main lodge. The suites each have a bedroom with one queen-size bed and a separate sitting room; both rooms have ceiling fans. The suites also have a full tiled bath but no balcony. These rooms are nice and roomy, and it is convenient to stay in the main lodge, where the restaurant and lobby are located. The single studio is identical to the suites but without a separate sitting room.

Bryce Canyon Lodge is a pleasant place to spend several days while you explore this national park. It sits in a heavily treed area with attractive vistas and numerous outdoor activities. The lodge is near Bryce Canyon.

A short walking trail from the front porch of the lodge leads to spectacular overlooks along the rim. An information desk in the hotel lobby provides information on the area and several tours that originate near the lodge. The main lodge building, with a restaurant and gift shop, is within easy walking distance of all the lodging facilities. The attractive restaurant has two large stone fireplaces and serves three meals daily. We suggest you choose the Western Cabins, especially if you plan to stay two or more nights.

Rooms: Doubles, triples, and quads. All rooms have a full bath.

Wheelchair Accessibility: Each of the two hotel units offers two first-floor end rooms with wheelchair accessibility. The buildings have ramp access, but the rooms are some distance from parking. A large bathroom has an extra-wide door and grab bars by the toilet. One room in each building has a roll-in shower while the other has a tub-shower combination. The main lodge, with the registration area, restaurant, and gift shop, has ramp access from the parking lot in the back. None of the Western Cabins or suites is wheelchair accessible.

Reservations: Xanterra Parks and Resorts, 6312 S. Fiddlers Green Circle, Suite 600N, Greenwood Village, CO 80111. Phone (888) 297-2757; fax (303) 297-3175; www.bryce canyonlodge.com. Reservations may be made up to thirteen months in advance. A deposit of one night's stay is required. Cancellation notice of forty-eight hours is required for a refund.

Rates: Western Cabins ($131); motel units ($126); suites ($141); studio ($111). Children sixteen and under stay free with an adult. Each additional person is $10 per night. Roll-aways are $10.00 and cribs are $5.00 per night.

Location: The lodge is near the north end of Bryce Canyon National Park, about 1.5 miles south of the visitor center that is located near the park entrance station. The lodge is within walking distance of the rim of the canyon.

Season: Bryce Canyon Lodge is open from April 1 through November 1. The park is open year-round.

Food: A full-service restaurant serves breakfast ($5.00-$9.50), lunch ($6.00-$9.00), and dinner ($14.00-$22.00). Beer and wine are available. A children's menu is available. Reservations are recommended for dinner. Groceries and

Bryce Canyon Lodge is the only remaining lodging facility constructed in this region in the 1920s by the Utah Parks Company, a subsidiary of the Union Pacific Railroad. The Union Pacific was interested in stimulating tourism to the region and competing against other railroads that were building similar facilities in Glacier National Park, Yellowstone National Park, and the South Rim of the Grand Canyon. The "U.P. loop" consisted of lodges at Zion National Park, the North Rim of the Grand Canyon, Bryce Canyon, and Cedar City, where a spur line connected to the Union Pacific main line in Lund. Unable to sell the operation, the Union Pacific in 1972 donated all of the Utah Parks Company's property, including lodges, cabins, curio shops, and service stations, to the National Park Service, which soon signed TWA Services, a subsidiary of Trans World Airlines, as concessioner.

snacks are available at a general store at Sunrise Point, about 1 mile from the lodge.

Transportation: Airlines serve Cedar City, St. George, and Salt Lake City, Utah, and Las Vegas, Nevada. Rental cars are available at each of these airports. Greyhound/Trailways serves St. George and Cedar City. Amtrak serves Salt Lake City.

Facilities: A full-service dining room and gift shop are in the main lodge building. A general store 1 mile north of the lodge near Sunrise Point has snacks and groceries.

Activities: The National Park Service conducts a variety of lectures, nature walks and talks, and slide presentations. A schedule with times is posted at the visitor center. Two-hour and half-day mule and horse trips into the canyon are offered daily. Information on these and other activities is available at the tour desk located in the lobby.

Zion National Park

S.R. 9 • Springdale, UT 84767 • (435) 722–3256 • www.nps.gov/zion

Zion National Park comprises approximately 147,000 acres of colorful canyons and mesas that create phenomenal shapes and landscapes. Scenic drives and trails provide access to canyons, sculpted rocks, cliffs, and rivers in one of the most beautiful areas operated by the National Park Service. Zion is in southwestern Utah, with the southwest entrance approximately 150 miles northeast of Las Vegas, Nevada.

The National Park Service operates a bus transportation system in Zion National Park. All visitors except those with confirmed reservations at Zion Lodge are required to use the system to access Zion Canyon. The entry fee to the park includes unlimited access to the free park shuttle system, which comprises two loops: the Springdale loop connects the town of Springdale with the visitor center and transportation center just inside the park entrance. The second loop operates from the visitor center to the end of Zion Canyon Scenic Drive. Zion Canyon Lodge is one of several stops on the Zion Canyon Scenic Drive shuttle. The Mount Carmel area on the park's east side remains accessible by vehicle. The drive is very beautiful but exceedingly slow. **Park Entrance Fee:** $20 per vehicle (all occupants) or $10 per person, good for seven days.

Lodging in Zion National Park: Zion has only one lodging facility inside the park. Zion Lodge is located on Zion Canyon Scenic Drive, north of Utah Highway 9, which crosses the southeastern section of the park. Driving Zion Canyon Scenic Road to the Zion Lodge requires a permit that must be displayed on the vehicle windshield. The permit can be obtained at the visitor center or, sometimes, at one of the entrance stations. Proof of a lodge room reservation is required to obtain a permit. Have proof of lodge registration handy when entering the park so you won't be required to locate a parking place at the busy visitor center. Additional lodging is available in the town of Springdale, just outside the southwest entrance.

ZION LODGE

Zion National Park • Springdale, UT 84767 • (435) 772–3213 • www.zionlodge.com

Motel Units at Zion Lodge

Zion National Park

Z ION LODGE COMPRISES A CENTRAL LODGE BUILD-ing that houses registration and dining facilities, plus seventeen separate but nearby buildings that provide a total of 121 rooms for overnight accommodations. No overnight rooms are in the main lodge building. The lodge is situated in a grassy area of cottonwood trees surrounded by the beautiful red sandstone cliffs that make this such a scenic national park. The North Fork of the Virgin River is across the road from the lodge. The wood and Navajo sandstone main lodge building is a one- and two-story, V-shaped, ranch-style structure that was constructed in 1966 on the site of the original lodge, which burned earlier in the year. The new lodge is attractive but does not have the majestic look of its sister lodges at Bryce Canyon and the

North Rim of the Grand Canyon. Zion Lodge is located 3 miles north of the main park road, on Zion Canyon Scenic Drive. The lodge is approximately 3.5 miles north of the National Park Service visitor center.

Three types of accommodations are available at Zion Lodge. All of the lodging is separate from but near the main lodge building. All rooms have heat, air-conditioning, carpeted floors, a telephone, and a hair dryer but no television. Forty Western Cabins each offer two double beds, a gas fireplace, and a full tiled bath. The cabins were constructed either two or four units to a building, in the 1930s, and the interiors were remodeled in 1997–1998. These wood-framed cabins with vaulted ceilings are very similar in design and size to the western log cabins in both Bryce Canyon and

A camp of wood-framed tents opened in 1916 on the site of Zion Lodge. The original lodge, designed by Gilbert Stanley Underwood (1890–1961), was constructed in 1925 for the Union Pacific Railroad, which wanted to promote tourism in southern Utah. The current Western Cabins were constructed in the late 1920s. Fire destroyed the main lodge during renovations in the winter of 1966. The present building, which underwent a major renovation in 1989–1990, was completed only three months after the fire.

the North Rim of the Grand Canyon. The cabins are closely clustered in the front and at the end of one of the motel buildings south of the main lodge. Each cabin has a private porch. Cabins that face west toward the parking lot offer a better location and view. These include cabins 505, 509, 516, 517, 518, 520, 522, 523, 528, and 529.

Seventy-five motel-type rooms are in two large, two-story motor lodge buildings, which were remodeled in 1998–1999. A stone fireplace is in the central lobby area of the larger of the two buildings. Rooms have two queen-size beds (some have only a single queen) and a full tiled bath. Each room has a private covered balcony with two chairs and a table. The rooms are accessed from an interior corridor that runs the length of each building. The best rooms for privacy and views are at the rear of the second floor of each building. These are all odd-numbered. Six two-room suites on the second floor of the motel buildings offer a bedroom with a king bed and a sitting room with a queen sofa bed, chairs, and a refrigerator. The suite includes two sinks and a bathroom with a toilet and combination shower-tub. Each suite has a large covered balcony with table and chairs.

The choice between a Western Cabin and a room in one of the two motel buildings is pretty much a toss-up. Rooms in the motel units are quite nice and offer more interior space than the Western Cabins, which are somewhat smaller than similar Western Cabins at Bryce Canyon and the North Rim of the Grand Canyon. If the nights will be cool and you enjoy a gas fireplace, then paying a few extra dollars for a Western Cabin is probably money well spent. Keep in mind, however, that the cabins are closely spaced and have relatively small front porches. The choice between the Western Cabins and other lodging is not nearly as clear-cut in Zion as at its sister parks, Bryce Canyon and the North Rim of the Grand Canyon.

Zion Lodge is a comfortable, quiet place to spend one or more days while you explore magnificent Zion National Park. The setting is both attractive and convenient. Be aware that summer months generally bring hot days to Zion, and daytime temperatures often reach 100° Fahrenheit. The main lodge has most of the facilities you will need for a stay in the park. A large grassy area in front of the lodge provides a nice place to

Navajo sandstone, which forms the canyon walls in Zion National Park, is a porous rock that absorbs rainfall. The moisture percolates through the rock and may require many decades (some say centuries) to reach the base of a large cliff. Perhaps the best example in Zion of this phenomenon is 2,000-foot Weeping Rock, where you can walk under the rock and feel the water dripping. Moisture seeping from the rock results in hanging gardens and spring wildflowers. Weeping Rock is accessed via a quarter-mile trail from Zion Canyon Scenic Drive north of Zion Lodge. This is a stop on the tram tour.

read a book, eat a picnic lunch, or lie on a blanket under a cottonwood tree. A lobby in front of the registration desk has chairs and benches for relaxing. A spacious, wood-paneled restaurant on the second floor serves three meals a day. The restaurant has large front windows that offer an outstanding view of the front grounds and colorful canyon walls surrounding the lodge. A large balcony is available for outside dining when weather and temperature permit. A cafe at the north end of the main lodge building serves pizza, sandwiches, and beverages and has patio seating. A coffee bar serves specialty coffees. The lodge also has a tour desk, auditorium, post office, and gift shop. A 0.6-mile paved trail to Lower Emerald Pools begins opposite Zion Lodge. The longer, 2-mile walk leads to Middle Emerald Pools. The free shuttle that traverses Zion Canyon Scenic Drive stops beside the lodge.

Rooms: Doubles, triples, and quads. All rooms have a full bath.

Wheelchair Accessibility: Four first-floor wheelchair-accessible rooms are in the motel building nearest the lodge registration building. These rooms have either one or two queen beds, and two of the rooms have bathrooms with roll-in showers. The other two rooms have a combination shower-tub with grab bars. Two Western Cabins offer partial wheelchair accessibility with ramp access, but the exterior and bathroom doorways are too small for wheelchair access. One of these Western Cabins has an extra large bathroom with grab bars. An elevator in the main lodge building provides wheelchair access to the restaurant on the second floor. Shuttle buses serving the lodge are equipped for wheelchair access.

Reservations: Xanterra Parks and Resorts, 6312 S. Fiddlers Green Circle, Suite 600N, Greenwood Village, CO 80111. Phone (888) 297-2757; fax (303) 297-3175. A deposit of one night's stay is required. A cancellation notice of forty-eight hours is required for a full refund.

Rates: Western Cabins ($143); motel ($133); suites ($149). All rates quoted are for two adults. Children sixteen and younger stay free. Each additional person is $10. Rollaways are $10.00 and cribs are $5.00 per night. Discount rates are offered December to mid-March, and special packages are also available in the off-season.

Location: Three miles north of the main park highway on Zion Canyon Scenic Drive.

Season: All of the units of Zion Lodge are open year-round. The lodge is often full from early April through October.

Food: An attractive restaurant on the second floor of the main lodge building serves breakfast buffet ($9.00) from 6:00 to 10:00 A.M., lunch ($7.00–$8.00) from 11:30 A.M. to 2:30 P.M., and dinner ($10.00–$20.00) from 5:00 to 10:00 P.M. Dinner reservations are required and should be made prior to or immediately upon arrival; otherwise you are likely to end up with a very early or very late dinner. Alcoholic beverages are served. A children's menu is available. A coffee bar in the lobby is open from 6:00 A.M. to 1:00 P.M. A cafe at the north end of the main lodge building offers outside dining with pizza, sandwiches, salads, ice cream, soft drinks, and beer from 11:00 A.M. to 7:00 P.M. in season. Groceries and restaurants are in the town of Springdale and can be reached via the free shuttle that stops beside the lodge.

Transportation: Scheduled airlines serve Cedar City, St. George, and Salt Lake City, Utah, and Las Vegas, Nevada, where rental cars are available. Scheduled bus service is available to St. George and Cedar City. Amtrak serves Salt Lake City.

Facilities: Post office, gift shop, restaurant, coffee bar, and cafe.

Activities: A tour desk in the main lodge building can arrange horseback rides and guided tours. Naturalist programs are offered throughout the park by National Park Service personnel. Schedules are posted at the front desk of the lodge and in the visitor center, which shows a fifteen-minute orientation film. Hiking is a popular activity in Zion National Park.

VIRGINIA

Shenandoah National Park

3655 U.S. Highway 211 East • Luray, VA 22835 • (540) 999–3500 • www.nps.gov/shen

Shenandoah National Park comprises 199,000 acres of forested mountains through an 80-mile stretch of the Blue Ridge Mountains. Most of the park's features lie alongside 105-mile Skyline Drive, a slow but scenic two-lane road that wanders along much of the crest of the mountain range. The road accesses lodges, campgrounds, and overlooks from the north entrance at Front Royal to the south entrance near Waynesboro, Virginia. The park brochure provided at entry stations identifies places of interest and park facilities according to mile markers alongside the west side of the road. The park has more than 500 miles of hiking trails, including a 101-mile stretch of the Appalachian Trail. Shenandoah National Park is located in northern Virginia, with the northern entrance some 60 miles west of Washington, D.C. The south entrance connects with the north end of the Blue Ridge Parkway. The northern half of the park tends to be the most crowded. Shenandoah National Park is the northern terminus for the Blue Ridge Parkway, which meanders through Virginia and North Carolina. The parkway is listed in the North Carolina section of this book. **Park Entrance Fee:** $10.00 per vehicle or $5.00 per person, good for seven days.

Lodging in Shenandoah National Park: Three locations in Shenandoah National Park provide lodging facilities, all of which are in the central section between mile markers 40 and 60. Big Meadows Lodge and Skyland Resort are relatively large complexes with historic lodge and cabins, and modern lodging units. Lewis Mountain Cabins is a very small facility with cabins only. All three facilities are operated by the same concessioner, ARAMARK.

Reservations for All Lodging Facilities: ARAMARK Convention and Tourism Services, P. O. Box 727, Luray, VA 22835. Phone (800) 999–4714 or (540) 743–5108; fax (540) 743–7883; www.visitshenandoah.com. The first night's deposit by check is required within ten days of booking a reservation. Full refund of deposit requires a seventy-two-hour advance cancellation.

Transportation: Scheduled airline service is available to several towns surrounding Shenandoah National Park, including Washington, D.C. (use Dulles), and Charlottesville and Harrisonburg, Virginia. Bus service is available to Waynesboro, just outside the south entrance to the park, and Amtrak (800–872–7245) provides passenger rail service to Charlottesville, Virginia. No public transportation is available in the park.

Shenandoah National Park

Front Royal

Dickey Ridge

522

Compton Gap

Bentonville

Gravel Springs Gap

211 522

Mathews Arm

Washington, VA

Elkwallow

340

Sperryville

522

Thornton Gap

81

Luray

Panorama

231

211

BUS 340

Skyland

Skyland Resort

340

Stanley

Big Meadows Lodge

Big Meadows

Byrd

Lewis Mountain Cabins

Madison

Shenandoah

Lewis Mountain

Elkton

230

29

33

Swift Run Gap

Standardsville

33

33

340

Simmons Gap

Loft Mountain

Grottoes

Dundo Group Camp

810

Appalachian Trail

340

64

Rockfish Gap

Crozet

Waynesboro

250

Charlottesville

64

Miles

0   5   10

N
W   E
S

BIG MEADOWS LODGE

P.O. Box 727 • Luray, VA 22835 • (540) 999–2221 • www.visitshenandoah.com

*One-Story Lodging Unit
at Big Meadows Lodge*

BIG MEADOWS LODGE IS A COMPLEX CONSISTING OF a historic main lodge building plus five cabins, all of which were constructed in 1939, and six one- and two-story lodge buildings that together offer a total of ninety-seven rooms. All of the buildings are in close proximity so that guests have an easy walk from any of the rooms to the main lodge, which houses an attractive dining room, a large greatroom, and a downstairs taproom, or tavern. Excellent views of the Shenandoah Valley are available from the dining room, the greatroom, and a large stone porch that runs across the backside of the main lodge. The main lodge also has overnight rooms on three floors. Registration parking is just outside the building, and adequate parking is near most of the lodging units. Big Meadows is in a heavily forested area at an altitude of 3,510 feet and is located at milepost 51, about midway between the north and south entrances to Shenandoah National Park. The northern entry point to Big Meadows is via U.S. Highway 211 from Luray, Virginia. The lodge is 15 miles north of Swift Run Gap Entrance and U.S. Highway 33.

Big Meadows Lodge offers five categories of accommodations: main lodge rooms (rooms in the main building), cabins, lodge rooms, mini-suites, and suites. All of the rooms have a private bathroom, carpeting, wood paneling, and heat, but no air-conditioning or telephones. Only suites and mini-suites have a television, and only the cabins, suites, and mini-suites have a fireplace. The main lodge has twenty-five relatively small rooms on three floors. Most of these rooms have one double bed or two twin beds and will accommodate two persons only. Two larger rooms have two double beds and one room has a queen-size bed. Each room in the main lodge has a private bathroom with a tub, a shower, or both. Rooms 1 through 6 on the main floor provide good valley views. Rooms on the upper floor have dormers and are entered from an interior hallway that is accessed from a stairway in the lobby of the main lodge and also from an outside doorway. An elevator in the greatroom provides access to the bottom floor and the taproom but not to second-floor rooms. As in many older hotels and lodging buildings, the main lodge at Big Meadows has some quirky and interesting rooms. One of these is 13 and 14, which has two separate bedrooms and two separate bathrooms. It can only be rented as one room because of the single fire escape. Room 23 on the second floor has a private stairway and a good valley view but is above the kitchen and its associated noises.

Six one- and two-story lodge buildings house sixty-two rooms in a combination of suites, mini-suites, and standard lodge rooms. Rooms in each category have a balcony or patio with a table and chairs. Four one-story lodge buildings sit end to end on a wooded hillside. Three of these buildings (Piedmont, Blackrock, and Hawksbill) were constructed in the 1940s, while the other (Crescent Rock) offers only mini-suites and was built in 1986. The standard lodge rooms in these one-story buildings have two double beds and are relatively small. The rooms each have a private bathroom, most with a combination shower-tub, although a few have a shower only. Two rooms in Piedmont have two bedrooms while most of the rest of the standard lodge rooms have connecting doors. Two newer two-story lodge buildings (Doubletop and Rapidan) sit on a hillside overlooking the valley. Rooms in these buildings are larger and rent for slightly more than rooms in the one-story units. In addition, they each have a private balcony or patio that offers good valley views, especially from the second floor. Rooms on the second floor of these two buildings have a vaulted ceiling and ceiling fan.

Ten mini-suites in the Crescent Rock building each have one large room with a vaulted ceiling, a stone fireplace (wood provided), a television, coffeemaker, and a nice balcony with table and chairs. Eight of the mini-suites have a king-size bed and a sofa bed, while the other two, which are wheelchair accessible, have one double bed and chairs. The six suites each have two rooms, a small bedroom with either two double beds or one king, plus a large living room with a stone fireplace, chairs, a sofa bed, a small refrigerator, a coffee-

maker, and a private balcony. The suites are situated at the ends of three one-story lodge buildings and connecting doors allow the addition of another bedroom (at an extra charge) to make a two-bedroom suite.

Five wooden duplex buildings provide ten cabin rooms near the main lodge. The cabins sit in a grassy area surrounded by trees and offer no particularly good views. Each cabin has paneled walls, carpeting, a stone fireplace with wood provided, and connecting doors, so both cabins in a building can be rented as a single unit. Each has a small bathroom with a shower only. All except one cabin have one bedroom, most with a double bed, although a few have two twin beds. One cabin has two bedrooms, one with a double bed and the other with two twins. This unit has a bath and a half but rents for only $5.00 per night more than the one-bedroom units. The cabins are quite small and only one (120) has a large screened front porch. The other cabins have chairs on the lawn near the front steps.

With all these lodging options, where will you stay? If the season is right and you enjoy a fireplace,

Big Meadows Lodge, named for a nearby grassy meadow, is constructed of stones cut from the Massanutten Mountains across the Shenandoah Valley. Built by Civilian Conservation Corps and mountain labor, the lodge was completed in 1939 and is listed on the National Register of Historic Places. Paneling in the bedrooms and the dining room came from the native chestnut trees that once grew here on the Blue Ridge but were virtually wiped out by the 1930s blight. Beams in the lounge and dining room are native oak. Heavy cement shingles protect the building from the harsh mountain winters.

choose one of the cabins. These are relatively small but nicely spaced and close to the main lodge. If you don't care about a fireplace or the season isn't right for a fire, our suggestion would be a second-floor room in one of the two-story lodge buildings, Doubletop or Rapidan. Choose a room on the second floor of Doubletop and you will only have to climb a half flight of stairs. The disadvantage of these buildings is that they are not directly next to a parking lot. Compared to rooms in the one-story lodge buildings, these rooms are larger and offer a great view for a few dollars more. If you want to splurge, choose one of the ten mini-suites in Crescent Rock. We like these better than the more expensive suites.

Big Meadows Lodge is a relaxing place to spend several days, especially in the fall when the morning air is crisp and trees present their parade of brilliant colors. The greatroom in the main lodge retains its original 1930s appearance, with a large stone fireplace, a row of rocking chairs, handcrafted furniture including sofas and chairs, and outstanding vistas from large picture windows. Here you can enjoy a good book, play a board game, or just sit and enjoy the scenery. Or maybe you will want to walk out back and enjoy the view from a chair on the stone patio. The attractive dining room, with its beamed vaulted ceiling and a wall of windows overlooking the valley, is a wonderful place to linger over a cup of coffee or a trout dinner. Activities include guided hikes, ranger programs at the nearby campground, and numerous special events such as Virginia wine tasting weekends and craft demonstrations. Nightly entertainment is offered in the taproom. The large National Park Service visitor center near the entrance to Big Meadows offers exhibits, information, and several video presentations. Large windows provide terrific views. A nearby general store sells camping equipment, limited groceries, and fast-food items.

Rooms: Doubles, triples, and quads. Suites will accommodate up to six adults. Connecting rooms are available in the main lodge and in one of the regular lodging units. All rooms have a private bath, although some have only a shower or a tub.

Wheelchair Accessibility: Three rooms, two mini-suites, and one regular lodge room are wheelchair accessible. The mini-suites in Crescent Rock have ramp access, one double bed in a very large room, and a bathroom with a wide doorway, grab bars, a combination shower-tub, and a high toilet. The main lodge room, with a double bed, has ramp access and a bathroom with a wide doorway, a roll-in shower, and a high toilet with grab bars. The dining room and taproom are wheelchair accessible.

Rates: Main lodge ($67–$114); cabins ($85–$90); lodge units ($85–$96); mini-suites ($124); suites ($127). Higher rates for weekends and daily in October. Rates quoted are for two adults. Each additional adult in a lodge room is $10.00 per night. Children under sixteen years of age stay free. Special packages are offered seasonally.

Location: At milepost 51.2, about midway on Skyline Drive between the north and south entrances to Shenandoah National Park.

Season: Last week in April to last week of October.

Food: A full-service dining room serves breakfast ($5.00–$7.50), lunch ($5.00–$9.00), and dinner ($9.00–$26.00). Beer and wine are available. A children's menu is available. A taproom opens each afternoon to serve appetizers, sandwiches, pizza, and chili. A convenience store at the entrance to Big Meadows has limited groceries and a coffee shop that serves breakfast and fast-food items including burgers and fries from 9:00 A.M. to 8:00 P.M.

Facilities: Restaurant, gift and craft shop, taproom, conference room, and a nice playground area for children. A gas station, coffee shop, convenience store, and National Park Service visitor center are at the nearby Big Meadows Wayside.

Activities: Hiking, National Park Service hikes and programs. Special events are coordinated throughout the season by the concessioner. Call (800) 999–4714 or visit the Web site.

LEWIS MOUNTAIN CABINS

P.O. Box 727 • Luray, VA 22835 • (540) 999–2255 • www.visitshenandoah.com

*A Duplex Cabin
at Lewis Mountain Cabins*

Lewis Mountain is one of the smallest lodging units in all the national parks. The entire complex consists of one building with a registration desk and a small store, seven one-story structures that provide a total of nine overnight rooms, and a hikers' cabin. Lewis Mountain Cabins has no lobby, dining room, swimming pool, or cocktail lounge. A small parking lot is beside the registration building, and all the cabins are a short walk away. A loading area is in front of each cabin. The entire complex is in a heavily forested area with no particularly good views but a lot of quiet and privacy. Lewis Mountain Cabins is at mile marker 57.5, in the central section of Shenandoah National Park. It is about 6 miles south of Big Meadows.

The nine cabins at Lewis Mountain date from the 1930s but are well maintained both inside and out. Each has wood paneling, hardwood floors, electric heat, and private baths with a shower, with the exception of one two-bedroom wheelchair-accessible cabin that has a combination shower-tub. The cabins do not have air-conditioning, telephone, or television. Each cabin has a small front porch with two chairs plus a covered picnic pavilion with a table, barbecue pit, electric

light, and electrical outlets. Wood is not provided but is available for purchase at the store. Two of the buildings are constructed as duplexes, with two cabin rooms per unit. These four cabin rooms each have one double bed. Five of the buildings have two bedrooms, one on each side of a bathroom. The two-bedroom units, which cost about $25 per night more than the one-bedroom duplex cabins, have a double bed in each bedroom. The single hikers' cabin with two bunk beds has a potbellied stove

In the early 1940s, Virginia still had "separate but equal" facilities for African Americans. The Lewis Mountain area was originally designated for blacks and called Lewis Mountain Negro Area. The National Park Service was responsible for caring for the campground, picnic area, and utilities, while the concessioner constructed the original five cabins. An additional two cabins were brought in later.

but no bath or running water. Public bathrooms are located in the store and the nearby campground. Bunk beds have mattresses, but guests must supply their own linens for the hikers' cabin.

Lewis Mountain Cabins is the smallest and one of the least expensive lodging options in Shenandoah National Park. This is an especially inviting place where you can take an evening stroll through the adjacent picnic area or along a stretch of the Appalachian Trail that runs beside the nearby campground. Sitting on the front porch of cabin 8 early one morning, we watched a young bear come out of the woods, climb a tree, look around, climb down, and then search the complex for something to eat. What a great way to start the morning! With only one double bed, the cabins provide adequate interior space and the separate covered patio is a nice place to grill steaks. Don't forget to bring food to cook because the small store across the road offers limited groceries. Big Meadows is only a short distance north on Skyline Drive if you decide to eat at a restaurant. Cabin 10 has one double bed and offers the most quiet and privacy with a front porch that is next to the woods. Cabin 1 and 2 (the five two-bedroom cabins are each assigned two numbers) is probably the best choice if you want two rooms. If you anticipate good weather and want to save money, choose the hikers' cabin for $25 per night. This unit is small but has a nice covered patio with a picnic table. Besides, who wants to stay inside at such a nice location in the Blue Ridge Mountains?

Rooms: Doubles, triples, and quads. Each cabin has a private bathroom.

Wheelchair Accessibility: One cabin has ramp access and an extra large bathroom that has a wide door, a high toilet, and a combination shower-tub with a tub chair and grab bars. The store, showers, and laundry are wheelchair accessible.

Rates: Single-bedroom cabins ($71); two-bedroom cabins ($97); hikers' cabin ($25). Higher prices are charged on weekend nights and during October. Special packages are available seasonally.

Location: Between mile marker 57 and 58, near the midpoint of Skyline Drive. Lewis Mountain is about 6 miles south of Big Meadows.

Season: First week in May to the last weekend in October. The cabins tend to be full on all weekends and during July, August, and the first part of October.

Food: No restaurant or other dining facilities are at Lewis Mountain. A small store with limited groceries is in the registration building.

Facilities: Small store, pay showers, and laundry facility.

Activities: Hiking.

SKYLAND RESORT

P.O. Box 727 • Luray, VA 22835 • (540) 999–2211 • www.visitshenandoah.com

Laurel Building at Skyland Resort

SKYLAND RESORT IS A WIDE-RANGING COMPLEX OF approximately three dozen one- and two-story structures, including twenty-six buildings and cabins that provide overnight accommodations. Lodging buildings range from freestanding rustic cabins constructed in the early 1900s to a modern two-story motel-type building with twenty rooms. Some of the buildings sit on a bluff, others are along a wooded hillside, but most are on a plateau overlooking the beautiful Shenandoah Valley. The registration building at the top of the hill has a small, comfortable lobby with chairs, tables, a television, and a wall of windows offering an outstanding view of the Shenandoah Valley. An adjacent building has a craft and gift shop, a taproom, a small lounge area, and a nice dining room with windows that provide a valley view. Chairs on a patio area between the two buildings offer a pleasant place to sit and view the valley. Lodging structures are scattered about a wide area, although three lodge buildings on the top of the hill are near the registration and dining buildings. Many of the remaining buildings and cabins are down a hill and some distance from the dining room. Many, but not all, of the 178 rooms at Skyland Resort offer good views of the valley. Some have great views from private balconies, while views from other rooms are blocked by trees or nearby buildings. Skyland Resort is at mile marker 42, 10 miles north of Big Meadows in the central section of Shenandoah National Park. Situated at 3,680 feet, it is at the highest point on Skyline Drive.

The lodging complex offers four classes of accommodations: lodge rooms, cabins, family cabins, and suites. A wide range of prices applies to each category depending on size, view, and beds. All the rooms have wood paneling, a private bathroom, a coffeemaker, and heat, but no air-conditioning or telephone. The six suites and about half the lodge rooms each have a television. Most rooms at Skyland Resort are in a series of sixteen one- and two-story lodge buildings that sit on a bluff on the edge of a plateau and overlook the valley.

These buildings vary in size and age, but most have two double beds and a private bathroom with a combination shower-tub. All the lodge rooms have either a balcony or a patio. Views vary depending on where the building is located and whether trees are between the building and the valley. An excellent and relatively private view of the valley is available from a large corner room (73) on the ground floor in the Shenandoah building. This is one of our favorite lodge rooms. A suite on the second floor of the same building offers a similar view at a higher price. Staying in a room at Shenandoah requires walking an uphill grade from the parking lot. Two-story Laurel, constructed in the late 1980s, is one of the two newest buildings in the complex. Each room has two double beds and a private balcony that generally offers excellent valley views. Choosing a second-floor room in this building would be a good choice. Another good choice would be the second floor of the Pinnacles building, which is closer to the dining room. Both Pinnacles and Laurel sit on hillsides, so entry is easier to a second-floor room than a first-floor room. Raven's Nest is the only lodge building with rooms that have king beds. Parking for this

The Skyland area was originally developed in the 1850s to mine copper. Surrounding timber was used to make charcoal for a copper smelter. It was not until 1886 that the son of one of the original mine owners considered the possibility of developing the area as a resort. By the early 1900s Skyland had a dining hall, a recreation hall, bathhouses, and bungalows, all paid for by the sale of cabin sites and loans. The developer ran Skyland as a concessioner for the National Park Service until 1937.

building is down a hill, so climbing is required to reach the building from the parking lot.

The least expensive accommodations at Skyland Resort are twenty cabins in ten historic buildings constructed between 1906 and 1922. Most of the cabins have a bathroom with a shower only and a small porch with chairs. The cabins tend to have small windows and dark, paneled interiors. None of the cabins has a television. The units are scattered among trees, and most do not offer a view of the valley. In addition, most are not close to the registration building or dining room. Cabins differ in both size and beds, ranging from six small units with one double bed to a large freestanding unit with a separate bedroom, kitchenette, a gas fireplace, and a large front porch. The latter, cabin 68, also called Byrd's Nest, is our pick of the cabins even though it doesn't offer a valley view. Cabin 173, with a queen bed and separate living room fronted by a large picture window, offers a commanding view of the valley. This unit does not have a balcony but is a good choice.

Three cabins were restored and converted in 2005 from multiple-family units back to their original status as freestanding cabins. Now classified as family cabins, these units have either one or two separate bedrooms and each features a living room, a large porch with a picnic table, and a kitchenette with a sink, microwave, small refrigerator, and eating utensils. One of the family cabins can sleep six adults while the other two sleep four. Two of these units have a gas fireplace. Family cabins rent for about twice the rate of most other Skyland cabins.

Six suites each comprise two rooms on the end of four lodge buildings. Four of the suites are in buildings near the dining room and two are in buildings down the hill on a plateau. Each suite offers a living room with a sofa bed and a wood-burning fireplace (wood provided), plus a separate bedroom. Beds vary from a double plus a twin to two queens. The two suites down the hill offer a view of the valley, but the four suites

nearer the registration building each have a balcony with valley views blocked by trees.

Skyland Resort, the largest lodging facility in Shenandoah National Park, offers accommodations for a wide range of tastes, from historic cabins for visitors who want to experience the rich history of this region to modern lodge rooms for people who want to enjoy the natural beauty of the Blue Ridge Mountains, but in style. This is a place where people come for weddings, family reunions, honeymoons, and weekend rest periods. A conference hall convenient to many of the cabins and lodge rooms can be reserved (fee charged) for planned gatherings. Your main decisions in choosing a room will be lodge room or cabin, valley view or nature view, and double beds, queen beds, or king bed. Lodging units are spread over a fairly wide area, so if location and/or view is an important consideration, be certain this is stated when making a reservation. Activities at Skyland and nearby locations include horseback riding, pony rides, guided hikes, ranger programs, and special events such as craft displays, workshops, and festivals sponsored by the concessioner. The resort includes an attractive dining room that serves three meals a day and has a wide range of menu options. A large taproom serves salads, soups, sandwiches, and pizza beginning in the early afternoon. Nightly entertainment is offered here.

Rooms: Doubles, triples, and quads. Some suites sleep up to five, and one family cabin accommodates up to six adults. Some rooms, including the suites, can connect with adjacent rooms. All rooms have a private bath with a shower or a combination shower-tub.

Wheelchair Accessibility: Four lodge rooms in Pinnacles (nearest the dining room) and two in Laurel (the newest building at Skyland Resort) are wheelchair accessible, with ramp access, wide bathroom doorways, a high toilet, and a combination shower-tub with grab bars. One family cabin has ramp access, wide doorways, and a bathroom with grab bars and a roll-in shower. The restaurant and craft/gift shop each have ramp access.

Rates: Lodge units ($85–$110); cabins ($62–$107); suites

($119–$165); family cabins ($210-$220). Higher rates for weekends and daily in October. Lodge rooms, cabins, and four suites are priced for two adults; family cabins and two suites are priced for four adults. Each additional person is $10.00 per night. Children under sixteen stay free. Special packages are offered seasonally.

Location: At milepost 42, about midway on Skyline Drive between the north and south entrances to Shenandoah National Park. Skyland is the northernmost lodging facility in the park.

Season: End of March to the end of November.

Food: An attractive dining room serves breakfast ($5.00–$7.50), lunch ($5.00–$9.00), and dinner ($9.00–$26.00). Beer and wine are available. A children's menu is available. An adjacent taproom serves appetizers, soups, salads, sandwiches, and pizza beginning in the early afternoon.

Facilities: Restaurant, taproom, craft and gift shop, conference hall (fee), large children's playground, stables, trails.

Activities: Hiking, horseback riding, pony rides, National Park Service ranger-led programs, nightly entertainment. Special events are coordinated throughout the season by the concessioner. Call (800) 999–4714 or visit the Web site.

WASHINGTON

Mount Rainier National Park

Tahoma Woods, Star Route • Ashford, WA 98304 • (360) 569–2211• www.nps.gov/mora

Mount Rainier National Park encompasses 235,625 acres, including the greatest single-peak glacial system in the United States. This is one of the most popular mountain-climbing areas in the country. Mount Rainier, the ancient volcano at the center of the park, is surrounded by snow, forests, and subalpine flowered meadows. Visitor centers are at Sunrise, Ohanapecosh, Paradise, and Longmire, the latter being the park's oldest developed area. The Sunrise visitor center, at 6,400 feet, is the highest point in the park reached by road. The road from the Nisqually Entrance in the park's southwest corner to Longmire is considered one of the world's most beautiful forest roads. Mount Rainier National Park is in southwestern Washington, 89 miles south of Seattle. It is 64 miles west of the town of Yakima, Washington. **Park Entrance Fee:** $10.00 per vehicle or $5.00 per person, good for seven days.

Lodging in Mount Rainier National Park: Mount Rainier has two inns that each offer very different lodging experiences. National Park Inn is a small, cozy lodge in a heavily forested area with a view of Mount Rainier. The much larger and busier Paradise Inn offers more of an alpine experience, at a higher altitude and with better mountain views. Despite the different environments, the two lodges are both in the southern end of the park and only about 13 miles apart.

NATIONAL PARK INN

Mount Rainier National Park • Longmire, WA 98397 • (360) 569–2275
www.guestservices.com/rainier

Mount Rainier National Park

NATIONAL PARK INN IS A SMALL BUT NICE TWO-story wooden lodge with twenty-five overnight rooms, all but two of which are on the second floor. The inn is at an altitude of 2,700 feet, surrounded by an old-growth forest of Douglas fir, western red cedar, and western hemlock. National Park Inn retains the character of an early 1900s lodge even though the building has been completely modernized. The inn is entered from a large parking area in back of the building. The lodge is on Washington Highway 706, 6 miles from the southwest entrance to Mount Rainier National Park. It is 13 winding miles from the much larger inn at Paradise.

The twenty-five rooms at National Park Inn are all very different in terms of size, beds, and bathrooms. In general, the rooms are comfortable but small. Two suites each have two rooms, one with a double bed and the other with two twin beds. All of the rooms have

The current National Park Inn was the annex of the original lodge, most of which burned in 1926. The inn was subsequently reopened and underwent a major remodeling in 1936. Another extensive renovation occurred in 1989, when the inn was essentially rebuilt from the ground up for reopening in May 1990. The adjacent building currently housing the gift shop was constructed in 1911 and is the only structure at this location that is still on its original site.

heat, window fans, coffeemakers, hair dryers, and bathrobes, but no air-conditioning, telephone, or television. All but seven rooms have private baths, which have a tub, shower, or both. Rooms without a private bathroom have an in-room sink and access to community showers and baths on the second floor. Beds range from one queen to two double beds. Although the rooms can be quite dissimilar, with the exception of the two suites, the cost for two adults depends only on whether or not a room has a private bath. Rooms with a bath cost about $35 per night more than rooms without a private bath. Room 7 has a bath and is much larger than average. Rooms 6, 8, and 10, with a bath, and 12 and 14, without a bath, which are along the front of the building, have a good view of Mount Rainier when the mountain isn't shrouded in clouds. All rooms are entered from an inside corridor that is accessed via a stairway from the lobby area. No elevator is available. Two handicap-accessible rooms are on the first floor.

National Park Inn is much smaller and cozier than the lodge at Paradise. It is a comfortable place to rest overnight or to stay for several days. There aren't a lot of people here and activities in the immediate vicinity

are minimal, but if you desire a comfortable and quiet place to read a book, get to know your spouse and kids, or just recharge your batteries, the National Park Inn can't be beat. A large covered porch with numerous chairs runs the length of the building. A guest lounge just off the check-in area has a large stone fireplace, sofas, tables, chairs, games, and puzzles. Complimentary tea and cookies or scones are served here each afternoon. An informal dining room on the opposite side of the lobby serves three meals a day. A tiny post office is located in a "closet" next to the registration desk. The general store next door sells gifts, limited groceries, beer, and wine. A National Park Service visitor center and a museum with exhibits on geology and wildlife are only a short walk from the inn.

Rooms: Doubles, triples, and quads. Eighteen of the twenty-five rooms have private baths. Community baths are on the second floor.

Wheelchair Accessibility: The inn has two ADA compliant rooms on the first floor where the registration desk, guest lounge, and dining room are located.

Reservations: Mount Rainier Guest Services, P.O. Box 108, Ashford, WA 98304-0108. Phone (360) 569–2275; fax (360) 569–2770. Credit card guarantee required when the reservation is made. Cancellation requires seven days' notice plus a $15 handling fee. Less than seven days' notice results in a charge for one night's room rate plus tax.

Rates: Rooms with baths ($132); rooms without baths ($98). Rates quoted are for two adults. Two-room unit with bath ($181). Rates are for three adults. Each additonal person is $15. Children under two stay free with an adult, using existing bedding in the room. Special winter packages are available October through April.

Location: Six miles from the southwest entrance to Mount Rainier National Park on WA 706. The inn is 13 miles from Paradise, the park's other lodge.

Season: Open all year.

Food: A pleasant dining room on the main floor is open for breakfast ($5.00–$8.00), lunch ($7.00–$9.00), and dinner ($13.00–$19.00). A children's menu is available. Snacks and drinks may be purchased at the gift shop/store next door.

Transportation: The nearest major airport is SeaTac, located between Seattle and Tacoma, Washington, where rental cars are available. Amtrak also serves these cities. Two ground shuttle services operate between Seattle and Mount Rainier National Park. They are Rainier Overland Shuttle (360-569-0851) and Rainier Shuttle (360–569–2331).

Facilities: Dining room, post office, general store that sells gifts and some food items, museum, National Park Service visitor center, hiker information center. The store rents cross-country ski equipment during winter months. Lessons are available. Gasoline is not available in the park but may be purchased at Ashford and Elbe.

Activities: Hiking, fishing, ranger-guided walks, snowshoeing, cross-country skiing.

PARADISE INN

Mount Rainier National Park • Paradise, WA 98398 • (360) 569–2275
www.guestservices.com/rainier

Main Lodge at Paradise Inn

Paradise Inn is expected to be closed for renovations during the 2006 and 2007 seasons.

PARADISE INN IS A LARGE WOODEN TWO-STORY lodge building with an attached four-story annex that offers some of the most striking views of the park's snow-covered peaks, including Mount Rainier. The inn has 117 rooms, most of which are in the annex that is reached via an enclosed walkway from the lobby of the main building. The primary structure was completed in 1917, and the annex was added in the 1920s. Paradise Inn is located at the base of Mount Rainier at an altitude of 5,400 feet, in the southern end of Mount Rainier National Park, 19 miles from the park's southwest entrance station.

The inn is on a hill such that the outside entry to the lobby is the hotel's third floor. An immense stone fireplace is at each end of the huge two-story lobby, which has a vaulted ceiling and runs most of the length of the building. The lobby is filled with tables, benches, sofas, and stuffed chairs. Massive log beams frame a mezzanine that wraps around the inside of the floor above. The large parking lot is often crowded, so it is best to temporarily park beside the entrance to unload luggage. Assistance with luggage can be requested at the registration desk. There are no elevators, so access to all guest rooms other than those on the third floor requires climbing stairs.

Paradise Inn has several categories of rooms, all of which have heat but no air-conditioning, telephone, or television. The thirty-one least expensive rooms without private bath are all in the main lodge building. These very small rooms (approximately 8 feet by 12 feet, including a small open closet area) have a sink and beds ranging from two twin beds to one double bed, to one double plus a single. Room 469 does not have a private bath and is quite large, with three double beds. It is the only room in the hotel that can hold six people without adding a rollaway. Room 470, also without a private bathroom, is somewhat larger than average and has a double bed plus a futon. It is next to the stairway, which may result in additional noise. The thirty-one rooms without a bath share two showers, one men's restroom, and one women's restroom. Additional restrooms are on the floor below near the stairway. The next room classification includes seventy-four rooms with bath, nearly all of which are in the annex. Bathrooms have a tub, shower, or both. Rooms have two twin beds, a double plus a twin bed, two double beds, or one queen-size bed.

Ten rooms have two bedrooms and one bath. One bedroom has a double bed, a queen, or a double plus a twin, and the other has two twins. The bath is in a small hallway and accessible from either bedroom. These rooms have the added amenity of a coffeemaker and rent for about $60 per night more than the one bedroom with a bath, so you might consider one of these if you are traveling with children. Paradise also offers two suites, each with a bedroom with a queen-size bed, a separate sitting room with a futon, a refrigerator, a coffeemaker, and a private bath.

Rooms in both the main lodge building and the annex offer varying views, but none have a particularly good view of Mount Rainier. When making a reservation you should consider that rooms in the annex are on four floors, and there is no elevator. Thus, you may be required to climb two flights of stairs each time you go to or from your room. Ask for a room on the third floor (the hotel entry level) if you want to avoid climbing stairs. Rooms 317 and 319, each with two double beds, enjoy a large window area that offers good views

The original structure of Paradise Inn, including the existing lobby, dining room, kitchen, three storerooms, and guest rooms above the dining room, was constructed in 1917 of Alaskan cedar salvaged from standing dead timber resulting from a nearby fire in 1885. The huge logs were hauled by horse-drawn wagons from an area near Narada Falls and Canyon Rim to the present site. The ceiling-high cedar logs and attached bracing were added later to support the roof under the heavy snowfalls in the Paradise area. The original inn offered thirty-three rooms, and the attached annex was added in the 1920s. Most of the lobby's woodwork was done by a German carpenter, who used only an adze in his work. He also built an unusual piano and a huge grandfather clock, which remain in the lobby.

of a mountain range. Room 411 allows guests to look out the window while taking a bath.

Paradise Inn is a classic national park lodge. At an altitude of 5,400 feet, this area can be quite cool and foggy, even during summer. Paradise is a heavily visited area of Mount Rainier National Park, and lots of people, both guests and visitors, seem to constantly browse through the lobby area. Tables and chairs on two sides of the mezzanine offer a more relaxing place to read, play cards, or just people-watch. Complimentary tea and cookies are served for guests here each afternoon from 3:00 to 5:00. An attractive 200-seat dining room with a beamed ceiling is just off the lobby on the main floor. A few entrées served are not found on most menus, such as Buffalo Stew, a luncheon item, and Buffalo Meatloaf with Jack Daniel's Sauce, which is on the dinner menu. A lounge, gift shop, snack bar, and post office are on the same floor. A large visitor center within walking distance of the lodge also has an observation floor, exhibits, a grill, and gift shops. The area around Paradise is noted for many varieties of sub-alpine flowers, which bloom in July and August as the snow is melting.

Rooms: Singles, doubles, triples, and quads. Not all rooms have private baths.

Wheelchair Accessibility: Five rooms on the entry floor of the annex each have two twin beds and a large bathroom. The bathroom includes a wide bathroom door and a combination shower-tub with grab bars. The five wheelchair-accessible rooms are classified as basic rooms with a private bath. Disabled parking spaces are near the front door of the hotel.

Reservations: Mount Rainier Guest Services, P.O. Box 108, Ashford, WA 98304-0108. Phone (360) 569–2275; fax (360) 569–2770. A credit card guarantee is required when the reservations are made. A minimum of seven days' notice must be given for a full refund less a $15 handling fee. Less than seven days' notice results in a charge for one night's room rate plus tax.

Rates: Rooms without a bath ($92); rooms with a bath ($137); two-room units with a bath ($194); suites with sitting room ($211). Rates for two-room units and suites are for three adults. Each additional person is $15. Children under two stay free with an adult, utilizing existing bedding in the room.

Location: Paradise Inn is on Highway 706, 19 miles from the southwest entrance to Mount Rainier National Park.

Season: The lodge is open from mid-May through the first part of October, depending on weather.

Food: A large dining room seats 200 and offers breakfast ($7.00–$9.00), lunch ($6.00–$13.00), and dinner ($11.00–$20.00) daily, with a special Sunday brunch. Alcoholic beverages are available. No reservations are taken. A children's menu is available. A grill with sandwiches, hamburgers, soups, and beverages is located in the visitor center and open from 10:00 A.M. to 7:00 P.M.

Transportation: The nearest major airport is SeaTac, located between Seattle and Tacoma, Washington, where rental cars are available. Amtrak also serves these cities. Two ground shuttle services operate between Seattle and Mount Rainier National Park. They are Rainier Overland Shuttle (360-569-0851) and Rainier Shuttle (360–569-2331).

Facilities: Restaurant, gift shop, post office, lounge, snack bar, hiker information center, and nearby National Park Service visitor center. Gasoline is not available in the park but may be purchased at Ashford and Elbe.

Activities: Hiking, guided walks, evening programs in the lobby, fishing, mountain climbing, snowshoeing, cross-country skiing, snowboarding, and tubing.

North Cascades National Park
Lake Chelan National Recreation Area
Ross Lake National Recreation Area
810 State Route 20 • Sedro-Woolley, WA 98284 • (360) 856–5700 • www.nps.gov/noca

The North Cascades National Park complex, covering 1,069 square miles, offers magnificent alpine scenery that is unmatched in the continental United States. Heavy precipitation has produced alpine lakes, waterfalls, ice caps, more than 300 glaciers, and glacier-carved canyons such as Stehekin (Native American for "the way through") that sits at the head of 55-mile-long Lake Chelan. Compared to many of the other national parks, this scenic park is relatively wild and uncrowded. The park complex is located in northern Washington (the north boundary borders on Canada). Primary access to the area is via Washington State Route 20, which bisects the park through a portion of the Ross Lake section. **Park Entrance Fee:** No charge.

North Cascades National Park/Lake Chelan National Recreation Area
Ross Lake National Recreation Area

BRITISH COLUMBIA

WASHINGTON

Skagit River

To Hope, B.C.

CANADA

UNITED STATES

Hozomeen

N

W   E

S

NORTH CASCADES
NATIONAL PARK

NORTH UNIT

Ross Lake

ROSS LAKE
NAT. REC.
AREA

OKANOGAN
NATIONAL
FOREST

Pacific Crest National Scenic Trail

**Ross Lake
Resort**

Diablo

Newhalem

*Baker
Lake*

*North Cascades Hwy.
(Closed in Winter)*

Colonial
Creek

North Cascades

20

*To
Mazama*

*To
Concrete*

Marblemount

NORTH CASCADES
NATIONAL PARK

SOUTH UNIT

Skagit River

20

Rockport

MOUNT BAKER–
SNOQUALMIE
NATIONAL FOREST

LAKE CHELAN
NAT. REC.
AREA

530

Darrington

0   5   10
Miles

**Stehekin
Valley Ranch**

**North Cascades
Stehekin Lodge**

WENATCHEE
NAT. FOREST

Stehekin
Landing

Lake Chelan

*Toll Ferry
to/from
Chelan*

Lodging in North Cascades National Park Service Complex: Three major lodging facilities are in the North Cascades National Park Complex. Two of the three are in or near the village of Stehekin at the north end of Lake Chelan in Lake Chelan National Recreation Area. The other is at the south end of Ross Lake in Ross Lake National Recreation Area. Stehekin Valley Ranch is a privately owned facility surrounded by the North Cascades National Park Complex but is unregulated by the National Park Service. In addition, a smaller lodging facility (Silver Bay Inn Resort with two cabins, a house, and one room; phone 509–687–3142; or email stehekin@silver bayinn.com) and several privately owned cabins, often with vehicles, are also available for rent near Stehekin. For information on the area, call Lake Chelan Chamber of Commerce at (800) 4–CHELAN. When traveling to Stehekin, keep in mind that no ATMs are available, and not all businesses accept credit cards.

The lodging facilities at Stehekin are reached only via commercial boats or floatplanes that leave from the town of Chelan or Field's Point Landing. The largest and least expensive boat (approximately $32 round-trip) takes four hours one way and leaves Chelan each morning at 8:30. A faster and more expensive boat ($51 round-trip) takes two and a quarter hours and leaves at the same time. The fastest boat ($96 round-trip) makes two daily round-trips and takes one and a quarter hours each way. All three boats are operated by the same company, Lake Chelan Boat Company. Reservations are recommended on the two faster boats. For information, call (509) 682–4584, or visit the Web site at www.ladyofthelake.com. You will save money and see more by selecting the slower boat, Lady of the Lake II. This is probably the best choice on your first trip to Stehekin. The scenery between Chelan and Stehekin is beautiful, and the captain sometimes approaches the shoreline when wild animals are spotted. For those in a hurry, floatplanes are available for round-trips ($139) or one way ($89), with flights taking approximately thirty minutes. Chelan Airways offers several transportation options, including fly/boat trips that allow flying one way and taking a chartered boat the other way ($129). The charter boat trip takes approximately two hours. For information about air transportation contact Chelan Airways at (509) 682–5065 or check the firm's Web site at www.chelanairways.com. For reservations call (509) 682-5555.

The only other national park lodging facility in the North Cascades Complex is Ross Lake Resort in Ross Lake National Recreation Area. This resort consists of floating cabins, and guests must carry in all food because no food service of any kind is available at or near the resort. Ross Lake Resort is reached via State Route 20, which bisects the North Cascades Complex. Most guests choose to take the combination ferry/truck/speedboat route from near Diablo Dam, 65 miles east of Burlington on State Route 20. To get to the free parking area, cross Diablo Dam and turn right to park in the resort parking lot. A sign on State Route 20 indicates the turnoff. The ferry, operated by Seattle City Light and departing each day at 8:30 A.M. and 3:00 P.M., takes you to the end of Diablo Lake. The charge is $5.00 per person each way, payable in cash. A maximum of three carry-ons per person is permitted. You will then be met by the resort truck, which will carry you and your luggage on a winding gravel road to Ross Lake ($3.00 each way, payable at the resort). From there you will transfer to a speedboat that quickly crosses the lake and delivers you directly to your assigned cabin. No reservations are necessary for either the ferry or the truck. Guests interested in hiking to the resort can park their vehicle on State Route 20 at milepost 134 (the Ross Lake/Ross Dam trailhead). It is a 1-mile hike down the trail to the gravel road and another mile to the boat docking area across the lake from the resort. The last power pole beside the road has a telephone that can be used to call the resort for pickup (dial 82–31974; $1.00 charge per person).

NORTH CASCADES STEHEKIN LODGE

P.O. Box 457 • Chelan, WA 98816 • (509) 682–4494 • www.stehekin.com

NORTH CASCADES STEHEKIN LODGE COMPRISES seven wooden buildings, six of which have a total of twenty-eight overnight units. The registration desk is inside the store across a small parking area and up a flight of stairs from the boat dock. The store and restaurant are fronted by a wooden deck with chairs and picnic tables. A registration sign is above the entrance. A restaurant in an adjacent building is the only structure in the complex that does not have accommodations. The lodge is on the east bank near the north terminus of Lake Chelan, across the road from the boat dock. There are also a laundry, post office, a few stores, and a large National Park Service visitor center. Shuttle service and tours for the Stehekin Valley begin near the dock.

A total of twenty-eight units of various sizes and configurations are available at the lodge. All of the rooms have a private bath with a shower or a combination shower-tub, heat, and electricity but no telephone, television, or air-conditioning. Ten standard rooms, eight of which are above the store, are the least expensive. These small rooms do not have a balcony or offer a view of the lake, but a sitting area with books, games, and puzzles at the end of the hallway has a good view

of the lake. Standard rooms have either one queen-size or two twin beds. Standard rooms 5 and 6 on the lower floor of an A-frame building have nice interiors and are preferable to rooms above the store.

Eleven lakeview rooms in a wooden, two-story motel-style building next to the restaurant are larger than standard rooms. Each lakeview room has at least one large window and a balcony facing Lake Chelan. Three of these rooms are larger and rent for approximately $25 per night more than the other eight rooms. The five first-floor rooms, 9 through 13, have a significantly larger balcony than the upstairs units. The eight regular-size lakeview rooms each have either a king bed or a queen bed plus a twin sofa bed. Beds in the three large lakeview rooms range from one queen plus a queen sofa bed to two queen beds plus a queen sofa bed.

Seven housekeeping units have a kitchen with a stove, oven, refrigerator/freezer, coffeemaker, toaster, and all utensils including pots and pans. These seven units are in five different buildings. One unit two flights above the store (no elevator) has two bedrooms plus a living room and sleeps six with the sofa bed. This unit has large windows facing the lake but no deck and can become uncomfortably warm during July and August. A freestanding wooden building with a large deck and wheelchair accessibility has two bedrooms and a living room and can sleep six with two twin sofa beds. Two separate A-frame buildings each sleep six, with a bedroom and living room plus an upstairs bedroom. Each A-frame has a large deck facing the lake on the main floor, which is one flight above ground level. Views from the decks are somewhat obstructed by buildings. The three other housekeeping units are in a triplex building with a large deck. Smaller units 2 and 3 each sleep three people with a king bed and a twin sofa bed. Unit 4 is larger and can sleep six in one bedroom and a separate living area. All three units have a deck facing the lake.

We believe the lakeview rooms are the best choice for two adults not interested in cooking. They offer a good view of Lake Chelan and are worth the nominal price difference compared to the smaller standard rooms. For families, housekeeping unit 1 with two bedrooms, a living room, and kitchen is best, although some people might prefer the ambience of one of the two A-frame units. Keep in mind that few grocery items are available for sale at Stehekin, so you must bring food if you wish to use the kitchen of a housekeeping unit. If you purchase groceries at the Safeway store in Chelan the day before you are to depart for Stehekin, the store will box and deliver your groceries to the appropriate boat.

North Cascades Stehekin Lodge is a convenient and comfortable place to spend a night or two. You might want to take the morning boat from Chelan, stay an evening, then return the morning or afternoon of the following day. The lodge restaurant offers three meals a day, including breakfast buffet and an evening buffet. Shuttle service is available to Stehekin Valley Ranch, which provides an alternative for dining. North Cascades Stehekin Lodge serves as the center for Stehekin activities, including boat and bicycle rentals, snowshoe rental in the winter, bus tours, and hikes. Buses for tours of the valley leave from the lodge.

Rooms: Doubles, triples, quads, with a few housekeeping units sleeping up to six.

Wheelchair Accessibility: Two units at the lodge are wheelchair accessible. One lakeview room has a large bathroom with a wide doorway. The room has one queen, and the bathroom has grab bars by the toilet and in the combination shower-tub. The freestanding housekeeping cabin has ramp access and an extra wide doorway to both the cabin and the large bathroom, which has grab bars by the toilet and in the combination shower-tub. An electric lift on the dock provides wheelchair access to the store, the restaurant, and the rooms.

Reservations: North Cascades Stehekin Lodge, P.O. Box 457, Chelan, WA 98816. Call (509) 682–4494. Payment in full is required to book a reservation. Cancellation of sleeping units requires fourteen days' notice. Housekeeping unit cancellation requires thirty days' notice.

Rates: Standard rooms ($99); lakeview rooms ($111–$135); housekeeping units ($128–$146). Rates quoted are for two persons. Each additional adult is $10 per night. Rates for children six through eleven are an additional $5.00 per night.

North Cascades Stehekin Lodge is not the only lodging facility to have served the public at Stehekin. The small Argonaut Hotel with several rooms and a store was under construction, when in 1892 it was sold to Merritt Field, who built a three-story hotel that could house one hundred guests in fifty rooms. Faced with flooding as a result of the proposed Lake Chelan Dam, Field sold the hotel in 1915 to the Great Northern Railroad, which continued operations until 1927 when the building was demolished. Timber and beams from the hotel were used to construct the Golden West Lodge farther up the hill, which operated here until 1971 when it was sold to the National Park Service, which currently utilizes the building as a visitor center. The current North Cascades Stehekin Lodge is a conglomeration of two hotels that were acquired by the National Park Service in 1968.

Children under six stay free. Reduced rates of approximately $20 per room per night are offered from October 16 to June 14, excluding Memorial Day weekend. Special fall, winter, and spring packages are offered along with a Hiker's Special. Check the Web site at www.stehekin.com.

Location: Next to the Stehekin boat dock.

Season: The lodge is open all year, although services, lodging, and facilities are fully operational only from mid-June to mid-October and during the Memorial Day weekend. Only the seven housekeeping units are open year-round. Restaurant hours are reduced, or the restaurant is closed at various times during fall, winter, and spring. Check with the lodge about specific dates.

Food: An adjacent restaurant offers a breakfast buffet ($7.00), lunch ($5.00–$7.00), and dinner ($13.00–$16.00). Dinner reservations are required. Beer and wine are served. A children's menu is available. A small store sells milk, chips, beer, and wine. The Valley Shuttle offers transportation to Stehekin Valley Ranch, which is open for dinner.

Transportation: Major airports are in Seattle and Spokane, Washington, where rental cars are available. The lodge is reached from Chelan only via boat or floatplane.

Facilities: Dining room, convenience store, craft store, post office, laundry, National Park Service visitor center, marina, and boat and bicycle rentals. Snowshoe rentals in winter.

Activities: Hiking, fishing, boating, cycling.

STEHEKIN VALLEY RANCH

P.O. Box 36 • Stehekin, WA 98852 • (800) 536–0745 • www.stehekin.biz

Wood Cabin with a Canvas Roof at Stehekin Valley Ranch

STEHEKIN VALLEY RANCH IS AN ISOLATED LODGING complex that includes a two-story dining hall, fourteen wooden cabins, a corral, and a small sporting goods shop. The buildings sit in a grove of maple trees next to a large pasture and are surrounded by mountains. The cabins are a short walk from the dining hall, which includes a small registration/gift shop area, a loft reading room, separate men's and women's bathhouses, and an attractive log-beamed dining area with three massive picnic tables and a wood stove. The location offers outstanding views and access to great hiking, rafting, and fishing in a restful and friendly atmosphere. Three meals a day, including an excellent dinner, are included in the price of a room, with the exception of the two housekeeping cabins. There are no televisions or telephones, and cell phones do not work at the ranch. Stehekin Valley Ranch is 9 miles north of the public boat dock at Stehekin and is reached via a free shuttle bus from the dock.

Lodging at the ranch is in three types of cabins. Seven older cabins, constructed in 1983, are wood sided with heavy canvas roofs. These cabins have cement floors, screens, and canvas shades (no glass) as window coverings, unfinished interiors, and no heat, electricity, or running water. The seven differ in size, with cabin 5 being smallest and having one double bed and cabins 1 and 2 being largest and each having a double bed plus three twin beds. The other four canvas-covered cabins each have either a double plus two twins or a queen plus one twin. Community bathroom facilities including shower rooms are on the first floor of the main building, a short walk from all the cabins. A kerosene lantern in each cabin provides the only artificial source of light, so you will want to bring a flashlight if you will be staying in one of these cabins. Despite the rustic appearance, these units are clean and comfortable, and the choice of many regular guests. Five of the seven cabins (cabins 1 though 5) are directly beside the pasture and provide an excellent view of the mountains. Cabins 11 and 12 are higher on the hill with views that are obstructed by other cabins.

Five larger wooden cabins with metal roofs were constructed in the mid-1990s. Each of these cabins has a painted cement floor, an unfinished interior, and a large front porch with chairs. Sliding windows with screens are on the front and two sides of the buildings. These cabins also have electric lights, an electrical outlet in the bathroom, and a private bathroom with a shower, but they do not have heat. Beds in three of these cabins include one queen-size and two twin beds. Cabins 9 and 10 are newer and larger with a loft bedroom that has two twin beds and a downstairs futon and queen-size bed. The five newer metal-roofed cabins are larger, brighter, and more comfortable than the older canvas-covered cabins. They are situated, however, behind five of the canvas-roofed cabins, which block their view of the pasture and mountains.

Guests can prepare their own meals when staying in two log cabins that will open in 2006. These units, similar in size to the smaller metal-roofed cabins, have finished interiors, one queen bed, a private bathroom, and a kitchen with a sink, stove, oven, refrigerator, cookware,

and tableware. A vehicle is provided for guests (pay only for fuel used). Meals are not included in the price of these two cabins, although guests can pay extra and eat in the dining hall.

The choice of a cabin depends in large part on whether you want a private bathroom. The five metal-roofed cabins cost about $10 per person more per day but offer more interior space, a private bathroom, and are likely to be more comfortable in cool or rainy weather. On the other hand, the canvas-covered cabins may offer more of the ambience you seek from this type vacation. The dining hall and loft reading room are always open if you want to play cards, converse with other guests, or read.

Stehekin Valley Ranch is a fun place to stay, with lots of outdoor activities, including river rafting, kayaking horseback riding, mountain biking, fishing, and hiking. Three-hour trail rides leave each morning and afternoon from the nearby corral. Riding lessons are offered to anyone six years and older. Mountain bikes are available for rent. Guests at Stehekin Valley Ranch enjoy free use of the shuttle that connects Stehekin Landing with the ranch. The shuttle also stops at the bakery and Rainbow

Hugh Courtney, grandfather of the current owners of Stehekin Valley Ranch, homesteaded fifty-two acres in the Stehekin area in 1916. One of his sons, Ray, purchased the twenty-acre dairy farm where the ranch is currently located and started a successful pack trip business. Six of Ray's children are currently involved in a variety of businesses, including the operation of the ranch. The present lodging operation commenced in 1983 with the construction of the main building and canvas-roofed cabins. Stehekin Valley Ranch is on private land that is surrounded by Lake Chelan National Recreation Area.

Falls. Hiking trails begin at High Bridge, which is on the route of the Pacific Coast Scenic Trail.

The dining room, with its three extra-large dining tables, provides a great atmosphere for enjoying some exceptional meals of fish, chicken, and steak. Best of all are the homemade pies served each evening. After dinner, relax on the porch outside the dining room or walk up the stairs to a small loft reading room. Guests sometimes linger in the dining room to chat, read, or play board games.

Rooms: Fourteen individual cabins, most of which sleep up to four people. Two larger cabins can sleep up to six. Seven canvas-roofed cabins have no private bath. Seven cabins, two with a kitchen, have a private bath with shower.

Wheelchair Accessibility: None of the cabins is wheelchair accessible.

Reservations: Write P.O. Box 881, Chelan, WA 98816. Call (800) 536–0745. A deposit of 50 percent of the total is required at the time the reservation is made. Cancellation in writing of twenty-one days is required for 75 percent refund. No refunds for later cancellations.

Rates: Canvas-covered cabins ($75 per adult, $55 per child ages four to twelve, $15 per child ages one to three); cabins with bath (two adult minimum, $85 per adult, $65 per child age four to twelve, $20 per child age one to three); cabins with bath and kitchen ($125 per night or $700 per week for two persons). Discounts are available for stays of three or more nights. Meals are included for all cabins except the two with kitchens. Pack-

ages that include a variety of activities such as rafting and horseback riding are available.

Location: Nine miles north of Stehekin Landing. A free shuttle service for guests of the ranch operates four round-trips daily between Stehekin Landing and the ranch.

Season: Mid-June to early October.

Food: Three meals a day are included in the price of the room. Breakfast includes meat, eggs, pancakes, French toast, oatmeal, and fruit, among other items. Lunch choices include hamburgers, soup, and the makings for cold-meat sandwiches. Guests can make sack lunches after breakfast. The dinner is outstanding, with a choice of steak, chicken, fish, and a daily special. The homemade pie for dessert is world class. Vegetarian meals are available. Alcoholic beverages are not available, but guests may bring their own. Groceries that are purchased at the Safeway store in Chelan the day before you are to depart for Stehekin will be boxed and delivered to the appropriate boat the next day.

Transportation: Major airports are in Seattle and Spokane, Washington, where rental cars are available. Scheduled boat service is available to Stehekin Landing from Chelan. Floatplanes are available at Chelan. A valley shuttle system operates every three hours beginning at 8:15 A.M. between Stehekin Landing and Stehekin Valley Ranch. The shuttle also stops at the bakery and other points along the road.

Facilities: Dining room, small gift shop, outdoor store, reading room, and a bicycle rental.

Activities: Fishing, hiking, river rafting, kayaking, trail rides, riding lessons, ultralight backpacking and gear classes, mountain trips, bicycling, volleyball, horseshoes.

ROSS LAKE RESORT

503 Diablo Street • Rockport, WA 98283 • (206) 386–4437 • www.rosslakeresort.com

ROSS LAKE RESORT IS ONE OF THE MOST UNUSUAL lodging facilities in a national park. It consists of a row of floating cabins, bunkhouses, and support buildings along the shoreline of 22-mile-long Ross Lake. The rustic looking, shake-sided cabins and bunkhouses are constructed on wooden docks attached to huge cedar logs that float on the water and are cabled to shore. The floating base allows the cabins to rise and fall with the water level of the lake.

Ross Lake Resort caters to people who love to fish, boat, hike, and just relax. The resort also includes an office, small marina area, and associated outbuildings. It is located in a wild and beautiful area of the state so you shouldn't be surprised to see the resort owner scare off an inquisitive black bear that has walked out of the woods behind the cabins. Guests do not have access to television, radio, or the Internet, and even your cell phone will be out of range. The isolation

Peak Cabin and Modern Cabin at Ross Lake Resort

alone makes the resort a refreshing place to visit. The lake and mountain views from large windows along the front of each cabin make it even better.

The resort is located at the base of Ross Lake, a short distance up from Ross Dam. Access is via Highway 20, which bisects North Cascades National Park Complex. Guests must either hike 2 miles to a boat-pick-up point across from the resort or utilize scheduled transportation by ferry/flatbed truck /speedboat to reach the resort. Keep in mind that guests MUST BRING ALL OF THEIR OWN FOOD BECAUSE NO FOOD SERVICE OF ANY KIND IS AVAILABLE AT OR NEAR THE RESORT.

Four classes of accommodations are offered at Ross Lake Resort: Private Bunkhouse rooms, Little Cabins, Modern Cabins, and Peak Cabins. None have a telephone or television. All have woodstove or electric heat, private bathrooms, and kitchens with pots, pans, plates, utensils, coffeemaker, and a toaster. The cabins with woodstoves have plenty of firewood and an axe. Two Adirondack chairs in which to relax and enjoy the fantastic view of the lake and mountains are in front of or beside each cabin. Several charcoal grills are near the cabins and charcoal can be purchased at the office.

The three Private Bunkhouse rooms were built in 1982 and are reproductions of the bunkhouses used by the dam construction crews. Each unit consists of one large room with four bunk beds (eight total beds), a large table with chairs, and a woodstove. The kitchen includes an electric stovetop (no oven) and a full-size refrigerator. These are typically rented to large families or groups who come here to fish.

The two Little Cabins, constructed as a duplex, both have two bunk beds in an area separate from the kitchen. The kitchen includes a stove, oven, small refrigerator, woodstove, and a table with chairs. These

Ross Lake Resort evolved from numerous floating cabins that were built on the lake to house workers engaged in logging and the construction of nearby Ross Dam. The dam was completed in 1949 and the power station was added several years later. Although the current cabins are modern, an adventurous atmosphere remains for resort guests.

are nicely done and are the smallest and least expensive of the three types of cabins.

The eight Modern Cabins were constructed over a ten-year period, with the last unit completed in 1971. All have since been remodeled. Each cabin has an open front room with a kitchen area that includes a stove, oven, a full-size refrigerator, and a large table with six padded chairs. Six of the eight Modern Cabins have two single beds and a woodstove in the front room, while the other two have electric heat (rather than a woodstove) and three single beds. (Remember to specify your wishes when making reservations if a woodstove is an important part of your vacation enjoyment.) There is a bunk bed in a very small bedroom between the front room and the bathroom. This area is handy luggage storage for couples who sleep in the front room.

The most expensive accommodations are the two Peak Cabins constructed in 1996. These large, two-story cabins have electric heat plus a woodstove. They are the only accommodations with a complete kitchen, including a microwave and dishwasher, and a full-size bathroom with a combination shower-tub. The front room has a sofa bed, a cushioned chair, and a large table with chairs. A small bedroom off the front room includes a single bed and a bunk bed. The loft area, a major attraction for many guests, includes a queen bed, two single beds, and a cushioned chair.

Ross Lake Resort is a restful place in a setting that is as beautiful as you will find in any national park. Guests typically spend most of their stay boating, fishing, hiking, and reading. There are few distractions to keep you from enjoying a relaxing lifestyle. Sit in front of your cabin sipping a favorite beverage, reading a book by your favorite author, and taking in mountain views across the lake. It is best to visit when you can stay for several days because transportation to and from the resort is limited to twice a day in each direction. You are unlikely to enjoy much relaxation if you arrive at 4:00 P.M. one afternoon and leave at 8:30 A.M. the next morning. Even choosing the 2:30 P.M. departure

doesn't allow sufficient time to appreciate this beautiful part of Washington.

Choosing among the four classes of accommodations is mostly determined by the number of people who will be included in your group. All of the accommodations, except the bunkhouses, have large front windows that provide an outstanding view of the lake and mountains. The two Peak Cabins offer considerably more room and are situated at the far end of the row so that few other guests will be traipsing in front of your cabin. On the other hand, two people are easily accommodated in one of the Little Cabins, which are not only less expensive, but situated so that other guests must walk behind, rather than in front of, your cabin.

Rooms: The least expensive accommodations, the Little Cabins, offer bedding for up to four guests but are better suited for a couple or a couple with one or two small children. The Modern Cabins can accommodate up to six people with the use of a rollaway bed but are more comfortable for two to four people. The Peak Cabins can accommodate up to nine people but are better suited for two couples or a couple with three or four children. Each Bunkhouse holds up to eight people, but they had better be good friends.

Wheelchair Accessibility: Each of the two Peak Cabins has a small ramp by the entry door, a large bathroom with a wide doorway, and grab bars in the bathtub. A tub/shower stool is available.

Reservations: Ross Lake Resort, 503 Diablo Street, Rockport, WA 98283. Phone (206) 386–4437. A required deposit is based on the cabin classification and number of nights requested. A cancellation notice of thirty days is required for a refund, less a $10 fee.

Rates: Private Bunkhouse ($154.00 for up to six people; $8.00 each additional person); Little Cabin ($100.00 for two people; $6.00 each additional person); Modern Cabin ($121.00 for two people; $10.00 each additional person); Peak Cabin ($213.00 for up to four people; $15.00 each additional person). Children four and under stay free. Rates are reduced in June and on Sunday through Thursday during the fall with a boat rental.

Location: Approximately 130 miles northeast of Seattle, Washington, via Interstate 5 and Washington Highway 20. The resort sits directly on Ross Lake just above Ross Dam.

Season: Mid-June through the end of October.

Food: No stores or restaurants of any kind are at or near the resort. Visitors must carry in their own food and beverages. Candy, soft drinks, and ice are sold in the office.

Transportation: The nearest major airport is in Seattle, where rental cars are available. The resort is not accessible by road. Seattle City Light provides ferry service from near Diablo Dam just off WA 20 to a dock at the end of Diablo Lake (fee).

From there Ross Lake Resort operates a truck (fee), which carries you to the resort's speedboat.

Facilities: Canoes, single and double kayaks, and 14-foot motor boats are available for rent. A fuel barge and limited repair facilities are at the marina. A small paperback lending library is in the office.

Activities: Hiking, fishing, boating. Fishing licenses are sold at the office. Fishing gear is available for rent.

Olympic National Park

600 East Park Avenue • Port Angeles, WA 98362 • (360) 565–3130

www.nps.gov/olym/home.htm

Olympic National Park covers 1,442 square miles of mountain wilderness and includes active glaciers, 57 miles of scenic ocean shore, and the finest remnant of Pacific Northwest rain forest. The strip of the park along the Pacific Ocean has some of the most primitive coastline in the continental United States. Olympic National Park is composed of two sections, located in the northwest corner of Washington. Main access is via U.S. Highway 101, although roads penetrate only the perimeter of the park. **Park Entrance Fee:** $10.00 per vehicle or $5.00 per person, good for seven days.

Lodging in Olympic National Park: The park has four facilities with overnight accommodations. Kalaloch Lodge is located directly on the coast and is perfect for beach walkers. Sol Duc Hot Springs Resort is great for those who want to spend time relaxing in a hot mineral bath. Lake Crescent Lodge and Log Cabin Resort are situated in heavily wooded areas on opposite sides of beautiful Lake Crescent. We have also included charming Lake Quinault Lodge, which is across Lake Quinault from the park's southern boundary.

KALALOCH LODGE

157151 Highway 101 • Forks, WA 98331 • (360) 962–2271 or (866) 525–2562

www.visitkalaloch.com

Main Lodge Building at Kalaloch Lodge

Olympic National Park

Strait of Juan de Fuca

Port Angeles

Pioneer Memorial Museum

Deer Park

Hurricane Ridge

Elwha

Altaire

Storm King

Log Cabin Resort

Fairholm

Lake Crescent

Sol Duc

Lake Crescent Lodge

Sol Duc Hot Springs Resort

Hoh Rain Forest

MOUNT OLYMPUS

Dosewallips

Staircase

Graves Creek

North Fork

Quinault Rain Forest

Lake Quinault Lodge

Quinault Lake

To Hoquiam & Aberdeen

Queets

USFS/NPS Information Station

Forks

Kalaloch Lodge

Kalaloch

South Beach

Ozette

Ozette Lake

Mora

Rialto Beach

Pacific Ocean

N
W   E
S

Miles

0   5   10

Kalaloch Lodge is a complex of wooden buildings that include a main lodge, cabins, a motel-style unit, and a store, all situated on a bluff overlooking the Pacific Ocean. Only a few overnight rooms are in the main lodge building. The registration desk for all rooms is in the gift shop of the main lodge, which is on Highway 101. This building also has the restaurant. All of the cabins and other lodging units are adjacent to and within easy walking distance of the main lodge. Kalaloch Lodge is located on U.S. 101, 35 miles south of Forks, Washington. The lodge is 95 miles southwest of Port Angeles, Washington.

The lodge offers a total of sixty-four guest rooms in four categories, all of which have a coffeemaker, electric heat, and a private bath but no telephone, air-conditioning, or television (except the suites in the main lodge). The main lodge building has ten guest rooms, including two suites. All but one of the rooms are on the second floor and are accessed from a central hallway that is reached from a stairway in the lobby. These rooms each have a bath with a shower but no tub. Room size varies, with five rooms having one queen-size bed and other rooms having up to one queen, one double, and two single beds. Each of the suites has a combination living room–bedroom with one king-size bed and a sofa bed. Becker's Suite, which has a fireplace, is only rented as a suite during the summer months; during the remainder of the year, it is used as a library/reading room for the lodge guests. Rooms 1 (on the first floor), 6, 7, and 8 and the suites provide an ocean view. Rooms 5 and 9, with one queen, one double, and two single beds each, are quite large, but are located above the kitchen and can be noisy. Five rooms, including 5 and 9, can only be rented on site.

The two-story Seacrest House has six regular rooms, plus four suites. This building sits behind two bluff cabins. The six regular motel-style rooms are very spacious and have two queen-size beds and a private bath with a shower but no tub. Each room has its own covered patio or balcony and large windows that face the ocean but do not provide an ocean view. Three suites have a sitting room with a fireplace (wood provided) and two separate bedrooms with one double and one queen-size bed plus a sofa bed. One bedroom and the sitting room have large windows. The fourth suite is one large room with a fireplace, a queen bed, and a futon.

Twenty bluff cabins, most of which were refurbished in 1999, offer covered back porches and a great view of the ocean. Approximately half these cabins have a single room with two queen beds or

The current Kalaloch Lodge sits on the site of an earlier lodging facility constructed in the late 1920s by Charles Becker, who had acquired forty acres just south of Kalaloch Creek. Becker's operation included a home, lodge, and several frame cabins constructed on the bluff overlooking the ocean. Additional cabins were constructed between 1934 and 1936 following completion of Highway 101. The owner added additional cabins and moved some of the existing cabins back from the bluff following World War II, during which the resort was occupied by the U.S. Coast Guard. Between 1950 and 1954 Becker erected a new main lodge building, which remains in use today. In 1978 the National Park Service purchased the Becker operation and renamed it Kalaloch Lodge. Within four years a new concessioner had completed construction of twenty-two log cabins that have become a major part of the current operation. ARAMARK Corporation won the contract to manage Kalaloch Lodge in 1989.

one queen bed plus a futon. The remainder each have either one or two separate bedrooms with bedding that can sleep from six to eight persons. All but six of the bluff cabins have kitchens with a sink, stove, refrigerator, oven, pots, pans, plates, glasses, cups, and utensils. When reserving a bluff cabin keep in mind that some have a woodstove, some have a kitchen, and the larger units have both.

Sitting directly behind the bluff cabins are twenty-four log cabins with exteriors that have been sided with cedar and interiors that retain exposed log walls. These are very nice cabins with tiled floors, vaulted ceilings, and a kitchen with a refrigerator, stove, sink, and table with four chairs. All but four of the cabins have a woodstove (small bundle of wood provided). The other four have an oven. Most of these cabins have one bedroom with a queen bed plus another queen bed in a separate living area that also has a love seat. Two larger log cabins have two bedrooms, each with a queen bed and a living room with a sofa bed. These two cabins can sleep six. Although none of these cabins sits on the bluff, cabins 25, 26, and 27 provide an ocean view when standing by the front windows. Parking is directly in front of or beside each cabin.

Kalaloch Lodge is a great place to stay if you want to experience the Pacific Ocean. The roar of the sea can be heard from your room. A wide sandy beach just below the bluff can be reached via an easy trail. The water is relatively cold and there are riptides, so you probably won't want to swim, but walks along the beach are one of the pleasures of staying here. National Park Service rangers lead daily walks along the beach and to various points in the park during the summer months. The main lodge building has a very attractive restaurant with big windows overlooking the ocean. Keep in mind that this coastal area is often breezy and can get quite foggy, so be prepared for the possibility of chilly weather. Of course, the wind, fog, and cool air are all part of the experience of a visit to the Pacific Northwest.

Rooms: Doubles, triples, and quads. A few cabins can hold more than four persons. All rooms have a private bath, although most have a shower but no tub.

Wheelchair Accessibility: One unit of a duplex bluff cabin is wheelchair accessible with a wide bathroom door and a roll-in shower. Grab bars are around the toilet. A ramp at the main lodge building provides access to the restaurant.

Reservations: Kalaloch Lodge, 157151 Highway 101, Forks, WA 98331-9396. Phone (866) 525–2562 or (360) 962–2271; or online at www.visitkalaloch.com. A deposit of one night's stay is required. A cancellation notice of seventy-two hours is required for a refund less a $10 fee.

Rates: Two sets of rates apply to all rooms; peak rates are from early June through September, plus all weekends and holidays. Off-peak rates are 25 to 50 percent less. Lodge rooms ($143); lodge suites ($265); Seacrest House regular rooms ($153); Seacrest suites ($163-$174); bluff cabins ($184–$275, depending on size); log cabins ($165–$184, depending on size). Rates quoted are for two persons. Each additional person is $12 per night. Children under five years old stay free.

Location: Directly on the Pacific Ocean, 35 miles south of Forks, Washington, on US 101.

Season: Kalaloch Lodge is open year-round.

Food: A restaurant serves breakfast ($5.00–$9.00), lunch ($7.00–$11.00), and dinner ($7.00–$26.00). Dinner reservations are required. Alcoholic beverages are served. A children's menu is available. Limited groceries including beer and wine can be purchased at the store beside the main lodge building.

Transportation: The nearest major city with scheduled air and train service is Olympia, Washington, where rental cars are available.

Facilities: Restaurant, gift shop, gas station, and small store.

Activities: Walking, beachcombing, whale watching, kite flying, and surf fishing. Ranger-guided walks are offered each day during summer months.

Pets: Pets are allowed in cabins only for $12.50 per pet, pet night.

LAKE CRESCENT LODGE

416 Lake Crescent Road • Port Angeles, WA 98363 • (360) 928–3211
www.lakecrescentlodge.com

*Main Lodge Building
at Lake Crescent Lodge*

LAKE CRESCENT LODGE COMPRISES A CLASSIC MAIN lodge building surrounded at each end by several types of cabins and one- and two-story motel structures. The main wooden lodge, constructed in 1916 as the Singer Tavern, has only five overnight rooms, all upstairs and without a private bath. All other accommodations are separate but near the main lodge. The entire complex is situated on the south shore of Lake Crescent among giant hemlock and fir trees in the shadow of Mount Storm King. Registration for all lodging at Lake Crescent Lodge is just inside the door of the main building in the lobby area highlighted by a huge stone fireplace. A gift shop, a restaurant, a lounge, and a beautiful sunroom are also on the main floor of the same building. Virtually all the accommodations, including the cabins, offer a view of beautiful Lake Crescent. Lake Crescent Lodge is located 21 miles west of Port Angeles, Washington, just off U.S. Highway 101.

The lodge offers several types of accommodations. All rooms have hair dryers, coffeemakers, and heat but no air-conditioning, television, or telephone. All rooms except those in the main lodge have a private bath. Pets are permitted in the Roosevelt Fireplace Cottages and the

Singer Tavern Cottages. Parking is convenient to all the rooms. The least expensive accommodations are the five relatively small rooms on the second floor of the main lodge building. These rooms are entered from an interior hallway via a lobby stairway. All have a double bed but no private bathroom. Two shower rooms and two small bathrooms are in the hallway. All five rooms are on the west side of the building and offer a terrific view of Lake Crescent and mountains on the opposite shore.

The four Roosevelt Fireplace Cottages, two with one room and the other two with a living room plus a bedroom, were constructed from 1945–1947. These units are very nice, with hardwood floors, wood interiors, a small refrigerator, and a stone fireplace (wood provided). All four cottages are on the shore of Lake Crescent and at the opposite end of the main lodge building from the other cabins and motor lodge buildings. This location provides more privacy and quiet compared to other accommodations in the complex. These are the most expensive and by far the most desirable accommodations at Lake Crescent. With only four units available, they are also the most difficult to reserve. The two one-room Roosevelt Fireplace units are in a

Lake Crescent Lodge was completed in 1915 and initially called Singer's Lake Crescent Tavern after owner Avery Singer. The current enclosed porch facing the lake was originally part of a long veranda that wrapped around the north and west faces of the building. The gift shop occupies the former dining room. Singer built a row of sixteen cabins the same year and subsequently added a row of frame tents that were later converted to cabins. Lodge guests arrived via boat until 1922 when the road from Port Angeles was extended along the south shore of the lake. The sunroom has a photo of the original lodge, which Singer sold in 1927. Lake Crescent Lodge has hosted luminaries such as Henry Ford, Frank Sinatra, William O. Douglas, Robert Kennedy, and, of course, President Franklin D. Roosevelt.

duplex wood-frame building. They each have two queen beds, a sofa, and two chairs. The two cottages with two rooms are freestanding and have one queen in the living area and two double beds in the bedroom.

Thirteen one- and two-bedroom Singer Tavern Cottages are constructed two or three units to a building. The current reconstructed cottages retain the scale and historic character of the original cabins that were torn down in the 1980s. Each shake-sided cottage has a covered porch with chairs, and all but one (cottage 19) offer a good porch view of Lake Crescent. The cottages sit side-by-side in a large grassy area adjacent to the main lodge building. These cottages have large interiors with hardwood floors. The bathrooms, with a combination shower-tub, are quite nice. Ten of the cottages are one-bedroom units with two queen beds. The three two-bedroom cottages with one bathroom have two queen beds in one room and a queen plus a twin bed in the other room. The two-bedroom units provide double the space but don't cost a great deal

more than the one-bedroom units. Singer Tavern Cottages 20 and 21 sit closest to the lake and to the parking lot but can suffer from the noise of substantial foot traffic during busy summer months. Cabin 5 is nearest to the main lodge but backs up to a parking area.

Three separate buildings house motor lodge rooms. The Marymere Lodge is a one-story motel-type, cement-block-and-wood-frame building with ten rooms that each have large front and back windows. This building was constructed in 1959 and has direct access to the lake and provides excellent lake views. A covered porch with chairs runs across the lake side of the building. Each room is relatively large and has two double beds and a tiled bath with a combination shower-tub.

The two-story wood-frame Storm King Motor Lodge, built in 1962, is situated among trees back from the lake, but its ten rooms each provide a relatively good lake view. The rooms are fairly small and each has a queen bed and a balcony or patio with chairs. Each room has a private bath with a tiled shower. Two-story Pyramid Mountain Lodge, constructed in 1991, offers the newest lodging in the complex. This attractive wooden building sits back from the lake on a hill in the trees. Each of its ten rooms has a covered balcony or patio that looks out over a grassy area leading to Lake Crescent. The rooms each have two queen beds and a tiled bathroom with a combination shower-tub. Rooms on the top floor have vaulted ceilings and offer a superior balcony view.

The five second-floor rooms in the main lodge offer the best value if you don't mind using a common bathroom. These rooms are relatively small, but the front windows offer picture-postcard views of one of the country's most beautiful lakes. Plus, there is a special feeling about staying in the main lodge building. The Roosevelt Fireplace Cottages are by far the nicest accommodations and worth the extra $30 per night compared to the Singer Tavern Cottages. Among the motor lodge units we would choose Marymere, where you can lie in your bed and look out at the lake.

A visit to Lake Crescent Lodge will almost certainly be an enjoyable experience no matter which accommodation you choose. The lodge offers a quiet atmosphere in a picturesque setting and is one of our favorite places to stay. Arrive early in the afternoon so that you can spend time relaxing in a chair on the grassy lawn and read a book while stealing glances at the lake. If you need to expend some energy, rent one of the rowboats and enjoy a different view of the lodge and surrounding mountains. The award-winning dining room was recently remodeled and offers some of the best food served in any national park lodge.

Rooms: Doubles, triples, and quads in most units. Some units hold up to seven persons. All rooms outside the main lodge building have private bathrooms.

Wheelchair Accessibility: One first-floor room at Pyramid Mountain Lodge is the only handicap-accessible room at Lake Crescent Lodge. This room has one queen bed and a large bathroom with a wide doorway and a combination shower-tub with grab bars. A paved path leads to the room from wheelchair parking that is some distance away.

Reservations: Lake Crescent Lodge, 416 Lake Crescent Road, Port Angeles, WA 98363-8672. Phone (360) 928–3211, ext. 10. A deposit of one night's stay is required. Cancellation seven days prior to scheduled arrival is required for a refund less a $15 fee. Reservation modifications also incur a $15 fee.

Rates: High season (late-May through late-September)/low season (remainder of the season): Historic lodge rooms ($85/$68); Singer Tavern Cottages: one-room ($165/$132); two-room ($195/$156); Roosevelt Fireplace Cottages: one-room ($203/$163); two-room ($211/$169); Pyramid Motor Lodge ($145/$116); Storm King Motor Lodge ($132/$106); Marymere ($137/$110). Rates quoted are for two persons. Rollaways, cribs, and additional persons are $12 extra per night. Children under six years of age stay free.

Location: Twenty-one miles west of Port Angeles, Washington, on US 101.

Season: Late April through October. The Roosevelt Fireplace Cottages and the Singer Tavern Cottages are open on winter weekends, but no dining service is available.

Food: A dining room on the main floor serves breakfast ($5.50–$8.00), lunch ($6.00–$10.00), and dinner ($10.00–$26.00) from late April through October. Alcoholic beverages are available in the lounge and dining room.

Transportation: Scheduled airline service is in Port Angeles, Washington, where rental cars are available. A city bus from Port Angeles to the lodge operates daily during the summer.

Facilities: Boat rental, restaurant, lounge, swimming beach, and gift shop. Wireless Internet is available in the lobby.

Activities: Swimming, hiking, boating, fishing.

Pets: Pets are allowed only in the cottages for $12 per pet, per night.

LAKE QUINAULT LODGE

P.O. Box 7 • Quinault, WA 98575 • (360) 288–2900 • www.visitlakequinault.com

Lake Quinault Lodge is a complex of four shake-covered buildings, including a two-story main lodge that has the registration desk/gift shop, dining room, lobby area, indoor heated swimming pool, and men's and women's dry saunas. The main lodge has guest rooms on both floors, but most rooms are in three buildings situated on either side of the main lodge building. The lodge is in the middle of a rain forest, on a hill overlooking the south shore of Lake Quinault. The beautiful setting includes a large lawn that leads to the lake. Eighty-year-old native redwood trees are near the lodge. Lake Quinault Lodge is on South Shore Road, 2 miles east of U.S. Highway 101. The turnoff from US 101 is 40 miles north of the town of Hoquiam. The lodge is in Olympic National Forest, across the lake from Olympic National Park. We have included this lodge because of its proximity to the park.

Lake Quinault Lodge offers four types of rooms, all with a coffeemaker, heat, and a private bathroom but no air-conditioning or telephone. Televisions are only in the lakeside units. None of the buildings has an elevator. The main lodge building was constructed in 1926 with thirty-one guest rooms, including two connecting rooms on the main floor that can be rented together as a suite. Rooms in the main lodge differ in view and configuration but are generally smaller than rooms in the three other buildings. These rooms have ceiling fans and beds that vary from one queen to two double beds. About half the rooms offer a lake view and rent for approximately $30 extra per night compared to rooms on the opposite side that face the road and front drive. Rooms 102, 104, and 106 on the front side have windows that face a nearby roof and offer absolutely no views. Rooms 102 and 104 share a connecting door and can be rented as a suite. You may also want to avoid rooms 206 and 208, which are above the kitchen and can be noisy. These are generally rented only to walk-ins, who are informed of the problem. For many returning guests, a corner room, 223, with two windows and a lake view, is a favorite. Room 107, another corner

The first log structure to accommodate travelers to Quinault was built in the 1890s. Another facility, Lakeside Inn, was constructed here in 1923. The inn eventually changed its name to The Annex (now the Boathouse) following the construction of Lake Quinault Lodge in 1926. Even though lumber, glass, fixtures, and furniture had to be hauled over 50 miles of dirt road, the lodge was completed in only ten weeks at a cost of $90,000. Guests can still view original stenciled designs on the beamed ceiling of the lobby. Lake Quinault Lodge's most famous guest was President Franklin D. Roosevelt, who visited here in 1937, one year before the creation of Olympic National Park.

room with a lake view, is directly below room 223. Several other rooms in the main lodge offer excellent views of the lake.

Adjacent to the main lodge, the Boathouse, constructed in 1923 and the only remaining original building, offers nine rooms that vary in size and view. Rooms in the Boathouse are paneled in pine and were refurbished in 2002. Beds vary from one queen to two doubles plus a queen-size futon. This rectangular wooden building with rooms on all four sides has a large covered porch around three sides and is reminiscent of an old western bunkhouse. Each room has a private bathroom with a shower but no tub. Some rooms face the lake and rent for approximately $15 per night extra. Room 304, with a lake view, is particularly large, with two double beds, a queen futon, and a table with four chairs. Room 308, on the backside, has a partition that separates a bedroom and sitting area that has a queen futon. One suite (room 309) on the second floor of the Boathouse has a large sitting room with furniture that includes two chair futons that can each be made into a very small bed for a child. This room also has a kitchen area with a small refrigerator and a sink along with a dining table and four chairs. A separate bedroom has a queen bed, and two rollaways are available. A large bathroom has a shower but no tub. The Boathouse is the only building at Lake Quinault Lodge in which pets are permitted. This is a positive if you have a pet but can be a negative if your neighbor has a barking dog.

At the other end of the main lodge building and connected by a covered walkway are two side-by-side wooden buildings that house sixteen fireplace units. These attractive two-story buildings were constructed in 1972 and refurbished in 1999–2000. The fireplace units are the most expensive and considered by most guests to be the nicest rooms at Lake Quinault Lodge. The rooms are quite large, and each contains a gas fireplace, one queen-size bed, one queen sofa bed, and a full bath with a combination shower-tub. Fireplace units each have a large private balcony or patio facing the lake, but views from the first floor of both buildings tend to be obstructed by trees and bushes, giving guests the feeling of being in a private garden. Second-floor rooms 226 through 230 offer outstanding lake views. Parking is directly in front of the two buildings with fireplace rooms. Try for a second-floor room if you don't mind climbing a flight of stairs.

On the far side of the Boathouse are two shake-sided modern-style buildings that house thirty-six lakeside units. These three-story buildings were constructed in 1990 and have nicely furnished rooms that are spacious, although not quite as large as the fireplace units. Each room has either two double beds or a king bed, a sofa bed, a television, and a small private balcony that faces the lake. As previously mentioned, these are the only rooms at Lake Quinault Lodge that have televisions. These units are closest to the lake, although lake views from the windows and balconies are mostly blocked by nearby cedar and fir trees. Twelve lakeside

rooms have connecting doors so that two rooms, one with a king bed and the other with two double beds, can be rented as a suite. Noise can filter through the closed doors, so you may want to avoid rooms with connecting doors if you only require one room. Lakeside rooms are entered from an outside walkway on each floor, reached from either a stairway or a series of ramps. No elevator is in either Lakeside building so a room on the third floor will require climbing two flights of stairs or toting luggage up an extended ramp system.

Lake Quinault Lodge offers plenty to do in a scenic outdoor setting. It is a wonderful place to spend several days or a week. The spacious lobby with a large brick fireplace and windows that overlook the lake is one of the most comfortable common areas you will find in any national park lodge. It is perfect for reading, playing board games or completing jigsaw puzzles, conversing with friends, or just enjoying the fire on a rainy day. When the weather clears, move out to a chair on the spacious back porch or on the lawn. Activities range from games such as badminton and volleyball, to swimming in the lake or indoor pool, to canoeing. The main lodge dining room has two walls of large windows that offer a great view of the lake. A service bar in the lobby sells coffee, espresso, beer, wine, cocktails, and other beverages. Across the road from the lodge, a country store sells general merchandise, sandwiches, and groceries. The thirty-minute loop drive around Lake Quinault offers a good view of the rain forest and the possibility of an elk sighting.

Rooms: Doubles, triples, and quads. A few rooms sleep more than four. Each room has a private bath, with the majority having a combination shower-tub, although some rooms have either a bathtub or a shower, but not both.

Wheelchair Accessibility: Two first-floor lakeside rooms with one queen bed are ADA compliant. Ramp access at the front of the main lodge building provides wheelchair access to the registration area, restaurant, and lobby area.

Reservations: Lake Quinault Lodge, P.O. Box 7, Quinault, WA 98575-0007. Phone (800) 562–6672 or (360) 288–2900;

or visit www.visitlakequinault.com. First night's payment is required. A twenty-four-hour cancellation notice is required for full refund less a $10 cancellation fee.

Rates: Rates are seasonal. Peak rates apply from mid-June through September, plus all holidays. Value season rates apply the remainder of the year. Lakeside rooms ($158/$117); Lakeside suites ($316/$234); Main Lodge lake view ($148/$107); Main Lodge woodside ($117/$80); Main Lodge suite ($234/$160); Fireplace units ($183/$133); Boathouse lake view ($133/$80); Boathouse woodside ($117/$70); Boathouse suite ($255/$199). Rates quoted are for two adults; each additional person is $10. Children under five stay free. Special packages are offered during the winter months.

Location: On the south shore of Lake Quinault, 2 miles east of US 101 on South Shore Road.

Season: The lodge is open year-round.

Food: The dining room serves breakfast ($6.00–$15.00), lunch ($8.00–$19.00), and dinner ($13.00–$39.00). Reserva-tions are required for dinner. A general store across the road serves hamburgers, pizza, sandwiches, ice cream, and beverages including espresso and milk shakes. It also sells groceries, beer, and wine.

Transportation: The nearest scheduled air and rail service is in Seattle, where rental cars are available.

Facilities: Heated indoor pool, men's and women's dry saunas, recreation room, canoe, kayak, seacycle, and row-boat rentals, swimming beach, auditorium, restaurant, service bar, gift shop, gas station, and general store.

Activities: Guided walks, canoeing, kayaking, seacycling, boating, badminton, volleyball, croquet, horseshoes, and evening programs are popular during summer. Fishing, hik-ing, swimming, Ping-Pong, pool, video games, and board games are available year-round. Massage therapy is avail-able on weekends and holidays.

Pets: Pets are allowed only in the Boathouse at $10 per night, per pet.

Log Cabin Resort

3183 East Beach Road • Port Angeles, WA 98363 • (360) 928–3325 • www.logcabinresort.net

Chalets at Log Cabin Resort

Log Cabin Resort is a complex of freestanding cabins and linked A-frame chalets scattered in front of and beside a main lodge building that houses motel-type rooms. The one-story wooden main lodge, constructed in the 1950s, houses the registration desk, a restaurant, a cafe, a lobby, and a small store, and has lots of antiques. There's a parking lot immediately in front of the lodge; other parking is near the chalets and cabins. Virtually all of the cabins and rooms offer great views of beautiful Lake Crescent and the mountains on

Log Cabin Resort is on the site of the former Log Hotel (also known as Log Cabin Hotel or Hotel Piedmont), the first hotel built on Lake Crescent. The two-story Log Hotel was constructed of peeled cedar logs and had an attached observation tower that was also built of logs. The hotel burned in 1932, and the present Log Cabin Resort was built in the early 1950s on the same site.

\|/

the southern shore. Log Cabin Resort is located in the far northern section of Olympic National Park, on the north shore of Lake Crescent. It is 21 miles west of Port Angeles, Washington, 3.5 miles off U.S. Highway 101 on East Beach Road.

The resort offers four types of accommodations. All of the rooms have electric heat but no air-conditioning, television, or telephone. The main lodge building has four attached motel-type rooms that each have one queen-size bed, one queen-size futon, a private bath with a shower but no tub, and a kitchen area with a sink and a small refrigerator. (No cooking or eating utensils are provided.) These rooms are paneled and have a large back window that provides a view of Lake Crescent. A table and two chairs are beside the window and a back door that opens to a private patio with table and chairs. The rooms are entered through an outside door directly beside the parking lot.

Beside the lodge along the shoreline are two buildings that each have six attached A-frame rooms with small lofts. These rooms have a double bed, a futon, a kitchen sink, and a refrigerator, but no cooking or eating utensils are provided. A second double bed is in the loft reached via a stairway. A private bathroom has a shower. Windows across the back allow good lake views from both the downstairs and the loft. A cement

patio across the back of both buildings has a picnic table and grill for each room.

Eight rustic cabins constructed in 1928, three with kitchens, are available in a variety of sizes, with several types of beds that range upward from a double and a single bed. The cabins each have a private bath with either a shower or a tub. Each cabin has a covered front porch with chairs that allow guests a good view of the lake and mountains. The three cabins with kitchens each have a stove, oven, sink, and refrigerator, but no cooking or eating utensils are provided. Six of the cabins are arranged in a semi-circle on a grassy hillside overlooking the lake. A picnic table is in front of each cabin. The least expensive accommodation is four relatively new camping log cabins with electricity but no plumbing. Each cabin has two double beds, but guests are required to provide their own bedding or it can be rented. Outside each cabin is a picnic table and a fire barrel. A common bathroom with showers is located just behind the cabins.

Log Cabin Resort is a fun place to spend several days in a magnificent mountain and lake setting inside Olympic National Park. Guests have plenty to do, with a roped lake swimming area just beside the lodge, boat rentals (canoes, paddleboats, and rowboats), and fishing. A 4-mile-long trail along an old railroad bed beside the lake passes by the resort. A nicely decorated restaurant, which serves breakfast and dinner, has a wall of windows that overlooks the lake. A patio area directly in back of the main lodge is available for outside dining. A cafe, the Soda Jerk, serves hot dogs, espresso, other beverages, and ice cream from 8:00 A.M. to 8:00 P.M. The store also sells snack foods and beverages.

Rooms: Singles, doubles, triples, and quads. The A-frame chalets and some of the cabins can hold up to six persons.

Wheelchair Accessibility: No wheelchair-accessible rooms are available at the resort.

Reservations: 3183 East Beach Road, Port Angeles, WA

98363. Phone (360) 928–3325; fax (360) 928–2088. A deposit of one night's stay is required. A cancellation notice of seventy-two hours is required for a full refund less a $15 fee.

Rates: Lodge rooms ($110); A-frame chalet ($134); cabins ($82–$98); camping log cabins ($53). Rates quoted are for two adults. Each additional person is $12 per night in all lodgings, with the exception of the camping cabins where each additional person is $6.00. Children six and under stay free.

Location: The resort is 18 miles west of Port Angeles, Washington, on US 101, 3.5 miles on East Beach Road on the north shore of Lake Crescent.

Season: April 1 to September 30.

Food: An attractive dining room in the main lodge serves breakfast ($6.00–$10.00) and dinner ($11.00–$19.00). Alco-

holic beverages are served. A cafe serves hot dogs, espresso, other beverages, and ice cream from 8:00 A.M. to 8:00 P.M.; microwaveable foods are sold in the store and a microwave is available for use.

Transportation: The nearest scheduled air service is in Port Angeles, where rental cars are available. A Port Angeles city bus stops at the resort twice a day, at 1:00 and 6:00 P.M.

Facilities: Swimming beach, boat rental, boat launch, gift shop, limited groceries, laundry, and fishing supplies.

Activities: Fishing, hiking, boating, swimming.

Pets: Pets are allowed in the cabins only. There is a $10 fee per pet, per day, along with a pet deposit of $35.

SOL DUC HOT SPRINGS RESORT

P.O. 2169 • Port Angeles, WA 98362 • (866) 476–5382 • www.visitsolduc.com

Cabin at Sol Duc Hot Springs Resort

SOL DUC (A NATIVE AMERICAN TERM MEANING "sparkling water") Hot Springs Resort includes a single two-story wooden lodge building constructed in the 1980s and twenty-nine modern wooden buildings, for a total of thirty-two rooms. The former owner's home is available for group rental. No overnight accommodations are in the main lodge building, which houses the registration desk, a very small lobby area, a gift shop, a small convenience store, a restaurant, and rest rooms. The resort is known primarily for more than twenty hot

mineral springs that feed pools located behind the lodge. A swimming pool is in the same complex. The resort is situated in the Sol Duc River Valley, surrounded by the heavily treed mountains of Olympic National Park. Sol Duc Hot Springs Resort is 42 miles west of Port Angeles, Washington, in the northwest corner of Olympic National Park. It is on a paved road 12 miles southeast of U.S. Highway 101.

Sol Duc Hot Springs Resort offers thirty-two wood-frame cabins and one house constructed in the

The first hotel at Sol Duc Springs was opened in 1912. The elaborate hotel, constructed by a man who claimed the mineral springs had cured him of a fatal illness, included tennis courts, bowling alleys, golf links, a theater, and a three-story sanatorium with beds for one hundred patients. Unfortunately, sparks from the fireplace ignited the shingle roof and burned down the hotel only four years after its completion. According to legend, the fire short-circuited the hotel's wiring, causing the organ to begin playing Beethoven's "Funeral March" while the building was burning.

early 1980s. All of the cabins have a shake roof and covered front porch with a bench seat. The cabins are clustered in a large grassy area in front of the main lodge building. Sliding windows are on the front and back walls of each cabin. Twenty-six cabins are free-standing units, while six cabins are in duplex buildings near the main lodge. Other than the duplex units, all the cabins are virtually identical, with two queen beds or two double beds, finished interior walls, carpeted floors, electric heat, a table and four chairs, and a full bathroom with a combination shower-tub. No telephones, air-conditioning, or televisions are in any of the cabins. The interiors of the cabins are similar to, but maybe a little larger than, most motel rooms. Three duplex units comprising six cabins each have two double beds and a kitchen area furnished with a sink, refrigerator and freezer, stove, and oven. These units are near the main lodge and rent for about $20 per night more than cabins without a kitchen. Cabins in the duplex buildings have approximately the same interior space as the freestanding cabins. Parking is available near all of the cabins so that handling luggage isn't a

problem. A three-bedroom house with two baths, a full kitchen, a living room, family room, and sunroom is available for group rental. All of the living space is on the second floor.

Most visitors take advantage of the natural hot springs. The resort has three circular pools of hot mineral water and a regular heated swimming pool, all located behind the main lodge building. The largest hot-water pool and a small shallow pool for children each have mineral water at a temperature of 99° to 101° Fahrenheit. Another small pool has mineral water at a

According to Quileute Indian legend, dragon tears are the source of the hot springs at Sol Duc. Whether dragon tears or natural phenomena, the hot springs have drawn people to this area for many years. In the early 1900s the springs were claimed by Theodore Moritz, who said the hot mineral water helped him recuperate from an injury in the woods. In the early 1920s the third owner of this property built two pools, a 50-by-150-foot freshwater pool without heat and a 50-by-60-foot hot springs pool. The sides of these pools were knocked out in 1984 and replaced by the four pools currently in use. The three mineral pools include a wading pool with water at 99° Fahrenheit, the fountain pool with a temperature of 101° Fahrenheit, and a soaking pool with a 104° Fahrenheit temperature. The large freshwater swimming pool utilizes a heat exchanger, and water temperature varies depending on the weather and outside temperature. Admission to the pool area includes use of all the pools. Wheelchair access is available to the fountain pool and freshwater pool. Wheelchairs can be borrowed on-site.

temperature of 104° Fahrenheit. These pools are relatively shallow and designed for sitting and walking, not swimming. A larger swimming pool in the same complex has regular water that is heated. Both the larger mineral water pool and the swimming pool have ramps for wheelchair access. The mineral water pools and the swimming pool are available without charge to resort cabin guests; other visitors can use the facilities for a fee.

Sol Duc Hot Springs Resort is a good place to unwind. You can hike in the morning, soak in the mineral water pool after lunch, get a professional massage in the late afternoon, take a nap in your cabin, then walk to the lodge for supper. After that, it's time for a good night's sleep so you can start all over again the next morning. A restaurant in the main lodge serves breakfast and dinner, while lunch is available at a deli beside the pool. Plenty of hiking trails near the resort lead into the rain forest and to the beautiful Sol Duc Falls. Evening programs on natural history are occasionally offered at the nearby campground by National Park Service rangers.

Rooms: Doubles, triples, and quads. All rooms have a full bath. A three-bedroom house with two full bathrooms should be available for the 2006 season.

Wheelchair Accessibility: Three freestanding cabins without a kitchen are wheelchair accessible with an entry ramp, a wide bathroom doorway, and grab bars around the combination shower-tub. No grab bars are by the toilet. A ramp allows entry to the main lodge building and restaurant. Wheelchair access is available to one hot mineral pool and the freshwater pool. Wheelchairs are available for loan.

Reservations: Sol Duc Hot Springs Resort, P.O. Box 2169, Port Angeles, WA 98362. Phone (866) 476–5382. A deposit of one-night's stay is required. A cancellation notice of forty-eight hours is required for a full refund less an $8.00 fee.

Rates: Cabin without kitchen ($119). Cabins with kitchen ($139). Rates quoted are for two persons. Each additional person is $20 per night. Children under four stay free.

Location: Twelve miles southeast of US 101. The resort is in the northern part of Olympic National Park, 42 miles from Port Angeles, Washington.

Season: The lodge is open to overnight guests from April 1 to October 31. The restaurant is open from early May to late September.

Food: A restaurant in the main lodge building serves breakfast ($5.00–$8.00) and dinner ($15.00–$20.00). Beer and wine are available. Sandwiches and beverages are available at the poolside deli from 11:00 A.M. to 4:00 P.M. during the summer. Hours are extended to 6:00 P.M. in the spring and fall. A few groceries, beer, and wine are sold near the registration desk.

Transportation: No public transportation is available to the lodge. Port Angeles, Washington, is the nearest city with scheduled air service and rental vehicles.

Facilities: Heated swimming pool, heated mineral pools, restaurant (summer), deli, gift shop, convenience store, and licensed massage practitioners.

Activities: Swimming, hiking, fishing, and soaking in mineral baths. Occasional evening National Park Service campfire programs.

Pets: Pets are allowed in the cabins for $10 per pet, per night. They are not allowed in the pool area or on the trails.

WYOMING

Grand Teton National Park/
John D. Rockefeller, Jr., Memorial Parkway

P.O. Drawer 170 • Moose, WY 83012 • (307) 739–3300 • www.nps/gov/grte/ • www.nps.gov/jodr/

Grand Teton National Park, which covers nearly 310,000 acres, includes the famous Teton Range, considered by many as the most beautiful mountain range in the United States. The park's three visitor centers are at Moose, Jenny Lake, and Colter Bay. A visitor center jointly operated by the U.S. Forest Service and the City of Jackson is at the north end of Jackson. The 24,000-acre John D. Rockefeller, Jr., Memorial Parkway is a 7½ -mile corridor that links the south entrance of Yellowstone National Park with the north entrance to Grand Teton National Park. The Snake River, which flows through both parks, offers excellent float trips. The two parks are in northwestern Wyoming, directly south of the West Thumb area of Yellowstone National Park. **Park Entrance Fee:** $20 per vehicle, $15 per motorcycle, or $10 per person, good for seven days. This entrance fee also covers Yellowstone National Park.

Lodging in Grand Teton National Park: Grand Teton National Park and the John D. Rockefeller, Jr., Memorial Parkway together provide a total of seven lodging facilities. Flagg Ranch Village is the only one of the seven that is located in the parkway, which lies between Grand Teton and Yellowstone. Triangle X Ranch, the only working dude ranch in a national park, is the most unusual lodging facility in the park, and maybe in any park. The least expensive facilities are at Colter Bay. The view rooms at Jackson Lake Lodge are some of the most upscale accommodations. Jenny Lake Lodge, with a four-diamond rating, is a quaint facility but is relatively expensive, even considering that horseback riding, bicycles, breakfast, and a five-course dinner are included in the price.

COLTER BAY VILLAGE

P.O. Box 240 • Moran, WY 83013 • (307) 543–3100 • www.gtlc.com

Cabins at Colter Bay Village

Grand Teton National Park/
John D. Rockefeller, Jr., Memorial Parkway

YELLOWSTONE NATIONAL PARK

Flagg Ranch
Resort

JOHN D. ROCKEFELLER, JR.,
MEMORIAL PARKWAY

89
287
191

Lizard Creek

BRIDGER-
TETON
NATIONAL
FOREST

GRAND TETON
NATIONAL
PARK

Jackson Lake

Leeks
Marina

Jackson Lake
Lodge

CARIBOU-
TARGHEE
NATIONAL
FOREST

Colter Bay
Village

Signal
Mountain

Signal
Mountain
Lodge

Moran
Junction

26   287

Leigh
Lake

Teton Park Rd.

Jenny
Lake

Jenny Lake
Lodge

Triangle
X Ranch

TETON RANGE

Moose

Dornan's Spur Ranch
Log Cabins

Snake River

Jackson Hole Airport

Kelly

Gros
Ventre

Teton
Village

Gros Ventre
Junction

Moose-Wilson Rd.

N
W   E
S

0   5   10
Miles

22

26
89
191

To Jackson

Colter Bay Village, a major recreation center for Grand Teton National Park, includes a grocery store, gift and tackle shop, laundromat, the steak and pasta house, cafe court, and gas station. The lodging facility at Colter Bay consists of 166 rooms in log cabins and sixty-six tent cabins. RV sites and a campground are also available. Colter Bay has no hotel, motel, or main lodge building. A small cabin rental office handles registration for the log cabins, while a separate office farther down the road takes care of registration for the tent cabins. The two types of accommodations are in separate areas, but both are near the restaurants and other facilities of Colter Bay Village. The lodging facilities here are the least expensive in Grand Teton National Park. Colter Bay Village is located on the shore of Jackson Lake, about 15 miles south of the north entrance to Grand Teton National Park.

Colter Bay has two very different types of accommodations. The least expensive lodging is in sixty-six tent cabins. This lodging is about as basic as you will find outside your own tent. The tent cabins are constructed of two canvas walls and a canvas roof connected to two log walls. The cabins each contain a wood stove (wood is not provided but can be purchased), electric light, and two sets of bunk beds with thin vinyl-covered mattresses. A picnic table is on a canvas-covered porch just outside the front door. Guests are responsible for everything else, including sheets, blankets, pillows, and utensils. Sleeping bags, cots, blankets, and pillows can be rented at the registration office. Two rest room facilities without showers are in the immediate area. Showers (fee) are available at a nearby laundry facility. The tent cabins are on a hill and offer views of pine trees, and a few sites have limited views of the Tetons.

Colter Bay also has 166 mostly log cabins clustered on a hillside of pine trees, grass, wildflowers, and weeds along paved roads behind the commercial center. All cabins other than two semiprivate dorm units have a private bath with a shower and all have heat.

The well-maintained cabins are of varying sizes and ages, with vaulted log-beamed ceilings, attractive log or wood interiors, and linoleum floors (only one-room cabins 401 and 403, and two-room cabin 405 have carpeting). None of the cabins has a television or telephone. Parking is immediately in front of each unit.

Most of the one-room cabins are constructed as duplex units, although a few are freestanding, and one particularly long building includes six cabins. Only a few of these cabins have a front porch. Beds range from one double to two doubles plus a single. Cabins 637 and 639 are each freestanding, with a nice porch overhang. Unit 212, with floor to ceiling windows on one wall, was once an artist's studio and is the most unusual cabin at Colter Bay. One-room cabin 471 was constructed more than one hundred years ago and is the oldest cabin in the Colter Bay complex.

Forty-two cabins each have two rooms, most with a bedroom on each side of a common bathroom. The majority of two-room cabins are freestanding and have a very small front porch. About half of these cabins have a double bed in one room and two twin beds in the other room. Units 617 and 810 in this group sit on a hill and offer more privacy than most other cabins, although staying in either unit will involve a little climbing. The other two-room cabins are somewhat larger, have two double beds in each room, and are priced somewhat higher, but the price includes up to four adults. Cabins 1031, 1035, 1039, 1043, and 1055 in this group are particularly desirable because they are on a dead-end road and back up to a wooded area.

Two log buildings in the cabin area offer a total of nine rooms without private bath. These semiprivate dorm rooms are nice, but occupants must use a community bathroom. Four units in one building each have two twin beds and a hallway bathroom. Five units in a nearby building behind the restaurant are smaller, with one double bed. Bathrooms here must be entered from outside the building. The building with twin-bed units is far more desirable because the rooms

Most of the buildings at Colter Bay Village were moved here from other locations around the Jackson Hole area. At one time Jackson Hole had many small dude ranches and tourist resorts, typically consisting of a central lodge building and five to thirty log cabins. After Grand Teton National Park was expanded in 1950 with a gift of 34,000 acres from John D. Rockefeller, Jr., most of the old lodges were closed and many of the cabins were moved via flatbed truck to Colter Bay, where the cabins were modernized with new roofs, electricity, and plumbing. In fact, the existing Colter Bay cabin office was once the old store at Square G Ranch that was located just north of Jenny Lake. The ranch also supplied many of Colter Bay's cabins. Other cabins came from the old Teton Lodge at Moran, the old Jackson Lake Lodge, and the Circle H Guest Ranch. Cabins from several other old resorts were moved to Colter Bay during the 1960s. A written history of each cabin at Colter Bay is framed and posted inside the building. Guests may ask the front desk for a keepsake history of the cabin in which they stayed.

are bigger (especially rooms 460 and 466), the bathroom is inside, and the location is quieter. A guest lounge with couches, chairs, and game tables is next door. Keep in mind that these buildings have no insulation between rooms, so guests are likely to hear conversations in adjacent rooms. This is the major drawback to a room in one of these two buildings.

Colter Bay Village is a pleasant place to spend several days in Grand Teton National Park. Although the main village area, with a marina, restaurants, gift shops, grocery store, laundry facility with showers

(fee), and the National Park Service visitor center, is generally bustling with people and vehicles, the lodging is far enough away to escape most of the noise and congestion. At the same time, it is close enough that guests can avail themselves of the facilities. If you don't mind a room without a private bath, the semiprivate dorm rooms are the best value, at half the price you will pay for the smallest cabin and about the same price as a tent cabin, where you have to supply your own bedding and pay for a shower that is some distance away. Colter Bay Village offers a variety of activities, including horseback riding, raft trips, fishing, lake cruises, and boating. A pool at Jackson Lake Lodge is available to Colter Bay guests.

Rooms: Doubles, triples, and quads. A few two-bedroom units can accommodate up to eight persons. Most of the cabins have a private bath. None of the tent cabins has a private bath.

Wheelchair Accessibility: Three wheelchair-accessible cabins each have asphalt paths to the doorway and a bathroom with a wide doorway, grab bars, and a shower with a slight lip and a fold-down seat. These rooms are on each side of the guest lounge. Both restaurants and the accompanying bathrooms are wheelchair accessible, as are the grocery store and the convenience store at the gas station.

Reservations: Grand Teton Lodge Company, P.O. Box 240, Moran, WY 83013. Phone (800) 628–9988, (307) 543–3100. A one-night deposit is required. A cancellation notice of three days is required for a refund less a $15 fee.

Rates: Tent cabins ($37); semiprivate dorm cabins ($38); one-room cabins ($75–$112); two-room cabins ($118–$140). Rates quoted are for two persons with the exception of the larger two-room cabins where rates are quoted for four adults. Each additional person is $5.00 per night in tent cabins, $9.00 per night in log cabins. Children eleven and under stay free with an adult.

Location: North section of Grand Teton National Park, 40 miles north of Jackson, Wyoming.

Season: Late May to late September for log cabins. Early June to early September for tent cabins.

Food: Colter Bay has two eating establishments. The Chuckwagon Steak & Pasta House serves a continental breakfast ($7.50) and a full breakfast buffet ($10.50), lunch ($7.00-$10.00), and dinner ($11.00–$20.00). The John Colter Café Court serves soups, salads, sandwiches, and pizza ($5.00–$8.00). A grocery store in the village sells bakery items, deli sandwiches, and ice cream in addition to a fairly extensive line of groceries, beer, and wine.

Transportation: The nearest scheduled air service is in Jackson, Wyoming, where rental cars are available. With advance notice, a shuttle from Jackson Lake Lodge will meet flights. A shuttle (fee charged) operates between Colter Bay and Jackson Lake Lodge.

Facilities: Restaurant, food court, grocery store, gift shop, tackle shop, stables, marina, boat rental, service station, laundromat, National Park Service visitor center with museum and gift shop. Internet service is available in the registration building.

Activities: Hiking, fishing, boating, boat cruises, horseback riding, float trips, bus tours to Yellowstone National Park and through Grand Teton National Park, ranger/naturalist talks and walks during the day, evening campfire programs. The swimming pool at Jackson Lake Lodge is available to registered guests from Colter Bay Village.

Pets: Pets are allowed in some cabins.

DORNAN'S SPUR RANCH LOG CABINS

P.O. Box 39 • Moose, WY 83012 • (307) 733–2522 • www.dornans.com

DORNAN'S SPUR RANCH IS A LODGING COMPLEX OF twelve modern log cabins clustered in a courtyard behind a log registration building. The cabins are down a small hill from Dornan's, a small commercial center, which includes a grocery and outdoor restaurant. The entire complex sits in a basin next to the Snake River. Parking is beside the registration building and a short distance from the cabins. Two-wheel carts are available to transport luggage along paved walkways leading to each of the cabins. The cabins are on privately owned land within the boundaries of Grand Teton National Park. Dornan's is located near the south end of the park, at Moose Junction.

The twelve modern duplex log cabins at Dornan's were constructed in 1992. All the cabins have a combination living room/kitchen area, a full bathroom with a combination shower-tub, and either one or two bedrooms. The kitchen area has a table and chairs. The bedrooms have one queen-size bed with a down comforter, and the living room has a sofa bed. An extra comforter is in the closet. Each cabin has a door off the living room that leads to a small covered wooden deck

> *Dornan's is probably most famous for the gourmet grocery and large wine selection. The grocery has a deli, a bakery, and a selection of gourmet specialty foods. Next door, the liquor store offers 1,500 choices of wine. The chuck wagon dinner offers all you can eat of ribs, roast beef, and stew, beginning at 5:00 P.M.*

\||/

with table and chairs. A charcoal grill (but not charcoal) is on the porch. The cabins have been sited so that most of the decks offer a view of the magnificent Tetons. The cabins also sit close to the famous Snake River. One duplex unit houses Cascade and Garnet, two one-bedroom cabins that are next to the river and provide excellent views of the mountains. Larkspur, a two-bedroom unit, has a patio that faces the river.

Even though the cabins are duplex units, we found that they were designed so that you won't realize you have a neighbor in the same building. The cabins are roomy and have hardwood floors in the living room/kitchen, nice tile in the bathroom, and fully carpeted bedrooms. Voice mail service and Internet access is available in all units. The kitchen is fully equipped, with a full-size refrigerator, stove, oven, coffeemaker, toaster, dishes, and all utensils. All you need to bring is the food. Of course you can walk up the hill and purchase some nice sirloins at the gourmet grocery store. Folks, it doesn't get much better than this.

Dornan's log cabins are among the nicest accommodations in Grand Teton National Park. The cabins are a short walk from Dornan's small commercial area, which has a gas station, a gift shop, a sporting goods store, a chuck wagon restaurant, and a grocery with many specialty gourmet items. A bar/restaurant adjacent to a liquor store, with a sizable variety of wines, has large picture windows that offer spectacular views of the

Teton Mountain Range. Dornan's sells and rents various sports equipment and offers both scenic and whitewater float trips. The cabins are open during the winter.

Rooms: One-bedroom cabins can accommodate up to four persons. Two-bedroom units hold up to six. All cabins have a full bath and full kitchen.

Wheelchair Accessibility: One cabin has a boardwalk ramp and a bathroom with a wide doorway, a high toilet, grab bars, and a roll-in shower.

Reservations: Dornan's Spur Ranch Log Cabins, P.O. Box 39, Moose, WY 83012. Phone (307) 733–2522; fax (307) 739–9098. A deposit of three nights' stay is required during high season, and a deposit for one night is required for the low season. All cancellations result in a $50 charge plus forfeit of deposit if received less than thirty days prior to arrival.

Rates: Rates are seasonal. High-season rates apply Memorial Day Weekend to September 30 and Christmas through New Year's Day with a three-night minimum; one-bedroom cabin with one to two persons ($155), with three to four persons ($185); two-bedroom cabin with up to six persons ($230). Low-season rates for October 1 to Memorial Day Weekend with a one-night minimum: one-bedroom cabin with one to two persons ($125); with three to four persons ($150); two-bedroom cabin with up to six persons ($175).

Location: South end of Grand Teton National Park, at Moose Junction. The cabins are 12 miles north of Jackson, Wyoming.

Season: Open year-round.

Food: A chuck wagon outdoor restaurant serves breakfast ($8.50), lunch ($6.00–$9.50), and all-you-can-eat dinner ($14.00–$16.00; Saturday and Sunday, Prime Rib or twelve-ounce steak ($22.00) during summer months. A bar/restaurant serves salads, pizza, and pasta for lunch and dinner (hours vary); there is both inside and outside seating available. Groceries are available at the store.

Transportation: Air service is available to Jackson, Wyoming, where rental vehicles are available.

Facilities: Grocery, bar/restaurant, liquor store, outdoor restaurant, gift shop, fly-fishing store, gas station, and sports shop, with bicycle, canoe, and kayak rentals.

Activities: Hiking, fishing, scenic and whitewater float trips on the Snake River, canoeing, kayaking, mountain biking. Winter activities include cross-country skiing, downhill skiing, and snowmobiling.

FLAGG RANCH RESORT

P.O. Box 187 • Moran, WY 83013 • (307) 543–2861 • www.flaggranch.com

Cabin at Flagg Ranch Resort

FLAGG RANCH RESORT ENCOMPASSES A MODERN log-style main lodge building, ninety-two nearby modern log cabin rooms, a service station, and a campground with hookups. Registration for the cabins is just inside the front door of the main lodge, which itself has no accommodations. A large parking lot is in front of the lodge. The main lodge is quite attractive, with a lobby separated from the dining room by a large double-sided stone fireplace. In addition to the dining room and lobby, the main lodge houses a gift shop, grocery, lounge, and front desk. Flagg Ranch Resort is located at the north end of John D. Rockefeller, Jr., Memorial Parkway, 2 miles south of the south entrance to Yellowstone National Park and 5 miles north of the north entrance to Grand Teton National Park.

Thirty wooden buildings constructed in 1995 with metal roofs and log-style exteriors house ninety-two cabin-style hotel rooms. The cabin complex sits on a bluff that overlooks the Snake River Valley, although the river itself is visible from only a few of the cabin patios. The buildings, constructed as either duplexes or quads, are clustered in a natural setting of rocks, dirt,

weeds, grass, and wildflowers behind a large parking area that is approximately a quarter mile from the main lodge parking. The buildings are nicely spaced, and the cabins are insulated, so you are unlikely to be bothered by noise from guests in an adjoining cabin. A series of cement walkways lead from the parking area, where two-wheeled luggage carts are kept. The cabins are far enough from the main lodge and restaurant that many guests drive between the two locations.

All the cabins are rented in one of two classifications: view and nonview. View cabins rent for $10 per night extra and are in the back of the complex nearest the bluff and most distant from the parking area. View rooms each have a patio facing the Snake River Valley. All ninety-two cabins are the same size, with some having one king bed and others two queen beds. Each cabin has a private bathroom with a combination shower-tub (with the exception of three wheelchair-accessible cabins, which have roll-in showers), gas heat, a vaulted ceiling, and a finished interior that is similar to that found in a large and nicely furnished motel room. Each cabin also has a coffeemaker and a tele-

Flagg Ranch was established between 1910 and 1916 at its present location by an early guide and pioneer in this area, which is believed to have been a favorite camping spot for both native tribes and fur trappers. The ranch is the oldest continually operating resort in the upper Jackson Hole area. It has served as both a dude ranch and a lodging facility, offering overnight accommodations to early trappers and present-day travelers. The ranch name is derived from the flag that flew from the Snake River Military Station, once located here.

Several activities are available for guests, including interpretive tours to Yellowstone and Grand Teton National Parks, one-hour guided trail rides, a 10-mile scenic float trip, and a 3-mile whitewater rafting trip. The road between the town of Jackson and Flagg Ranch is open during winter months. With prior notice, Flagg Ranch will furnish transportation (fee charged) from several locations including the Jackson airport and Teton Village to the ranch. Check with the ranch for information. Winter equipment rentals are available at the ranch. Snowcoaches from Yellowstone provide transportation between Flagg Ranch and the Old Faithful area; Old Faithful Snow Lodge is open during winter months.

Rooms: Doubles, triples, and quads. All rooms have a private bath with a combination shower-tub.

Wheelchair Accessibility: Three nonview cabins nearest the parking are wheelchair accessible, with a large bathroom that has a wide doorway, grab bars, a high toilet, and a roll-in shower. The main lodge and restaurant are also wheelchair accessible.

Reservations: Flagg Ranch Resort, P.O. Box 187, Moran, WY 83013. Phone (800) 443–2311 or (307) 543–2861; fax (307) 543–2356. A deposit of one-night's stay (or two-nights' stay for multiple nights) is required. A cancellation notice of six days is required for a full refund, less a $25 cancellation fee.

Rates: Nonview ($150), view ($160). Rates quoted are for two adults. Children seventeen and under stay free.

Location: North end of John D. Rockefeller, Jr., Memorial Parkway, 2 miles south of the south entrance to Yellowstone National Park.

Season: Mid-May through mid-October.

Food: A full-service restaurant offers breakfast ($5.00–$10.00), lunch ($7.00–$10.00), and dinner ($11.00–$20.00). Alcoholic beverages are served in the dining room. A children's menu is available. A lounge adjacent to the dining room serves appetizers. Groceries are available at a small store in the main lodge.

Transportation: The nearest scheduled air service is in Jackson, Wyoming.

Facilities: Restaurant, cocktail lounge, gift shop, grocery store, gas station, coin laundry.

phone. None of the rooms has air-conditioning, a television, or a kitchenette. Cabins have a covered cement patio with rocking chairs.

The cabins at Flagg Ranch are modern, clean, and comfortable. Each is identical in interior size and furnishings, so you are only required to choose between a view or nonview cabin and between two queen beds or one king bed. We don't know about your bed preference, but we suggest you spring for a view room that has larger windows and a patio that faces nature instead of your neighbor. The slight difference in cost is especially worthwhile if you will be spending considerable time in your cabin. Keep in mind that the cabins with a view are most distant from the parking lot, but with the luggage carts the difference in distance isn't really a problem. We enjoyed sitting on the patio, reading a book, and being able to see the beauty of the Wyoming landscape uninterrupted by other cabins. A trail behind the cabins leads along the edge of the bluff and down to the Snake River.

Flagg Ranch offers modern, comfortable lodging at a convenient location between Yellowstone and Grand Teton National Parks. The cabins are relatively large, and the main lodge building has an attractive western decor.

Activities: Hiking, whitewater rafting, float trips, trail rides, guided fishing trips, interpretive tours to Yellowstone National Park and Grand Teton National Park. Winter activities include snowmobiling.

Pets: Pets are permitted in the cabins at an additional fee of $10 per day, per pet.

JACKSON LAKE LODGE

Grand Teton Lodge Company • P.O. Box 250 • Moran, WY 83013 • (307) 543–3100
www.gtlc.com

Main Lodge Building at Jackson Lake Lodge

JACKSON LAKE LODGE INCLUDES A VERY LARGE CENTRAL lodge building flanked by numerous multiple-unit wooden buildings that house cottage units. These cottages are hidden from view by surrounding trees. Overnight rooms are also on the third floor of the lodge. The three-story cement lodge sits on a bluff overlooking a large willow meadow and Jackson Lake, both of which are highlighted by the spectacular Teton mountain range. Registration is just inside the main entrance. The lodge building has a large second-floor lobby with two corner fireplaces, many comfortable chairs and sofas, Native American artifacts scattered throughout, and a two-story wall of windows with a picture-perfect view of the Tetons. The lodge also has a dining room, grill, cocktail lounge, gift shop, apparel shop featuring fine western and adventure wear, and a T-shirt shop—all on the second floor; an art gallery on the third-floor balcony has tables and chairs and a great view. A large parking lot is just behind the lodge, and plentiful parking is near each of the cottage units. Arriving guests can use the entrance drive to register and, for guests who will be staying in the lodge, drop off luggage. An elevator is in the lodge. Jackson Lake Lodge is located on the east side of Jackson Lake, 5 miles northwest of Moran Junction, about 35 miles north of the town of Jackson.

The lodge offers four basic types of Rooms: view rooms, lodge rooms, cottages, and suites. All rooms have heat, a telephone with data port, voice mail, iron and ironing board, hair dryer, and a private bath but no television or air-conditioning. Cottages comprise the vast majority of the 385 rooms at the Jackson Lake complex. The thirty-seven rooms in the main lodge, all on the third floor, are mostly alike except for the view. Rooms on the west side of the building, with large windows that provide great views of the Tetons, cost a little over $100 more per night than similar rooms on the east side. All the rooms have two double beds with a full bathroom. The more costly view rooms also have a small refrigerator, a wet bar,

The Amoretti Inn, the original lodge constructed in 1922 at this site, included a main lodge building and thirty cabins. The lodge, which stood near where the 900 building of the current lodge is located, boasted of indoor plumbing in its log cabins. The name was changed to Jackson Lake Lodge in the late 1920s. The old lodge continued to provide overnight rooms until the new Jackson Lake Lodge was completed in June 1955. The old cabins were then moved to Colter Bay, where they were renovated and are still in use today.

a coffeemaker, a ceiling fan, and down comforters on the beds. All the rooms in the lodge are quite large and attractively decorated, but none has a balcony. The main lodge building has one suite with a sitting area with a sofa and chairs, one king-size bed, a whirlpool bathtub, a formal cherrywood dining table, a wet bar, and a full-size refrigerator. The suite offers a panoramic view of the mountains.

The 347 cottage rooms each have two double beds, comfortable furniture, ceiling fans, and a full bath. These cottages are quite roomy (bigger than rooms in the main lodge), most have a vaulted beamed ceiling, and they are attractively decorated and considerably nicer than a typical motel room. Most of the cottages are in a series of one-story wood-frame buildings of eight to twenty rooms that back up to one another. The buildings are in a nicely landscaped area with lots of vegetation including fir and aspen trees. Many cottages have a front porch but do not offer a mountain or lake view. Most odd-numbered cottages in the 100 and 200 buildings do not have a front porch and are less desirable. One two-story and four one-story buildings offer cottages with a private back patio or balcony and rent for $7.00 extra per night. Cottages 123 and 125 in this category both have a patio that offers a partial view of the Tetons. Three two-story

cottage buildings offer forty-six units with a private balcony or patio that faces the Tetons. Other than three corner suites in these buildings, these are the premiere cottage units and rent for about $60 per night more than cottages with a back patio but no mountain view. Rooms on the second floor each have a balcony and a vaulted interior ceiling with a fan, while first-floor rooms have a regular ceiling and a back patio fronted by a small grassy area. No elevators are in the two-story cottage buildings. Three suites in one of the two-story view buildings have a double-size room, two bathrooms, one with a whirlpool tub and one with a shower, a king- or queen-size bed plus a Murphy bed. One of these suites (room 911) has a full kitchen and wraparound balcony. We believe the best value is rooms in the lodge without a mountain view, which rent for $32 per night less than any other accommodations at Jackson Lake Lodge. These are nice rooms, and guests can enjoy a great view of the Tetons by walking down one flight of stairs to the second-floor lobby. If you want to splurge for a room with a view we suggest you choose one of the mountain view cottages, which have a private balcony or patio facing the mountains. One of the great pleasures of staying in one of these units is sitting on your back patio and enjoying the magnificent panorama of Jackson Lake against a background of the Tetons. The mountain view cottages each have a large back window that allows a similar view. The back patio or balcony, along with the ease of getting your luggage into the room, makes these a better choice than the view rooms in the lodge, which actually cost a little more.

Jackson Lake Lodge is a pleasant place to stay, especially if you enjoy spectacular scenery and abundant wildlife. The location offers unsurpassed views, and all of the rooms in the complex are relatively large and comfortable. Several choices are available for dining, and the main dining room on the second floor has western-theme murals and large windows with views that rival those of the lobby. The chef will even cook fish that you catch and clean. The lounge, on the opposite side of the lobby from the dining room, has two walls of windows with views of the Tetons. The lodge also offers more stores than are usually found in a national park lodge. A variety of activities are available, including swimming in a heated pool, horseback riding, float trips, and park bus tours.

Rooms: Doubles, triples, and quads. All rooms have a private bath.

Wheelchair Accessibility: Wheelchair-accessible rooms are in both the lodge and the cottages. One nonview room in the lodge has a large bathroom with grab bars, a high toilet, and a shower with a seat and a slight lip along the bottom entry. A lodge room with a mountain view has a wide bathroom door, a high toilet, grab bars, and a combination shower-tub. An elevator operates from the registration area on the lower floor to the third floor, where lodge rooms are located. Eighteen cottage units each have ramp access and a wheelchair-accessible bathroom with a combination shower-tub. Some of the wheelchair-accessible cottage units offer a mountain view.

Reservations: Grand Teton Lodge Company, P.O. Box 250, Moran, WY 83013. Phone (800) 628–9988, (307) 543–3100. If staying two or more nights, a two-night deposit is required. A seven-day cancellation is required for deposit refund less a $30 fee.

Rates: Main lodge: nonview ($141); view ($249); cottages/patios nonview ($173–$181); view rooms ($239); suites ($425–$575). Rates quoted are for two persons. Each additional person is $10 per night. Children eleven and under stay free.

Location: Jackson Lake Lodge is located on the eastern shore of Jackson Lake, 5 miles northwest of Moran Junction, about 24 miles north of the town of Moose.

Season: Mid-May through early October.

Food: The main dining room serves bakery items or a breakfast buffet ($12.30), lunch ($9.00–$11.00), and dinner ($19.00–$32.00). Next door, the Pioneer Grill, with U-shaped counters, serves breakfast ($7.00–$9.00), lunch ($8.00–$10.00), and dinner ($8.00–$20.00). A pool grill with sandwiches, pizza, and ice cream is open for lunch during July and August. An all-you-can-eat barbecue ($20) is offered Sunday through Friday evenings, weather permitting. A cappucino/espresso cart is open during the morning hours in the lobby.

Transportation: The nearest airport is 28 miles south, in Jackson, Wyoming, where rental cars are available. A shuttle service (fee charged) operates several times a day between Jackson and the Jackson Lake Lodge, reservations suggested (800–628–9988).

Facilities: Dining room, grill, cocktail lounge, gift shops, apparel shop, newsstand, tour desk, outdoor heated swimming pool, service station, stable, medical clinic, conference facilities. Wireless Internet is available in the lobby.

Activities: Horseback riding, swimming, Snake River float trips, hiking, evening ranger/naturalist programs, boat curises on Jackson Lake, bus tours to Yellowstone National Park and through Grand Teton National Park.

Pets: Pets are allowed in some cottages.

JENNY LAKE LODGE

P.O. Box 240 • Moran, WY 83013 • (307) 733–4647 • www.gtlc.com

Cabin at
Jenny Lake Lodge

Jenny Lake Lodge features a main log lodge building on a grassy area and thirty-seven log cabins. The complex is located at the base of the Tetons, across the road from beautiful Jenny Lake. The main lodge building, with hardwood floors and vaulted ceilings, houses the registration desk, the dining room, and a cozy lobby with stuffed furniture and a large stone fireplace. Lobby and some dining room windows provide good mountain views. A wooden front deck has chairs and benches that face the mountains. A few of the cabins are freestanding, but most are duplex units. The cabins are nicely spaced in an area of pine trees. The facility is quaint, quiet, well maintained, and expensive. Unlike cabin rates at most other national park facilities, the rates here include breakfast, a five-course dinner, the use of bicycles, and for those so inclined, horseback riding. Lunch is also served for an extra charge. Jenny Lake Lodge is located in the middle of Grand Teton National Park, about 20 miles north of Jackson, Wyoming.

Jenny Lake Lodge has been awarded four diamonds by the American Automobile Association, indicating that it is one of the more upscale lodging units in the United States, let alone in a national park. For example, each cabin is named for a wildflower and has an original watercolor painting of the respective flower. The flower is also painted on a few bathroom tiles. The beds are covered with handmade quilts and down comforters, and robes, an iron and ironing board, and a hair dryer are provided in each cabin.

Two types of cabin accommodations are available at the lodge. Each cabin has a log-beamed vaulted ceiling, hardwood floors, heat, ceiling fan, a small refrigerator, coffeemaker, a telephone, and a private bath with a combination shower-tub but no air-conditioning or television. Thirty-one one-room cabins vary somewhat in decor, view, and bed configuration, which ranges from one queen-size bed, to a queen-size and a twin, to one king-size bed. Each cabin has a covered front porch with two rocking chairs. Some of the cabins face

Jenny Lake Lodge is the descendant of a small 1920s dude ranch called Danny Ranch on the same site. Five cabins and a portion of the original main lodge building remain as part of the existing complex, which gained its current name in 1952. The original log building now houses the lodge dining room. Cabins have been modernized and added to over the years. A major restoration was undertaken in the late 1980s, and four new cabins were added in 1993.

the mountain range and offer good views from the front porch. Six suites each have a wood stove (wood provided) and sofa bed in the sitting area or living room and an in-wall safe. Five of the suites have two rooms, a living room, and a bedroom. One suite consists of one very large room with a whirlpool tub and a large private patio. The suites have either a king or two queen beds.

Jenny Lake is a wonderful place where you can relax, hike, and sightsee without worrying about much of anything. The rustic nature of the lodge and cabins provides a taste of the West but with style. Two meals a day, bicycles, and horseback riding are included, the chef will cook any fish you catch, and a valet will take care of your laundry for a nominal charge. Guests of Jenny Lake Lodge have free use of the swimming pools at Jackson Lake Lodge and the Jackson Hole Golf and Tennis Club. Fly into Jackson and the staff will, with prior notice, pick you up. The only downside to Jenny Lake Lodge is the expense. On the other hand, if cost isn't a factor, this is your place to enjoy the Tetons and nature in luxury.

Rooms: Singles, doubles, triples, and quads. All cabins have a full bathroom.

Wheelchair Accessibility: Two cabins each have ramp access and a bathroom with grab bars and a combination shower-tub. The registration building, where the dining room is, is wheelchair accessible with ramp access.

Reservations: Grand Teton Lodge Company, P.O. Box 240, Moran, WY 83013. Phone (800) 628–9988 or (307) 733–4647. Up to a three-day deposit is required for stays of three days or more. Four-week cancellation is required for a refund less a $40 fee.

Rates: Cabin: one person ($385); two persons ($475); suites: one or two persons ($635–$680). Each additional person is $140 a day. Children two years and under stay free with an adult. Breakfast and dinner are included in the price.

Location: Midsection of Grand Teton National Park, approximately 20 miles north of Jackson, Wyoming.

Season: First part of June to early October.

Food: A cozy dining room serves breakfast, lunch, and a five-course dinner. Breakfast and dinner are included in the price of a room.

Transportation: Daily air service is available from Denver, Colorado, and Salt Lake City, Utah, to Jackson, Wyoming, where rental vehicles are available.

Facilities: Dining room, stables, bicycles, gift shop, concierge service. Guests have free use of the swimming pools at Jackson Lake Lodge and the Jackson Hole Golf and Tennis Club. A National Park Service visitor center is 3 miles away.

Activities: Hiking, fishing, horseback riding, Snake River float trips, and bicycling. Guided walks and evening campfire programs originate at the National Park Service visitor center.

SIGNAL MOUNTAIN LODGE

P.O. Box 50 • Moran, WY 83103 • (307) 543–2831 • www.signalmtnlodge.com

Rustic Log Cabins at Signal Mountain Lodge

SIGNAL MOUNTAIN LODGE IS A MEDIUM-SIZE COMmercial and lodging complex with seventy-nine cabin units plus support structures including a registration building, a separate restaurant/gift shop, a marina with rental boats, and a gas station/convenience store with limited supplies and groceries. The backside of the registration building houses a comfortable and generally uncrowded lounge with couches, stuffed chairs, tables, a stone fireplace, and large windows that offer terrific views of Jackson Lake and the Teton Range. A separate and somewhat smaller room in the front of the building has a television, a small library, and a collection of games and puzzles. The adjacent building houses an attractive restaurant and a grill, both of which offer lake and mountain views. The same building also includes a lounge, T-shirt shop, and one of the nicest gift shops in any national park lodge. Signal Mountain Lodge is in an attractive location 7 miles west of the Moran national park entrance station and about 4 miles south of Jackson Lake Lodge.

The lodge offers fives types of cabins that are constructed two, three, or four to a building with the exception of one large freestanding unit. All of the cabins have a covered porch with chairs or a picnic table, carpeting, electric heat, a telephone, and a full tiled bathroom with a combination shower-tub, but no television or air-conditioning. The cabins are within easy walking distance of the registration building, the restaurant, and the store. The least expensive rooms are one-room rustic cabins with beds that range from one double to two doubles plus a sofa bed. Five of these units with one double bed have a gas fireplace. The two-room rustic cabins can accommodate from four to six guests with beds that range from two doubles to three double beds. Both one- and two-room rustics are priced according to the beds available in the cabins. Some of the cabins have a good view of the lake while other cabins have views obstructed by trees or other cabins. Two-room rustic cabins 136, 138, 142, 143, and 144 sit a short distance from the lakeshore and offer great lake views from the porches. Two-room cabin 102 sits on a hill and offers a partial mountain view. One-room cabins 129, 146, and 147 provide partial lake views. Avoid one-room cabin 107 and two-room cabin 112, which each have a porch directly on the road.

Sixteen larger Country Rooms offer more modern motel-style lodging with two queen beds or one king, a small refrigerator, a microwave, and a coffeemaker. Three Deluxe Country Rooms, all in the same building, have a living room and separate bedroom with one king bed. These units also have a gas fireplace. All but one of the Country Rooms sit back from the lake and offer minimal views. Country Room 137 is sandwiched between two two-room cabins and has a private porch that offers a good lake view. We would choose this over the other twelve units in this classification. Twenty-eight Lakefront Retreats are constructed four units to a building, with two units up and two unit units down. These large two-room units have a living room/kitchen with sofa bed, microwave, two-burner stove, coffeemaker, refrigerator, and limited cookware and utensils. A separate bedroom has either two queen beds or a king bed. These sit directly on Jackson Lake and

Today's Signal Mountain Lodge was a small fishing camp that went through several owners before being purchased in 1932 by Charles Wort, a homesteader who had plans to make this a fishing resort. The Worts sold the lodge in 1940 in order to build an upscale hotel in Jackson. The new owners financed construction of the current guest cabins, convenience store, and registration building during the forty years they owned the property.

are the only accommodations at Signal Mountain Lodge that offer excellent views of both Jackson Lake and the Teton Range. The upper units of each building are closer to parking, offer better views, and are priced $10 per night more than the bottom units. Request upper Lakefront unit 152 or lower unit 151, which offer the best views.

Larger groups can be accommodated in a family bungalow with two units that can be rented either as a whole or separately. One unit comprises a bedroom with two queen beds, as well as a separate kitchen/living room with a sofa bed, microwave, stove top, oven, coffeemaker, full-size refrigerator, and limited cookware and utensils. The attached one-room unit has a king bed, sofa bed, small refrigerator, microwave, and coffeemaker. The building has a large deck with chairs and a picnic table. One large Home Away from Home cabin has three rooms including a bedroom with two queen beds, a living/dining room with a sofa bed and gas fireplace, and a kitchen with limited cookware and utensils. This unit also has a laundry area.

Signal Mountain Lodge is a relatively quiet facility situated in a beautiful area of Grand Teton National Park. Rooms here are more rustic and less expensive than at nearby Jackson Lake Lodge, but the vistas are just as impressive. Plus, it is directly on the lake so you can walk a short distance to take a swim or rent a canoe or kayak. Located approximately midway between the town of Jackson and Yellowstone National Park, it is a good base from which to explore both Grand Teton and Yellowstone.

Rooms: Doubles, triples, and quads. Several rooms with a sofa bed can handle up to six persons. All rooms have a private bath.

Wheelchair Accessibility: No cabins are designated as wheelchair accessible. A few cabins have ramp access, but bathrooms have not been modified to facilitate wheelchair accessibility. The restaurant, grill, and lounge are wheelchair accessible.

Reservations: Signal Mountain Lodge accepts reservations only by phone. Phone (307) 543–2831 Monday through Friday from 8:00 A.M. to 5:00 P.M. MST. The reservation line is open twenty-four hours daily from May through early October. A deposit of one night's stay is required. Cancellation notice of seven days is required for refund of deposit less an administrative fee of $10 per room per night of the stay that is canceled (to a maximum of $50 per room).

Rates: Rustic Log Cabins: one room ($99–$126); with a fireplace ($129); two rooms ($142–$148); Country Rooms ($132); Deluxe Country Rooms ($179); Lakefront Retreats ($199–$210); family bungalow–one room ($140), two

rooms ($215); Home Away from Home ($255). Rates are by the room and not the number of occupants. Rollaways are $15 per night.

Location: On Jackson Lake, 7 miles west of Moran Junction and 35 miles north of Jackson.

Season: Mid-May to mid-October.

Food: The Peaks Restaurant serves dinner only ($16–$33). Alcoholic beverages are available. The adjacent Trapper Grill offers breakfast ($6.00–$9.00), lunch and dinner ($7.00–$14.00). Food from the grill is also served in the lounge and on the outside deck. Limited groceries, beer, and wine are available in the convenience store. Eleven miles north, Leeks Pizzeria serves pizza, pasta, and sandwiches.

Transportation: The nearest scheduled air service is in Jackson, Wyoming, where rental vehicles are available.

Facilities: Restaurant, grill, lounge, gift shop, clothing store, convenience store, laundromat, and gas station. Marina with powerboat, canoe, and kayak rentals.

Activities: Boating, canoeing, kayaking, fishing, hiking, guided fishing trips, guided sailboat tours, evening naturalist programs, float trips.

Pets: Pets are permitted in all of the units except the upper Lakefront Retreats for a charge of $10 per pet, per night.

TRIANGLE X RANCH

2 Triangle X Ranch Road • Moose, WY 83012 • (307) 733–2183 • www.trianglex.com

One-Bedroom and Two-Bedroom Cabins at Triangle X Ranch

TRIANGLE X RANCH IS THE ONLY OPERATING DUDE ranch in a national park. It has also been used as the location for several movies, including John Wayne's first picture and the classic western *Shane*. The ranch has all of the buildings you would expect in a working ranch, as well as twenty freestanding log or wood-frame cabins that provide overnight accommodations. The ranch is on a hill overlooking Jackson Hole and the Teton Mountain Range. One of the many buildings in the ranch complex has the dining room and a living room with a fireplace. All of the cabins are within a short walking distance of the dining room. During the peak season of June through August the Triangle X requires a minimum stay of one week beginning and ending on Sunday. Reduced minimum stays are required during other times of the year. The ranch is particularly appealing to people who enjoy horseback riding, since this is the main activity for guests. Triangle X Ranch is on the eastern side of Grand Teton National Park, 25 miles north of Jackson, Wyoming, just off U.S. Highways 26, 89, and 191. It is 6 miles south of Moran Junction.

Triangle X Ranch has served as home to four generations of the same family. The ranch was purchased by John S. Turner in the summer of 1926. Turner started construction of his home and welcomed guests the same summer. The ranch was self-sufficient, with refrigeration provided by ice cut from nearby ponds and stored in piles of sawdust. In the late 1920s Turner sold the property to a land company owned by John D. Rockefeller, who eventually donated the land to the federal government. Today the grandsons of John Turner operate the ranch as a concessionaire of the National Park Service.

A total of twenty log or wood-frame cabins are available for guests. All of the cabins have electricity, heat, and a private bathroom with a combination shower-tub but no telephone or television. Cabins are available with one, two, and three bedrooms. The two- and three-bedroom units each have two full bathrooms. In general, most bedrooms have either two twin beds or one queen bed. While all cabins have a very rustic outside appearance, the interiors are quite nice, with paneled walls and heavy pine furniture. Most of the ceilings are slightly vaulted. Each cabin has a covered front porch with chairs and views of the Tetons.

Triangle X Ranch is a wonderful place to stay if you enjoy mountain scenery, horseback riding, and an overall western experience. With each guest spending an entire week at the ranch, it is a certainty you will make some friends during your stay here. Three meals a day, each announced by a ringing of the dinner bell, are served family-style and included in the price of a room. A typical dinner includes a main entree, a green salad, several vegetables, home-baked bread, and a dessert. Daily horseback riding (except for Sundays) is also included in the price of a room. Each guest is assigned his or her own horse at the beginning of the week's stay. The evenings each have a different scheduled activity, including square dancing, ranger talks, cookouts, and campfire gatherings. Triangle X offers float trips and pack trips at extra cost.

Children five to twelve receive special attention at Triangle X. They eat in a separate dining room from teenagers and adults, and their activities, including horseback riding, are especially designed for their age group.

Winter brings a different environment with different activities. The ranch reduces the required stay to two nights, and a shuttle service is available without charge to the Jackson Hole airport and to the Jackson Hole Ski Resort. Triangle X provides complimentary cross-country skis and snowshoes. In addition, guided snowmobile trips can be arranged (fee charged). An outdoor hot tub is available for guests. More formal gourmet meals are served during the winter season. Dinner includes three to four courses, with several entree choices.

Rooms: One to three persons in a one-bedroom unit; three to five persons in a two-bedroom unit; five to six persons in a three-bedroom cabin. All cabins have a private bath with a combination shower-tub.

Wheelchair Accessibility: One cabin has ramp access to the front door and a bathroom with a wide doorway, grab bars, and a roll-in shower. The dining room building also has ramp access.

Reservations: Triangle X Ranch, 2 Triangle X Ranch Road, Moose, WY 83012. Phone (307) 733–2183; fax (307) 733–8685. Minimum stay of one week during June, July, and August. Four days at other times during the summer season. A two-day minimum is required during the winter season. Required deposit of 35 percent of total cost. Credit cards are not accepted during the summer season. When a cancellation occurs, a refund is given if the cabin can be filled.

Rates: All rates are per person. One-bedroom cabin (one person $1,800, two persons $1,485, three persons $1,270); two-bedroom cabin (three persons $1,590, four persons $1,380, five persons $1,270); three-bedroom cabin (five persons $1,430, six persons $1,270). Prices reduced before June 1 and after September 1. Winter rates are $105 per night per person. A 15 percent service charge is added to all bills. Summer rates include three meals a day, horseback riding, and all ranch activities.

Location: East side of Grand Teton National Park, 25 miles north of Jackson, Wyoming. The ranch is 6 miles south of Moran Junction, on U.S. Highways 26, 89, and 191.

Season: Summer Season: late May to the first week in November. Winter Season: December 26 to mid-March.

Food: Three meals a day are served in the ranch dining room. Meals are included in the quoted rates for both summer and winter seasons.

Transportation: Scheduled airlines serve Jackson Hole, Wyoming, where rental vehicles are available. Salt Lake City, Utah, is the nearest large airport.

Facilities: Corrals, dining room, laundry, gift shop.

Activities: Summer: Horseback riding, breakfast and dinner cookouts, square dancing, fishing, hiking. Optional services offered (fee): float trips, fishing trips, pack trips (minimum of four days), and hunting trips (ten days). Winter: Cross-country skiing, snowmobiling, snowshoeing, wildlife viewing, or just relaxing in the outdoor hot tub. Downhill skiing is available at three resorts in the area.

Yellowstone National Park

P.O. Box 168 • Yellowstone National Park, WY 82190 • (307) 344–7381 • www.nps.gov/yell

Yellowstone National Park, the world's first and probably best-known national park, comprises nearly 3,400 square miles of lakes, waterfalls, mountains, and some 10,000 geysers and hot springs. The park has almost 300 miles of roads. Most of the major attractions are near Grand Loop Road, which makes a figure eight in the park's central area. The road's east side provides access to canyons, mountains, and waterfalls, while the west side leads to areas of thermal activity. Most of the park is in the northwestern corner of Wyoming, with overlapping strips in Montana and Idaho. **Park Entrance Fee:** $20.00 per vehicle, $15.00 per motorcycle, or $5.00 per person, good for seven days. This entrance fee also covers Grand Teton National Park and the connecting parkway.

Lodging in Yellowstone National Park: Yellowstone has nine separate lodging facilities scattered about the park. One is near the north entrance, one is in the northeast section, one is in the canyon area, two are in Lake Village on the north shore of Lake Yellowstone, one is 20 miles inside the south entrance, and three are in the Old Faithful area. The lodges offer a wide choice of accommodations that range from rustic cabins without a private bathroom to a modern upscale lodge with handcrafted furniture. Likewise, prices range from what you are likely to pay for a

Yellowstone National Park

Miles
0   5   10   15

To Livingston

To Bozeman

Gardiner

89

191

Mammoth Hot Springs

Mammoth Hot Springs Hotel and Cabins

To Quake Lake

287

Indian Creek

To Ashton

Norris

20

West Yellowstone

Madison

Roosevelt Lodge Cabins

Tower Fall

MONTANA
WYOMING

Silver Gate

Pebble Creek

Slough Creek

212

To Red Lodge

Canyon

Canyon Lodge and Cabins

Fishing Bridge

Lake Village

Bridge Bay

Old Faithful Inn

See map

Yellowstone Lake

Lake Yellowstone Hotel and Cabins

Lake Lodge Cabins

14 16 20

To Cody

MONTANA
WYOMING

Lewis Lake

Grant Village

N

W   E

S

IDAHO
WYOMING

Bechler

89

191

287

47

To Ashton

To Jackson

To Madison Junction

Geyser Hill

Service Station

Store

Old Faithful Geyser

Old Faithful Lodge Cabins

Old Faithful Inn

Ranger Station

West Parking

Store

Post Office

East Parking

Picnic Area

Old Faithful Snow Lodge and Cabins

To West Thumb

Motel 6 in rural America to the price of a nice hotel room in a major city. Much of Yellowstone's lodging consists of cabins in four categories. In ascending order of quality and cost, cabins are classified as Budget (rustic, small, no private bathroom), Pioneer (rustic, small, private bathroom), Frontier (small or mid-size, nicer interior, private bathroom), and Western (nicest, larger than Frontier, private bathroom). The cabins are generally quite old, but the interiors have often been refurbished. In general, we find the cabins to have nicer interiors than indicated by the condition of the exteriors.

Mammoth Hot Springs Hotel and Cabins, near the north entrance, offers a historic hotel and rustic cabins, both of which have rooms with and without private bathrooms.

Roosevelt Lodge Cabins, in the northeast section of the park, has rustic cabins with and without private bathrooms. Roosevelt offers some of the least expensive lodging in Yellowstone.

Canyon Lodge and Cabins, a very large facility centrally located midway between the east and west entrances, includes two modern lodge buildings with a total of eighty-one rooms plus four types of cabins, each with a private bathroom.

Lake Village, on the east side of the park, has two separate but nearby lodging facilities. Lake Yellowstone Hotel and Cabins provides 110 recently renovated Frontier Cabins plus an elegant old hotel that was completely redone in the early 1990s. Nearby, Lake Lodge Cabins has 186 cabins that range from rustic to reasonably modern.

Grant Village, near the park's south entrance from Grand Teton National Park, has six relatively modern motel-type buildings with nearly 300 rooms. This is our least favorite place to stay.

The Old Faithful Area has three different lodging facilities, including the famous Old Faithful Inn, with 327 rooms including many in the original structure, or "Old House," plus larger and more upscale rooms in two newer wings. Nearby, less well-known Old Faithful Lodge Cabins offers cabins with and without private bathrooms at relatively inexpensive rates. Old Faithful Snow Lodge and Cabins, behind its more famous sister hotel, has two classes of cabins plus one hundred rooms in one of the newest and nicest hotels in the park. The cabins at Snow Lodge are larger and less closely clustered compared to the cabins at Old Faithful Lodge Cabins.

When choosing a lodging facility remember that Yellowstone encompasses a very large area, and visiting different sections of the park can entail unexpectedly long driving times. Distances are substantial, but planning to visit another area of the park on the basis of mileage alone can result in underestimating the time required in a vehicle. Traffic can be heavy, animal watching causes bottlenecks, and the park seems to be in an endless cycle of road repair that often slows traffic to a standstill. Thus, you might consider staying in more than one location, especially if you will be visiting for more than a couple of days. Every first-time visitor to Yellowstone will certainly want to spend time in the Old Faithful area, which offers a good base for exploring the park's geyser country. Another place to consider is Canyon Village, which serves as a convenient location for exploring an entirely different part of the park, including beautiful Yellowstone Falls. The Lake Village area enjoys a more relaxed atmosphere and is one of our favorite sections of the park. In fact, Lake Yellowstone Hotel is probably our favorite place to stay in the park. Likewise, Roosevelt and Mammoth are interesting places in their own right.

All nine of the lodging facilities are operated by the same firm, so the registration desk at any of the lodges can determine whether vacancies exist at any of the other locations. Yellowstone is very busy, so it is important to make reservations as early as possible. If you are unable to obtain a reservation when you first call, it may pay to call periodically, because openings may become available due to cancellations. You may be able to obtain a room as a walk-in, although you aren't likely to have much choice regarding the location, facility, or cost.

Reservations for All Accommodations Inside the Park: Yellowstone National Park Lodges (operated by Xanterra Parks & Resorts), Reservations Office, P.O. Box 168, Yellowstone National Park, WY 82190. Phone (307) 344–7311; fax (307) 344–7456; or book on the Web site, www.TravelYellowstone.com. Deposit is required for first night's lodging at each location where you will be staying. Cancellation notice of forty-eight hours during the summer season required for refund of deposit. Fourteen days' advance notice required for cancellation of winter reservations. If traveling in an off-season, be sure to inquire about seasonal specials, such as Early Bird, Fall, and Winter Kickoff specials.

Transportation: Scheduled airlines serve Bozeman, Montana, on the northwest side; West Yellowstone, Montana, on the west side; Cody, Wyoming, on the east side; Jackson, Wyoming, south of Grand Teton National Park, and Billings, Montana, which is 129 miles to the northeast. Rental vehicles are available at all five locations. Scheduled shuttle service is available to Bozeman and Livingston, Montana. Bus service operates between Cody and the park. No public transportation system operates within Yellowstone National Park, although scenic bus tours along the upper and lower loop roads are scheduled from various lodging locations in the park. Heavy traffic, poor road conditions, and seemingly continual repairs can make driving in Yellowstone an aggravating affair.

Snowcoaches operate during winter months between Old Faithful and West Yellowstone (three hours one-way), Mammoth (four hours one-way), and Flagg Ranch (three and one-half hours one-way). Within the park, only Old Faithful Snow Lodge and Mammoth Hotel are open during winter months. The road from Livingston to Mammoth is open year-round. Transportation is available between Jackson and Flagg Ranch during winter months. Most of the transportation mentioned above operates only once per day.

CANYON LODGE AND CABINS

Yellowstone National Park, WY 82190 • (307) 344–7331 • www.TravelYellowstone.com

Dunraven Lodge at Canyon Lodge and Cabins

CANYON LODGE IS A LARGE COMMERCIAL COMPLEX that includes hundreds of cabins and two newer lodge buildings. Most of the 562 rooms at Canyon Lodge are one-story cabins constructed four to eight to a building. The village also has a large general store/ coffee shop, restaurant, cafeteria, lounge, gas station, post office, and gift shops. This is a busy commercial center of the park, but most of the overnight rooms are far enough away that you will be able to enjoy a relatively quiet stay.

It is also large enough that you will have a hike, or you may prefer driving, to the restaurant, depending on the location of your cabin. The registration desk is in a separate building near the gift shop and restaurant. After registering, you will need to drive to your room. The village takes its name from the Grand Canyon of the Yellowstone River, a half mile away. Canyon Village is near the center of the park, 42 miles from the east entrance and 40 miles from the west entrance at West Yellowstone.

Canyon Lodge and Cabins has five types of accommodations. All of the rooms have heat and private baths but no telephone, television, or air-conditioning. Adequate parking is available near all the rooms. The least expensive and most plentiful lodging at Canyon are almost 400 Economy, Pioneer, and Frontier Cabins built in the 1950s. These cabins are constructed either six or eight to a building and clustered in two large loops behind the commercial complex. Cabins in all three categories are essentially identical except for upgrades. Each cabin has a very small bathroom with a shower. The cabins come in two sizes, regardless of category, with two twins in small units and usually two doubles in larger units. An Economy Cabin with two double beds is larger than the more expensive Frontier Cabin with two twin beds. A cabin might be upgraded to a more expensive category because of new carpet, new beds, or a new roof. In many instances it is difficult to determine which type of cabin you are in other than by the price. Even housekeeping employees sometimes have difficulty knowing if a cabin is Economy, Pioneer, or Frontier without looking at the rate card on the door

Eighty-four Western Cabins are constructed four or six units to a building. These units were built in 1969 and are quite a bit larger than cabins in the other three categories. Twenty Western Cabins in four buildings were extensively renovated in 2005. These units (#1 through #10, #53 through #58, and #81 through #84) are much nicer but rent at the same rate. Additional Western cabins may be renovated during the next couple of years.

Two relatively new rustic-style lodge buildings with steep shake roofs and dormers offer eighty-one nearly identical rooms, each with two double beds (except for seven wheelchair rooms and two rooms on the fourth floor of Dunraven), a carpeted floor, attractive pine furniture, and a bathroom with a combination shower-tub. The rooms have coffeemakers and electric heat but no air-conditioning, telephone, or television.

Canyon Lodge is within walking distance of the North Rim of the Grand Canyon of the Yellowstone. A half-mile trail leads from cabin P26 to the North Rim's Grandview Point. From here North Rim Trail leads either 1 mile northeast to Inspiration Point or about 1 mile southwest to the Lower Falls. The entire North Rim Trail, which begins at South Rim Drive Bridge and ends at Inspiration Point, is slightly less than 3 miles, and a portion of it is paved. A variety of trails are also on the south side of the canyon.

Public telephones, vending machines, and ice machines are in each of the two buildings. The two lodge buildings are adjacent to one another and connected by a short walkway. Adequate parking is near the entrances to both buildings. The oldest of the two, Cascade Lodge, was constructed in 1993 and has thirty-seven rooms on three floors. The newer Dunraven Lodge was completed in 1999 and has forty-four rooms on four floors. Dunraven is built on a small hillside and is entered on the second floor. The first floor has rooms on only one side. Only Dunraven has an elevator, and an attractive lobby with a steepled ceiling is on the second floor. The lobby is for use by guests of both lodge buildings. The rooms in these two lodges are by far the nicest accommodations in the Canyon complex.

If you are traveling on a tight budget, select an Economy or Pioneer cabin with two double beds. This will put you in one of the larger units at low cost. The Economy cabins at Canyon are the lowest priced lodging in Yellowstone. For those seeking more upscale accommodations, we would choose either of the lodge units over a Western Cabin. Of the two, you might want to select the newer Dunraven Lodge because it has an elevator. Try for second- or third-floor rooms on the south side (odd-numbered rooms) that face the woods rather than the parking lot. Dunraven rooms on the fourth floor are somewhat smaller than rooms on the other floors. Rooms on the third floor of Cascade, especially 305 and 307, are larger and offer views of the woods.

Canyon Lodge and Cabins is the most centrally located of all the lodging facilities at Yellowstone National Park, so it is a perfect place to settle in and explore this large park. Canyon Village offers just about anything you desire when you return from a long day of touring. The location, number of lodging places, and variety of facilities make this a very busy place. A restaurant, cafeteria, coffee shop, and picnic shop offer an array of meals and prices. You will also find gift shops, a sporting goods store, and a large general store with books, supplies, gifts, and groceries. A cocktail lounge with a large fireplace and post office are also in the village. A renovated National Park Service visitor center will open in 2006. Stables are available for horseback riding.

Rooms: Doubles, triples, and quads. All rooms have a private bath.

Wheelchair Accessibility: A total of seven wheelchair-accessible rooms are in the two lodge buildings. Each room has a double bed and a bathroom with a wide doorway, high toilet, grab bars, and a roll-in shower. None of the cabins is wheelchair accessible.

Rates: Economy Cabins ($45); Pioneer Cabins ($61); Frontier Cabins ($83); Western Cabins ($121); lodge rooms ($142). Each additional person is $10 per night. Children eleven and under stay free.

Location: Near the middle of Yellowstone National Park, 40 miles from the west entrance at West Yellowstone.

Season: June through mid-September.

Food: Several eating options are available in the Canyon commercial center, which is a long walk from the two lodge buildings and many of the cabins. A dining room offers breakfast ($5.00–$9.00), lunch ($6.00–$9.00), and dinner ($12.00–$19.00). A less expensive cafeteria serves three meals a day with dinner costing from $6.00–$16.00. The picnic shop serves sandwiches, salads, drinks, and ice cream. A coffee shop in the general store building serves breakfast, salads, sandwiches, hamburgers, ice cream, and beverages. A lounge serves appetizers.

Facilities: Restaurant, cafeteria, picnic shop, coffee shop, lounge, gift shop, laundry, general store with groceries, sporting goods store, post office, gas station, stables, National Park Service visitor center.

Activities: Horseback riding, hiking, motor coach excursions, evening ranger program.

GRANT VILLAGE

Yellowstone National Park, WY 82190 • (307) 344–7311 • www.TravelYellowstone.com

Grant Village, Lodge Building A

GRANT VILLAGE INCLUDES A REGISTRATION BUILD-Ging plus six modern two-story lodge buildings, each with about fifty rooms. The wooden lodge buildings, constructed from 1982 to 1984, sit staggered across a hillside above the south shore of the West Thumb of Yellowstone Lake. Rooms on each side of the building are entered from a central corridor on each floor. Half the rooms in each of the six lodge buildings face the lake, although lake views are obscured by pine trees. Each building has a small first-floor lobby with chairs, while the four newer buildings, A, D, E, and F, also have a small second-floor lobby with tables and chairs. Adequate parking is directly beside each building. There are no elevators in the buildings, but bell service is available at the registration building. Grant Village is located in the south end of Yellowstone, in the West Thumb area. It is the southernmost lodging facility in the park, 20 miles north of the south entrance to Yellowstone.

All of the rooms at Grant Village have heat, a telephone, a private bath, and rent for the same price. Most bathrooms have a shower, but some offer a combination shower-tub. None of the rooms have air-conditioning, a television, or a balcony. All rooms are of good size, but approximately 200 rooms in the four newer buildings noted above are a little larger. We advise you request a room in one of the two newer buildings, A or F, that are closest to Lake Yellowstone. A room facing the lake rather than the parking lot is more desirable even though views of the lake are obscured by trees. Ask for the second floor if you don't mind climbing a flight of stairs. The eight corner rooms in each of the four newer buildings have an extra side window.

Grant Village is a good place to spend a restful night at Yellowstone, especially if you are arriving late or will be leaving from the park's south entrance. The village is away from the park's heavily visited tourist areas and free from the congestion they attract. Another advantage is that the village is only 19 miles from the park's main attraction, Old Faithful. In addition to lodging, Grant Village also has a post office, a gift shop, a service station, laundry facilities, a boat launch, and a National Park Service visitor center. Three eating establishments with varying menus and prices are separate but only a short walk from the lodges. The Grant Village Dining Room near Lodge A serves three meals a day. It is an unusual building, with a high vaulted wooden ceiling and windows that offer a view of Yellowstone Lake. A cozy cocktail lounge is just off the entrance area. A less expensive restaurant, Lake House, is directly on the lake and serves a buffet breakfast and pizza and pasta for dinner. Windows on three sides of the building provide good views of the lake. A general store near the registration building houses a grill that serves breakfast, sandwiches, ice cream, and beverages. A salad bar is also available.

Rooms: Doubles, triples, and quads. All rooms have a private bath with shower or combination shower-tub.

Wheelchair Accessibility: Two rooms on the first floor of each building are wheelchair accessible, with a wide bathroom doorway, a high toilet, a roll-in shower, and grab bars. Each of these twelve rooms has one double bed.

Rates: Room ($116). Rates are quoted for two adults. Each additional person is $10 per night. Children eleven and under stay free.

Location: At the south end of the park, 20 miles north of the south entrance.

Season: The end of May through the first of October.

Food: Grant Village Dining Room serves a breakfast buffet ($9.00), menu items ($5.00–$8.00), lunch ($7.00–$10.00), and dinner ($12.00–$21.00) in an attractive building. Lake House serves a breakfast buffet ($7.50) and dinner ($6.00–$18.00) only. A grill in the general store serves breakfast, salads, sandwiches, and beverages. The store also has a good offering of groceries.

Facilities: Two restaurants, cocktail lounge, grill, general store, gift shop, service station, boat ramp, picnic area, post office, laundry, National Park Service visitor center.

Activities: Hiking, fishing, evening ranger programs at the amphitheater.

LAKE LODGE CABINS

Yellowstone National Park, WY 82190 • (307) 344–7311 • www.TravelYellowstone.com

Pioneer Cabins at Lake Lodge Cabins

LAKE LODGE CABINS IS A COMPLEX CONSISTING OF a large log lodge building with a registration desk and support services, plus 186 wood cabins situated on a hill overlooking the lodge. No guest rooms are in the main registration building, which has a cafeteria, a gift shop, a cocktail lounge, and a large lobby area with two large gas fireplaces. The lodge building has a massive covered front porch with chairs and overlooks Yellowstone Lake. The entire complex sits back from the lake, and the cabins offer no lake views. Parking is in front of each cabin unit. The lodge is located at Lake Village, in the eastern section of Yellowstone National Park. It is 30 miles from the park's east entrance station.

Lake Lodge Cabins offers two types of cabin accommodations. All of the cabins have heat and private bath with shower, with a few cabins having a combination shower-tub. There is no air-conditioning, telephone, or television in any of the cabins. Most of the cabins are constructed four to a building, although a few buildings have two units and others have six. The least expensive alternative is the eighty-six Pioneer Cabins that sit in an area devoid of trees. The smallest Pioneer units have one double bed; larger units have two double beds. These cabins look very rustic on the outside, but the interior is fairly nice, with paneled walls and carpeting. A limited number of these cabins are being extensively refurbished each year. As of 2005, D11–D20 had been completed. The refurbishment includes a new foundation, a new interior, and removal of lowered ceiling tiles to reveal the original vaulted ceiling.

One hundred Western cabins are identical to those at Canyon Lodge and Cabins. All are the same size and come with two double beds or two double beds and a single bed. These cabins are bigger than the

Lake Lodge was constructed during the 1920s to provide mid-level accommodations to travelers who didn't want to tent camp but who couldn't afford the more expensive hotels. The East Wing was added as a dining area (currently the cafeteria) in 1926, and the West Wing was built as a dance hall (now an employee recreation hall) in the same year. The front porch of Lake Lodge was added in 1929.

Pioneer units and cost about twice as much. All cabins have private bathrooms, most having a shower only, but a few have a combination shower-tub. The layouts differ from building to building but a majority of Western cabins have windows in two walls. Western cabins toward the rear of the complex (units G, H, and J) are spaced farther apart and are surrounded by trees.

Lake Lodge Cabins provides modestly priced accommodations. The Lake Village area is very scenic and relatively quiet, at least compared with the Old Faithful area. These are also the closest accommodations to Fishing Bridge and Bridge Bay Marina. The less expensive Pioneer Cabins are a good value, especially if you are able to get one of the refurbished units.

Rooms: Doubles, triples, and quads. A few rooms have a single bed for a fifth person. All cabins have private baths.

Wheelchair Accessibility: No cabins are designated wheelchair accessible.

Rates: Pioneer cabins ($61); Western cabins ($121). Rates quoted are for two adults. Each additional person is $10 per night. Children eleven and under stay free with an adult.

Location: On the north shore of Yellowstone Lake, in the east-central section of Yellowstone National Park. The lodge is approximately 30 miles from the east park entrance and 43 miles from the south entrance.

Season: Mid-June to mid-September.

Food: A cafeteria is open for breakfast ($3.00–$6.00), lunch/dinner ($5.00–$9.00). A nearby general store has limited groceries and a counter that serves breakfast, salads, sandwiches, soups, ice cream, and beverages. Nearby Lake Yellowstone Hotel has a lovely dining room and a small deli.

Facilities: Gift shop, laundry, cafeteria, cocktail lounge. A general store is a short walk from the lodge. Nearby Lake Yellowstone Hotel offers additional facilities.

Activities: Hiking, fishing. Nearby Bridge Bay Marina offers boat tours on Lake Yellowstone, boat rentals, and fishing guides.

LAKE YELLOWSTONE HOTEL AND CABINS

Yellowstone National Park, WY 82190 • (307) 344–7311 • www.TravelYellowstone.com

LAKE YELLOWSTONE HOTEL AND CABINS COMPRISES a three- and four-story hotel building, an adjacent two-story annex, and 110 closely clustered cabin units that are located behind the hotel. The hotel, annex, and cabins offer a total of 304 rooms. The large hotel is the oldest hotel in the park today. An extensive renovation to return the hotel to its 1920s appearance was completed in 1991. The first floor houses the registration desk, lobby, dining room, lobby bar, and gift shop. The wonderful lobby and sunroom, with some of the hotel's original wicker furniture, has large windows that over-look Yellowstone Lake. The 1920s-era dining room has large windows on the south and west walls. A drive to the front of the hotel provides access for registration and dropping off luggage. The parking area is on the back side of the hotel. Lake Yellowstone Hotel and Cabins is located in the east-central portion of Yellowstone National Park, on the north shore of Yellowstone Lake. It is 30 miles from the east entrance to the park.

The main hotel, often called Lake Hotel, has 158 rooms in two wings, one on each side of the main lobby. An elevator is in the East Wing, and bell service is available. All of the rooms are attractively decorated and each has heat, a full tiled bathroom, a fan, and a telephone, but no air-conditioning or television. Room size and beds vary, but the largest rooms are in the three-story West Wing, while the best lake views are from end rooms of the East Wing. An elevator in the East Wing makes it easy to haul luggage to a fourth-floor room where you enjoy the best views and nobody is walking above. We recommend even-numbered rooms 430 to 460. Beds range from one to three queen-size beds, although a few rooms have two double beds. Other than one second-floor suite, all rooms in the hotel, regardless of size and beds, are priced according to whether they are on the front or back of the hotel. Rooms on the front rent for an extra $13 per night, which we believe is money well spent. The Presidential Suite on the corner of the second floor has a queen bed in each of two large bedrooms, two full bathrooms, and a large living room with a coffeemaker, wet bar, and refrigerator stocked with snacks and sodas. The suite is large and as nice as you will find in any historic hotel. In the West Wing, room 100 with one queen bed is a good choice. In general, requesting a room with two queen beds means you are likely to end up with a larger room at no additional cost.

The two-story annex, which was once used as employee housing, has thirty-six rooms that are nearly as nice as rooms in the main hotel but rent for $55 less

Construction on Lake Yellowstone Hotel began in 1889 in an area once populated by native tribes, fur trappers, and mountain men. The first guests arrived two years later. Additions engineered by the architect of Old Faithful Inn in the early 1900s nearly tripled the number of rooms at the hotel to 210. The East Wing, with 113 additional rooms, was completed in the early 1920s and the sunroom was added in 1924. The hotel had fallen into disrepair by the 1980s, when a decade-long renovation was initiated to return the building to its glory years of the 1920s.

per night. Annex rooms have heat, a telephone, and a private bathroom with a combination shower-tub (except for four wheelchair-accessible rooms, which have a roll-in shower), but no air-conditioning or television. A small lobby with several stuffed chairs is on the first floor. Beds in annex rooms consist of either one or two doubles. Rooms with two double beds are generally larger but rent for the same price. None of the rooms in the annex offers particularly good views, although those on the east side provide views of pine trees, while rooms on the west side overlook the parking lot. The annex rooms probably offer a better value than rooms in the main hotel, especially if you can get a larger room with two double beds on the east side. If you book a room in the annex, this is what you should request.

The Frontier Cabins were built in the 1940s and renovated from 2002 to 2005. They are closely clustered in an area devoid of trees behind the hotel and away from the lake. Most of the cabins are constructed as duplex units, with rooms that back up to one another. The remaining cabins are freestanding units. All the cabins are approximately the same size and have a nicely finished interior with carpeting, two double beds, and a private bathroom with a shower. If you decide to book a cabin, request freestanding units 49, 50, or 51, which sit at the end of the complex and face the lake and trees. In addition, you will avoid noise from guests in an adjoining room.

Lake Yellowstone Hotel is a quiet place to spend your vacation in Yellowstone National Park. The hotel captures the ambience of an earlier period and is reminiscent of Yosemite's even older Wawona Hotel. The airy and bright lobby area is a great place to read a book, with occasional glances out the windows at the lake. A pianist or string quartet play here most evenings. The equally delightful dining room, just off the lobby, offers three meals a day. A small deli, just down the hall, serves sandwiches, soup, and beverages. The hotel and cabins are a short walk from a general store and Lake Lodge Cabins, which offers a cafeteria and laundry facilities. If you want an inexpensive place to stay, choose the cabins. If you want to experience Yellowstone in a grand old hotel, opt for a room in the main hotel.

Rooms: Doubles, triples, and quads. A few rooms sleep up to six. All rooms, including cabins, have private bathrooms.

Wheelchair Accessibility: Four first-floor rooms in the annex and five Frontier Cabins are ADA compliant. The dining room in the main hotel is wheelchair accessible, with ramp access into the building.

Rates: Frontier Cabins ($101); Annex ($124); hotel: back ($179); front ($192); suite ($443). Children eleven and under stay free. Each additional person is $10 per night.

Location: East-central section of the park, on the north shore of Yellowstone Lake. The hotel is 30 miles from the park's east entrance.

Season: From mid-May to first of October.

Food: A 1920s-era hotel dining room serves breakfast ($7.00–$10.50), lunch ($7.00–$13.00), and dinner ($16.00–$33.00). A breakfast buffet ($10.25) is served daily. A children's menu is available. A deli on the first floor opens from 10:30 A.M. to 9:00 P.M. for sandwiches, soups, and beverages. A cafeteria at Lake Lodge Cabins, a short walk from the hotel, serves three meals a day. A nearby general store has limited groceries and a counter that serves breakfast, sandwiches, soups, salads, ice cream, and beverages.

Facilities: Clinic, dining room, lobby bar, small deli, gift shop, ATM, post office. Nearby is a general store. Lake Lodge Cabins has a cafeteria and laundry facilities.

Activities: Hiking, fishing, photo tour, sunset tour, evening music in the hotel lobby. Nearby Bridge Bay Marina offers boat tours on Lake Yellowstone, boat rentals, and fishing guides.

MAMMOTH HOT SPRINGS HOTEL AND CABINS

Yellowstone National Park, WY 82190 • (307) 344–7311 • www.TravelYellowstone.com

IF YOU HAVE EVER WANTED TO STAY AT AN OLD ARMY fort, then Mammoth Hot Springs Hotels and Cabins is your place. The hotel is adjacent to buildings that were once part of a small military post that served as headquarters for the U.S. Army when it was in charge of this park. Some of the original Army buildings continue in use as administrative offices for personnel of the National Park Service. The current lodging complex at Mammoth comprises a four-story hotel plus 115 cabin units that together provide a total of 212 rooms.

Registration for all lodging is in the first-floor lobby of the hotel. Bell service is available at the front desk. The cabin units are clustered along the roads and in grassy areas behind the hotel. Each cabin has its own parking area. Mammoth Hot Springs Hotel and Cabins is located near the north entrance to Yellowstone National Park, 5 miles south of Gardiner, Montana.

The lodging complex offers various types of rooms, both in the hotel and in the cabins. Ninety-seven hotel rooms each have steam heat and telephone but no air-conditioning or television (with the exception of the suites). An elevator is near the registration desk. The hotel has sixty-eight rooms with private bath that rent for about $25 per night more than twenty-nine rooms without private bath. Community bath and shower rooms are on each floor. Rooms without a bath have two double beds. Regular hotel rooms with bath have a double and a single bed or two double beds. Some bathrooms have a tub, some have a shower, and some have both. Corner rooms 230, 231, 330, and 331 each have a full bath and rent for the same price but are quite a bit larger than other rooms with a bath. The hotel has two suites, one each on the third and fourth floors, each about the size of two regular rooms. These have a bedroom and separate sitting room. The suites each have a television and coffeemaker, and guests receive a basket of fruit and a newspaper. The fourth-floor suite has two bathrooms, one with a shower-tub combination. The third-floor suite has one bathroom with a shower but no tub.

The cabin units, both with and without a private bath, are either freestanding or duplex units. All cabins have nearly identical living space (not counting the small bathroom in the Frontier cabins), finished interiors, two double beds, a sink with hot and cold water, and a covered front porch with chairs. Frontier cabins have a shower and toilet and rent for about $30 extra per

The hotel and cabins currently operating at Mammoth are only the latest chapter in a long history of lodging in this area. The first crude hotel in the park was built at Mammoth in 1871. The much larger and more elaborate National Hotel was constructed here in 1883. An annex that was added to the National Hotel in 1911 serves as the main lodging section of today's Mammoth Hot Springs Hotel. The remainder of the old National Hotel was torn down. The current hotel's front section containing the lobby, a map room, and a gift shop was added in 1936–1937, one year before the first ninety-six cabins were completed behind the hotel.

night compared to Budget cabins without a bath. Four of the Frontier cabins with one queen bed each have a large hot tub on a private porch and rent for an additional $70 per night. These hot tubs can be rented by the hour during winter months. All of the cabins front either on a road or around a grassy area. The latter are preferred, and we recommend Budget cabins C26, C27, and C30. Frontier cabins B14, B15, B16, C46, and C49 are recommended if you desire a private bath. Each of these cabins is freestanding, fronts on a grassy area, and enjoys morning sun. A13 and A14, one Frontier and one Budget cabin, are in a duplex building. This is a good choice for a family that needs more than one cabin since both rooms will have access to a bathroom without being charged for two bathroom cabins.

Mammoth Hot Springs Hotel and Cabins is in a unique and interesting section of Yellowstone. It's fun to walk around the area and view the historic buildings. We prefer the cabins listed above to rooms in the hotel. The cabins allow you to relax on your own front porch, and parking beside each cabin makes loading and unloading luggage less of a chore. An interesting dining room across the street, decorated in a kind of Art Deco style, serves three meals a day. Windows overlook the old military parade ground, which is in front of the hotel. A grill offering breakfast and a variety of fast-food items is adjacent to the dining room in the same building. A general store next door sells supplies, limited groceries, beer, wine, and spirits. A National Park Service visitor center in one of the old military buildings has exhibits on the park's early history. On the downside, Mammoth is at the extreme north end of the park, some distance away from Old Faithful and many of Yellowstone's other popular sites. This means that a stay at Mammoth is likely to result in additional driving.

Rooms: Doubles, triples, and quads. Many hotel rooms and cabins have private baths.

Wheelchair Accessibility: The hotel has a ramp to the elevator that provides access to all floors. Two rooms in the hotel and four cabin units, each with a roll-in shower and one queen bed, are designated as wheelchair accessible. The restaurant across the street from the hotel is wheelchair accessible, with access through the grill on the opposite side of the building.

Rates: Budget Cabins ($65); Frontier Cabins ($94); Frontier Cabins with hot tubs ($164); hotel rooms without bath ($75); hotel rooms with bath ($99); suites ($301). Rates quoted are for two persons except suites, which are for up to four. Each additional person is $10 per night. Children eleven and under stay free. Special packages are offered during the winter season.

Location: North end of Yellowstone National Park, 5 miles south of Gardiner, Montana.

Season: Summer season is from mid-May to mid-October. Winter season is from mid-December to early March. During winter months, only the hotel is open. The hot tub cabins are open to rent by the hour.

Food: A large dining room across the street from the hotel offers breakfast ($5.00–$9.50), lunch ($7.00–$11.00), and dinner ($13.00–$22.00). Alcoholic beverages are served. A children's menu is available. A grill next to the dining room sells breakfast, a variety of fast-food items, soups, salads, and ice cream. A general store sells ice cream, beverages, limited groceries, and alcoholic beverages.

Facilities: Restaurant, cocktail lounge, espresso bar in lobby, grill, gift shop, general store, post office, National Park Service visitor center. Winter Season: ski shop, ice-skating rink, and skate and snowshoe rental.

Activities: Walking on the boardwalk that winds through the hot springs area, walking among the historic buildings at Mammoth (printed guide available), hiking, evening programs. Winter activities include ice skating, guided snowshoe touring, cross-country skiing, snowmobiling, guided snowmobile touring, snowcoach rides.

OLD FAITHFUL INN

Yellowstone National Park, WY 82190 • (307) 344–7311 • www.TravelYellowstone.com

OLD FAITHFUL INN IS THE MOST FAMOUS OF ALL the national park lodges. The structure's unique appearance is so familiar that the Disney Company constructed a replica of the inn for its Disney World theme park. The hotel is well maintained, and all of the facilities, including the rooms, are clean and comfortable. The large lobby, with log beams and a vaulted ceiling that soars 77 feet above the first floor, has multiple overhanging balconies. A mezzanine with chairs, tables, and sofas wraps around the entire second floor. Oddly shaped logs are used as decoration and for support of the railings and log beams. A huge clock ticks away on the front of a massive, four-sided stone fireplace that highlights the lobby. An attractive restaurant and lounge are entered from the back of the lobby.

The inn doesn't directly face Old Faithful, but arriving guests are likely to discover that the famous geyser is the first thing they see as they drive up to the front door to unload their luggage. Good views of Old Faithful are obtained from several locations in the hotel, including the large second-floor porch and a few of the lodging rooms. All of the lodging rooms are in the older main section and the two attached wings. No cabins or separate buildings are part of the hotel, although two other lodging facilities with cabins are nearby. The registration desk for Old Faithful Inn is to the left as you enter the lobby. Bell service is available to assist with luggage. A large parking area is in front of the hotel, a relatively short walk from the entrance. Lodging rooms are on three floors in the Old House (the original structure) and the East Wing, and on four floors in the West Wing. One elevator is in each wing, but these are relatively slow, so you may end up climbing several flights of stairs depending upon where your room is located. Old Faithful Inn is in the southwest portion of Yellowstone National Park, 30 miles from the entrance station at West Yellowstone.

The inn offers 327 rooms that vary in size, views, bathroom facilities, and configuration. Accommodations range from Old House rooms without private

The Northern Pacific Railroad financed the construction of Old Faithful Inn, which provided lodging for the large number of tourists coming to this area by train. The hotel that would cost approximately $140,000 was to replace the Upper Geyser Basin Hotel, which had been lost to fire. Old Faithful Inn was constructed in three phases: the original Old House was completed in 1903; the east wing was constructed in 1913–14; and the Y-shaped west wing was added in 1927. Numerous modifications have taken place over the years.

bath in the original central log building to relatively large, recently remodeled rooms with private bath in each of the wings. Room rates vary accordingly. All of the rooms have heat, but none have air-conditioning or television. Only the rooms in the east and west wings have telephones. Pay phones are in the hotel wings.

The least expensive rooms in Old Faithful Inn are in the original Old House section of the building. Although these rooms tend to be dark, and can also be noisy if they are located close to the busy lobby, the log or rough-hewn wood hallways and interior walls of rooms provide the ambience of a rustic national park lodge. Most of the eighty-nine rooms in the Old House are without a private bathroom. Guests in these rooms must use one of the community bathrooms located on each corridor of this section of the building. Rooms in the Old House are all different and interesting. Some are small with one double bed while others are quite large with two doubles or two doubles plus a single. First-floor rooms have interior log walls, while rooms on the second and third floors have walls of rough-hewn pine. Baths often have claw-foot bathtubs, and a few have pull-chain toilets. If requesting an

Old House room, keep in mind that there are no showers on the first floor, and guests staying in first-floor rooms without a bath are required to use second-floor shower rooms. Some of the best Old House rooms are without a private bathroom, such as corner room 229, which offers the best view of the Old Faithful geyser, and room 46, a large, rustic corner room with corner window seats. Room 243 has a unique shape and is entered from a short private stairway. The best rooms with a bath are 8 and 108, both of which have two bedrooms. Room 127 is large, offers a view of the geyser basin, and has a unique bathroom. President Clinton stayed in room 127 during his visit to Old Faithful. It is best to avoid rooms 1 through 6, which are in a hallway with a bathroom that is heavily used by nonguests.

The largest rooms in Old Faithful Inn are in the East Wing. Beds range from a double plus a single to two doubles. Rooms 1012, 1020, 1024, and corresponding rooms on the second and third floors offer good views of Old Faithful geyser. Three L-shaped mini-suites in this wing each have two queen beds and a separate sitting area with a coffeemaker, a daily newspaper, and a refrigerator stocked with snacks. Six two-room suites with windows facing Old Faithful each have two queen beds and a separate sitting room. The suites offer the same amenities as described for the mini-suites, including upgraded bathrooms.

Recently renovated West Wing rooms have nice tiled bathrooms and beds that range from one double to two queens. Rooms facing the front of the hotel are somewhat larger and more expensive than rooms on the opposite side of the hallway. Although they entail a longer walk from the elevator and lobby, we like corner rooms 2073 and 2074, and corresponding rooms on the third and fourth floors. These rooms are at the end the corridor and subject to less noise and foot traffic. They also provide additional light and better views by having windows in two walls.

Old Faithful Inn is the classic national park lodge where you should stay at least one night. It is convenient

to the geysers and a good base for exploring this section of the park. Be aware that, during the summer, the inn is a busy place and the Old Faithful area is congested. Both guests and visitors constantly roam through the lobby, the mezzanine, and the second-floor porch, so if you are seeking quiet, this isn't the place. On the other hand, you've got to see Old Faithful, so you might as well do it from where you are staying.

Rooms: Doubles, triples, and quads. A few rooms in the Old House can sleep up to five persons. Most but not all of the rooms have a private bath.

Wheelchair Accessibility: Four wheelchair-accessible rooms each have a bathroom with a wide doorway and a combination shower-tub with grab bars. Two of the rooms have two single beds, and the other two rooms have a double plus a single bed.

Rates: Old House rooms without private bath ($81); rooms with private bath ($106–$192), depending on size, location, and view; semi-suites ($290); suites ($385). Most rates quoted are for two persons, with the exception of the two-room units in the Old House, the semi-suites, and the suites, where the price is for four persons. Each additional person is $10 per night. Children eleven and under stay free when staying with an adult.

Location: Southwest section of Yellowstone National Park, 30 miles from the entrance station at West Yellowstone.

Season: Old House renovations are expected to shorten the 2006 season to July through September. A longer season is projected for 2007.

Food: A dining room on the main floor serves a breakfast buffet ($9.00), breakfast menu ($5.00–$8.00), lunch buffet ($11.25), lunch menu ($7.00–$9.50), and dinner ($15.00–$30.00); reservations are required. A children's menu is available. The snack shop offers sandwiches, fast-food items, and ice cream; a lunch counter in the adjacent general store serves breakfast, salads, sandwiches, hamburgers, soup, ice cream, and beverages. Other eating facilities are nearby.

Facilities: Restaurant, snack bar, tour desk, gift shop, ATM. Many additional facilities, including a gas station, gift shops, stores, and restaurants, are in the immediate area.

Activities: Walking through nearby geyser area, guided tours of the inn, hiking.

OLD FAITHFUL LODGE CABINS

Yellowstone National Park, WY 82190 • (307) 344–7311• www.TravelYellowstone.com

Frontier Cabins at Old Faithful Lodge Cabins

OLD FAITHFUL LODGE CABINS CONSISTS OF A main lodge building and 97 cabins, usually constructed two to four to a building. The main lodge was constructed in the late 1920s and has no overnight accommodations. The cabins are behind and to one side of the main lodge, which houses the registration desk. The impressive lobby area has large windows that provide an excellent view of Old Faithful. A big stone fireplace is surrounded with chairs and tables for eating, visiting, and viewing. The main building also has a food court, ice cream shop, bake shop, and gift shop. Old Faithful Lodge Cabins is in the southwest section of Yellowstone National Park, 30 miles from the west entrance at West Yellowstone. It is a short walk from the better-known Old Faithful Inn.

The lodge offers cabins in two classifications, Budget and Frontier. All of the cabins were remodeled in 2002 and have finished interiors, heat, electricity, and carpeted floors, but only Frontier Cabins have a private bathroom. Keep in mind that the cabins are not insulated, so the small electric heaters may prove inadequate when the outside temperature is low, as may be the case in the spring and fall. The cabins are clustered closely together behind the main lodge in an area with much paving and few trees. A few of the cabins front on a river, while several others face the geyser basin. Most, however,

offer no particularly good views. Cabins in either classification are the best values in the Old Faithful area.

The least expensive rooms in the Old Faithful area are thirty-five Budget Cabins, which have a hot-and-cold water sink but no bathroom facilities. Toilets and sinks are in two community bathrooms and also in the main lodge building. Shower facilities are in the main lodge building, which is not particularly close to any of the cabins. Beds in Budget Cabins are either a double bed plus a single bed or two double beds. Cabins in this classification are all the same size, so units with two doubles have less floor space for you and your belongings. All except two Budget Cabins are constructed as duplex units with connecting doors, a feature that may appeal to families. If you plan to choose a cabin without a bath, we suggest units 221 through 225, which sit on a small bluff overlooking the river in the back of the complex. These offer more privacy and a good view but are some distance from the showers. Budget cabins 200, 201, 203, 205, 207, and 209 are nearest the geyser basin, but trees obstruct views of Old Faithful. Budget cabins 226 and 235 are the only freestanding units in this classification, which means you will probably enjoy more quiet. Both are away from the river but close to a community bathroom.

Sixty-one Frontier Cabins are mostly constructed as duplex units. These units have a sink in the room and a

Boardwalks and unpaved paths meander through Upper Geyser Basin, near Old Faithful Lodge Cabins. A boardwalk that begins near the lodge leads around Old Faithful geyser and through a large area of pools, geysers, and hot springs. One path is designated for both people and bicycles. One 3-mile loop leads to Morning Glory Pool and returns to the lodge. Both shorter and longer trails are in the basin area.

private bathroom with a toilet and shower. Bedding is either one double or a double plus a single. The Frontier Cabins with a double and a single are somewhat larger in size but priced the same as cabins in the same class with one double bed. Essentially, most of the Frontier Cabins are the same size as Budget Cabins but have a private bathroom. Frontier units 114, 141, and 144 are the only freestanding cabins in this classification. Cabin 114 faces Old Faithful geyser but is in the front of the complex and is subject to a heavy traffic flow.

Old Faithful Lodge Cabins offers basic but relatively inexpensive accommodations. The main lodge has a large food court serving lunch and dinner. Items include

salads, pasta, hot and cold sandwiches, and prime rib. A small bakery sells muffins, cinnamon rolls, and other baked goods, as well as coffee. This is the nearest lodge to Old Faithful geyser, which can be viewed through three massive picture windows in the lobby. The lodge sits close by the more famous Old Faithful Inn, which offers what may be America's most picturesque lobby.

Rooms: Doubles, triples, and a few quads. More than half the cabins have a private bath.

Wheelchair Accessibility: One double-size Frontier Cabin, 228, has ramp access and a bathroom with a wide doorway and a roll-in shower. Grab bars are beside the elevated toilet. One budget cabin has ramp access.

Rates: Budget cabins without bath ($57); Frontier cabins ($85). Rates quoted are for two persons. Each additional person is $10 per night. Children eleven and under stay free with an adult.

Location: Southwest section of Yellowstone National Park, 30 miles from the entrance station at West Yellowstone.

Season: Mid-May to October.

Food: A large food court offers lunch ($4.50–$10.00) and dinner ($7.00–$16.00). Two snack shops serve bakery goods, breakfast burritos, ice cream, yogurt, and espresso.

Facilities: Food court, snack shops, tour desk, gift shop. Many stores and restaurants are in the immediate vicinity.

Activities: Walking through the geyser area, hiking.

OLD FAITHFUL SNOW LODGE AND CABINS

Yellowstone National Park, WY 82190 • (307) 344–7311 • www.TravelYellowstone.com

OLD FAITHFUL SNOW LODGE AND CABINS consists of a single three-story main lodge building plus thirty-four wooden cabins that are located near, but not immediately beside, the lodge. The lodge offers a dining room, grill, cocktail lounge, gift shop, and an impressive two-story lobby with huge wood beams and a large gas fireplace. A second-floor mezzanine with chairs and a table overlooks the lobby. Lamps and chandeliers throughout the building and the guest rooms feature animal motifs. Craftsmen created many of the furnishings in the lobby, lounge, and restaurant. Even much of the woodwork includes inlaid animal figures. The rustic design of the lodge fits in well with better known Old Faithful Inn, which is nearby. Old Faithful Snow Lodge and Cabins is in the Old Faithful area of Yellowstone, 30 miles from the west entrance at West Yellowstone. The lodge is across a large parking area from Old Faithful Inn. Plenty of parking is available near the lodge and beside the cabins. Registration for the lodge and the cabins is at the main desk of the lodge building.

Snow Lodge is the first full-service hotel (dining rooms, lobby, gift shop, etc.) built in Yellowstone National Park since Canyon Lodge was completed in 1911 (and has since burned). The complex has one hundred similar but not identical rooms that are all rented at the same rate. The new lodge building replaces the previous Snow Lodge that was demolished in 1998. Each room in the new lodge is large, with two double beds (with the exception of the wheelchair-accessible rooms), and a built-in wooden closet. Heavy wooden shutters swing out to cover the windows. A padded window seat is in a few of the rooms. All rooms have a full bath with a combination shower-tub, a telephone, coffeemaker, and heat but no air conditioning.

The complex is in a relatively quiet section of the Old Faithful area, but the location does not lend itself to great views from any of the rooms. There are elevators in the lodge and bell service is available to assist with luggage. We recommend that you try to book rooms 2037,

Old Faithful Snow Lodge and Cabins and Mammoth Hot Springs Hotel are the only two facilities that offer winter accommodations. Reservations should be made well in advance of your planned arrival. Only Mammoth is accessible by car. Old Faithful Snow Lodge is accessible only by over-the-snow vehicles from West Yellowstone, Mammoth, and Flagg Ranch on the south end. Skiing, snowshoeing, and ice skating (Mammoth) are popular activities. Ski rentals, waxes, trail maps, and other equipment are available at both locations.

2039, 2041, and the three corresponding rooms on the third floor, which are larger but rent for the same rate as all other rooms in the lodge. Rooms on the second floor have larger windows than third-floor rooms.

Two categories of cabins are rented at Snow Lodge. All the cabins sit in a gravel area of sparse vegetation. The least expensive are the ten Frontier Cabins with one or two double beds. Cabins 706 and 707, each with one double bed, are quite a bit smaller than the other eight Frontier Cabins. They all rent for the same price, so try to get two doubles if you book a Frontier Cabin. These cabins are roomy and nicely finished. They do not have a porch. Each cabin has a private bath with shower but no tub. Twenty-four Western Cabins are somewhat larger and nicer than the Frontier units. These are constructed four to a building; each cabin has a small covered porch, two double beds, and a full bath with a combination shower-tub. We believe the Frontier Cabins with two double beds are a better value than the Western Cabins.

Old Faithful Snow Lodge and Cabins offers something for everyone. Those on a tight budget can choose a Frontier Cabin. Others who are willing to spend more can sleep in one of the nicest lodging units in any national park. The lodge is only one of two Yellowstone lodging units (Mammoth is the other) open during the winter. The Snow Lodge complex is in a central location from which to explore a major thermal area of the park. It is also convenient to a National Park Service visitor center and various stores. An exceptionally attractive dining room with a western motif has a large gas fireplace and handcrafted furnishings. Some unique meal offerings are included on a menu that rivals that of the Old Faithful Inn. A small grill near the front of the lodge serves fast-food items. Another restaurant in Old Faithful Inn and a cafeteria in Old Faithful Lodge are only a short walk from the cabins or main building of Snow Lodge.

Rooms: Doubles, triples, and quads. All rooms have a private bath.

Wheelchair Accessibility: Five first-floor rooms in the lodge, each with one double and one single bed, are wheelchair accessible. Each room has a bathroom with a wide doorway, grab bars, and a roll-in shower. One Western Cabin has ramp access and a bathroom with grab bars and a tub/shower combination.

Rates: Frontier Cabins ($83); Western Cabins ($121); Snow Lodge rooms ($161). Rates quoted are for two persons. Each additional person is $10 per night. Children eleven and under stay free.

Location: Southwest section of Yellowstone, 30 miles southeast of the west entrance at West Yellowstone.

Season: Summer season is from early May to early November. Winter season is from mid-December to mid-March. The cabins are closed in winter. No roads are open to this location during winter months.

Food: A dining room serves a breakfast buffet ($9.00), breakfast menu ($5.00–$8.00), lunch ($7.00–$11.00), and dinner ($15.00–$30.00). A grill serves breakfast ($3.00–$4.00) and fast food for lunch/dinner ($3.00–$7.00). Another dining room, a cafeteria, and a general store with limited groceries and a grill are nearby.

Facilities: Dining room, grill, cocktail lounge, and gift shop. Other nearby facilities include a clinic, general store, visitor center, and post office. Winter sports equipment rental is available during winter months.

Activities: Hiking, walking through the nearby geyser area, and tours. Winter activities include snowcoach tours, guided ski tours, cross-country skiing, snowshoeing, and snowmobiling.

ROOSEVELT LODGE CABINS

Yellowstone National Park, WY 82190 • (307) 344–7311 • www.TravelYellowstone.com

Frontier Cabins at Roosevelt Lodge Cabins

Named for an area that served as a favorite campsite for President Theodore Roosevelt, Roosevelt Lodge Cabins includes a log registration and dining building and an adjacent small store. These two structures are surrounded on three sides by rustic wood cabins that were constructed mostly in the 1920s. The main building has a registration desk flanked on one side by a lobby and a large stone fireplace and on the other side by a family-style dining room. Rocking chairs fill a covered front porch that runs the length of the building. The lodging complex is situated on a hill surrounded by pine trees and overlooking a valley with a background of mountains. The relatively isolated location places the lodge away from the congestion that plagues other such facilities in the park. Roosevelt Lodge Cabins is in the northeast corner of Yellowstone National Park, 23 miles southeast of the north entrance near Mammoth and 29 miles west of the northeast entrance to Yellowstone.

Roosevelt Lodge Cabins provides a total of eighty wood-frame cabins in the smallest lodging complex in Yellowstone National Park. All overnight accommodations are in the freestanding cabins, which have vaulted ceilings, shake roofs, and wood floors. None has

The location of Roosevelt Lodge Cabins has served as a home for previous lodging facilities. John Yancy, an early entrepreneur to this area, built the Pleasant Valley Hotel in 1884 near the site where today's Old West Cookout takes place. Yancy died in 1903, and the hotel burned three years later. This same year saw the construction of the Roosevelt Tent Camp, which had wood-floored, candy-striped canvas tents. The current lodge was completed in 1920, and the cabins were added during the same decade.

air-conditioning, a television, telephone, or porch. The cabins are closely clustered in an area of trees, grass, gravel, and weeds, surrounded by hills. They are near a small store and the log registration building that houses the dining room. Adequate parking is in front of the dining room and directly in front of or beside each cabin.

The least expensive units at Roosevelt Lodge Cabins are sixty Rough Rider Cabins, which have a wood stove and no water or private bathroom. Two manufactured wood logs are provided per night to heat the cabin. The two logs are likely to be insufficient for a cold evening, and additional logs must be purchased. Three modern community bathrooms with showers are scattered among the cabins. Most of the Rough Rider Cabins are small freestanding buildings with wood floors and one double bed. The interior has adequate space for luggage and other belongings. These cabins each have two small screened windows to provide ventilation and outside light, which results in relatively dark interiors. Some Rough Rider units are in larger cabins that have either two or three double beds. The units with two double beds offer a spacious interior, while those with three double beds are pretty crowded. Rough Rider Cabin 5 is the exception, with two rooms and three double beds. This is the only cabin in the complex with two rooms. Keep in mind that all cabins in the Rough Rider classification rent for the same price regardless of size.

Fourteen Frontier Cabins with a private bath and heat have nicely finished interiors. They are the same size as the larger Rough Rider Cabins and have a much nicer inside appearance than you would expect from viewing the cabin exterior. Each Frontier unit (other than two wheelchair Frontier Cabins) has two double beds and four windows that let in more exterior light than the smaller Rough Rider units. The Frontier Cabins are in a small cluster among the Rough Rider Cabins.

The choice between the two types of cabins will depend primarily on how much you are willing to pay

Roosevelt Lodge Cabins is well-known for its "Roosevelt's Old West Cookout." Participants depart for Pleasant Valley from the Roosevelt Corral each day in a wagon or on horseback. Different rates are charged depending on whether you choose the wagon ride, the one-hour horseback ride, or the two-hour horseback ride. The cookout includes a steak dinner and entertainment and is very popular, so reservations should be made well in advance, especially if you choose one of the two horseback rides. Reservations for the cookout can be made at the same time you reserve a room.

\\/

for a private bathroom and a heater. If you don't think they are worth $37 extra, request a less expensive Rough Rider Cabin. Rough Rider Cabin 5 is a bargain, with two rooms and three double beds. This unit also has a front porch and is the end unit in a row of cabins. Unfortunately, it is some distance from a bathroom. We especially like the location of Rough Rider Cabin 115, bordered on two sides by a creek. Cabins 111, 113, and 114 are also on the creek but not in quite as good a location as 115. These are four smaller cabins, each with one double bed. You might also consider requesting a Rough Rider Cabin with two double beds, in which case you are likely to end up with one of the larger cabins in this classification. None of the Frontier Cabins is preferable to any other, although all have finished and comfortable interiors that make them considerably nicer than most of the Rough Rider Cabins.

Roosevelt Lodge Cabins offers basic accommodations at nominal cost in a quiet area near the Lamar Valley, where wolves are frequently sighted. The Frontier Cabins are comfortable, and the Rough Rider Cabins are inexpensive. The main registration and restaurant building, of log construction, has an attractive lobby with a hardwood floor, wicker furniture, and a large stone fireplace. A lobby bar in one corner serves alcoholic beverages beginning in the late afternoon. The covered porch is a great place to sit in a rocking chair and watch the sun rise, spend part of an afternoon, or relax after an evening meal. The informal country-style dining area specializes in BBQ ribs and fish. Horseback riding and stagecoach rides are available at the nearby corral.

Rooms: Doubles, triples, and quads. A few cabins hold up to six adults. Most of the cabins do not have a private bath.

Wheelchair Accessibility: Two Frontier Cabins each have ramp access and an extra large bathroom with a high toilet and a roll-in shower. The restaurant is wheelchair accessible via a ramp to the front door of the registration building, which also has a bathroom that is wheelchair accessible.

Rates: Rough Rider cabins without bath ($57); Frontier cabins ($94). Rates quoted are for two persons. Each additional person is $10 per night. Children eleven and under stay free.

Location: Northeast section of Yellowstone, 23 miles southeast of the north entrance.

Season: Mid-June through early September.

Food: A dining room serves breakfast ($5.00–$8.00), lunch ($6.00–$10.00), and dinner ($10.00–$21.00). Alcoholic beverages are served. A children's menu is available. An Old West Cookout via horseback ($60.00) or covered wagon ($50.00) is offered each evening, rain or shine. Limited groceries are sold at a small store.

Facilities: Store, dining room, lobby bar, gift counter, stables, gas station.

Activities: Hiking, guided trail rides, stagecoach rides.

INDEX OF LODGE NAMES

About the Authors

David and Kay Scott have spent twenty-eight summers touring America's national park areas. Most of these trips were in a series of four Volkswagen campers. Four summers have been devoted to staying in and experiencing America's national park lodges. The initial 1996 lodge trip allowed them to gather information for the first edition of this book. Three subsequent lodge trips, the latest in 2005, provided material to update and expand the content of the current edition.

David and Kay are also the authors of Globe Pequot's *Guide to the National Park Areas: Eastern States* and *Guide to the National Park Areas: Western States.* They have discussed national park travel on numerous radio programs and have appeared twice on NBC's *Today*, once from Yellowstone National Park and again from Grand Canyon National Park. David and Kay live in Valdosta, Georgia, where David is a professor of finance at Valdosta State University and Kay is retired from the public schools. David is also the author of two dozen finance books including *Wall Street Words* and *David Scott's Guides*, a series of personal finance and investing books.